Storied Lives

Storied Lives

The Cultural Politics of Self-Understanding

GEORGE C. ROSENWALD &

RICHARD L. OCHBERG

EDITORS

Yale University Press New Haven and London

Designed by Sonia L. Scanlon.
Set in Times Roman type by
The Composing Room of Michigan, Inc.,
Grand Rapids, Michigan.
Printed in the United States of America by
Book Crafters, Inc., Chelsea, Michigan.

Library of Congress Cataloging-in-Publication Data
Storied lives : the cultural politics of self-
  understanding / George C. Rosenwald and
  Richard L. Ochberg, editors.
        p.   cm.
    Includes bibliographical references and index.
    ISBN 0-300-05455-6 (alk. paper)
    1. Identity (Psychology)   2. Biography—
Psychological aspects.   3. Psychology—
Biographical methods.   4. Social sciences—
Biographical methods.   5. Discourse analysis,
Narrative.   6. Self-presentation.   I. Rosenwald,
George C., 1932– .   II. Ochberg, Richard L.,
1950– .
    BF697.S844   1992
    920—dc20   91-38345
                                              CIP

A catalogue record for this book is available from the British
Library.

The paper in this book meets the guidelines for
permanence and durability of the Committee on
Production Guidelines for Book Longevity of the
Council on Library Resources.

10 9 8 7 6 5 4 3 2 1

We dedicate this book to our parents,

Maximilian and Rachel Rosenwald &

Gerald, Belle, and Anne Ochberg

Contents

Acknowledgments

This book has benefited from the advice and inspiration of a wider circle of contributors than appears in the contents. In particular, we thank Ken Gergen, who first encouraged us to draw this collection together. Daniel Bertaux introduced us to like-minded colleagues in Europe. Rico Ainslie, Ellen Fredericks, Bob Green, Michael Jackson, and Tod Sloan were members of the original group at the University of Michigan who, in weekly meetings over several years, helped us to elaborate a perspective on lives and stories. Gladys Topkis, our editor at Yale, steered us home. Most important: a book of this sort, dealing with self-understandings not only revealed but fashioned and enlarged in conversation, raises more profoundly than most the ambiguity of authorship. In this spirit we wish not only to thank the many informants who shared their life-stories with us, but to acknowledge that they are our first circle of authors.

GEORGE C. ROSENWALD

RICHARD L. OCHBERG

Introduction: Life Stories, Cultural Politics, and Self-Understanding

T his book presents a series of diverse investigations into the stories people tell about their lives. Here are studies of the way couples talk about their children—or their childlessness; of factory workers, craftsmen, and artists talking about their work. Black women describe feeling caught between their allegiance to minority culture and the embrace, half desired and half distrusted, of American homogeneity. Women recount their struggle to rescue a sense of autonomy in a culture that undermines it by the very plot lines it makes available. And one study at the extreme—where genocide makes all human experience untellable—tests the limits of narrative self-exploration.

But this book is not intended as an anthology of human experience. An argument indebted to a critical theory of society (Geuss, 1981; Horkheimer, 1972; Wellmer, 1971) motivated us to undertake it, and the reader will have to judge whether the following chapters substantiate the view we present. Our argument, in brief, is this: First, the stories people tell about themselves are interesting not only for the events and characters they describe but also for something in the construction of the stories themselves. How individuals recount their histories—what they emphasize and omit, their stance as protagonists or victims, the relationship the story establishes between teller and audience—all shape what individuals can claim of their own lives. Personal stories are not merely a way of telling someone (or oneself) about one's life; they are the means by which identities may be fashioned. It is this formative—and sometimes deformative—power of life stories that makes them important. This approach to personal accounts has for some time been bringing psychology, sociology, anthropology, and literary studies closer together.

Second, we believe that this self-formative power of personal narrative may be constrained or stunted. As psychoanalytic experience suggests, the misfortunes of childhood may censor both memory and desire, impoverishing both the narrative past and how that narrative might seize the future. This limitation is, however, only partly a matter of individual misfortune. We assume that all stories are told and that all self-understanding is realized within the narrative frames each culture provides its members. These frames of intelligibility determine and limit the power of personal narrative. This step in our argument implies a skeptical attitude toward personal accounts.

Third, we imagine that it is possible, though surely difficult, to enlarge the range of personal narrative. Individuals and communities may become aware of the political-cultural conditions that have led to the circumscription of discourse. If a critique of these conditions occurs widely, it may alter not only how individuals construe their own identities but also how they talk to one another and indirectly the social order itself. Discourse mediates between the fate of the individual and the larger order of things.

From Realism to Narrativity

The study of life stories is by no means novel. Psychologists, sociologists, and anthropologists have long used the autobiographies of informants as a window into their experience and their social conditions (Allport, 1965; Shaw, 1938; Lewis, 1961). From today's perspective, however, these classic studies seem ambiguously perched between the traditional interests of empiricism—the program of constructing an encompassing theory on a base of value-neutral facts—and those associated with the turn to hermeneutics—the recognition that the precipitates of human experience do not speak for themselves but gain their significance through subjective and intersubjective interpretation (Blecher, 1980; Walzer, 1987). True, the traditional studies drew their evidence (and much of their vivacity) from what the Chicago sociologists called the informant's "own story." Still, it was the events themselves, not the stories told about them, that were intended to command our attention. Lewis and Shaw viewed life histories as reports from the front lines of poverty and oppression, intended to supplement the aggregate statistics and abstract formulas of social science, much as photographs bring to life the grey type of the morning paper. Like photographs, these histories were intended to be read as objective descriptions, different only in format from the descriptions of social science. In the past twenty years, however, a new conception of personal report (and of social science itself) has entered the scene. As a result, personal accounts are now read with an eye not just to the scenes they describe but to the process, product, and consequences of reportage itself.

Although a full account of the recent "interpretive turn" in social science (Rabinow and Sullivan, 1979) lies beyond our present purpose, we recognize several factors that may explain it. First is the loss of faith in the empiricist program noted in several disciplines. Specifically, the theory-free observation base is no longer a credible supposition. Interpretation enters every moment of scientific inquiry, especially in the social sciences, and this undermines the older logic linking theory and hypothesis testing (Hanson, 1973; Roth, 1987; Taylor, 1979). What is more, it has been suggested that social theorists concoct stories, if only implicitly, whenever they conceptualize human experience and behavior (Gergen and Gergen, 1986; Landau, 1984), and these are said to be culturally constrained.

A second impetus to the study of narrative originates in the humanities, where a new hermeneutic self-consciousness has transformed theories of criticism and history (Gadamer, 1989; White, 1978). It is no longer plausible to present the scholar as servant of what he or she studies. Rather, the scholar is its maker and characteristically its partisan maker. The relation between accounts of the world and the world of which they give us account is no longer treated as simply representational, mimetic. Historians are not people whose writings approach ever more closely a final best account. Rather, they write commentaries on previous accounts and regard them as improvements—by which is meant, among other things, that the later accounts address the problems of the present more successfully than earlier ones would have done (Rorty, 1982). According to this view, the development of all knowledge of the world must be shown not by a graph approaching the asymptote of truth but by a story relating the instigating problematics to the concepts, models, interpretations, plots, and theories put forward. Put bluntly, it means that the growth of any knowledge does not unfold the structure of the world but is itself a history.

The third source of the current interest in narrative accounts stems, we believe, from the recent struggle for the rights of the disenfranchised. The call for recognition of women, minorities, and Third World cultures has commonly taken the form of personal accounts of suffering and redemption. The women's movement, in particular, has called attention not only to objective measures of oppression (for example, inequalities of pay and promotion) but also to the pervasive misapprehension of women's tacit worldview by androcentric theory (Belenky, 1986; Gilligan, 1982).

These developments have done more than renew interest in life narratives: We now listen with a different style of attention. It is no longer plausible to regard the events informants describe as intelligible without further inquiry into the background assumptions of the speakers and their audiences.

At first glance this modern skepticism about the objectivity of narratives seems to throw the whole interpretive enterprise in doubt. Why take an interest in life stories if their truth cannot be warranted? The objection is well taken if "truth" in the realist sense is the target. But to the investigator of psychological or cultural representation, the object of study is not the "true" event, as it might have been recorded by some panel of disinterested observers, but the construction of that event within a personal and social history. In short, what interests us most is precisely what the realist finds most discomfiting—the factitiousness of the tale. In the form a particular narrator gives to a history we read the more or less abiding concerns and constraints of the individual and his or her community.

From this angle the study of narrative offers another promise than that of traditional empiricism, which assumed that objective events have equally objective histories and attempted to discover the causes and the ultimate control of political and psychological outcomes. By contrast, narrative criticism assumes that histories are continually reinvented in the service of contemporary psychological and political aims and attempts to widen the horizon of what can be recounted and imagined.

This turn to narratology has by no means replaced the realist school. Even today the vast majority of interview research uses personal accounts to document the realities of otherwise unfamiliar ways of living. Thus, Rubin's *Worlds of Pain* (1976) is intended as a report on working-class life, not as an analysis of working-class consciousness. Daniel Levinson, too, regards interviews as a basis for generalizing "a construction of the life course." This does not mean that he ignores problems of interpretation: "A poor biography depicts its protagonist as saint or villain, as merely a product of his times, a creation of his unconscious or a sequence of reactions without individuality" (Levinson, 1978, pp. 15–16). But the production of the personal account is regarded as unproblematic in itself and as allowing us a more or less unobstructed view of the subject's life.

A valuable survey of life-history research in anthropology recounts the variety of problems commonly investigated by means of personal accounts—"basic character," socialization, deviance, life cycle—but concedes that "questions of personal identity . . . have scarcely been undertaken on a cross-cultural basis" (Langness and Frank, 1981, p. 81). It further appears that the formal vulnerability of personal narratives to cultural strains, with which we are concerned, has not been fully recognized. On the whole, the traditional posture of descriptive realism still holds center stage.

Only gradually is scholarship turning our attention in a different direction. Recent works in anthropology (Rosaldo, 1989), sociology (Bertaux, 1981), psychology (Sarbin, 1986), and women's studies (Personal Narratives Group, 1989) explore self-explanations from post-objectivist perspectives and assign them a new place in social science.

Narrative and Social Existence

At first glance this turn to narratology might seem to be a turn from social analysis toward the scrutiny of individual subjectivity. After all, life stories are told by individuals and fashioned by individual consciousness. In fact, however, theoretical interest has not turned its back on culture and society. Most narratologists—and all those who are represented in this volume—assume that the explanations individuals offer of their lives are inevitably shaped by the prevailing norms of discourse within which they operate. That institutions have enormous power over the behavior and life chances of individuals has long been recognized. Now the cultural interpretation of self-explanation potentially carries this thought a step further: social influence shapes not only public action but also private self-understanding. To the degree that this is true, social control takes on a more ominous aspect. For now it appears that the alternatives one recognizes as possible or moral are constrained in the marrow of individual self-representation. Those strictures in turn limit personal and political emancipation.

In view of these contingencies one might expect narratology to enter an alliance with the critical theory of society. Together they would undertake to describe and conceptualize how social ideology is individually appropriated in the construction of life histories and selves. In fact, this has hardly happened at all except in feminist studies. The resistance to such an alliance arises, we believe, from the traditional distinction between fact and story. As long as interview research was thought to give us a direct view of life events, critical judgment seemed possible. One could agree that poverty or ethnic prejudice was oppressive. But when attention shifted from the "what" to the "how" of reportage, the critical focus blurred. One might note the choices and tactics narrators deploy and voice one's admiration of their skill, but one never dared judge one rendition inferior to another.

The dismantling of the realist position has shattered the image of life stories as the mirror of life events. When Allport, Shaw, or Lewis reported life histories—how one episode of a life leads coherently into another—that coherence was assumed to dwell within the events themselves. It is precisely this assumption that modern narratology suspends. We now believe that at least in the spheres of psychological and social consciousness, coherence is imposed by the work of story makers (Cohler, 1982). The logic with which one event leads into another is not simply "out there," waiting to be recognized by any disinterested observer. Instead, coherence derives from the tacit assumptions of plausibility that shape the way each story maker weaves the fragmentary episodes of experience into a history.

In this view, social analysis yields to literary appreciation and to reverence for cultural variety. The hermeneutic position is today most emphatically asserted by those who would defend the legitimacy of noncanonical perspectives: What usually passes for universal, they argue, reflects the worldview only of the white, male elite, who until recently owned the academic empire. Feminists and minority theorists hold that what has long counted as significant (morally, intellectually, aesthetically) must be reevaluated against culturally specific coordinates. The charge of cultural imperialism has made us all leery of demanding that narratives framed within different models of discourse conform to our own notions of adequate form.

Nothing we say in this volume is intended to take lightly the force of this argument. Critical theory can have no quarrel with investigative practices that call attention to the integrity of cultural schemas. Nevertheless, we are reluctant to surrender the critical agenda that makes social science a potentially emancipatory endeavor. For it remains possible, we believe, for any system of discourse—even one that prides itself on having severed its bondage to another—to enshrine within itself the traces of its fealty and thereby to restrict the enlightenment and development of a community. For this reason, mere appreciation of others' beliefs is not the highest respect we can offer. For similar reasons we cannot agree that a life story is "good" if it "works" for the person who tells it. Functionalist criteria simply shift the focus of evaluation from the person to the world he or she inhabits. The virtues of modesty and tolerance are often invoked as brakes on critical analysis.

Our emphasis throughout this volume is on the formative effects of narratives. Stories give direction to lives. Since we do not propose to accept life stories uncritically, our interpretive posture lays special emphasis on the reasons and costs of stories' disfigurement. This critical posture receives its impetus from presuppositions of conflict—between the individual and society, between consciousness and repression, between desire and adaptation. Unfortunately, the decline of realism and the rise of narrative theory seem to lend themselves to the premature dissolution of this model of conflict. We believe that the following four critical issues must be theoretically and methodologically reconciled with the new spirit of tolerance.

First, the premise of critique requires us to explain how one story is better than another, how a story may be deficient, and how a later story can be said to improve on its predecessor. For the realist, the better story is the truer story, the one more consistent with the facts. But if this equation is discredited, does any ground remain for critical judgment?

The second issue concerns the relation between past and present. Life stories draw a connection between the events of yesterday and today; the subjective conviction of autobiographic coherence is intrinsic to a sense of identity. The modern narrative perspective, however, suggests that this coherence is an illusion—a tactical maneuver. How we formulate our autobiographies is said to depend on the predicaments in which we find ourselves at the moment.

But is the self-historicizing subject a mere opportunist who casually reinvents the past to serve the needs of the present? If so, then it becomes nearly impossible to think about the importance of memories, of repetition compulsion, of attempts to master the past in new self-liberating editions. The ideal of self-transparence is also devalued, since we can no longer understand how current endeavors arise out of past struggles. Baring one's heart becomes more and more indistinguishable from playing a confidence trick. These reservations do not lead us to restore realism. Rather we suggest that any adequate account of life stories ought to illuminate the connections among the series of narratives that any informant may construct over the course of a life.

The third problem concerns the relation between the individual and society. Life stories enter this discussion in the following way: Since all narratives are told within the paradigms deemed intelligible by their specific culture, any story may be viewed chiefly as the instantiation of the norms of discourse (Shotter and Gergen, 1989). The culture "speaks itself" through each individual's story.

The difficulty with this view is that it dissolves the tension between individual desire and social adaptation. True, desire (and the life stories in which it is represented) is inevitably shaped by the forms each culture provides. At the same time, desire strains against these forms. The silences, truncations, and confusions in stories as well as the occasional outbreaks of action contradicting an individual's "official" narrative, point out to us—and to the narrator, if only his or her recognition can be enlisted—what else might be said and sought.

The final problem concerns the relation between stories and practices. The empiricist holds that stories tell us about behavior and that behavior is what matters. Critical-interpretive theory points out that human action, individual or collective, is constituted by discourse and unintelligible apart from its interpretation (Taylor, 1979).

At its limit, however, this line of reasoning can be taken to support the notion that social life counts for nothing outside of discourse. On this tack the improvement of life can be accomplished if one tells a better story about it. But life is not merely talk; inequalities of opportunity, for example, are not redressed if individuals, or even whole classes, tell more "agentic," optimistic autobiographies. Changes in narrative are significant to the extent that they stir up changes in how we live. The relation between narratives and forms of life must therefore be the focus of a critical perspective.

Life Stories and Subjectivity

In collecting, organizing, and commenting on the chapters of this volume we drew on the following assumptions. The encounter between individual and society is played out on a field extending beyond that of pure narrativity. It involves and revolves around the cultural taming of desire and the reassertion of indomitable desire, channeled into individual and collective action upon the culture. Human nature, the materiality of life, is not reducible to the time-bound local forms that culture offers it. It seeks forever to escape these forms. This in essence is Freud's vision.

When we speak of subjectivity, we mean something more than the private and inaccessible. We mean rather that the character of spontaneity is never extinguished in the person and that desire enters at best reluctantly into compromises with social and cultural conventions. Subjectivity is the restless force that society seeks to master. This conception rules out social adaptation as an intrinsic terminus of human development and relegates it to the position of a forced settlement. Subjectivity is not the romantic fiction of a self prior to and safe from socialization. On the contrary, it is what bears the marks of the person's interaction with the world and seeks yet to erase them.

Political conditions, including those of self-understanding, are created and maintained by human action. To the large extent that they achieve autonomy and resist modification, they perpetuate typical self-understandings and misunderstandings. The restlessness of human desire threatens the permanence of such limitations and—proportionately—the predictability of lives (Dewey, 1960). Just as no one's life is designed in advance, there is more than a single life story to be told. This is reasonable because the stories people tell are not only about their lives but also part of their lives. What is told and what is lived promote each other— hence our title.

A life story is more than a recital of events. It is an organization of experience. In relating the elements of experience to each other and to the present telling, the teller asserts their meanings. Some stories reflexively mobilize tellers to new actions and thereby surmount and replace the existing meaning structure. Other stories perpetuate themselves by the redundant, self-certifying actions they instigate. Accordingly, the formative dynamic of personal accounts, which we touch on here, creates a certain instability in life histories, but one which only a historical realist would deplore. Historical truth does not founder chiefly on the unreliability of memory or the arbitrariness of an interpreter's reconstructive attempts, but on the reflective mutability of meanings themselves. The movement of a life cannot be stopped by a story. If human development is our paramount concern, then obsolescent, mutating stories must inevitably command our respect. To this we shall return in our last chapter.

Organization of the Chapters

This volume is divided into three parts, corresponding to the steps in our argument. Part I illustrates how personal narratives contribute to the formation of identity. Part II explores the constraints that specific political-cultural conditions impose on narrativity and thereby on identity. Part III takes up the possibility of critical insight mediating psychosocial emancipation. By addressing the psychic and social obstacles to formative discourse, subjects may overcome stagnancy and remobilize personal and social development. They may tell better stories and live fuller lives.

Part I: Life stories and identity

The six chapters in Part I may be read as a conversation about two principal ideas. First, a narrative is a way of organizing experience. A good story presents a coherent plot. The narrative "now" must grow plausibly out of what has come before and point the way to what might reasonably come next. This literary criterion has implications for identity as well. For in telling their stories individuals make claims about the coherence of their lives. In effect the storyteller says, "This person I am today is who I have been years becoming." Further, what is included and omitted from the account renders plausible the anticipated future.

The second way in which narratives contribute to identity concerns the relationship between the storyteller and the audience. The sense one has of being a "self" is partly one's sense of who one is in relation to others. In telling our story to another we establish who that other is (the one who will understand us, or forgive us, or become converted to our point of view). In turn, as the telling of the tale turns the listener into the audience required by the teller, the storyteller's identity is reaffirmed or even altered.

In chapter 1 Elliot Mishler illustrates the narrative work of coherence-making. His protagonist, a furniture maker, has wandered through various occupations before settling on his present vocation; he anticipates yet another shift. But he achieves a sense of personal coherence. The culturally specific logic underlying occupational choice—the chained "realms"—becomes a resource for this craftsman's narrative journey. While he provides us with an account we recognize as reasonable, he provides himself with the sense of a plausible identity—an identity held together by the sustaining recital of his guiding values.

But the solitary narrator does not have carte blanche to create coherence in any fashion whatsoever; stories are constrained by the productions and expectations of others. Because the stories we tell of our lives invariably touch upon the lives of those who matter to us, our self-accounts must be coordinated with the accounts others give of us and of themselves. Not that all must tell their stories in unison. But even in the differences a harmony must be audible; the ensemble of voices must add up to a workable whole. Further, this chorus of coordinated stories is framed by cultural expectations. What counts as a consonant whole is culturally determined and may change from time to time.

Chapter 2, by Stanley Rosenberg, Harriett Rosenberg, and Michael Farrell, describes a family whose members, first interviewed ten years ago, originally presented an ideal, unified picture of themselves. Ten years later, however, the family is torn apart by a daughter's defection. Each family member now tries to tell a history that will make sense of this experience, but each finds that this attempt is undermined. First, each account risks being undone by everyone else's discordant accounts. Second, each member (perhaps most clearly the father) is constrained to act and be understood within the prevailing cultural code that the authors call the Voice of the Father. Finally, narrative coherence is undermined by the ways that this father, following the changing mores of the 1960s and 1970s, has attempted to disavow paternal authority, though with apparently mixed motives and imperfect success. The coherence of the family story thus becomes multiply fractured—by the discord among individual stories and by the disintegration of a cultural norm. This chapter gives a first hint of how tensions in the society penetrate the family, converge on the growing child, and become fatefully preserved in the strain toward narrative harmony.

Whether the demand for coherence requires the narrator to coordinate his or her account with those of particular others or with the broader cultural model of intelligibility, this demand is commonly mediated by the narrator's regard for the audience and the interlocutory situation.

Susan Harding, in chapter 3, describes an interview with a Baptist minister who turned the occasion into an opportunity to bear witness. The climax of his personal account is the description of an accident in which he killed his son. Harding reads this man's story within a tradition of biblical fathers who sacrificed their sons. She argues further that the telling of the tale is the minister's second sacrifice: he surrenders the privacy of his grief so that he can win souls for God. By telling the story in this fashion the minister establishes a relationship with his audience. The allegory exerts an illocutionary force on Harding herself, placing her in the role of prospective convert. But the telling of the story thus affects more than just Harding's identity. By telling his story to a potential convert the minister reaffirms his own identity. He is no longer just a bereaved father but a man of God who, like God, sacrificed his son. In this way, the minister rescues himself from what might have been a sense-destroying tragedy and reclaims his identity in a world made meaningful by religious sacrifice.

So far we have assumed that narrative conventions empower the narrator in search of self-clarification and that a story's success in affecting an audience may ratify the speaker's self-understanding. But what are life-story tellers to do when unconventional circumstance places them at odds with conventional expectations? In chapter 4 Judith Modell interprets the stories told by mothers who surrendered their children for adoption but twenty years later hope to reestablish contact with them. These women face a litany of (implicit) charges—that they were irresponsible to have ever conceived the child, heartless to have surrendered it, self-indulgent to hope for reunion. In self-defense they now tell one another, at support group meetings, histories that emphasize their innocence, their unshakable devotion, and the social coercion that made surrender necessary. Their narrative strategy employs whatever images popular culture offers to redeem the legitimacy of old choices and new hopes. At the same time, Modell argues, the discrepancy between their experience and what the dominant society deems tellable directs our attention to a critique of cultural ideas of parenthood.

Unfortunately—and here our reading may differ from Modell's—these informants invite skepticism. Though we understand their motives, their stories seem to us one-sided. In retrospect, their love for their surrendered children appears to them wholeheartedly unambivalent. But did none of them consider that giving up a child would make school, career, marriage itself, more likely? Only at the end does one woman admit (but quickly, in passing), "You know, I thought that if I gave up the child my boyfriend would marry me. I have never told that to anyone before." This single remark betrays the unspoken subtext of these stories: women who hope, against public policy, to reestablish connections with lost children cannot acknowledge that they were ever ambivalent. Does it matter if narrators tell life stories that systematically exclude an impolitic portion of their history? These birthparents' accounts raise a general issue that runs through this book and, indeed, through the contemporary debate about narrative and historical truth (Spence, 1982). A story may tell us one thing officially but point our attention to another undeclared truth without which it rings false. Can coherence be bought at the expense of comprehensiveness or rhetorical success rest on self-deception?

The chapters by Harding and Modell both deal with the efforts of narrators to persuade an audience. Each assumes that this effort will be best served by narrative intelligibility. But is the readily understood always the best friend of self-formation? In chapter 5 Jeffrey Evans reminds us that what we can make clear to others does not necessarily serve our own development. He describes the balance choreographers seek between connecting with their audience and yet avoiding the shallow, untrustworthy understanding conveyed by words and stories. The world of dance offers the medium for this delicate negotiation. Modern choreographic culture promotes the tension between story telling and a narratively opaque, visceral connectedness. Evans's point is not simply that choreographers find physical movement more expressive than language but that their search for identity is in jeopardy when they are asked to give a transparent account of their commitments to an audience or interviewer.

This point, we believe, has more general paradoxical implications. Briefly, sociocentric theorists regard stories as the realization and display of a culture's narrational norms. In this view, however meritorious compared with the older mimetic theory, these theorists overlook the tension that may arise when occasional speakers, in self-conscious dissent, seek to revise these norms by simultaneously and artfully invoking *and* violating them: the limits of what our audience is ready to accept may hinder our as well as their development. Yet if our development is to be socially meaningful and consequential, we *must* be heard.

We conclude Part I with a transitional chapter. The personal accounts discussed so far aim to persuade listeners and to extract reactions of some sort. These reactions partly determine the success of the story. This means that a narrative cannot be formative if the narrator encounters an incredulous audience. In chapter 6 Ruth Behar illustrates one way this can happen. Esperanza, a poor Mexican woman accused by her village of sorcery, attempts to win redemption by having her listener carry her story across the border. What does she imagine will happen when her story is read, say, in Chicago? Sometimes she thinks it will be like confession—like a sin confessed up the line of priests and bishops and cardinals, to the ears of God himself. But then she falters, "No, no one would believe it."

Esperanza's doubt has two implications. One is that only a priest, but not an anthropologist, can absolve a sinner. The second point refers to another larger paradox—namely, that those who understand her perfectly, the members of her community, will not forgive her because they know too much, while those "beyond the river" cannot forgive her because they will not understand her story. In various degrees this paradox marks the ultimate isolation of every storyteller from the audience he or she needs. The "terms of exchange" between teller and listener control the emerging story.

The typical structure of Western autobiography is the history of a conversion as modeled by the *Confessions of St. Augustine*. We are forever telling how we became what we are by leaving behind what we were (Freccero, 1986). For confessors we seek out strangers. But can and will strangers take our sins, our suffering, from us? Esperanza discovers that what makes her a stranger in her own culture cannot be helped by a stranger. She cannot extract a significant acceptance from the stranger any more than she can from her own community. In a reversal of the adage, she cannot understand in herself what has not been forgiven by others. We may take this as an irreducible human predicament. By comparison, the difficulties we take up in Part II are of quite another sort. Here we are concerned with specific political-cultural conditions of self-understanding and their implications for the development of selfhood.

Part II: Cultural politics and the constraint of narrative identity

In the first chapter of Part II, Mary Gergen takes a fresh look at the assumptions of "plot." It is a reasonable assumption that coherent life stories contribute to that "subjective conviction of self-sameness over time" that is so central a feature of identity (Erikson, 1968). But Gergen argues that our assumptions about the coherent, pointed plot lines of conventional narrative form may be largely androcentric. Women's stories (and women's identities) are built around the significant relationships in their lives. This difference affects not only the contents of stories—men talk about careers and women about relationships—but their formal structure as well. Men's stories point single-mindedly toward a goal; women's are digressive and complex. What Gergen presents is not merely a new entry in the catalog of gender differences. Rather, she points to narrative conventions that have formative consequences: by giving personal development intelligible form, gender-specific templates determine how men and women are able to imagine and conduct their lives. For better or worse, life stories will make history, and thus their shaping power must interest the social historian as well as the student of narrative.

Gergen, who deals with published autobiographies, reminds us that the range of possible self-definitions is not determined chiefly in intimate conversational settings as suggested up to this point but inheres in the very grammar of what is sayable. Nowhere is this more evident than in Henry Greenspan's study of

Holocaust survivors. Greenspan argues that survivors' experiences are fundamentally untellable. No language exists to render what they have undergone. Instead, he suggests, their lives become a kind of text as they put on display, before an eye-averting audience, what language cannot articulate and listeners cannot bear hearing.

Cultural values are not less influential merely because they are not yet firmly in place. On the contrary, as chapters 9 and 10 show, value changes may split the smooth surface of old grammar just as tectonic shifts split the earth's crust. Discourse becomes twisted by the tug of the new against the old, clearing away old obstructions as well as opening up hazardous new crevasses. Some subjects, especially those caught in the historical splitting of older value configurations, as subcultures alter their relation to the larger culture, attempt to forge new models of intelligibility.

But new genres do not invariably empower. Aaron Gresson's informants, two black women who have been in intimate relationships with white men, attempt to tell their stories in a way that would make "color" nothing more than pigment. In so doing, each ignores the history and current reality of racial oppression. Their narratives can be read as attempts to hasten a genre—to invent new language without regard to the larger political reality in which their stories unfold. They relate their experience as though racial unity had already been achieved. But their attempts dissolve. Both women find themselves not only abandoned by but also unintelligible to their friends and families and even, we suspect, themselves.

The self-consciousness of a culture continually reforms its public discourse and the informing notions of good and evil. Before such values become securely established so that they exert their formative effect on lives "from within"— through primary socialization—their influence is that of a looming admonition, a threat to moral comfort. Barbara Walkover reports in Chapter 10 on couples contemplating the prospects of parenthood. Their accounts reveal many of the common forms of ambivalence, weighing the enrichment offspring bring to one's life against the awesome responsibility and loss of freedom a child entails. These self-doubts and fears are aggravated by the intrusion of a cultural morality that demands perfection in child rearing and threatens ignominy on those who fail. These prospective parents' stirrings of hope are all but squelched by the intimidating code of approved child rearing. As a result, reflection and self-development are apt to be frozen.

Part III: Critical awakenings and the renewal of narrative identity

Whereas Part I features the self-formative power of life stories and Part II the damage done to narrative self-understanding by oppressive social conditions, Part III takes up the question of liberation. Under what conditions can narrators transform and transcend the psychic and social obstacles that constrain them? Self-understanding cannot thrive in isolation from narrative norms. Even when it negates these, it must therefore, like any act of defiance, borrow from that which it rejects. In this part we explore whether—and if so, how—an understanding of what constrains us can ease the pursuit of fuller stories and fuller lives.

As chapters in this book will show, the obstacles encountered by the striving for development are entrenched in social conditions and in the psyches of each individual. Accordingly, the chapters in this part do not describe unfettered emancipation but rather the continual struggle of liberative insight against cultural and intrapsychic resistance.

Throughout this introduction we have spoken of "better" and "worse" life stories, aided or deformed by more or less restrictive narrative models. This evaluative stance, we recognize, is at odds with the prevailing ethic of accepting as subjectively true whatever self stories narrators propose. We have continually justified our critical posture in terms of a larger emancipatory interest. But what, concretely, does it mean to say that one version of a life story is better than another? Barring the realist criterion, what does "progress" look like?

Jacquelyn Wiersma describes a transformation in one woman's life history. In her original version Karen portrays herself as merely responsive to other people's ideas about how she should live. Her progress from faculty wife to scholarly authority is passive. But over several tellings her authorial voice grows stronger. The fact that she had motives of her own grows clearer, and with this change she reclaims not only her past itinerary but also her ambition for the future.

The transformation Wiersma describes is relevant to a point raised earlier by Gergen's chapter. At first, Karen's story lacks inner purpose and displays no outward signs of continuity. She seems to drift through a series of choices pressed on her by others. Such passivity is not an inevitable accompaniment of a social-relational or group-centered definition of the self. By the end of her journey—at least so far as we can follow it—Karen has rediscovered the connections in her own history and, with this, the steadiness of her own purpose. Her narrative becomes better in a literary sense: The plot becomes more coherent even while retaining the traces of her deep and moving concern for and engagement with others. She becomes more active without becoming more egocentric. And with this recovery of narrative coherence her life has reacquired a previously arrested momentum. This illustrates what we mean by progress.

Karen's story is not an unqualified victory, however. It ends with her reencountering the brute facts of academic sexism, the immediate incarnation of the broader social problem that made her original self-mystifying story necessary in the first place. Her liberation is thus only partial. She is now stimulated to struggle against the very real social obstacles that continue to confront her.

In Karen's case psychological liberation paved the way to social insight and engagement. For Catherine, the protagonist of Richard Ochberg's chapter, insight seemingly proceeds in the opposite direction. In high school Catherine found herself unable to convince others (and perhaps herself) that she could be both feminine and ambitious. Her solution was to divide her life, keeping boyfriends and classmates ignorant of her success in a radically compartmentalized life. But this solution threatened her identity; she felt "rotten to the core." Only after a stint in the Peace Corps in Africa could she recognize that the segregation of femininity and competence is a product of urban American culture; this social insight released her to reunite her divided images of herself and transform the earlier attitude of defiance into a legitimate and constructive dissent.

Neither Karen nor Catherine could simply declare herself free of social restriction. In Karen's case, society reasserted its claim in the form of external pressure: the faculty at her university seemed indifferent or hostile to her success. Catherine, by contrast, struggled with an inner restraint. Freeing herself of American cultural identity left her feeling rootless. The complexity of her solution—a blend of respect for local traditions and for universal rights—illustrates a problem of cultural critique: those who would free themselves of their own culture's restrictions must find alternative conceptions of social engagement through which to develop their identities. This too makes liberation difficult.

Despite the difficulties faced by Catherine and Karen, the spirit of cultural critique is optimistic. Changing cultural values and discourse may open new paths for self-understanding and action. We see this whenever subjects can appropriate a new vocabulary to caption—and thus capture—an old but previously elusive species of suffering.

Catherine Riessman presents an interview with a woman for whom marital rape led eventually to divorce. The term *marital rape* is, of course, comparatively new; a victimized narrator can take for granted neither the support of the law nor the horrified sympathy of her audience. In a close analysis of narrative strategy Riessman shows how Tessa recounts her experience, skillfully constructing her story to capture her listeners.

However, this account contains a second story, which offers an instructive contrast. In recounting a later episode, when a broken promise triggered her own violent anger, Tessa appears to lose control of her own narrative artistry. Riessman argues that this reflects a cultural distinction. Women's victimization is increasingly tellable, but women's expression of violent anger continues to fall outside culturally sanctioned narrative form and, therefore, self-understanding.

As we have by now suggested several times, our outlook on the prospects for cultural critique is guardedly optimistic. Recent history, notably the examples of feminism and ethnic politics, suggests that social organization and individual self-understanding may indeed be liberated by a steadfast attack on what once seemed the "only natural" assumptions of discourse. Still, one should not imagine that the road to emancipation is easy, merely a matter of pointing out readily recognizable misconceptions. The resistance to which we refer runs deep—in social organization and in individual psychology. In fact, it is the alliance of these two that makes critical consciousness so difficult. The final chapter in this section exhibits the interplay of psychological and cultural resistance.

Randy Earnest attempts to enlist Pat, a factory worker at Chrysler, in a critique of the seemingly autocratic policies at the plant where he works. But Pat shows little interest. At each proffered political gambit he offers a defense of management. In warding the interviewer off, he shows a resourcefulness that does not spurn unreason. To reduce this to psychic or social categories leads us astray. Rather, we confront a complex interaction. Earnest tracks the parallels between Pat's resistance to political analysis—a resistance supported by the union's compromise with management—and the microworkings of psychodynamic defense. Patterns of avoiding psychic danger, rooted in the narrator's early life experience, converge with the politics of the workplace in obstructing Pat's understanding of his situation and, by extension, his pursuit of a more rewarding organization of the workplace.

We close with a word about the diversity of readings presented here. In setting out the ideas that organize this volume we have no doubt encouraged the expectation that our various contributors speak from common assumptions and purposes. As the reader will soon discover, this is hardly the case—and for good reason. There is no binding theory of narrative, no standard set of procedures comparable to those used in experimental social psychology, opinion survey, or psychophysical measurement. Investigators usually reach for narrative methods because of their evident power with respect to the topic at hand. The authors brought together here are an accurate reflection of the field of narrative studies. They, too, approach their subject matter from diverse disciplinary interests and theoretical orientations—feminist, Lacanian, Marxist, symbolic-interactionist, linguistic, psychodynamic. Only a few exercise a primary methodological interest. It is not surprising, therefore, that each of the chapters offers insights into a distinct topic by drawing on its author's own more or less explicit notions of how the tale bears on the teller or on the phenomena and experiences it relates. Thence the uncommon variety of topics and agendas between the covers of this volume.

To illustrate this conceptual diversity, every chapter recognizes that personal accounts are selective. But in some this is understood in terms of repression; ego-alien memories and desires are banished from conscious self-representation. In others, inclusion and omission, emphasis and minimization, are discussed as matters of narrative strategy. To cite another example of conceptual diversity, every one of our contributors recognizes the embeddedness of individual self-understanding in culturally conditioned discourse. But some go one step further in calling our attention to the protagonists' own understandings of their social situations. The narrators in some chapters speak in what are taken to be the "only natural" terms imaginable, leaving it to the reader to see how culturally or historically contingent those terms are. Other chapters feature narrators who are themselves becoming aware of their social predicament. In these narrators a degree of critical insight has been awakened.

We determined to let each essay speak for itself rather than to commandeer them under a single theoretical banner. It seemed to us that we would learn more about our theoretical project if we gathered investigations self-contained, independently conceived, and brought together from many quarters. Only in our own interpretive chapters, the introduction and the conclusion, and in the arrangement of the chapters would we impose our unifying framework over the essays to test whether it could contain them or whether they would burst its joints. The reader is invited to join us in reaching this verdict.

Is ours a useful perspective? Will it show us a way forward for academic research and, more important, for individual lives and public action? Although formal argument is inevitable—and will be resumed in the conclusion—we suspect that few readers will be persuaded by this alone. The proof, instead, lies in the practical demonstration of what this way of reading can illuminate. Herewith the pudding.

REFERENCES

Allport, Gordon W. 1965. *Letters from Jenny.* New York: Harcourt, Brace & World.
Belenky, Mary T. 1986. *Women's Ways of Knowing.* New York: Basic Books.
Bertaux, Daniel. 1981. *Biography and Society.* Beverly Hills, Calif.: Sage.
Bleicher, Josef. 1980. *Contemporary Hermeneutics.* London: Routledge & Kegan Paul.
Cohler, Bertram. 1982. "Personal Narrative and Life Course." In *Life-span Development and Behavior.* Edited by P. Baltes and O. Brim. Vol. 4. New York: Academic Press.
Dewey, John. 1960. "Time and Individuality." In *On Experience, Nature, and Freedom.* Indianapolis: Bobbs-Merrill.
Erikson, Erik H. 1968. *Identity: Youth and Crisis.* New York: W. W. Norton.
Freccero, John. 1986. "Autobiography and Narrative." In *Reconstructing Individualism.* Edited by T. C. Heller, M. Sosna, and D. E. Wellbery. Stanford: Stanford University Press.
Gadamer, Hans-Georg. 1989. *Truth and Method.* New York: Crossroad.
Gergen, Kenneth J., and Mary M. Gergen. 1986. "Narrative Form and the Construction of Psychological Science." In *Narrative Psychology.* Edited by T. R. Sarbin. New York: Praeger.
Geuss, Raymond. 1981. *The Idea of a Critical Theory: Habermas and the Frankfurt School.* Cambridge: Cambridge University Press.
Gilligan, Carol. 1982. *In a Different Voice.* Cambridge, Mass.: Harvard University Press.
Hanson, Norman R. 1973. "Observation." In *Theories and Observation in Science.* Edited by R. E. Grandy. Englewood Cliffs, N.J.: Prentice-Hall.
Horkheimer, Max. 1972. "Traditional and Critical Theory." In *Critical Theory: Selected Essays.* New York: Herder and Herder.
Landau, Misia. 1984. "Human Evolution as Narrative." *American Scientist* 72:262–268.
Langness, Lewis L., and Gelya Frank. 1981. *Lives.* Novato, Calif.: Chandler and Sharp.
Levinson, Daniel. 1978. *Seasons of a Man's Life.* New York: Alfred A. Knopf.
Lewis, Oscar. 1961. *The Children of Sanchez.* New York: Random House.

Personal Narratives Group. 1989. *Interpreting Women's Lives: Feminist Theory and Personal Narratives*. Bloomington: Indiana University Press.

Rabinow, Paul, and William Sullivan. 1979. *Interpretive Social Science*. Berkeley: University of California Press.

Rorty, Richard. 1982. *Consequences of Pragmatism*. Minneapolis: University of Minnesota Press.

Rosaldo, Renato. 1989. *Culture and Truth: The Remaking of Social Analysis*. Boston: Beacon Press.

Roth, Paul. 1987. *Meaning and Method in the Social Sciences*. Ithaca, N.Y.: Cornell University Press.

Rubin, Lillian. 1976. *Worlds of Pain: Life in the Working Class Family*. New York: Basic Books.

Sarbin, Theodore. 1986. *Narrative Psychology: The Storied Nature of Human Conduct*. New York: Praeger.

Shaw, Clifford. 1938. *The Jack-Roller: A Delinquent Boy's Own Story*. Chicago: University of Chicago Press.

Shotter, John, and Kenneth J. Gergen. 1989. *Texts of Identity*. London: Sage.

Spence, Donald P. 1982. *Narrative Truth and Historical Truth: Meaning and Interpretation in Psychoanalysis*. New York: W. W. Norton.

Taylor, Charles. 1979. "Interpretation and the Sciences of Man." In *Interpretive Social Science: A Reader*. Edited by P. Rabinow and W. M. Sullivan. Berkeley: University of California Press.

Walzer, Michael. 1987. *Interpretation and Social Criticism*. Cambridge, Mass.: Harvard University Press.

Wellmer, Albrecht. 1971. *Critical Theory of Society*. New York: Herder and Herder.

White, Hayden. 1978. *Tropics of Discourse*. Baltimore: Johns Hopkins University Press.

I

Life Stories and Identity

ELLIOT G. MISHLER

1 Work, Identity, and Narrative: An Artist-Craftsman's Story

Labour not only produces commodities; it also produces itself and the workers as a commodity. . . . The estrangement of the object of labour merely summarizes the estrangement, the alienation in the activity of labour itself. . . . [The worker] therefore does not confirm himself in his work, but denies himself, feels miserable and not happy, does not develop free mental and physical energy, but mortifies his flesh and ruins his mind. Hence the worker feels himself only when he is not working. . . . His labour is . . . not the satisfaction of a need but a mere means to satisfy needs outside itself. . . . It belongs not to him but to another, and . . . in it he belongs not to himself but to another.—Karl Marx ([1844] 1975, 323–326)

The pleasure which ought to go with the making of every piece of handicraft has for its basis the keen interest which every healthy man takes in healthy life, and is compounded, it seems to me, chiefly of three elements; variety, hope of creation and the self-respect which comes of a sense of usefulness; to which must be added that mysterious bodily pleasure which goes with the deft exercise of the bodily powers. . . . Now this compound pleasure in handiwork I claim as the birthright of all workmen. I say that if they lack any part of it they will be so far degraded, but if they lack it altogether they are, so far as their work goes, I will not say slaves, the word would not be strong enough, but machines more or less conscious of their own unhappiness.—William Morris (1883, 174)

Craftsmanship as a fully idealized model of work gratification involves six major features: There is no ulterior motive in work other than the product being made

I have had the good fortune to have colleagues who could leaven their criticism with constructive suggestions and encouragement. In particular, discussions over the past few years of various approaches to narrative analysis with members of my Research Seminar and the MIDAS Narrative Study Group have influenced the development of my work. I would like to acknowledge the suggestions of: Jane Attanucci, Darlene Douglas-Steele, Rosanna Hertz, Allyssa McCabe, Catherine Riessman, and Dennie Wolf. This paper has also benefited from close readings of earlier drafts by Vicky Steinitz, Katherine Young, and the editors of this volume. I also wish to thank Fred Wharton and the other craftspersons who trusted me with their stories. Without their graciousness, cooperation, and interest there would be no work to report.

and the processes of its creation. The details of daily work are meaningful because they are not detached in the worker's mind from the product of the work. The worker is free to control his working action. The craftsman is thus able to learn from his work; and to use and develop his capacities and skills in its prosecution. There is no split of work and play, or work and culture. The crafts-man's way of livelihood determines and infuses his entire mode of being.
—*C. Wright Mills (1951, 220)*

These observations—by Marx on alienated labor, Morris on the craftsman ideal, and Mills on a model of craftsmanship—span a hundred years. They trace the history of a radical, social, and political critique of the human impacts of industrialization and a modern capitalist economic system. This critical perspective, contrasting the experiences and consequences of crafts work with currently dominant modes of work, informs this study of identity formation among contemporary craftspersons.

The central task for craftspersons is how to sustain their commitment to and motivation for a nonalienated form of work in an inhospitable sociocultural eco-nomic environment. Faced by market demands and the need to earn a living, they must forge an identity grounded in motives for autonomy and control and guided by the values of Morris's craftsman ideal—of work as creative, varied, and useful. Further, they have to balance a crafts "mode of being" with the demands of family and social relationships. Finally, they have to choose a particular crafts identity from among those available at this time, when there are competing perspectives on the meaning of the "crafts."

I shall refer to the process through which individuals define and resolve these problems over the life course as identity formation, which is made visible and becomes available for analysis through personal narratives—that is, individuals' retrospective "tellings" of their histories. Such narratives were elicited in this study from a small but varied group of craftspersons—furniture makers, glass-makers, potters, weavers—through unstructured, in-depth life-history inter-views.

In this chapter, I present and apply a model for narrative analysis to one artist-furniture maker's account of his work history, focusing on his achievement of a particular craft identity. His achieved identity is his personal solution to general problems faced by all craftspersons, but it is not idiosyncratic. Other artist-craftspersons' narratives display remarkable parallels. For this reason, I view his identity path—the plot of his narrative—as paradigmatic.

A Model for the Analysis of Work-Identity Narratives

The model of narrative analysis applied here has two complementary components. The first represents the narrative structurally as a set of abstract "realms" of

WORK IDENTITY REALMS

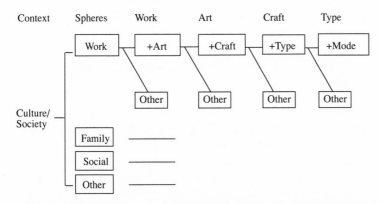

Figure 1.1. The Structure of Crafts Work Identities: Realms and Choices
This decision tree represents a set of logical, hierarchically ordered choices among successive realms within the sphere of Work. Alternatives in each realm are contingent on prior
choices. Achievement of a work identity as an artist-craftsperson is marked as a sequence of
positive choices. Other spheres and their associated part-identities are noted but not specified. The sociocultural context is the basic frame, defining the range of spheres, realms,
and choices for identity formation. (The terms *frame* and *realm* are borrowed from Young's
[1984, 1987] elegant model of narrative analysis.)

possible choices within the sphere of work. These "realms" are hierarchically
ordered from Art to Craft to Type and Mode of craft. This is shown schematically
in figure 1.1.

Space limitations preclude detailed explication, but a few features of this representation require brief comment. First, the "realms" specified and their ordering
are based on and generalized from artist-craftspersons' work-history narratives.
This is the set of culturally defined occupational choices for a subgroup of
craftspersons who are, in turn, a subcategory of artists. This structural component
of the model links individuals' choices to the sociocultural context. Other types of
craftspersons and other occupations, with different realms and choices, would
display different "structures." The model, therefore, provides a framework for
comparative and multiple-case studies.[1]

Second, this structure is an analytic abstraction. It represents a logical, hierarchical ordering among a set of choices, each prior one framing and partitioning
successive ones. Thus, choosing Art [+Art] within the Work realm frames the
next pair of possible choices between the Crafts [+Craft] and other work within
the realm of Art [+Other]. This logical ordering does not correspond to temporally ordered sequences of choices in actual work histories. The historical-
biographic dimension is represented in the second component, shown in figure

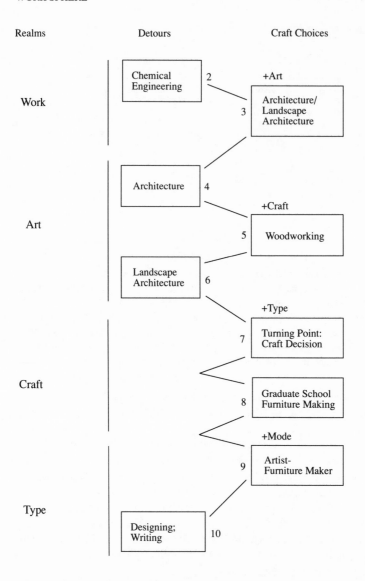

Figure 1.2. The Path to a Craft Identity: An Artist-Furniture Maker
The work history of an artist-furniture maker is represented as a sequence of choices
between and within different work-identity realms. "Detours" are "off" the path to his
current identity; "craft" choices are "on-line." The numbering of choices corresponds to the
actual sequence shown in his work-history narrative (table 1.1).

1.2, which outlines the occupational career of an artist-furniture maker I call Fred Wharton.

Fred Wharton's path to his achieved identity as an artist-furniture maker [#9] displays shifts back and forth within and between the realms represented structurally in figure 1.1. The principal distinction among these recursive moves or embedded cycles (Bremond [1966] 1980; also Grosse, 1978) is between off-line choices, or "detours," and on-line ones leading to his current identity and mode of work.

Categorizing choices as "on-line" or "off-line" is a critical analytic step in my interpretive approach to identity formation. It is guided by two assumptions: (1) the account is retrospective, and categorization depends on Fred Wharton's current view of a choice as having led to or away from his achieved identity; (2) the specific realms of the framing context within which a choice is made, rather than its particular features, determine whether it is "on-line" or "off-line." Thus, architecture and landscape architecture as college majors are on-line [+Art] choices within the Work realm [#3], but are redefined as detours when chosen within the Art realm [Other: #4 and #6].

Finally, the path is open to the future. He is considering a change in his mode of work, in which writing on furniture design and designing furniture for large-scale production may become more primary. I have tentatively classified this as a detour [#10], but will return below to its ambiguity of placement.

The two complementary components of this model of narrative analysis—the structure of logical alternatives and the path followed—parallel the distinction made by linguists between paradigmatic and syntagmatic aspects of discourse, for example, Jakobson's (1960) vertical and horizontal axes of language and Ricoeur's (1981) nonchronological and chronological dimensions of narrative. Although some structuralist theorists view the first as the "deep" and the second as the "surface" level of analysis, I am in accord with Ricoeur's view that these dimensions are both necessary and interdependent. One cannot have a narrative without both of them, but neither is analytically subordinate to the other.

The Narrativization of Identity Formation

Cohler (1982) argues that a personal narrative, "recounted at any point," imposes an intelligible and followable order on an "inherently unpredictable" life course and "represents the most internally consistent interpretation of presently understood past, experienced present, and anticipated future at that time" (pp. 206–207). Slavney and McHugh (1984), discussing how life stories function in clinical medicine and psychiatry, take a similar position: "A life story is a plausible, chronological, and coherent narrative that reconstructs the development of the present state of affairs. It starts at a certain time in the patient's life and draws together particular information about him into a linear perspective that makes his current distress seem the logical and sometimes even the inevitable outcome of his past" (p. 279; also McHugh and Slavney, 1983). This perspective, on the reconstructive nature and coherence function of personal narratives, is adopted here. It suggests that an analysis of identity formation should begin with a narrator's present sense of herself or himself, since the past is viewed in its light.

From Fred Wharton's interview, I extracted those sections where he talked about his jobs and his reasons for entering and leaving them, and arranged them chronologically. In this way, I "constructed" his work-history narrative. In doing so, I am selecting for study the "order of occurrence" or the order of the "told" rather than the "order of the telling" (Goodman, 1980). This analytic step is unavoidable in any interpretation of the life course, particularly in interview research where the "order of the telling" reflects the contingencies of interaction between interviewers and respondents. This step alerts us to the active role of the researcher in reconstructing a subject's account as a narrative—that is, as an analytic object that becomes the basis for interpretation.[2]

Telling us about how and why he changed course at different points in his life, Fred Wharton accounts plausibly and coherently for how his current identity is grounded in his work history. Each episode has the three-stage structure proposed in many models of narrative analysis (Mishler, 1986b): a problematic situation, action, and resolution. Following Bremond's model (Bremond, [1966] 1980; Grosse, 1978), which allows for recursions and embedded cycles, we may treat the episodes as "chained" together and reconstruct his account as an extended narrative.

I began my interview with Wharton, as with other respondents, by briefly stating my aims in the study, emphasizing that the interview would be open-ended and unstructured, giving him primary control over its content. I said that I wanted to "talk" with "craftspeople" about their work, how they came to be doing what they do, their problems and how they deal with them, and "what's involved in the kind of life you lead, that's related to—ah to being in the crafts. ah Those sorts of questions."

He responded immediately to my opening remarks without waiting for a specific question. His first statement is a significant clue as to how he defines his identity, a definition that will feature thematically in his narrative: "All right. I—I hope this is going to be of benefit to you, in that ah I don't consider myself just a craftsperson. I consider myself a designer, um committed to craftsmanship [laughs] in a way. ah And I do a—a number of things. And ah ah I do lead a partial life as a craftsman."

Later, after his roughly chronological account of his work history, I returned to his distinction between a craftsman and a designer, asking what he means and how this compares to the usual and hotly debated contrast within the craftsworld between a craftsperson and an artist.

That distinction between artists and craftspersons is this endless discussion that goes on and on and on in schools, and between professionals, and all that. And ah to me a craftsperson and an artist are synonymous, if you're looking at those you respect as good craftspeople. Not people who are just churning out objects, but people who are um doing personal work and ah doing ah progressive work. Whether they're—whether they're painters, or whether they're ceramic people, that doesn't matter.

Then I asked him, "Does it have to do with one-of-a-kind as compared to multiple copies of an object? Or—?"

"It has to do probably with their input into creating the object, rather than um ah being given a design, or being given something to copy and produce, and just giv-giving with their manual skills, as opposed to their intellect and their creativity."

I then said, "But now the designer contrasts with the craftsperson that you were mentioning."

"I would think that the—the final distinction between a designer and a craftsperson or an artist would be that the artist or craftsperson are making something—um looking for the best word that—um making something that revolves around their personal interests, whether it's an emotional thing or whether it's a visual thing. ah Where a designer is taking into consideration—ah making something that would appeal to more people. Okay? That ah is problem solving."

Thus, artists or craftspersons are doing it for themselves, whereas designers must be attentive to "whether other people can respond to it ah in a—ah in a ah real positive way. Or whether it's affordable, or whether anyone would want to make it."

This duality in his work identity, as primarily a designer but leading a "partial life as a craftsman," recurs as he talks about various transitions. Although differing in orientation, both designers and artist-craftspersons retain control over the conception and design of what they make. Maintaining such control is a pervasive theme, and the dialectic between work for oneself and for others motivates his career and occupational choices.

Thus, of his change in college major, he says:

I decided I wanted to do something else [than chemical engineering] and wasn't sure what. And I was really intrigued with ah environments and houses and decided I wanted to be an architect. And after a year I found out that that was—that was a dream. That architects didn't design houses. [laughs] They couldn't afford to spend the time designing houses, for the most part. . . . I was searching for something to do and found landscape architecture, which seemed somewhat appealing to me. . . . I ah enjoyed seeing the kinds of projects they worked on. It seemed that had more potential of um well actually doing design work, and ah having control over design.

Young architects, he observes, were likely to work for large firms where designs would have to be "approved by your boss, and by a cost estimator, and whatever design input you had anyway probably changed around and controlled. So ah it [laughs] it didn't seem really appealing to me." Further, the "majority" of architects would have to work for "fifteen or twenty years before they had any sort of design control."

I then asked, "But—but in landscape architecture you thought there'd be more direct control?"

"And there is. A faster—I believe a faster control. ah The kinds of projects you worked on were a little bit smaller in scale. . . . And you know that buildings just—you know just require the input of so many people. Wherein the courtyard behind the building doesn't. You have much more control with that."

Later, when he left the landscape architecture firm for graduate school in furniture making [#7], his personal "interests" as an artist became more prominent.

I made the ah decision to ah go into furniture, just in that I had an intuitive sense about woodworking, which I didn't about landscape architecture. uh Some landscape architects . . . they'd go to a nursery and select trees. Just the right kind of tree. And they'd bring it to the site, and they'd position it just in the right place, and have it rotated just the right way. They had it—a real sense of—of how that should be. And I didn't. uh Whereas if—in—talking about woodworking, I—I knew exactly looking at a board whether it should be used for a tabletop or a table leg. I just knew that. Felt very comfortable with it.

His artistic interests remained central for the three years of graduate school training where "totally investing" himself in the "furniture world as a craftsman" he got a degree in crafts: "Treating furniture as an art form. A lot of the things I did weren't ah heavily involved in a functional way. I mean I wasn't concerned with that as much as a visual impact of a piece."

His successive "on-line" choices trace a path of increasing specification, shown in figure 1.2 and table 1.1: from his initial entry into the "design world" through college majors in architecture and landscape architecture [#3], learning woodworking skills [#5], going to graduate school for training in furniture making "as an art form" [#7, #8], to his current work and identity as an artist-furniture maker [#9].

His motives for these choices closely parallel those features of nonalienated labor, the pleasures of handicraft, and the model of craftsmanship to which I called attention earlier. Thus, he emphasizes the self-directed nature of his work, where the making of an object as well as its design are under his own control. He also has a persistent drive to do creative work, which includes variety and is "progressive," providing for and expressing a continuous process of learning and development.

Table 1.1

Achieving a Craft Identity: The Narrative of an Artist-Furniture Maker

Narrative Episodes	*Identity Narrative: Interview Excerpts*
1. Origins	"My beginnings were in—uh I did a little bit of woodworking when I was a kid, mostly with wooden boats."
2. Detour₁	[Chemical Engineering] "I'm one of those people really vague about what I wanted to do. I—I entered—I got accepted to college as a chemical engineer, because I was interested in plastics at the time."
3. Art World	[Architecture/Landscape Architecture] "I decided I wanted to do something else. . . . I started in an undergraduate program as an architect and then became a landscape architect, and became involved in the design world in that way."
4. Detour₂	[Architecture] "And ah after school I had a job for a while with a firm. ah The firm . . . collapsed. Folded. And uh I met an architect, and he and I decided to design some geodesic domes, and do that kind of thing."
5. Craft Skills	[Woodworking] "And I met a third-generation craftsman in Indiana, who uh allowed me to share his shop space with— And ah that's when I really started to do woodworking. . . . But he just knew so much technically, and I learned an awful lot."
6. Detour₃	[Landscape Architecture] ".hh Well uh several things happened after ah close to two years. . . . And I felt like I was being locked into Milltown, Indiana, for the rest of my life. . . . And I felt like I was wasting all my—my ah schooling as a landscape architect. So at that time Sarah and I moved to ah Granit, where I started working as a landscape architect. And I did that for five and a half years."
7. Turning Point	[Craft Decision] "And ah it just wasn't what I wanted to do for the rest of my life. . . . So I did a search, and uh decided to go to

(*continued*)

Table 1.1
(*Continued*)

	graduate school in furniture. . . . And the older I got the more I found I—I didn't have enough—as much time or energy outside my—my career so to speak, to devote to that [woodworking]. . . . I made the—ah the decision to, ah, go into furniture. Just in that I had an intuitive sense about woodworking, which I didn't about landscape architecture."
8. Preparation	[Graduate School/Furniture Making] "And I ended up um . . opting to go to Griswold for—to Midwest State University, um, because I liked the—ah the artistic involvement. It was a Fine Arts program. And uh I spent a year there and then I decided t' change programs. Went to Anderson University in Glenside for another two years . . hh So three years altogether, totally investing myself in—in ah the furniture world as a craftsman. Got a—a degree in crafts, .hh ah treating furniture as an art form."
9. Craft Identity	[Artist-Furniture Maker] "What I didn't—what I didn't ah . . think about too much was, ah . . . . . . what kind of, ah, options there were in a real sense, on getting a degree in—in crafts. . . . I—I thought well I'd—I'd pursue a teaching job. . . . And I did get the one in—at Graylin. . . . I started teaching at the school, and, ah, ... I collected more equipment and set up the shop here. . . . Started doing some shows and commission work, and that all went pretty well."
10. Detour₄ Future	[Designing; Writing] "My expectations of what I wanted out of life changed. And I worked a lot. I mean I—I—my—my whole life I've worked a lot. ah And—ah that didn't bother me until probably around uh three years ago, ah, where I guess I . . . I keep doing this, and there are other things I want to do. . . . My work is .hh so time consuming, so labor intensive, that it's very difficult to get any—ah any financial reward from it. You can get by. I mean you can make a living. And you can—and you can exist. But I want to do a bit more than that. . . . Three years ago . . . I was in a meeting at the publishers.

(*continued*)

Table 1.1
(*Continued*)

... And I said, you know you people need some design articles in your magazine. . . . The book editor said, 'Why don't you write a book about it?' . . . I set off on doing an outline and sample chapters. . . . And ah the book got accepted. And I've been working on that. . . . And that should be ah ah relatively a good change for me, ah probably both my financial situation, or as a matter of reputation. . . .

What kind of design issues are important today? And I think that's—that's an issue that I'm—I'm wanting to deal with next, when I say I—I'd like to do some design in a production sense, because most people I know of are just dealing with style. . . . Dealing with style seems silly right now. . . . And the same with furniture people. So is there another step that can be taken on a broad scale, that improves our situation. To get the people more options of what they have, of what they live with, what they can afford, and how it can be better used."

Note: The numbering of the narrative episodes and their summary characterizations in brackets, "[ ]," correspond to the ordering and labeling of identity path choices in figure 1.2. In these illustrative excerpts, elisions from the complete text of the interview are marked by ". . .".

This aesthetic motive, distinctive to the arts and the art-framed crafts,[3] plays a significant role in Fred Wharton's narrative and is central to his identity. He expresses it directly in response to my question about what kept him "at it" when he wasn't earning a living or wasn't sure where the work was going: "Initially my drive to make what I considered beautiful objects was—ah was just something I had to do. Was—there was no other choice."

Different motives appear in his "off-line" choices. They reflect other "part-identities" in other life spheres and focus on earning enough money to sustain a more satisfying family and personal life. About his shift from woodworking to a job in landscape architecture in another city [#6], he says:

.hh well uh several things happened after ah close to two years. One was that I started buying a tremendous amount of material. Lumber . . . like—like piles and piles of lumber, stacked out on a farm field. And machinery. And I felt like I was being locked into Milltown, Indiana, for the rest of my life. And uh I also uh had a minor accident on a machine, and I started worrying about my hands. And I felt like I was wasting all my—my ah schooling, as a landscape architect. So at that time Sarah and I moved to ah Granit, where I started working as a landscape architect, and did that for five and a half years.

Although he "wasn't totally happy with that profession," he ended up working for "a good firm, 'n good projects, and .hh all that." However, "It just wasn't what I wanted to do for the rest of my life." As we know, this marks the Turning Point [#7] in his career, initiating training in furniture making. It was not, however, a decision made in a vacuum. As he says, in response to my question about this, he had continued with woodworking, but as a side involvement. "I did what I could. I uh had my tools. I had small shop spaces here and there. . . . And the older I got, the more I found I—I didn't have enough—as much time or energy outside my— my career so to speak, to devote to that. So—ah I made—I made that deci- sion. . . . I made the—ah the decision to ah go into furniture."

From other information in the interview, we learn that his wife completed her training and started her career when he was working in landscape architecture. He does not mention, and I failed to ask, whether the timing of his decision was related to her having established herself in her career by then. Sarah continued living in Granit during the time he was away at graduate school. This was also when their son was in elementary school.

He supported himself in graduate school through odd jobs and fellowships, and Sarah supported herself through her own work. This financial arrangement of keeping incomes separate and sharing household expenses continues into the present, when Sarah earns more than he does: "That ah direction took off ah when I went out to graduate school, and the—ah ah we started getting used to taking care of ourselves financially, as much as possible." Having known "each other since junior high school" and been "married for quite a long time," he feels "pretty comfortable" with this "income division." It gives him a "sense of pride, in what you should do to take care of yourself, you know. And I don't like the idea feeling like I'm being supported."

This suggests that their mutually recognized abilities to "take care" of them- selves may have been a factor in his deciding to give up a stable job with a secure income for graduate school—a decision he made without thinking too much about "what kind of, ah, options there were, in a real sense," although he "was very optimistic about that," but he "didn't look at it in terms of dollars and cents, so to speak."

His narrative extends into the future [#10]. He is writing a book, a "visual guide to designing furniture" for the "guy who has a shop in his garage." His aim is to "educate people about design," to foster "aesthetic awareness." He also wants to work "on a different scale," designing for factory production.

The direction I want to take with ah the kind of work I do, is not doing one-of- a-kind pieces, that are really hard to do, or really time consuming, but try to— try to invest myself in—um in design that—that is affordable by people. More people. ah That works real well, and that also um has some visual integrity. That I think is innovative, or—you know or special. And that probably is a bigger challenge than ah doing work like that, where virtually anything goes.

He would build only the "prototype," "an actual piece," "and then hopefully someone else would make the other, ah, thousand whatever."

My labeling of these intended changes as a detour [#10] is tentative. It reflects the anchoring of my analysis in his present achieved identity, the vantage point from which he has reconstructed his "past." His "future" is "off-line" in the same way as his earlier job in landscape architecture. I am treating his future, anticipated but still unrealized, as part of his history. However, were I to reinterview Fred Wharton in five years, his "new" identity would be the point of departure, and the structure of his narrative might be quite different, with choices redefined and realigned. These observations reflect a key assumption of my approach—namely, that personal narratives are contextually contingent in a double sense: responsive to and embedded in both the current life circumstances of the teller and the situation of the "telling" (Mishler, 1979, 1986a, 1986b; see also Schafer, 1980 and Smith, 1980).

His motives for change are another source of uncertainty in assessing the identity implications of his plans. Clearly, writing about and designing furniture for large-scale production are consistent with his lifelong aesthetic interest and drive. Further, his insistence that he himself will make the "prototype" reflects his deep, continuing commitment to crafts work, to the actual "making" of the object. On these grounds, we might perhaps view his future plans as a respecification of his present work identity rather than as a detour.

He is, however, also impelled by conflicts among other motives. Essentially, at this time in his life, he experiences an imbalance among competing and mutually exclusive desires and needs. These conflicts drive his narrative forward into a future that he hopes will resolve them and restore a satisfactory balance. One conflict is between the intense effort his work requires and the inadequacy of financial rewards. Another is between the dominating role of work in his life and the pursuit of other pleasures, for which he now has neither time nor money. A third is between his "drive" to make one-of-a-kind "beautiful objects" and an expanded interest in increasing "visual awareness" and general concern about the ecological impact of design. His future identity represents a complex resolution of these multiple and interdependent conflicts.

The disparity between the "time-consuming" and "labor-intensive" requirements of his work and his earnings is not a new problem. In the year prior to the interview, his gross income from sales of pieces that he had designed and made was $6,500—a typical annual return. Although he is well known and his work appears regularly in juried museum and gallery shows, his income from his crafts work is roughly the same as the average for a national sample of all types of craftspersons (Cerf et al., 1982a, 1982b). As is also true of them, another job provides his "primary" income, in his case as a teacher.

This long-standing problem recently took on new meaning: "That ah didn't bother me until probably around three years ago. . . . There are other things I want to do. I want to travel. And I found a sport that I absolutely loved. . . . And I didn't have enough time to devote to that, or even money to buy the equipment that I wanted to buy." Though he can "get by," "make a living," and "exist" on his income, he wants "to do a little more than that." He also points to another significant change in his life: "I was getting close on thirty-nine now. You know I was getting close to what I considered being—getting old. [laughs] And ah I know—you know this is—this has gotta change, you know. It's gotta get easier."

There has also been a shift in the relative emphasis he places on personal gratifications from others' responses to his work and its more general social and cultural effects: "For me there's another facet of why I made things, which is now ah not a reason any more. And that—there was a real thrill of making work and having it exhibited in a gallery, and ah having people, um pay attention to my work. And after a number of years, there's—that thrill isn' there anymore." His desire to "get the approval of my peers, or ah the people that I ah idolized" has "become unimportant to me to a large degree. And ah I would like to see a little bit of a financial reward behind there, more of a financial reward behind it. So um I'm very careful now about why I start making things."

Becoming more salient, on the other hand, is his interest in educating the general public, who "don't understand the difference" in quality between handmade, well-designed furniture and mass-produced pieces, and are unwilling to pay the price differential. He also wants to raise the awareness of both furniture makers and the public about the ecological consequences of different materials and different ways of making furniture.

This analysis has highlighted the significance for this artist-craftsman's identity of specific motives—for autonomy, control, and creativity in his work. These correspond to the features of nonalienated labor, limned in the theoretical tradition represented by Marx, Morris, and Mills. Conflicts among these and other motives and their resolutions have been located within certain framing contexts: historical and cultural definitions of arts and crafts as spheres of work, economic and market constraints on the earning potential of crafts work, and family roles and obligations.

Each life is more than one story, and each story has many versions. No particular "telling" can be captured fully in any single analysis, however detailed and complex. Nonetheless, I believe that applying the two-level model of narrative analysis to Fred Wharton's account of his work history has led to a context-sensitive interpretation of how he shaped and reshaped his work identity over time and how he achieved a sense of coherence and continuity through changes in motives and life circumstances. Further, we have learned how his particular way of narrativizing his life is both a resource and an achievement, serving to sustain his commitment to a nonalienated form of work. Finally, this interpretation is both empirically grounded in his own ways of telling and understanding, and theoretically relevant to general issues of adult identity formation.

Discussion: Identity Formation and Personal Narratives

Within the perspective informing this study, the dialectic between narrativization of one's life and identity formation is the central dynamic. This is a specification of the argument advanced by Cohler and others that personal narratives serve a "coherence" function. In how Fred Wharton retrospectively narrativizes his occupational history, he achieves coherence and continuity in his sense of himself as an artist-craftsperson. His "strategy of emplotment" (White, 1973; 1987) allows him to tell his life story as a series of temporally ordered episodes in which transitions can be "explained" as efforts to resolve conflicting motives and pursue certain aims. Discontinuities in his career, the "detours," are embedded within the primary trajectory. They do not disturb the coherence of the narrative because they are "chained," in Bremond's term, to both prior and succeeding episodes by adequate "reasons."

My reconstruction of his story displays the essential markers of the well-structured narrative in the Western cultural tradition: a temporally ordered series of events (Labov, 1972; Labov and Waletzky, 1967), coherence at several levels (Agar and Hobbs, 1982), and the basic agent-conflict-action structure (Rumelhart, 1975, 1977). Finally, the story has a "point"—it is not merely a chronicle of successive events. His currently achieved work identity as an artist-furniture maker, combined with his future plans, is an understandable conclusion to the story; at the same time, it is the source of our understanding of the story as a "path."

The success of any story—that is, its telling/hearing as a coherent and meaningful account—depends on presuppositions about the required features of narratives that are shared by narrators and their audiences, including, in this case, me in my dual roles as interviewer and analyst and, for its "retelling" in this chapter, other readers as well. This points to the importance of the interview situation and the role of the interviewer. These relatively neglected topics are central to my approach, and attending to them allows us to appreciate how shared cultural conventions about narratives enter into their production and are not simply brought in at the stage of analysis. That is, Fred Wharton's narrative is a version of his life that was jointly constructed in the interview situation. It reflects my active participation—how I let him know that his "story" made sense, how and when I asked him to fill in "missing" pieces, as well as how I failed to ask for further information. These effects are not a function of my idiosyncratic interviewing style but are inherent to all interview situations (Mishler, 1986a; 1986b).

This complex dialectic between researcher and subject in the construction and interpretation of personal narratives brings the critical problem of validity into the foreground. For many investigators engaged in one or another variant of qualitative or inquiry-guided research, the "mysteries" of interpretation appear to be viewed as virtues. Rejection of traditional research methods has been accompanied by dismissal of the problem. Unfortunately, it cannot simply be wished away. The task is to develop an approach more in tune with interpretive studies that would have the aim of demystifying the process by making it as explicit and visible as possible. The analysis presented in this paper is intended as a step in this direction. The work of interpretation has been displayed so that others can assess its relative plausibility, credibility, and trustworthiness vis-à-vis other competing interpretations.[4]

Finally, it is important to note differences between my model of identity formation and dominant trends in this area of research.[5] These differences are as follows: (1) I focused on identity formation rather than on identity development; (2) I examined a "part identity" rather than an individual's total identity; (3) I located the dynamics of identity formation in conflicts between contextually grounded and culturally defined motives rather than in presumed universal motives; (4) I viewed identity formation as an active, constructive process rather than as a static result of how underlying conflicts are resolved.

The principal reason for favoring the concept of identity formation over identity development is that the latter is now encumbered with two assumptions about which I have serious reservations. These are: (1) earlier conflicts and their resolutions set limits on later ones and, as well, earlier ones "explain" later ones (for a recent example, see Ochberg, 1988); and (2) there is a series of sequentially ordered universal "tasks" that everyone confronts, leading to a set of "stages" through which all must pass.

The reigning perspective, deriving from Erikson's seminal work on identity (1950, 1959), is stated clearly and succinctly by Stewart, Franz, and Layton (1988) in their study of identity changes with age through analyses of personal documents: "According to Erikson . . . beginning with adolescence, the developing individual confronts, in turn, issues of identity, intimacy, generativity, and integrity, each stage building on the resolution of earlier stages. The adult stage issues, like those of the childhood stages, correspond with typical demands made on all individuals at approximately the same age by society, by physiological growth, and by psychological changes. As each developmental stage is resolved, the ego gains strengths which are fundamental to the next stage" (p. 43; see Levinson et al., 1978, for a similar position).

My own view is that identity changes in adulthood do not follow the fixed, linear path of a universal stage model. Their trajectories involve detours, recursions, embedded cycles, that are responsive to culturally framed and socially situated alternatives. I have tried to show this process at work in Fred Wharton's career. For this reason, I would argue that it is more productive to use the open-ended concept of identity formation in studies of adults, with an emphasis on the person as an active agent and subject, rather than as the passive object of universal forces.[6]

A closely related point is that we need to take more seriously the cultural and social complexity of adult lives. All of us live simultaneously in different spheres—our work, family, and social worlds. Each sphere makes different demands and has its own categories of valued and disvalued actions. For example, we have all observed the disparity between how someone "is" in her or his family and how she or he "is" at work. Just as the notion of continuity through the life span must be treated as problematic rather than as given—that is, as an empirical question—so must the associated notion that the personality is "unified" through one master identity. If we begin with part identities we may be able to construct useful theories about how conflicts among them might or might not be resolved and whether some form of integration might or might not be achieved.

The aims of this brief discussion have been to make explicit several assumptions of my approach and to raise some questions about the study of adult identity through the analysis of life-history narratives. The work is demanding and there are many unresolved problems, but it offers exciting opportunities for new discoveries. Through such work, we may move a step closer to a theoretical understanding of the rich and complex ways in which we act as agents in the continuing and nonending process of making and remaking ourselves.

NOTES

1. In form and intent, this mode of representation draws inspiration from the structuralist tradition in linguistics and literary criticism, but it departs significantly from its search for universal categories. See Propp [1928] 1968; Levi-Strauss, 1963; Barthes, 1977; also Culler, 1975, for a critical survey and Martin, 1986, for structuralist analyses of narratives.
2. The "story" excerpted in table 1.1 is only one possible version or "reading" of the interview, reflecting my special interest in the achievement of a work identity. Others could be, but are not, drawn from the interview, for example, his marriage "story." Further, an alternative focus for different purposes on "how" a story is told would attend to the "order of the telling," that is, to what literary critics refer to as "sjuzhet" or "discours" rather than to the underlying plot of the "fabula" or "recit" (Culler, 1980). By focusing instead on the "order of the told," I am excluding the possibility of analyzing the linguistic strategies used by the teller to narrativize his life. For example, see Gee 1985, 1991; also Mishler, 1990.
3. On its absence in the industrial crafts, see Harper, 1987; Mishler, 1989.
4. For an extended discussion of validation in narrative research and other types of inquiry-guided studies, with a recommended approach based on the concept of exemplars, see Mishler, 1990. For an influential statement of the traditional approach to validation, see Campbell and Stanley, 1963, updated in Cook and Campbell, 1979. Instructive discussions of alternative formulations more relevant to qualitative research are in Katz, 1983; Lather, 1986; and Tagg, 1985.

5. For various approaches and the modal tendency, see Sarbin and Scheibe, 1983, and McAdams and Ochberg, 1988.
6. For related approaches, see the concept of "turnings" in Freeman, 1979, and Mandelbaum, 1973, and "second chances" in Kotre, 1984.

REFERENCES

Agar, Michael, and Jerry R. Hobbs. 1982. "Interpreting Discourse: Coherence and the Analysis of Ethnographic Interviews." *Discourse Processes* 5(1):1–32.

Barthes, Roland. 1977. "Introduction to the Structural Analysis of Narratives." In *Image, Music, Text,* by Roland Barthes. New York: Hill and Wang.

Bremond, Claude. [1966] 1980. "The Logic of Narrative Possibilities." *New Literary History* 11(3):387–411.

Campbell, Donald T., and Julian T. Stanley. 1963. "Experimental and Quasi-Experimental Designs for Research." In *Handbook of Research on Teaching,* edited by N. L. Gage. New York: Rand McNally.

Cerf, Georg, Constance F. Citro, Mathew Black, and Audrey McDonald. 1982a. *Methodology Report: Survey of Crafts-Artists.* Princeton, N.J.: Mathematica Policy Research (Report to National Endowment for the Arts, ERIC Report ED 226 110).

———. 1982b. *Crafts-Artists in the United States.* Princeton, N.J.: Mathematica Policy Research (Report to the National Endowment for the Arts, ERIC Report ED 226 111).

Cohler, Bertram J. 1982. "Personal Narrative and Life Course." In *Life-Span Development and Behavior,* vol. 4. Edited by Paul B. Baltes and Orville G. Brim, Jr. New York: Academic Press.

Cook, Thomas D., and Donald T. Campbell. 1979. *Quasi-Experimentation: Design and Analysis Issues for Field Settings.* Chicago: Rand McNally.

Culler, Jonathan. 1975. *Structuralist Poetics: Structuralism, Poetics, and the Study of Literature.* Ithaca, N.Y.: Cornell University Press.

———. 1980. "Fabula and Sjuzhet in the Analysis of Narrative: Some American Discussions." *Poetics Today* 1(3):27–37.

Erikson, Erik H. 1950. *Childhood and Society.* New York: W. W. Norton.

———. 1959. *Identity and the Life Cycle. Psychological Issues* 1(1), Monograph no. 1. New York: International Universities Press.

Freeman, James M. 1979. *Untouchable: An Indian Life History.* Stanford: Stanford University Press.

Gee, James P. 1985. "The Narrativization of Experience in the Oral Style." *Journal of Education* 167:9–35.

———. 1991. "A Linguistic Approach to Narrative." *Journal of Narrative and Life History* 1(1):15–39.

Goodman, Nelson. 1980. "Twisted Tales: Or, Story, Study, and Symphony." *Critical Inquiry* 7(1):103–119.

Grosse, Ernst U. 1978. "French Structuralist Views on Narrative Grammar." In *Current Trends in Textlinguistics.* Edited by Wolfgang U. Dressler. Berlin: Walter de Gruyter.

Harper, Douglas. 1987. *Working Knowledge: Skill and Community in a Small Shop.* Chicago: University of Chicago Press.

Jakobson, Roman. 1960. "Linguistics and Poetics." In *Style and Language*. Edited by Thomas Sebeok. Cambridge, Mass.: MIT Press.

Katz, Jack. 1983. "A Theory of Qualitative Methodology: The Social System of Analytic Fieldwork." In *Contemporary Field Research*. Edited by Robert M. Emerson. Boston: Little, Brown.

Kotre, John. 1984. *Outliving the Self: Generativity and the Interpretation of Lives*. Baltimore, Md.: Johns Hopkins University Press.

Labov, William. 1972. "The Transformation of Experience in Narrative Syntax." In *Language in the Inner City: Studies in the Black English Vernacular*. Edited by William Labov. Philadelphia: University of Pennsylvania Press.

Labov, William, and Joshua Waletzky. 1967. "Narrative Analysis: Oral Versions of Personal Experience." In *Essays on the Verbal and Visual Arts*. Edited by June Helms. Seattle: University of Washington Press.

Lather, Patti. 1986. "Issues of Validity in Openly Ideological Research: Between a Rock and a Soft Place." *Interchange* 17(4):63–84.

Levi-Strauss, Claude. 1963. *Structural Anthropology*. New York: Basic Books.

Levinson, Daniel J., Charlotte N. Darrow, Edward B. Klein, Maria H. Levinson, and Braxton McKee. 1978. *The Seasons of a Man's Life*. New York: Alfred A. Knopf.

Mandelbaum, David G. 1973. "The Study of Life History: Gandhi." *Current Anthropology* 14(3):177–206.

Martin, Wallace. 1986. *Recent Theories of Narrative*. Ithaca, N.Y.: Cornell University Press.

Marx, Karl. 1975. *Early Writings*. Edited by Quintin Hoare. New York: Vintage.

McAdams, Dan P., and Richard L. Ochberg, eds. 1988. *Psychobiography and Life Narratives*. Special Issue, *Journal of Personality* 56(1):1–326.

McHugh, Paul R., and Phillip R. Slavney. 1983. *The Perspectives of Psychiatry*. Baltimore, Md.: Johns Hopkins University Press.

Mills, C. Wright. 1951. *White Collar*. New York: Oxford University Press.

Mishler, Elliot G. 1979. "Meaning in Context: Is There Any Other Kind." *Harvard Educational Review* 49(1):1–19.

———. 1986a. "The Analysis of Interview Narratives." In *Narrative Psychology: The Storied Nature of Human Conduct*. Edited by Theodore R. Sarbin. New York: Praeger.

———. 1986b. *Research Interviewing: Context and Narrative*. Cambridge, Mass.: Harvard University Press.

———. 1989. Review of *Working Knowledge: Skill and Community in a Small Shop*, by Douglas Harper. *American Craft* 49(2):22, 28.

———. 1990. "Validation in Inquiry-Guided Research: The Role of Exemplars in Narrative Studies." *Harvard Educational Review* 60(4):415–442.

Morris, William. 1883. "Art Under Plutocracy." In *The Collected Works of William Morris*, vol. 23. *Signs of Change: Lectures on Socialism*. Edited by May Morris. New York: Russell and Russell, 1966.

Ochberg, Richard L. 1988. "Life Stories and the Psychosocial Construction of Careers." *Journal of Personality*, 56(1):173–204.

Propp, V. [1928] 1968. *Morphology of the Folktale*, 2d ed. Austin: University of Texas Press.

Ricoeur, Paul. 1981. *Hermeneutics and the Human Sciences: Essays on Language, Action, and Interpretation*. New York: Cambridge University Press.

Rumelhart, David E. 1975. "Notes on a Schema for Stories." In *Representation and Understanding: Studies in Cognitive Science*. Edited by Daniel G. Bobrow and Allan Collins. New York: Academic Press.

———. 1977. "Understanding and Summarizing Brief Stories." In *Reading: Perception and Comprehension*. Edited by David Leberge and S. Jay Samuels. Hillsdale, N.J.: Lawrence Erlbaum.

Sarbin, Theodore R., and Karl E. Scheibe, eds. 1983. *Studies in Social Identity*. New York: Praeger.

Schafer, Roy. 1980. "Narration in the Psychoanalytic Dialogue." *Critical Inquiry* 7:29–53.

Slavney, Phillip R., and Paul R. McHugh. 1984. "Life Stories and Meaningful Connections: Reflections on a Clinical Method in Psychiatry and Medicine." *Perspectives in Biology and Medicine* 27(2):279–288.

Smith, Barbara Herrnstein. 1980. "Narrative Versions, Narrative Theories." *Critical Inquiry* 7:212–236.

Stewart, Abigail J., Carol Franz, and Lynne Layton. 1988. "The Changing Self: Using Personal Documents to Study Lives." *Journal of Personality* 56(1):41–74.

Tagg, Stephen K. 1985. "Life Story Interviews and Their Interpretation." In *The Research Interview: Uses and Approaches*. Edited by Michael Brenner, Jennifer Brown, and David Canter. London: Academic Press.

White, Hayden. 1973. *Metahistory: The Historical Imagination in Nineteenth-Century Europe*. Baltimore, Md.: Johns Hopkins University Press.

———. 1987. *The Content of the Form: Narrative Discourse and Historical Representation*. Baltimore, Md.: Johns Hopkins University Press.

Young, Katharine. 1984. "Ontological Puzzles about Narrative." *Poetics* 13:239–259.

Young, Katharine Galloway. 1987. *Taleworlds and Storyrealms: The Phenomenology of Narrative*. Boston: Martinus Nijhoff.

STANLEY D. ROSENBERG

HARRIET J. ROSENBERG

MICHAEL P. FARRELL

2 In the Name of the Father

Berger and Kellner in a now classic article entitled "Marriage and the Construction of Reality" present an image of family dialogue in normal marriage. Their model of the "marital conversation" is an ongoing exchange, primarily between husband and wife, through which they create and maintain a "consistent reality" that determines "the imagery by which fellow men are viewed [and] the way in which one views oneself" (1964, 5). Such intimate and continual validation by a significant other, they argue, is a crucial mechanism for identity maintenance, creating opportunities for both affirmation and self-determination that are largely unattainable in less intimate spheres. They seem to think of the marital conversation as a sort of negotiated compromise, husband and wife reinforcing each other's somewhat arbitrary construals in ways that enhance the solidarity of their relationship while helping each other close out negative self-perceptions and existential doubt.

Oddly, Berger and Kellner's essay contains not a single example of in vivo marital conversation. As Wiley (1985) has pointed out, even as it was being published, this ideal view of marriage as a haven for the self was being challenged both by other writers, such as R. D. Laing, and by the weight of cultural change. The conversational text, by our current sensibility, must be understood as a text that functions to obscure its true meaning as an expression of desires the conversants cannot acknowledge or even truly understand (Ricoeur, 1974). In this sense, the marital conversation is not an innocent exercise in creating a livable mutual reality but is, rather, a form of ideology, carrying implications of "dissimulation and distortion" (Ricoeur, 1978) as well as "blindness and closedness" in its justification of a given system of authority and a given image of one's identity. The 1950s model of psychosocial development, most elegantly expressed in Erik Erikson's work, held forth a promise of identity attainment as a form of self-realization. The twin foci of this psychosocial achievement were career achievement and the development of stable, intimate relationships. Thus Erikson described identity as being manifested in "a mutual relation in that it connotes both a persistent sameness within one's self . . . and a persistent sharing of some kind of essential character with others" (1956, 57). Obviously, the nuclear family—and especially companionate marriage—is the ideal vehicle for such mutuality. Today the concept of identity—even as an ideal—is much more ambiguous. Jacques Lacan, for example, saw identity as an imaginary construct, a desperate antidote to a sense of internal fractionation, conflictual desire, and chaos. In Lacan, "The ego [or self] might give a feeling of permanence and stability to the subject, but this is an illusion" (Benvenuto and Kennedy, 1986, 62). Identity, that is, is realized in the register of the "imaginary" and is thus always riddled with apprehension and an awareness of its own deception.

The 1950s family, understanding itself and its purpose through the Eriksonian ideal, expected openness, mutuality, and fulfillment with and from one another. Any failure in this ideal would require explanation in terms of personal defect, faulty internal dynamics, or external pressures that have skewed family life. A crucial but often implicit component of this image of the nuclear family was a particular system of authority, reflected in and supported by an ideology of male dominance. The husband-father role was invested with enormous power, albeit within a complex set of expectations: the father was required to be competent, wise, nurturant, tactful, and generous. Reciprocally, wives and children were bound—by gratitude and by bonds of both emotional and practical dependency— to serve and obey the male breadwinner. The ideological transformations of the late 1960s, including the rise of the women's movement, represented a strident challenge to this "typical" system. Not only wives but children as well explicitly critiqued the value premises of the traditional nuclear family. Individual freedom, intimacy, and egalitarianism were asserted in opposition to traditions of parental obedience and generational hierarchy (Eiudson, 1979). These changes even became codified at the level of legislation and judicial reinterpretation of the rights of both wives and minor children. Having become legal persons, women and children were now much freer to experience and express feelings of inequality, conflict of interest, and encroachment on their sense of autonomy.

Today's family would not be startled by mutual frustration, anger, and dissolution—feelings that increasingly represent the acknowledged statistical norm. Lacanian subjects know themselves to be doomed to cycles of self-deception, suspicion, fear, and blame as each strives to defend the "identity" he or she knows not to be real and as each looks to the other to provide an unobtainable feeling of wholeness. In this sense, rereading "Marriage and the Construction of Reality" more than twenty-five years after its publication is a little like dusting off one's own album of wedding photographs. Nostalgia may also be tempered by a mild embarrassment: How could we have worn those tacky clothes or been that naïve? Berger and Kellner now seem to us an intriguing anachronism, a text "nestled in the time and family mentality of its period: that of the 1950s and early 1960s, . . . a period typified by a stable family, a fixed foreign policy, . . . and a clear route to success" (Wiley, 1985, 22). Rereading their text also raises other doubts. Were they giving us an accurate photograph of *temps perdu*, or were they engaging in artistic romanticization? What did their lighting tricks help to enhance or underplay? How much were the negatives retouched?

The marital conversation we will be "listening in on" in this chapter shadows, in an ironic way, the evolution of theoretical perspective on face-to-face discourse, the narrative task, and identity formation in the family. Like Erikson's model and Berger and Kellner's conception of family narrative, the marital conversation to be analyzed goes back to the 1950s, when Arthur and Sandy Russo first met. The conversational tenor between them has also moved from a tone of relative harmony and expressed mutual fulfillment to one of distrust, disguised anger, and ideologic struggle. The participants themselves now engage in a "hermeneutics of suspicion" (Ricoeur, 1974), questioning the intentionality and motivated distortions of their coparticipants in the marital conversation. Their reading of themselves and each other has become Lacanian. Before attempting to interpret the dynamics of this change, let us present some vignettes from an extended conversation in 1984 between the authors and the Russo family. These are excerpted from a daylong meeting with Mr. and Mrs. Russo and their younger child, seventeen-year-old Jimmy. Nancy, eight and a half years older, was not present for this particular discussion.

Arthur and Sandy Russo are in their early fifties, although they look younger. He is a journalist, working for the only newspaper in a small city some thirty miles from their home, and she is superintendent of schools for a very prosperous suburban school district. Sandy began her work in guidance and student personnel. Arthur continues to invest much emotional energy in his free-lance writing, seeing his newspaper job as something of a dead end and not commensurate with his abilities. The interview from which we quote is part of a longitudinal study of male adult development and family relationships. Subjects were drawn randomly to represent a full socioeconomic range of New England residents (see Farrell and Rosenberg, 1981). They were first contacted in 1972 or 1973 and then reinterviewed in 1984. The more recent interview is the focus of our current discussion.

During this meeting, the family members present spent several hours talking as a group about changes they had undergone since their previous contact with the interviewers, in the early 1970s. Each of these family members was then interviewed separately, giving them the opportunity to present their own narrative versions of family and personal history. This technique either corroborated or critiqued the official version of the "family narrative" as presented collectively.

In this discussion, we will juxtapose the group narrative (as presented in the joint interviews) to a parallel text generated by the Russos in the same format twelve years earlier and also to both individual commentaries at the first and second family interviews. Nancy Russo, twenty-six years old at the time of the second interview, was interviewed several weeks after the meeting with the other members of her family. As the discussion indicates, Nancy has become very disaffected from the family group and now resides in London. Despite the geographic separation and her refusal to spend much time with her parents, she remains involved in the familial debate over ideology and history. This investment made her quite willing to spend many hours talking with the interviewers about her parents, even though she was unwilling to talk with her parents.

Let us begin with the opening segment of the family discussion in the 1984 interview. Responding to the interviewer's request for information concerning the family's experiences since the last interview, the Russos began by describing the course of their daughter's life: she was graduated from college summa cum laude in English, established her own program for abused children in New York City, then moved to London. Still, her path has not been smooth.

Arthur: Yeah, but despite the academic ability, she's had kind of a hard time finding her place because she doesn't really have a good career orientation yet. She didn't have any help when she was doing the youth work and she got burned out very quickly. After she graduated, she took a lot of rather crummy jobs. Working in the mental health field. You know the kind of jobs you get in New York, taking care of welfare cases, the homeless, things like that.
Sandy: Halfway houses, community shelters for the homeless.
Interviewer: Was she doing that to explore those possibilities for a career or just to keep herself together financially?
Sandy: Both, I think. I mean, she was working in human services, all kinds of work, and that was what was available to people without a master's degree. And it turns out that the toughest work goes to the least experienced people, and I mean, the really front line dirty work and service work goes to, you know, inexperienced people like her and they burn out fast.
Interviewer: Did she get kind of demoralized at that idea?
Sandy: I think so. I think she gave up, even though I told her that counseling is not all that way, you know, not quite such tough things to do. She was thinking of going on to graduate school in clinical psychology when she worked, but she decided not to.
Interviewer: It sounds like in a way she combined both your interests, majored in English in college and then experimented with the counseling field. Is that something you discussed very much?
Sandy: Well, it's something that kind of, I guess looking back, kind of surprised us.
Arthur: Well, Jimmy's more practical. He's taking Greek, Latin, and French!
Interviewer: Has it been hard for you, felt like a big change for your family, to have one child not living in the country?
Arthur: Well, yes and no. There were troubles between us before she left. And it was fairly stormy. I think we get along better now. We went to visit her last Easter and I think it was very good.

Interviewer: What were the issues that were stormy?

Arthur: Well, when Nancy was, you know, she was very ill when she was much younger, and she was with me all the time. [They are referring to a congenital disorder that left Nancy unable to walk without crutches. This was corrected surgically, and she now is able to walk unaided.] I was working nights, odd hours, when she was little and could do a lot of work at home. So I spent a lot of time with her, trying to get her to walk again. I think we both neglected the emotional problems of her disorder. Certainly denied that there were any. And we were so concentrated on getting her to walk again, probably I overloaded her life. So did Sandy, and Nancy got sick of us, especially me. And, uh, that's only a partial explanation, I'm sure. It was very complex. But, ah, see she was in the hospital for months, needed several rounds of surgery and time recovering after each one. It was a very protective environment for both of us. I had, like almost agoraphobia for a while, I was reluctant to go out. I'd get up in the morning there and I'd work there, spend all day with her, and then come back late at night, after I'd been to work, to see her. I really avoided going on the streets anytime I didn't absolutely have to. When I had to go on the streets I was very nervous. I got over that, but I know what agoraphobia is.

Interviewer: How old was she when you began the corrective surgery?

Arthur: She was six, going on seven. Yeah, she was almost seven, yet she suffered a lot. She lost a lot in terms of freedom, development. . . . I think it was just too intense for all of us. It was very intense.

Interviewer: Do you think those scars were something that persisted?

Arthur: Always.

Interviewer: In what way did it come out?

Arthur: Well, we couldn't get along very well together. Um. Often there would be blowups. But, Sandy and I could never walk away very easily, I mean, you know, we should have probably have let go more easily. But we would beg her and things like that, you know, and I think that we were too much involved, all of us. Usually the big blowups were between me and Nancy, and it was very hard to get over them. There was a lot of troubles. But I think things have gotten a little bit better in the last few years.

Interviewer: (turning to Jimmy) Have you tried to help your sister stay close to the family, or is there enough difference in age where you're not that close?

Jimmy: That we're not . . . ?

Interviewer: Friends with each other.

Jimmy: I think that we got closer when she went away to college, and I would go visit her at college a lot, and I feel really close to her. Even though we hardly ever see each other, I haven't seen her for about a year, we write to each other a lot, and no, I feel very close to her. And I think that maybe if she'd lived with us for a longer period of time, we might not be as close, but I don't know. It hasn't really affected, ah, . . .

Interviewer: Your relationship.

Jimmy: Yeah.

Arthur: Oh, no, I think Jimmy has an excellent relationship with Nancy.

Jimmy: When she was having problems with Arthur, she would come to me a lot. Sometimes she wouldn't be speaking to Arthur and Sandy but she would always speak to me. It was hard on me, because I was only about, I was only about ten or so.

Arthur: He was the intermediary for everybody.

Jimmy: Yeah, and it was hard. It really was. She even wanted me to run away with her. She wanted me to come to London and live with her . . . of course I didn't want to do that. So it was hard for me for a while, but we really, we grew closer.

Interviewer: In what way do you think she felt bad about or angry with your parents?

Jimmy: Um, it was really hard for me to, I was real young when it was going on and I really didn't, kind of didn't want to understand what was going on, I mean I really, I don't know how old, about nine or so?

Sandy: Yeah.

Jimmy: And I didn't want to find out what was wrong. But I went to a session of theirs and I had a family, a group therapy thing, and I just remember that, I don't know, I never thought about what was wrong. I just, I guess I kinda just wanted to block myself out.

Interviewer: Um, hmm. It was too hard for a kid that age to be involved in it?

Jimmy: Yeah. And I just wanted everything to come out right.

Interviewer: Sandy, do you share Arthur's perception that this was an outgrowth of Nancy's . . . .

Sandy: Well, partly, yeah. I think that had a lot to do with it, and as Arthur said, we were both overprotective of her. You know, from the beginning, from the time she was a baby, I guess your first child, you know. And, ah, we, I guess we had a hard time accepting her anger at us. You know every, couldn't let it go and just let her be angry . . . get over it, things like that.

In some ways, this segment is similar to the the sorts of marital conversations Berger and Kellner seem to envision. These people are highly articulate, thoughtful, and working very hard to understand a distressing series of events in ways that will not be too damaging to the family's self-esteem. Jimmy seems to be quite willing to play his expected role according to Berger and Kellner's schema: children, they argue: "are taught from the beginning to speak precisely those lines that lend themselves to a supporting chorus, from their first invocations of 'Daddy' and 'Mummy' on to their adoption of the parents' ordering and typifying apparatus that now defines their world as well" (1964, 14).

In other respects, we seem to be entering into territory far darker and more complex than any these authors hinted at. As children mature, one envisions a marital conversation that could be drawn from an episode of "Father Knows Best": wry humor and good sense prevailing as the means of dealing with the petty traumas of affluent suburban life.

The Russos, in contrast, are dealing with real pain. In their narrative, it is not at all clear that things will "work out"—that the family will have a good laugh, hug one another, and adjourn to the dinner table. Today the marital conversation is serious business. The dissolution of the dyad and the family group is an omnipresent threat. As both Arthur and Sandy divulged in their individual interviews, they had gone through a trial separation some five years earlier, Sandy pushing for divorce and then finally relenting. Although they feel that their marriage is now stable, the intense closeness and commitment they testified to twelve years earlier is no longer discernible. The ideological center appears to be in danger of crumbling for the Russos as each of them (three physically present and one a dominant shadow in the room) struggles to work through his or her individual and collective sense of disappointment and betrayal. They currently seem to be working to salvage some viable ground, to recoup some of that assured sense of individual and family identity that characterized the narrative of the early 1970s.

One great difficulty the Russos are struggling with is the challenge to the family's self-definition from the events of the decade between the two interviews. The interview of 1973 presents a radically different tone, characterized by a buoyant confidence and optimism. Invoking a key family theme, for example, the Russos began the earlier interview by questioning their inclusion in the study. They clearly convey the belief that they are, individually and collectively, rather extraordinary people.

Arthur: I can't believe we were chosen in a random sample to be typical of anything. We're pretty unique in a lot of ways.
Sandy: (laughing) We're really going to skew your sample in a lot of ways.

Their commentary about their children, their marriage, and family life was extraordinarily positive in 1973:

Arthur: I really feel happy in this part of my life, especially lately, very happy. I remember coming back from a business trip a couple of months ago and pulling into the driveway and Sandy and the kids were waiting for me in the living room. And I walked in and I remember thinking, "Wow, it's nice to be connected to the universe at this point. You know, right here in this room with these people."

At another point, Sandy describes a vacation home they had recently purchased on a lake in rural Maine. They had acquired sixty acres of land and a rustic cabin along with the older lakefront home. Thus they could have old friends visit during the summer yet retain their privacy.

Sandy: It's like paradise to us up there. We have everything we've ever wanted when we get up in the morning and see the deer grazing at the edge of the lake and you can't see or hear another human being. You really can make your own paradise on earth.

Nancy, then a teenager, seems a particular point of pride for both of them.

Arthur: She's an amazing kid, filled with energy. She does all kinds of things. Last week we found out that she won the state essay contest they hold every year on topics related to civil rights. She has tremendous musical talent. We gave her piano lessons, but she has taught herself four instruments. She got so good on the flute that she was a soloist with the high school orchestra at the Christmas concert.

While Nancy seems to be apple of her father's eye, their six-year-old son appeared to be more quietly adored, the baby of the family. The Russos virtually competed with each other to hold and cuddle him. Each time he moved in and out of the room, parents and big sister would beam. The fall from this familial paradise is what must be explained and dealt with in the later narrative. The Russos struggle with the need to give coherence to this turn of events in a variety of ways. They no longer seem able to agree on how to describe or account for many aspects of their relationships. There is a certain proclivity to minimize and externalize blame for Nancy's plight and her anger toward them: "We get along better now"; "she doesn't really have a good career orientation yet"; "she didn't have any help when she was doing the youth work . . . got burned out." This minimization is, however, rather half-hearted. The pauses and unfinished sentences leave the observer wondering about things hinted at and unsaid. This segment of narrative tiptoes around issues of mutual blame, anger, and potential rejection. The group acts as if these issues are salient only for Nancy and are directed only at her father. Other segments of their individual and joint texts suggest that these issues are far more pervasive and that Nancy may in fact be enacting the sentiments of the rest of the group in her flight and her conflicted drive for separation.

In a dynamic that seems congruent with Ricoeur's analysis, it soon appears that the explicit account of Nancy's alienation from the family is, to a great degree, Arthur's account, or is at least one that minimizes the damage to his character. Behind such polite evasions as Jimmy's declaration that he "was real young . . . didn't want to understand . . . wanted to block myself out" is the lurking suggestion that he has a quite sophisticated awareness of his sister's gripes against their father. At the period of greatest acrimony, Nancy would call the house and ask to speak with Jimmy, not even acknowledging her parents by saying hello. She and Jimmy would then speak for hours, primarily about what an SOB Arthur was and how hard it was to live with their parents. Jimmy's silence about the content of these conversations is necessary to maintain the explanation of events being offered. Discretion is required because they all see making accusations against Arthur as a potentially explosive act, one that neither he nor the family would necessarily survive. Nancy's rage must thus be diluted, leading to equivocations and alibis that are only partially believable to Sandy, Jimmy, and Nancy. It should be noted, however, that even as hostility and rebellion against the familial hierarchy are simmering, a rather substantial core of family ideology still appears to be intact.

Part of the irony of this revolt, certainly from Arthur's perspective, is that he has always regarded himself as highly committed to egalitarianism and personal freedom. He is clearly shocked and disbelieving when accused of being domineering. The ideological changes of the 1970s and 1980s seem to have represented a challenge to the way the Russo family operated, even though Arthur and Sandy felt very much aligned with society's emergent ideals and what they implied for the rights of women and children. Any residual elements of traditional paternal authority almost seemed to become incendiary, especially to Nancy. As she matured into adolescence and young adulthood, she felt increasingly impelled to attack what she came to see as pockets of hypocrisy in Arthur's stated egalitarian ideals and his subtle use of unacknowledged controls. Certainly, the broader cultural movement toward questioning and challenging the legitimacy of paternal authority helped set the stage for this emerging familial struggle.

All narrative renderings converge on Nancy as the presence who dominates even in her absence. To understand the Russo family ideology and its meaning for each member one must come to grips with Nancy as sign and symbol (Ricoeur, 1970, 11–13). In a limited sense we can say that the signifier "Nancy" is paired for them all with a signified object: the person of their daughter and sister. Yet there is much less than a one-to-one correspondence between "Nancy" the signifier used by Arthur, "Nancy" as used by Sandy, the "Nancy" claimed as sister and best friend by Jimmy, and "Nancy" as she denotes herself. This was true even in 1973, before she became intensely involved in overt conflict with her parents; it has been amplified many times over as the dispute between Nancy and her father has escalated. The name "Nancy" has become a "sliding signifier" (Lacan, 1977) in the family code, standing at different moments for their suppressed rage, their felt specialness, or their collective feeling of being somehow lost. For the Russos, Nancy is the central symbol, the group icon, even as she stands for the very possibility of the group's dissolution. For each family member, Nancy is an extraordinarily polysemous signifier who evokes powerful ambivalence, representing in turn me and not-me, transcendence and defeat, sickness and power, liberation and bondage.

The descriptors in the family dialogue, as well those found in the individual interviews, make clear this confusion between the signifier "Nancy" and the signifiers "us" (family), "Arthur" (genius, domination), "Sandy" (suppressed potential, the feminine dilemma), and "Jimmy" (innocence, goodness). As Arthur testifies directly: "We were too much involved, all of us." Not only does Nancy carry and express parts of each of the others; the others also function as parts of her and of one another. Both their joint and individual narratives convey ambivalence and confusion about how merged they sometimes feel with an entangling familial mass of emotion, beliefs, and values.

Even as the Russos are aware of and dislike this fusion of identities, they appear conflicted about giving it up. Nancy's ironic commentary in a college essay on her youth expresses well this sense of entanglement: "Being repressed by parents who were in ten years of therapy in order to repress their desire to repress me has given me a unique slant on the experience of being neurotic." Part of what makes this conflict "neurotic" is the manner in which the drive for total, intense involvement in the emotional matrix of the family is often denied, disowned, or seen as the agenda of one member of the family (Arthur), although all members of the group express the same desire in differing ways. More specifically, Sandy and Jimmy typically take the stance of letting Nancy and Arthur slug it out, as if the battle between these two can decide for the others what the terms of their relationships will be. As spectators, Sandy and Jimmy superficially appear to be much cooler, more detached, and more in control than the others, but this apparent calm is purchased at the cost of feeling submerged and even oppressed, as if their identities must be found in the interstitial spaces not already dominated by the more assertive and volatile players. Jimmy, for example, seems to feel that Nancy has done all the risk taking the family can tolerate. Although he craves adventure, Nancy's experiences seem to foreclose for him the very possibility of risk: "I want to do, like really exciting things, but I also just want to, like lead a satisfying life, I guess. Not really an unstable life. Because of my sister's life, I don't think I could take that. She's very unsure about her future and she's twenty-six and still doesn't have a real job, a career. I mean, she's living in a hotel room because she couldn't afford to keep up her apartment, and her life just looks very unstable. I don't think I could take that." Moreover, Sandy and Jimmy's attempts to struggle with and against the family ideology—usually embodied in the voice of Arthur—seem never to feel very satisfying because they are usually expressed vicariously through the voice of Nancy.

Issues of intentionality, power, influence, and intimacy are expressed by and for all of them in the dense symbol "repression," which seems to refer to the most basic issues of selfhood and autonomy. Nancy expresses the dilemma of being unable even to identify her own self—her own desires—because they are so intertwined with and obscured by the desires and needs of her parents: "The thing is, I was supposed to do things, which if they had let me just kind of be myself, I probably would have wanted to do them anyway. But the weird thing is I was supposed to be that way. I was supposed to be, he would always say, I was constantly creative. I mean, I felt intensely guilty if I even turned on the TV set. I was never supposed to have needs, because I was supposed to get so much love I never needed anything material. They would call me like a consumer, a capitalist, a materialist when I would ask for the slightest thing." Nancy's confusion over whose desires she expresses with her choices and wishes is certainly shared by her parents, who recall some of the same events of her childhood and adolescence but with radically different interpretations. Arthur sees Nancy's aversion to television as another indicator of her superior, critical stance toward them. "She's totally into the natural, you know. She won't go near a color TV. She'll go and sit about fifty feet away in the kitchen while we're watching in the living room. None of us watch it very much, but she won't even let us put it on when she's in the living room. We have to warn her five minutes in advance so she gets out."

Nancy believes that she is prohibited from watching television lest she disappoint her parents (especially father): "Like he had these really strong child rearing views, like this is how things should be. And I always felt that I had to be, quote, this perfectly healthy, self-actualized child, unquote, or something so I wouldn't upset his philosophical views and just pull the rug out from under his feet." In Nancy's rendition, she sacrifices her own pleasure to protect Arthur. In Arthur's recounting, Nancy is protecting herself from corruption while he is made to suffer the humiliation of being shown up by his teenaged daughter.

Indeed, the confusion over whose wishes are being enacted by Nancy is mirrored by a confusion over who assumes the role of the parent and who assumes the role of the child; over who is master and who is slave. As Nancy writes in her essay: "I learned to act the 'therapeutically reared,' 'perfectly healthy child' model that they assumed I would be. I once heard Arthur brag at a party that his innovative and radical child rearing techniques had created a 'perfect child' and that 'the child is the father of the man.' My favorite fantasy at the time was that I was a twenty-two-year-old."

This struggle over being created by and for the other is indeed the essence of what Lacan (echoing Nancy's terms) calls the neurotic. In an essay entitled "The Neurotic's Individual Myth" (Lacan, 1979, 2), he sketches the ongoing dilemma of that fractionated, incomplete "self" attempting to find itself through achieving the love and admiration of the "other"—archetypically, the parent. Because this dynamic is so crucial to development, what we normally call ego is seen by Lacan as a false self shaped by the subject's perception of the desire of the other as structured in language. Schneiderman summarizes Lacan's view of this process as follows: "when he [the child] perceives that a parent desires an object that is other than he, he will want to be that object, to be the desired object. Second, when he perceives a parent desiring an object, he himself will then consider that object desirable. Here he will identify with the Other's desire" (1980, 5).

In other words, in order to become a self, the child asks the parent, "What do you want me to be?" or "What will make you love me the most?" Though Lacan sees this act of questioning as fundamental, he also sees it as fundamentally alienating. Surely Nancy's reconstruction of her own life attests to this struggle. She desires, on the one hand, to be "this perfectly healthy, self-actualized child"—the desire for recognition expressed in pride and love, which creates, on the other hand, its own antithesis. Nancy's success in enacting "the perfectly healthy child" breeds her subsequent resentment at being shaped by her parents' needs and fantasies. Nancy tells us that she came, rather precociously, to experience herself as not free to be—or even know—her self. As Nancy's commentary will testify, she came to feel that she could become a valued child only at the price of being captive to her parents' beliefs. This confusion between who she is, what her father wants her to be, and what her father himself wants to be or have is precisely the confusion Lacan sees as constitutive of human subjectivity.

But Nancy and Arthur seem also to go beyond Lacan, to enter realms and depths of complexity Lacan does not specifically schematize as part of the familial drama. In a brilliant move of transposition, Arthur turns Nancy into a kind of implacable parent—one whose love must be sought through a denigration of his self through acquiescence to her seemingly impossible demands. Each treats the other as that archetype of parental judgment and authority, which Lacan calls the Name of the Father.

It is in the Name of the Father, Lacan comments, that we must recognize the support of the symbolic function which, from the dawn of history, has identified the father's person with the figure of the law. This conception enables us to distinguish clearly "the unconscious effects of this function from the narcissistic relations, or even from the real relations that the subject sustains with the image and the action of the person who embodies it" (1977, 67).

Lacan's schema thus implies that Arthur and Nancy need not literally enact some implacable tyranny toward the other to be experienced as the tyrant. Each is impelled by his or her own sense of incompleteness to hear the voice of the other as representing "the paternal metaphor" (Lacan, 1977, 198) or "the Name of the Father." This symbolic use of the paternal principle is, for Lacan, quite independent of any actual behavior on the part of the real father (or father surrogate). Rather, it represents a set of structures—translated into prohibitions and injunctions—whereby the subject can at least imagine that he or she knows how to be both safe and loved. It is precisely because this symbolic use of each other cannot be correlated very well with Nancy's or Arthur's actions toward one another that we see continued puzzlement and revisionism in their testimony about each other. Arthur the "person" and Arthur as the "law whereby Nancy must live" are blurred images that shift, as Nancy will describe, from being utterly apart to being superimposed on each other.

Lacan's use of the term *law* can best be understood, for our purposes, as largely synonymous with Ricoeur's notion of ideology: the principles of power and legitimacy that structure the Russos' conception of their relations with one another. At this level, the text of their dialogue with one another is rife with contradictions and ambiguities—constructions and deconstructions of codes.

For example, even as she tells us of her parents' oppressive invasion of the very fundament of her being, Nancy also tells us of their refusal to wear the badges of authority or to exercise its prerogatives: "I never called them 'mother' or 'father.' If I did, they responded by calling me 'daughter.'" This abnegation of the badges of authority is juxtaposed for Nancy with implicit tyrannies that seemed the more devastating for their indirectness: "Even though they did not yell, slap, or otherwise exercise traditional parental modes of repression over me, I still got the message that some things made them very uncomfortable and confused and I had best avoid doing them. Lacking clear moral guidelines, I quickly grew sensitive to subtle clues of what seemed to be right and wrong."

The family narrative can thus be seen to contain several subplots, which appear to be somewhat mutually contradictory. For Nancy, her parents urging her to be free and to choose is a deceptive offer, one made in bad faith. She describes her father's words as having a feeling of insincerity. "I guess I always felt like he had a lot of intellectual ideas that were wonderful, but his heart wasn't really into them. And he had this kind of perfectionism and sort of superior attitude toward people that I always fought against. Especially because he kind of forced it down my throat. I always felt that I had to prove myself to him, that it wasn't okay to just be." She thus understands Arthur's words and actions as disguising a truer subtext, which states: "Without benefit of direct guidelines from me, learn what will make me proudest of you and most approving. Then do those things as if they were spontaneous expressions of your own desire." Nancy hears this message as demanding the most total and abject servitude, an expectation that she will be the slave who reads her master's desires even before the master speaks them.

From Nancy's point of view, Arthur is not playing fair in two distinct senses. First, he represents a kind of surplus dominance, forcing "perfectionism" and "a superior attitude . . . down [her] throat." Second, he is seen as abdicating his parental duty to lay down the terms by which Nancy can become an object who can attract his love. In substantiating this accusation, Nancy complains that nothing was forbidden, that she was encouraged to go out and explore for herself: "If it were a matter of the typical teenage rebellion kind of stuff, my parents had already done it. Premarital sex, drugs, that kind of stuff, they would just say, 'Great. Pass me the joint.' They actually encouraged me to experiment with premarital sex. How do you rebel against these totally liberated parents?" At the same time, Nancy thinks that her father was essentially up to something with all this nondirectiveness: "There was this kind of pressure . . . like for me to do music or art. . . . I felt that they were kind of subtly pushed on me."

The familial text, taken as a whole, offers contradictory evidence about Nancy's implied hypotheses. She is claiming that Arthur as Father knows quite well which Self he is wishing to create of Nancy but is operating in bad faith by pretending to encourage freedom. Her implication is that he has been assuaging his own narcissistic investment in an ideology he espouses but can't adhere to while enacting the tyrannical role he cannot admit to. Nancy, moreover, is not only appalled by what she sees as Arthur's hypocrisy but also enraged at the position it puts her in—

forcing her (as she reconstructs it) to pay exquisite attention to his every nuance of approval and disapproval in order to find love and escape his underground guilt-inducing stratagems.

Sandy and Jimmy seem to corroborate Nancy's allegations about her father's emotional manipulations. In his individual discussion following the family talk, Jimmy describes how his father continually opens things up to group decision making, only to force his preferences and beliefs on the rest of them. Early the previous summer, when Arthur was busy with work and could not get away, Sandy and Jimmy decided that they wanted to accept an invitation to join some friends who were renting a house on the outer banks of North Carolina for a couple of weeks. Although Arthur would never directly forbid them to go, Jimmy intuits that his father is basically too needy and possessive to let Sandy go away and leave him behind: "He's more dependent on her than she is on him. It's kind of hard to describe. I mean, I think he really depends on her and maybe on me too. Kind of like for support. He always resents her going off to meetings and stuff. He resents being left behind. He didn't want us to go to North Carolina and leave him. But what he said was that money was very tight and said we couldn't afford it. My father is very persuasive. He can talk you over to his side. . . . He's really an excellent arguer, I mean especially about political things, abortion or anything."

Sandy echoes the accusation that Arthur cloaks his striving to dominate behind his declarations of egalitarianism and freedom. In talking about the marriage, she comments: "Well, we've had our problems but we managed somehow to work them out. And I guess that there was a period when I was thinking of leaving. I felt that it was a little oppressive, Arthur was. He's more possessive than I am, and I felt it was too much sometimes. Well, you know, we talked it over and talked about divorce but we talked it out and got over it." Although Sandy seems to have come to terms with Arthur's demands, she fears that the example of their marriage will create continuing problems for Nancy: "I think Nancy has real difficulty envisioning marriage for herself. She wasn't sure that she wanted a long-term relationship. I mean she felt it would be too possessive, and that's probably something that she thinks about Arthur and me, that the relationship is a possessive kind of thing that she doesn't want." This fragment of testimony raises questions of how much Sandy is using Nancy to express her frustrations and to enact her need to find the freedom Arthur seems to foreclose.

Remarking about the interaction between Arthur and Nancy, Sandy tells us: "Arthur is kind of a strong personality and kind of in some ways a little insensitive to the kids . . . and Nancy would just stand up to him every time. She couldn't kind of let things go."

This corroborative testimony does not, however, close the case. As much as the rest of the family sees Arthur as demanding, intrusive, and domineering, they also identify with him. He is simultaneously stronger and weaker than the rest of them; an object of resentment, affection, admiration, and concern. Lacan suggests in

"The Neurotic's Individual Myth" that "a very special form of narcissistic splitting lies at the heart of the neurotic structure: that of a split in the psychic conception of the father so that he is idealized and denigrated at the same time, sought and fled simultaneously" (Ragland-Sullivan, 1987, 264). Even Arthur's most vocal critic acknowledges this ambivalence. Nancy reflects on her own split image of her father: "If you had asked me ten years ago, I would have been just totally negative and would not have been able to see the good stuff. He's very enthusiastic and has lots of charisma and has a good sense of humor. . . . And I really like his political views as much as I can understand them. Really, everything he thinks about the world is so much in advance of what most people his age think. I feel kind of lucky to have grown up in an atmosphere like that." Jimmy, as we have seen, also admires and identifies with his father's intelligence and verbal skills. When asked to describe his father, Jimmy seems to have unabashed hero worship: "Well, he's different from everyone else's dad. I guess the first thing I'd use to describe him, he's very intelligent, kind of bordering on genius. I mean, he knows about everything from Greek mythology to film directors to novelists. . . . He even took Latin. I mean, he's very knowledgeable in all subjects, like your basic Renaissance person." And Sandy indicates that in many ways Arthur has lived up to his pronouncements about what he believes in: "He has always been oriented toward the family being important and the love relationship with the children and me. That has always come first for him. And he has always been committed to an equal relationship, always done his share of the housework and child care and cooking."

A rather significant contradiction comes to the fore when we listen more closely to the children's testimony about their father's attempts to control and dominate them. When asked how he would like to raise his own children, Jimmy declares: "I think I'd do it a lot the same way I was brought up. I think I would impose more things on them, certain values. It's kind of hard to explain, but it seems to me the way I've grown up, I kind of got whatever I wanted and could do whatever I wanted. Nancy thought so too. She thought that she was given everything she wanted. She told me that there really weren't enough rules or limits set. She was allowed to be very free and so am I. But when I think about it, I think I'd be more comfortable if more limits were set, like curfews and stuff." Arthur's failing, as presented here, is not his subtle tyranny but the very real feeling of dread he may have engendered in them by a refusal to be the Father who states the Law through his injunctions.

The Russos' attempts to grapple with issues of power, authority, freedom, law, and intimacy also appear to shadow the cultural upheavals they have lived through. Like the countercultural ideology of the 1960s and 1970s, the Russos strove to abolish the principle of the Father in favor of the—perhaps utopian— ideal embodied in the "paradise" their Maine home seemed to represent. In that paradise, freedom would lead to mutual love, creativity, and growth. A family like theirs did not require strict rules of discipline; these could only inhibit their development and contaminate their relationships. Like many who grew up in that culture, the Russos now suffer from terrible disappointment and confusion. Freedom seemed to lead to conflict (between Arthur and Nancy as well as Arthur and Sandy), self-destructive excess (enacted most clearly in Nancy's adolescent eating disorder) and failure to adapt (embodied in Arthur's career stagnation, the couple's near divorce, and Nancy's inability to find a career direction or earn a decent living). At the same time, returning to an earlier model of the stern, patriarchal family is not a viable alternative. They now believe neither in freedom nor in authority and find themselves in limbo, asking alternately for controls and freedom, as if each were the only real conveyance of love and respect.

Both children, in different ways, feel paralyzed precisely because Arthur will not represent the force of Law who can help them crystallize a self, either in obedience or in opposition to his command. Nancy's parents are correct when they acknowledge: "She has had a hard time finding her place . . . ," but this appears to become almost a comic understatement when Nancy talks of her own identity struggles. She feels almost paralyzed about moving forward in life, even though she has changed cultures and radically cut off communication with her father. Nancy attempts to express this oppressive state of limbo by describing a recurrent dream: "I'm on the stage and looking out into the audience. Everybody else in the cast is very nonchalant and assured. They're real self-assured and joking around and everything, and I had no idea of what to do. And I just looked out into the audience and everyone, there were thousands of them, and every single person out there was my father, just looking at me, just expectantly. And I just completely freaked out." Nancy has placed herself on center stage in this dream scenario; she cannot understand what or how to be in the face of Arthur's vague expectation— that is, in relation to a lack of coercion.

Indeed, how much of Arthur's supposed covert manipulation is created by Nancy's need to find the Law in the absence of the Father who would pronounce it? She recalls: "I learned very early on that I was supposed to be mysterious and kind of hard to figure out. I wasn't going to be analyzed, I wasn't going to let them have that advantage. It was kind of like their happiness depended on my internal state of being, and I didn't like that feeling of connection between us. It was like even though I was encouraged to be independent, that their needing that connection with me was detrimental . . . I developed a technique to hold my own. It was directly counter to their technique. You would sort of read their minds before they could read yours." What Nancy "read" was that her parents' "identities depended on who I was. And I couldn't just lay back and chew bubble gum like other kids or else they'd dissolve." Nancy goes on to describe how unhappy she felt while acting out the role of the model, high-achieving, artistic adolescent: "I was really good at that point at keeping my negative side to myself. So they actually had no way of knowing how miserable I was. But I really wouldn't share anything with them about what was going on inside me, so they really couldn't read my mind, of course."

This last aside appears to cast doubt on the entire thrust of Nancy's explanatory structure. Her understanding of her family, of Arthur, and of herself is dependent on their abilities to "read" one another's unspoken intentions in an almost magical way. Indeed, Nancy's claim of oppression is based entirely on such finely honed empathic-intuitive skills. If such readings are vulnerable to ambiguity and misinterpretation, the admitted absence of more overt textual evidence for Arthur's domineering intentions makes us begin to question Nancy's justification for rejecting her father.

We begin to wonder if the text is an inverted one, Nancy attributing to her father intentions and demands that in ways she cannot acknowledge, Arthur being the one who scrambles desperately to win *her* love by becoming that perfect other she cannot specify. Both testify to the agony to which Nancy subjects him: "I don't see him a lot you know. I think he's a little bewildered by everything that's happened. Like, he used to have all the answers to everything. It's like something that Mark Twain said one time, that he used to have ten theories and no children and now he has ten children and no theories. Just, it's sad but I feel like he's been broken down in ways. He had this false pride initially and it had to break. You get the sense of brokenness from him now."

This particular reading is partially confirmed by Arthur: "The most painful thing in my life has been the trouble between me and my daughter. It's taken me a long, long time to try to get over the pain of that. You keep questioning what you could have done differently, the specific things I was wrong about. Sometimes I think it's just the way each of us was and is. You know how they say that character is fate." Nancy attempts to put this wound in an anonymous or agentless space: "He's been broken down." This seems to sidestep what the narrative underlines: she has broken him down and disabused him of his false pride. In this sense, she has enacted that stern Name of the Father role she had attributed to her father's unspoken intention. She would claim, at some level, that this has been an act of retribution, a way to even the score. Operating only from the level of the text presented, we are left much more at sea. Arthur appears at many points to have assumed the role of child, as Nancy says, searching for guidelines of love and forgiveness that will enable him to win back his daughter. Each of them feels, in this sense, doomed to fail the other and to torment the other by judging him or her as inadequate to be an object of desire. Nancy's essay once again expresses the doomed passion each seems to feel for the other, a passion that leaves them acutely aware of a lack that they must continue to suffer without the other: "His myth of me (I think) is that someday I will become the all-forgiving daughter who never loses control or gets hurt. My myth of him is that he will someday become accepting of both his and my feelings so that he won't need me to be happy all the time in order to feel good about himself." Each needs the other to liberate him or her by granting a self that feels fulfilling, yet each resents and fights the possibility of the other's owning his or her life in this way.

Although this dynamic is most overtly played out in the Arthur-Nancy axis of the family, we can observe that its primary structure characterizes each dyad and the relation of each participant to the family as a whole. Berger and Kellner are correct: the family is where each participant turns for a sense of self and of satisfaction. However, they lack Lacan's sophisticated awareness that no act or relationship can fulfill that hunger, no relationship or act "is totally satisfying." The Russos are more like Lacan's tortured souls for whom desire is "the place of the lack and its irreducibility. The object 'a' [desire] is a trace, a leftover, a remainder. We can summarize its concept by saying that it leaves something to be desired" (Schneiderman, 1980, 7). Unlike Berger and Kellner's rational entrepreneurs of love, the Russos cannot at this point accept what each of them gives the others but instead rage at the lack these exchanges entail. Each in turn becomes the Father who would determine the other as the price of love, only to reject the other as an insufficient object of desire. Each also in turn demands that the other play the Name of the Father, as in a repetition compulsion: "Tell me, once again, what it is I should be to harness your desire and show me what I should desire." As in a repetition compulsion, there is no mastery of the trauma. Whether they will be able to find expiation or cure in their marital conversation remains to be seen. Just as their current disenchantment was not foreseen in 1973, so the next turn of the plot line remains open to revision.

REFERENCES

Benvenuto, B., and R. Kennedy. 1986. *The Works of Jacques Lacan*. London: Free Association Books.

Berger, B., and H. Kellner. 1964. "Marriage and the Construction of Reality: An Exercise in the Microsociology of Knowledge." *Diogenes* 46:1–23.

Eiduson, B. 1979. "Emergent Families of the 1970s." In *The American Family*. Edited by P. Reiss and H. Hoffman. New York: Plenum.

Erikson, E. 1956. "The Problem of Ego Identity." *Journal of the American Psychoanalytic Association* 4(1):56–121.

Farrell, M. P., and S. D. Rosenberg. 1981. *Men at Midlife*. Dover, Mass.: Auburn House.

Lacan, J. 1966. *Ecrits*. Paris: Editions du Seuil.

———. [1966] 1977. *Ecrits: A Selection*. Translated by A. Sheridan. New York: W. W. Norton.

———. 1979. "The Neurotic's Individual Myth." *Psychoanalytic Quarterly* 48:405–425.

Ragland-Sullivan, E. 1987. *Jacques Lacan and the Philosophy of Psychoanalysis*. Urbana: University of Illinois Press.

Ricoeur, P. 1970. *Freud and Philosophy: An Essay on Interpretation*. New Haven: Yale University Press.

———. 1974. *The Conflict of Interpretation*. Evanston, Ill.: Northwestern University Press.

————. 1978. "Can There Be a Scientific Concept of Ideology?" In *Phenomenology and the Social Sciences: A Dialogue*. Edited by J. Bien. The Hague: Martinus Nijhoff.

Schneiderman, S. 1980. *Returning to Freud: Clinical Psychoanalysis in the School of Lacan*. New Haven: Yale University Press.

Wiley, N. F. 1985. "Marriage and the Construction of Reality: Then and Now." In *The Psychosocial Interior of the Family*. Edited by G. Handel. New York: Aldine.

3 The Afterlife of Stories:
Genesis of a Man of God

S tories are gifts, and the Reverend Cantrell gave me dozens of them as we sat in the study of his Covenant Baptist Church in Lynchburg, Virginia, one fall afternoon in 1982. With seductively poetic ease, he wove back and forth between the Bible and his life, fashioning tales of love and sacrifice and redemption. The drift was unmistakable, unavoidable: he was trying to convert me; he would ask me to accept Christ as my personal Savior. When the time came, he pinned me down with a few simple questions—"Do you know Christ as your personal Savior?" "Do you believe in God?" "What if you died today?" "Have you ever sensed the presence of God?" "Is he real?"—but let me go gracefully when I hesitated and squirmed. He told me two more little stories about men he knew, one who had missed his chance for salvation, the other, for marriage. Vaguely, I heard him telling me between the lines that my evasions left our exchange, our dialogue, hanging open, ominously incomplete, like a wound that would not heal, or the gift of love refused. Finally, he told me this unforgettable story.

Now if in this life, the Bible says, only we have hope, then we of all men are most miserable. But you see my life, my hope, is in the life to come, and I realize this life is a passing thing. Jeremiah says it's like a vapor. It appears but for a little while and then vanishes. We know how uncertain life is. We're just not sure how long things are going to go.

I went to work one morning. I had some work to do on a Saturday morning. And one of my sons was fourteen years old. And the other one was fifteen years old. And we got up that morning. And I went in, and I rassled with my son and rassled him out of bed, the one that was fourteen. And we got up that morning and ate breakfast. We opened the Word of God. We read and we prayed together as a family, my wife, my two sons, and I. And I went on to do that work that morning. It was a Saturday. And I had something I wanted to move. And I was operating a crane. And I accidentally killed him that morning.

And I looked at God. And I said, "Lord, you told me in your Word that all

For their comments on this chapter, I am grateful to Richard Ochberg, George Rosenwald, Joan Scott, Cynthia Sowers, and especially Ross Chambers, who noticed that the Reverend Cantrell's key witnessing tales were all "sacrifice stories."

things work together for good to those that love you, especially those that are called according to your purpose." And I said, "I've served you faithfully. And I've loved you. And I've given you my heart, my life, my soul, given you everything about me. And now I can't understand this, why you've taken my son."

And God didn't speak with a voice that I heard with my ear, but he spoke to my heart. He said, "Milton, you know maybe you don't understand what I've done at this particular time, but can you accept it?" And I said, "Yes, sir, I can accept it." And Susan, when I made that statement, and I settled that in my own heart, and I said, "Lord, I accept it though I don't understand it." I don't know where to say it came from other than that God gave it to me, but he gave me a peace in my soul. And I have not questioned it since.

Now I went and shared it with my wife. I said, "Shirley," I said, "God said all things would work together for the good to us because we love him." And she said basically the same thing I did. "Well, I don't understand this. This isn't good." But I said, "Yeah, but God said it is good." And I shared with her, and when I shared this with her, she came of the same opinion.

And we watched them close the casket on that little fellow and my, he was just super. I mean, he was almost my heartthrob, you know, that was my baby. And yet he died in my arms. And yet I looked at God and I said, "Lord, I'm going to love you if you take my other son. I'm going to love you if you take my wife. I'm going to love you if you take my health, if you strip me of everything I've got, I'm going to love you."

Now I'm saying that because, Susan, he is real. This is not mythology. I'm forty-six years old, and I'm no fool. God is alive. And his son lives in my heart.

Of all that I could give you or think of ever giving over to you, I hope that what we've talked about here today will help you make that decision, to let him come into your heart, and then he will be your tutor. And he'll instruct you in things that perhaps I've stumbled over today. Sometimes the vocabulary may not be appropriate to really describe the depth and the detail of the things that need to be said. But this is where the Holy Spirit can make intercession for us. The Bible says with groanings and utterings that we just cannot utter. I may miss something, but he'll bring it out. I may present something and you don't understand it. But he will reveal it to you. This is what the whole thing is about.

The Reverend Cantrell's final story was disturbing and disorienting in my unborn-again ear. After opening with a wistful, philosophic lull, he rapidly unfolded in a humble, staccato rhythm a string of homey details that terminated abruptly with his son's death, with Cantrell's accidentally killing his son that Saturday morning. The details disappeared, the narrative stopped, and he reported three subsequent dialogues, one with God, another with his wife, and, after they "watched them close the casket on that little fellow," again with God. And then he spoke to me about God's son, who lives in Milton's heart, that I might let God's son come into my heart.

The unborn-again listener wants to know more about Milton and Milton's son, not about God's son. How did the boy die? How did Milton *really* feel about it? What about his pain? His sorrow? His guilt? How could he speak with such spareness, such calm, and such calculation to a stranger about what could be the most tragic moment in his life? The dialogues with God and with his wife sound like cloaks that conceal what he must have felt. At best, they ring of reinterpretation, of a retrospective story, one that, Milton suggests, renders him at peace with his loss.

The unregenerate listener interrogates Milton's story as if it were a system of verbal clues about something outside itself—the tragic event, Milton's raw experience, the unmediated emotions of the moment, his subsequent effort to recover and reintegrate—and finds the story distinctly odd, choppy, suspiciously elusive. In contrast, the born-again listener, or one who is "coming under conviction," who is beginning to submit to the interpretive conventions of born-again culture, accepts Milton's story as "true" in the sense of being "an integral and dynamic component—an insistent dimension—of what is being narrated," rather than "a transparent envelope of the narrated events or an aesthetic embellishment of them" (Alter, 1982, 112). The story is not a system of clues to extranarrative realities (neither to prestoried emotions, experiences, and events, nor to posthoc psychological processes) but a generative moment in which the event, characters, narrator, feelings, motives, and moral and theological meanings are brought into existence through language. A faithful ear also would have heard a multidimensional, biblically storied universe of significance in Milton's words, cadence, phrases, story frames, and character references, as well as juxtaposition of dialogue and description.

Born-again discourse does not represent its speakers, its "believers," as existing prior to or apart from its Bible-based speech, its biblically framed stories—except in the past tense, when they were lost (unstoried) souls. Of course, we all live in a world in which "reason" and "empirical reality" are hegemonic notions, and if asked, born-again believers, like all reasonable people, will firmly assert that their language depicts reality as it is. But unlike, for example, speakers of secular psychological discourse, born-again idioms in practice do not presuppose (and, in presupposing, reproduce the assumption) that language "reflects" independently existing, prediscursive, outer and inner realities.

Born-again stories "speak" their narrators and their emotions, motives, and experiences into existence, and in this sense they are invariably "true" stories. The Reverend Cantrell's story of his son's death was the finale of a series of stories that spoke him into existence not only as a born-again believer but also as a gospel preacher, a Man of God (in the born-again idiom), a man anointed by God to win souls to Christ, to speak Christians into existence through his gospel preaching.

Being born-again means entering into a specific narrative culture and speaking one's self, one's life, one's world, in its terms, and it is the task of gospel preachers to transmit the authority, ability, and desire to speak born-again stories. They do so by "opening up" the Christian biblical canon and becoming a kind of third testament in their speech as well as in their actions. They emerge out of the web of biblical allusions of which their stories are an intersection, out of the aesthetics of the biblical shape of their stories, and out of the trail of biblically framed stories which came before and prefigured them. The web, the shape, and the trail are gifts that transcend the Reverend Cantrell's, or any preacher's, stories. They are the Word of God brought to life, and accepting them is a kind of incarnation, for it makes the Word flesh.

The Web of Allusions

Sumner Wemp arrived at Jerry Falwell's Lynchburg Baptist College (now Liberty University) and the Thomas Road (now Liberty) Home Bible Institute in the early 1970s, not long after Milton Cantrell had trained to become a preacher at the Institute. In *The Guide to Practical Pastoring,* Wemp admonished his students to "soak your soul in the Word of God. Saturate yourself with the blessed Book as Jeremiah did. He said, 'Thy words were found, and I did eat them; and the word was unto me the joy and rejoicing of mine heart.' (Jer. 15:16). Absorb it until it seeps into your every conversation. Let it flow out of your message as naturally as breathing. The Word of God will burn like a fire. It will break the hardest heart. It will cut to the quick" (Wemp, 1982, 212).

Wemp's advice illustrates itself obviously in the direct quotation from the book of Jeremiah and obliquely in the final string of metaphors: John the Baptist predicted Jesus (the Word made flesh) would "burn up the chaff with unquenchable fire" (Matt. 3:12 and Luke 3:7). Job (23:16) said, "God maketh my heart soft," and Jesus thrice lamented the "hard hearts" of those who saw and heard him and yet did not believe (Mark 8:17, 10:5, 16:14). God's word often "cuts" to the heart, the soul, the spirit (for example, Isa. 49:2, Acts 5:33, 7:54, Heb. 4:12).

Weaving biblical phrases in and out of speech is a craft Milton Cantrell learned well. He prefaced his story first by overtly paraphrasing Paul (1 Cor. 15:19): "If in this life only we have hope in Christ, we are of all men most miserable." And then he glossed James (4:14; attributed to Jeremiah): "Whereas ye know not what shall be on the morrow. For what is your life? It is even a vapor, that appeareth for a little time, and then vanisheth away." Later, in his conversation with God and with his wife, the Reverend Cantrell paraphrased Paul (Rom. 8:28) as if God had spoken the words to him: "And we know that all things work together for good to them that love God, to them who are the called according to his purpose."

Milton more obliquely quoted Paul (Phil. 4:7) when he accepted what God had done, even though he could not understand it: "And the peace of God, which

passeth all understanding, shall keep your hearts and minds through Christ Jesus."
When Milton told me, "I'm no fool. God is alive," he was reworking a line from
two of David's songs (Ps. 14:1, 53:1): "The fool hath said in his heart, there is no
God." And in Milton's final, prophetic words, he promised me what Paul had
promised the Romans (8:26): "Likewise the Spirit also helpeth our infirmities: for
we know not what we should pray for as we ought: but the Spirit itself maketh
intercession for us with groanings which cannot be uttered."

Such references are threads connecting Cantrell's speech to the Bible, splicing
God's Word and his own words, insinuating God's voice in his own. They quite
literally constitute him as a Man of God, a man who breathes life to God's Word, a
man whom God's Word breathes to life. These are but the tiniest of intertextualities in the Reverend Cantrell's story.

The Aesthetic Shape of the Story

Although the Reverend Cantrell's story conforms to distinctly Christian terms in
certain respects, most notably in its message, its aesthetic shape locates it squarely
in the tradition of Hebrew Scripture, or what Christians call the Old Testament.

The Reverend Cantrell opened his story with "now," "the quasi-temporal, quasi-
attitudinal indicator of emphasis" (Alter, 1982, 68) in Hebrew stories. In this
instance "now" marked the beginning of what would become his final story of our
afternoon together in his church study. The laconic pace of Milton's preamble and
story is another biblical convention, as is the narrative's parataxis, the series of
continuous terms linked by "and" (Alter, 1982, 7, 26). Cantrell's poetic rhythm
and "strategies of retardation" rendered the scene "ceremoniously"—not outside
the norms of biblical realism, yet with a distinct mythic lilt. They attract and focus
the listener's attention, and the string of "ands" specifically spotlights the links
between one term and another without specifying the connections, thus methodi-
cally leaving open the question of causal relationships and nodding narratively
toward the uncertainties and ambiguities of life (Alter, 1982, 125). The early
narrative details minimally established time, place, personages, and their family
relationships as well as succinctly characterizing the protagonist morally and
socially (a good and loving and faithful father), as would a "paradigmatic bible
story" (Alter, 1982, 80). The "characteristic rush of biblical narrative toward the
essential moment" (Alter, 1982, 161) via Cantrell's unnerving details comes to a
sudden halt in his final claim: "I accidentally killed him that morning."

Not "he was accidentally killed," but "I accidentally killed him." Alter notes that
"to understand a narrative art so bare of embellishment and explicit commentary,
one must constantly be aware [among other things] of . . . the richly expressive
function of syntax, which often carries the weight of meaning that, say, imagery
does in a novel" (Alter, 1982, 21). Because Cantrell did not seem to dwell on his
feelings in this dreadful moment, a psychologically minded interpreter might

suggest he was repressing his guilt. Yet, on closer inspection, in his specific turn of phrase, Cantrell precisely and unambiguously asserted his responsibility and innocence: "I accidentally killed him."

The abruptness of the shift at this point from narrative to dialogue is another redolent biblical cue. By opening a gap between what the listener expects to hear (more about what happened, more about what Milton felt) and hears, the gap stipulates what must be inferred, thus triggering a deeper interpretive engagement, pulling the listener in through the hole of the unsaid. The spare story about his son's death aside, Milton's expansive dialogue with God establishes in no uncertain terms what matters in this telling: neither his son's death nor Milton's responsibility for it, except insofar as they are grounds for what does matter—his response to those joint facts as revealed in his dialogue.

> The biblical writers . . . are often less concerned with actions themselves than with how individual character responds to actions or produces them; and direct speech is made the chief instrument for revealing the varied and at times nuanced relations of the personages to the actions in which they are implicated. . . . beginning with narration [Hebrew writers] move into dialogue, drawing back momentarily or at length to narrate again, but always centering on the sharply salient verbal intercourse of the characters, who act upon one another, discover themselves, affirm or expose their relation to God, through the force of [spoken] language (Alter, 1982, 66, 75).

Three dialogic segments follow Milton's narration of his son's death, and it is through them that Milton's character as a godly man and a Man of God are established and intensified.

He "killed his son" and "looked at God" without a pause. He quoted God's Word to God, testified to his faithfulness, and told him he could not understand "why you've taken my son." This parsing of the event sounds strange to the unbeliever's ear but rings true to the believer, thus forming another tiny moment of choice for one coming under conviction. Milton interpreted his son's death as a figment of his, Milton's, relationship with God, and his last remark indicated that God was ultimately responsible for this death. His son's death was something God had done to Milton. God, in effect, agreed and then simply asked Milton to accept it. And Milton accepted it, though he did not understand it. And God gave him peace in his soul. The space between what God asked and Milton accepted forms still another resonant juncture, a gap that unbelievers cannot bridge and believers can. The creative power of spoken words is established in biblical stories when a spoken instruction, "magically powerful speech," is followed by immediately completed action, "the results of speech" (Alter, 1982, 9). God's efficacy and Milton's election are jointly established in the swiftness and simplicity of their awesome exchange.

In Hebrew stories, dialogue and narration often interact to endow characters with a "degree of morally problematic interiority" (Alter, 1982, 29), whereas in Cantrell's story, as in the fundamental Baptist narrative tradition generally, the interplay works powerfully in the opposite direction, toward endowing characters with a degree of morally unproblematic interiority. The subsequent dialogues that Milton had with his wife and with God dramatically intensified this movement. Given an unquestioning "peace in his soul," Milton spoke to Shirley as God had spoken to him, bringing her "of the same opinion," with one striking difference: together they went beyond accepting what God has done and agreed that "it is good," as God said all would be to those that serve him faithfully. Together, again, they (and with them those who are listening) viewed the dead son, and then Milton recapitulated his love for his son, his son's death, and his faith, accentuating both his loss and his submission to God. Milton this time stated in three ways ("just super," "my heartthrob," "my baby") how much he cared for his son. Then he gravely etched the image of his son dying in his arms and declared ("I'm going to love you if") repeatedly his acceptance of God's taking everything he's got.

This was the end of the Old Testament portion of the Reverend Cantrell's story, aesthetically speaking. The literary devices used by Hebrew writers that Cantrell also deployed to generate event, character, sentiment, and meaning are: the strategic use of "now" and "and"; slowing the pace to focus attention; establishing time, place, characters, and relationships with minimal initial details; the hasty engagement with the crucial moment; auspicious shifts and gaps, which focus interpretive attention on motives and feelings; privileging dialogue over narration as the principal means of revealing (constructing) character; reiterating, with meaningful variations, key dialogue; and recapitulating (twice) the movement of the initial action-response.

Once again, the Reverend Cantrell emerges from his story a formidable Man of God, or, more precisely, God's Word.

The Trail of Stories That Came Before

The Reverend Cantrell's story echoes at least three major stories in the Bible, which thereby frame, fill out, and focus its interpretation for those willing to submit to born-again conventions.

The innuendos of Job in the Reverend Cantrell's story are strong. A good man suffers terrible loss, turns to God, and asks "why me?" But the story is played out in New, not Old, Testament terms. Job received lengthy and troubling counsel from his wife and friends and spoke to God many times, revealing a certain sense of self-righteousness before God answered. When God did speak back, he asked Job over sixty mortifying questions, which Job could not answer, beginning with "Where wast thou when I laid the foundations of the earth?" Finally, Job was humbled, accepted what he could not understand, and once more was blessed by God. The editors (under Jerry Falwell) of the *Liberty Bible Commentary* sum up the significance of Job's story as showing us that "there is a benevolent divine purpose running through the sufferings of the godly and that life's bitterest enigmas are reconcilable with this purpose did we but know the facts. . . . we are meant to see that there was an explanation, even though Job and his [wife and] friends did not know it, so that when baffling affliction comes to us we may believe that the same hold good in our own case—that there is a purpose for it in the counsel of heaven, and a foreknown outcome of blessing" (Falwell, 1982, 927).

The Reverend Cantrell's story moved across much of the same moral landscape but dispensed with the residual ambiguities communicated by the extravagant oratory and reiteration in Job's story, even when it is read through a born-again Christian lens. God answered Milton immediately after his first affliction and Job-like (though he quoted Paul) lament and made his point quite plainly. Milton instantly submitted, and as he accepted what he could not understand he was blessed with peace and his wife's conformity. Finally, he promised, in effect, to withstand the trials of Job, should God ask it of him.

Job, of course, lost his son, indeed lost ten children, but not by his own hand, and this loss, though it may have been his greatest, was only one among countless afflictions he suffered. The Reverend Cantrell's story most forcefully recalls the story of Abraham and Isaac and, inescapably, the story of Christ, of God's sacrificing his son. That the story of Job to some degree frames Cantrell's story is a reasonable inference, but the connection between his story and the two great biblical stories of ultimate sacrifice is one he made. A half hour before he told me about his son's death, Cantrell discussed both sacrifice stories and their relationship to each other in such a way that they not only commented in advance on his final story but "prefigured" it—looking backward, his final story seemed to "fulfill" the biblical stories of filial sacrifice. By setting up this dense and precisely nuanced system of intertextualities, which works something like a hall of implicating mirrors, the Reverend Cantrell instructed his listener in the deepest lessons of born-again (specifically fundamental Baptist) interpretation.

The Reverend Cantrell intertwined the stories of Abraham and Isaac and of Christ in the context of explaining the difference between the first birth, which depends on the mother, and the second, which depends on God. He located the second birth at Calvary, derived "forgiveness of sins" from "shedding of blood," shifted to Mount Moriah, interrupted at the crucial moment his telling of Isaac almost being sacrificed, somehow finished Isaac's story with Christ's, returned to Mount Moriah and let Isaac go, then returned to Calvary and explored its meaning for all humankind.

> Now where did the [second] birth take place at? It had to be a birth of such caliber that it had to take care of the whole world, and was a place called Calvary.
>
> Jesus, when he was dying, was shedding his blood, and the Old Testament

says that without the shedding of blood there is no remission, there can be no forgiveness for sin. So blood—the innocent—and God typified this in the animal sacrifices of the Old Testament. . . . And the blood was used to atone for their sins. . . .

Atonement means to cover, and the blood of the animals of the Old Testament typified one day that Christ would come, shed his blood, but then this blood, this blood being shed now, brings about redemption and not atonement, which is a temporal covering. For thousands of years the Jews, under the Mosaic economy, offered up sacrifices of animals—you've probably read that—and they did this because this was representative of one day a coming Savior.

You remember the incident in Exodus, about Abraham went to offer his son Isaac on Mount Moriah, and the Bible says that Isaac, the son, said "Father," he did not know what was going on, he said "here's the altar, here's the wood, here's the knife, here's the fire, but where's the sacrifice? Where's the lamb?" Abraham said, "My son, God himself shall provide a sacrifice. A lamb."

Now we go down several thousand years into the future, and John the Baptist, when he saw Jesus for the first time, he told the disciples that were with him, he said, "Behold, take a look, here is the lamb of God that will take away the sins of the world." And the lamb of God was Jesus Christ.

Of course, Isaac was not slain. There was a ram caught in the thicket, which was a type of substitution, so Jesus Christ died in my place as a substitution for me. . . .

So when Jesus died at Calvary, he said these words, he said, "Father, into thy hands I commend my spirit," and he said, "It's finished." Now the prophets of old prophesied that Jesus Christ would also say these words, that, when he looked back and he saw the travail of his soul, in Isaiah 53, that he was satisfied. . . .

Now, the Bible said Jesus said, "Father, it's finished," and the Bible said when he looked upon the travail of his soul because he was dying, when he looked upon the travail of his soul, he was satisfied that he had now made a way for every human being to look to him and live, after this life was over with.

Now here's the entire Bible and its economy coming together. For four thousand years of the Old Testament, they offered up blood sacrifices. Now all of this together, combined, typified one day a coming hope. They looked through the offering of the blood one day to Calvary.

You see, we're looking back to what Jesus did, nearly two thousand years ago, he died for us. The people on the other side look forward to his coming. Now of course they died, and many have died prior to my existence, but they all focus and by faith they all believe that he did die with a specific thought in mind, that was to redeem them, to give them salvation, to give them deliverance.

Through this compact, heavy-handed, but absolutely orthodox Calvinist reading of Calvary and Mount Moriah, the Reverend Cantrell implied not only a relation between the two stories (and sacrificial events) but also a relation between the New and Old Testaments, the contemporary reader and the Bible, and the believer and the Man of God. Simply put, what comes before prefigures, or "typifies," what comes after; what comes after fulfills, or completes, what came before. The relation between the prefigured and its fulfillment is not symbolic or literary. It is historical and theological. In born-again discourse, story and event are utterly inseparable; to speak of the story is to speak of the event. Through this mode of storytelling, Cantrell and many early Christian and Protestant preachers before him articulated a particular theory of causality and hence history, one that interprets, or posits, connections between events and persons (and stories) in terms of God's design and that generates a certain determinacy of meaning and a distinctive narrative point of view.

The Reverend Cantrell states a number of times that animal sacrifice and Abraham's willingness to sacrifice Isaac "typifies" or "represents" the sacrifice of Christ. This is, theologically speaking, a "typological" or "figural" reading and is one of the earliest, if not *the* earliest (Paul does it) and most aggressive versions of what is now called biblical literalism. Until recently, probably still when Milton Cantrell was studying for the ministry, preachers were formally taught typology as a Bible hermeneutic. Now they learn it more indirectly, as their listeners always learned it, in the course of preaching and witnessing, as the Reverend Cantrell taught me, and by studying books on "types," study Bibles (for example, by Scofield or Criswell), Bible commentaries, and devotional literature.

In his study Bible (one of the most popular among fundamental Baptists), W. A. Criswell said the events on Mount Moriah "gave a foreshadowing of the divine sacrifice to be made by the Heavenly Father and His only Son. . . . Almost certainly the event is . . . typological. Abraham, advancing up the slope of Mount Moriah, very possibly where Solomon's temple later stood, feels something of the agony of the Heavenly Father sacrificing His only son, Jesus. At the summit of Moriah, the type changes, and Isaac is a type of all lost and condemned men for whom a substitute ram, typical of Christ, is sacrificed" (Criswell, 1979, 33).

Isaac, in his willingness to be sacrificed (which is inferred from his silence later on when Abraham placed him, bound, upon the altar), prefigured Christ and then, once a substitute was found, all humankind. And Abraham's willingness and agony prefigured God's when the time came to sacrifice his son.

The Reverend Cantrell made roughly the same equations between Isaac and Christ and dramatically "completed" the space opened up by Isaac's question ("Where's the sacrifice?") with Christ, the lamb. When Abraham said, "My son, God himself shall provide a sacrifice, a lamb," he foreshadowed, in the sense of

foreknew, Christ's coming. John the Baptist, when he first saw Jesus, acknowledged that this was the man whom Abraham foresaw, "the lamb of God." When
the ram was caught, Isaac's type—whom Isaac prefigured—shifted from Christ
to all humankind.

The Reverend Cantrell indicated two other ways in which the relation of figure to
fulfillment applied in a general way to the relation between Old and New Testament events. First, regarding animal sacrifice: "Jews, under the Mosaic economy," offered up animals "because this was representative of one day a coming
Savior." It "typified one day a coming hope. They looked through the offering of
the blood one day to Calvary." Second, regarding Christ's final words: "Now the
prophets of old prophesied that Jesus Christ would also say these words . . . in
Isaiah 53, that he was satisfied."

The connection between Isaac's deliverance and Christ's sacrifice, "Mosaic"
animal sacrifices and the coming Savior, Isaiah's prophecy and Christ's dying
words, is not causal in the sense of the first somehow having brought about the
second but that the first revealed in advance, if incompletely, God's plan, God's
foreknowledge of what would come later. This is, of course, a stronger link
between two events than earthly causality, for much might intervene between
earthly cause and effect to change the outcome, but nothing interrupts God's plan,
by definition. Here is how Erich Auerbach put it in *Mimesis:* "In this conception,
an event on earth signifies not only itself but at the same time another, which it
predicts or confirms, without prejudice to the power of its concrete reality here and
now. The connection between occurrences is not regarded as primarily a
chronological or causal development but as a oneness within the divine plan, of
which all occurrences are parts and reflections. Their direct earthly connection is
of secondary importance, and often their interpretation can altogether dispense
with any knowledge of it" (Auerbach, 1953, 73).

Full-blown, figural interpretation enables preachers such as the Reverend
Cantrell (and most Christians before the nineteenth century) to understand "the
real world as formed by the sequence told by the biblical stories" (Frei, 1974, 1).

Figural interpretation is a specifically Christian reading of the Bible but bears
some comparison to the way Hebrew writers, according to Robert Alter, intended
some of their stories to be read. Hebrew Scripture is replete with parallel stories—
Alter calls them "type-scenes"—that recount several times, with significant variations, a crucial moment in the life of a protagonist, or cast different protagonists in
similar but not identical situations, for example, annunciations of a hero's birth to
a barren woman, or encounters at a well between a man and woman who are to be
betrothed. In deploying this and other techniques, Alter considers the essential
aim of Hebrew writers to have been "to produce a certain indeterminacy of
meaning, especially with regard to motive, moral character, and psychology. . . . Meaning, perhaps for the first time in narrative literature, was con-

ceived as a *process,* requiring continual revision—both in the ordinary sense and in the etymological sense of seeing-again—continual suspension of judgment, weighing of multiple alternatives, brooding over gaps in the information provided" (Alter, 1982, 12).

In Hebrew Scripture, type-scenes open up meaning, or the process of construing meaning. The Christian Bible, by contrast, at least through a typological, or figural, lens, shuts down the process in a way that produces the opposite effect: a certain determinacy of meaning. Through the eyes above all of orthodox Protestants, the New Testament establishes a "master type-story" for the "whole" Bible: the divine hero's self-sacrifice (or God the father's sacrifice of his divine son). The primary "purpose" of events recorded in the Old Testament was to prefigure, to foretell, that ultimate sacrifice. What is stressed is not human freedom, hence indeterminacy, but God's design, hence determinacy. So the Reverend Cantrell can say without an iota of doubt that "Jews, under the Mosaic economy" sacrificed animals *because* "they looked through the offering of the blood one day to Calvary," and that "the people on the other side" of Christ "look forward to his coming."

He can also say with equal assurance that "there was a ram caught in the thicket which was a type of substitution [for Isaac], so Jesus Christ died in my place as a substitution for me." And, "you see, we're looking back to what Jesus did, nearly two thousand years ago, he died for us." Those before Christ look forward, and those since look backward, and "they all believe that he did die with a specific thought in mind, that was to redeem them, to give them salvation, to give them deliverance."

In other words, the New Testament, read figurally, not only establishes "a point of view" from which to read the Old Testament, but one from which to "read" one's own life.[1] Here is how Hans Frei put it in *The Eclipse of Biblical Narrative:* "Not only was it possible for [any present reader], it was also his duty to fit himself into that world in which he was in any case a member, and he too did so in part by figural interpretation and in part of course by his mode of life. He was to see his disposition, his actions and passions, the shape of his own life as well as that of his era's events as figures of that storied world" (Frei, 1974, 3).

Toward the end of the exegesis quoted above, the Reverend Cantrell began to make clear his listener's place with respect to Abraham and Isaac and Christ, and his remarks immediately following made absolutely clear her place, her duty:

So John 3:16 says it's a mere act of believing, a mere act of faith, it's a look of faith. It's not works that we do, because when you apply works to it, the Bible says, you pollute it, you begin to incorporate yourself in as helping God. So when you were born, you couldn't help your mother the first time, and when you were born the second time, you couldn't help God, because the Bible said he died alone for us. So a mere look of faith, they looked forward and believed that he would, and I looked back and believed that he did, and we all focus at a place called Calvary and realize why he died.

Repeatedly, then, the Reverend Cantrell established the essential principle of figural thought: what comes after determines (the meaning of) what comes before. And he established its domain: the whole of history, including his life, and mine.

The Hall of Implications

Not long after this exposé of my right relationship to Calvary, the Reverend Cantrell inquired into my beliefs and found, mostly from what was not said, that I was unlikely to be convinced that afternoon that Christ died for me. From then on his talk led in a zigzag but steady fashion toward his sacrificing his own son for me, so that I might have eternal life. In doing so he set up a powerful, deeply compelling, figural sequence of sacrifice stories, from Abraham and Isaac, to Christ's passion, to his own terrible tale, a sequence that "looked forward with hope" to the next story—my own self-sacrifice of faith. I say it was "deeply compelling" because, although I did not convert, I was "brought under conviction" that afternoon. In my inner speech, I began, in a way that was beyond my conscious control, to acquire, to "submit" to, the conventions of born-again interpretation.[2] Let us now look down that sacrificial passage.

The Reverend Cantrell wanted his listener to understand that she, her life, bore the same relationship to the story of Christ's sacrifice that that story bore to the story of Abraham and Isaac. Her story would fulfill Christ's in the same way that Christ's fulfilled the Old Testament tale. The moment of salvation is precisely the moment when a lost soul realizes that Christ died "for you." Suddenly, the story of Calvary, the Bible as a whole, becomes "relevant." The context in which biblical stories are meaningful and the context of one's personal life collapse into each other, and the fusion evokes a sense of great insight, of miracle. All these stories are God speaking "to you."

More specifically, you stand in the same relation to the ram as Isaac did. The ram died in his stead. The lamb, Christ, died in your stead. This connection between stories (events) is established through a sense of incompleteness, of "something missing." Isaac fashioned the gap in the form of a question: "Where's the sacrifice?" And Cantrell answered that question, completed that story, with Christ's story, which in turn is also incomplete, divinely incomplete: Why did Christ die? Why did God sacrifice his son? Cantrell raised the question in this instance by answering it: Christ died for you and me, so that we might live. We, through a mere look of faith, "complete" the story of Christ. What comes after determines (the meaning of) what came before.

Milton's final story replicated the biblical stories in the obvious thematic sense (a father sacrifices his son), but the connection is not merely allusive; it is also figural. Milton's story fulfills Christ's, which fulfills Abraham's. Milton, like Abraham, like God himself, was willing to sacrifice his son in accordance with God's plan. But like their stories, his too is incomplete; it evokes a haunting sense of something missing. Why did Milton's son die? Or, more precisely given the typological sequence, whom did Milton's son die for? The answer, of course, has already been provided as well by the previous stories. He died for me. The Reverend Cantrell sacrificed his son, narratively speaking, for me. Through the cumulative pattern of his Bible-based storytelling that afternoon, Cantrell created a space for me to take responsibility, and feel responsible, for determining the meaning of his son's death.

That I owed him something, and what it was, and what I would receive in turn, was one of the last things the Reverend Cantrell made clear to me: "Of all that I could give you or think of ever giving over to you, I hope that what we've talked about here today will help you make that decision, to let him come into your heart, and then he will be your tutor." Cantrell had fashioned access to the pattern of history for me, and the only question remaining was, would I accept it? His final words to me, the tense of his verbs, suggested, prophesied, that I would: "he'll instruct you," "he'll bring it out to you," "he will reveal it to you." He forecast in this way, lightly, the outcome of the story anticipated by his own. "This is what the whole thing is about."

This is a heady set of story frames for lost souls to find themselves "looking back" through for the meaning of the moment. The figural story, like the Hebrew type-scene, is "not merely a way of formally recognizing a particular kind of narrative moment; it is also a means of attaching that moment to a larger pattern of historical and theological meaning" (Alter, 1982, 60). And, as biblically framed stories make remorselessly clear, the response, specifically the verbal response, is what matters: "In words each person reveals his distinctive nature, his willingness to enter into binding compacts with men and God, his ability to control others, to deceive them, to feel for them, and to respond to them. Spoken language is the substratum of everything human and divine that transpires in the Bible" (Alter, 1982, 70).

And, for born-again believers, speech is the substratum of everything that transpires out of the Bible as well. I left the Reverend Cantrell that afternoon owing him my spoken life.

Figural stories are an even headier set of frames through which preachers see themselves and are seen. They become, simply, God's living Word. Their lives, the stories of their trials and victories and sufferings and blessings, fulfill the biblical stories they tell in such a way as to frame their own, to prefigure them, to foretell them. The prophets prophesied Christ, and together, the prophets and the apostles prophesied preachers. When Jim Bakker compares himself to David (and Bathsheba), or Oral Roberts to Daniel in the lion's den, or Jerry Falwell to Paul preaching to the Gentiles, they are not plying a mere web of semantic allusions. In their world, story and event have not been torn apart—or perhaps we should say they are sewing them back up. Those biblical figures are not fictional or even historical "models," good to think with and that is all; they are "types." In aligning themselves with biblical figures, preachers (and believers) place themselves in the matrix of God's design and give all to understand that their words and actions are a further working out of God's plan for history.

From the point of view of unbelief, it is probably easier to understand how the authority and the ability to speak born-again stories are transmitted than it is to understand how the desire, the need, to speak them is evoked. Hard to grasp, it is simply put: you convert to born-again belief the moment you *know* that someone infinitely superior to you gave his life, or his son's life, to save your lowly life. It is the *knowledge* of ultimate, inexplicable, transcendent compassion that "saves" the unwashed, that ushers them into the born-again kingdom, not only licensing them to speak and according them the enabling point of view but also instilling in them a desire to repay the debt, to come to know and to obey and to become one with the one who gave them so much. Just before the Reverend Cantrell inquired into my beliefs, he, in the manner of Ezekiel, put the matter this way:

My birth, it belongs to God. God made me. And then, Paul said, "When I've been saved, I've been bought with a price." What was the price? His life at Calvary, that's what he gave for me. He ransomed me out of the, you might say, the slave markets of sin and brought me into a right relationship. And when I was unworthy, the Bible said, he loved me.

When I was wretched and naked, when I was borned—the prophets said it was like I was thrown out onto the ground. I had not been washed in salt. I had not been suppled. I had not been bathed in olive oil. I was laying there in my own blood, dying. And when he saw me, there was nothing about me that really made me desirable.

Yet he looked beyond all of my faults and saw my needs, and he come and he loved me and he died for me. And even made it available so that I could know this, and when I come to that knowledge I had no alternative but to want to run to the one that loved me. Because nobody had ever cared for me like Jesus. And that's about the size of the story. Nobody.

The Reverend Cantrell hoped that the storied gifts he offered his listener that afternoon in his study would engender in her the same poetic of desire, the same knowledge of divine love, that Christ's sacrifice evoked in him. "I was laying there in my own blood, dying. . . . yet he looked beyond all my faults and saw my needs, and he come and he loved me and he died for me." Cantrell's stories— above all, the story of his son's death—mingled with his sentimental, liquid language and the liminality of the moment, with the whole vibrating, escalating sequence of sacrificial implications his stories released, and with the thrill, the thrall, of being in the verbal hands of such a master, all together wrought a nearly irresistible desire to return his favors with a leap, "a mere look," of faith.

NOTES

1. Note that there are twelve "zigzags" between Old and New Testaments in Cantrell's exegesis. These moves, in addition to the specific typological connections, are the means by which Cantrell, and other preachers, teach believers how to read the Old Testament—by "looking back," through the New Testament. The New Testament determines the meaning of the Old.
2. I do not mean to imply anything like "brain-washing" here (see Harding, 1987, 168). Witnessing is a more focused, intense, consequential version of what happens in any conversation (all speakers endeavor to induce their point of view in their listeners), or when any intellectual discipline is taught, for example, anthropology, or literary criticism, or psychology.

REFERENCES

Alter, Robert. 1982. *The Art of Biblical Narrative*. New York: Basic Books.
Auerbach, Erich. 1953. *Mimesis: The Representation of Reality in Western Literature*. Princeton: Princeton University Press.
Criswell, W. A. 1979. *Criswell Study Bible*. Nashville, Tenn.: Thomas Nelson.
Falwell, Jerry, ed. 1982. *The Liberty Bible Commentary*. Lynchburg, Va.: The Old-Time Gospel Hour.
Frei, Hans. 1974. *The Eclipse of Biblical Narrative: A Study in Eighteenth- and Nineteenth-Century Hermeneutics*. New Haven: Yale University Press.
Harding, Susan. 1987. Convicted by the Holy Spirit: The Rhetoric of Fundamental Baptist Conversion. *American Ethnologist* 14:1.
Wemp, C. Sumner. 1982. *The Guide to Practical Pastoring*. Nashville, Tenn.: Thomas Nelson.
Willmington, Harold. 1981. *Willmington's Guide to the Bible*. Wheaton, Ill.: Tyndale House.

JUDITH MODELL

4 *"How Do You Introduce Yourself as a Childless Mother?" Birthparent Interpretations of Parenthood*

"I have a book in me." "Let me share with you my story." "Each time you tell your story, remember that you make a difference for someone." These are quotations from the CUB *Communicator,* newsletter of Concerned United Birthparents.[1] CUB began in 1976 as a support group for birthparents and over the years has become increasingly activist, arguing for changes in adoption policy and for the right of everyone to know blood relatives. CUB stands behind individuals who search for lost relatives, whether they are adoptees looking for birthparents, birthparents for their relinquished children, or adoptive parents searching for their adopted child's biological kin. An emphasis on talking about experiences connects these activities and purposes: sharing your story to help yourself and to "make a difference" to someone else. Birthparents who come "out of the closet"—a repeated CUB phrase—come out talking.

In this article I analyze the purpose and the content of birthparent narratives. I consider them an interpretation and critique of American cultural conventions about parenthood, family, and kinship (Martin, 1986, 197). The significance of this critique is sharpened by the particular vantage point of the narrators: they are parents without children. In exploring the implications of this phrase, birthparent narratives delineate the cultural values attached to parenthood and demonstrate the inconsistencies in these values as manifested in adoptive arrangements. From their "deviant" position—rejecting the conventional expectations of adoption by thinking about the relinquished child—birthparents construct an interpretation of these conventions. The thrust of their critique is that adoption, in which a parent by birth relinquishes a child to a parent by social designation, exposes inconsistencies in the values constitutive of parenthood in general.

The final form of this article owes much to the careful, attentive, and persistent reading of the editors. The argument and interpretations are my own but benefited from challenges along the way.

I proceed in the following way. First, I briefly describe the contemporary adoption reform movement, context for birthparent narratives. Then I analyze the narratives, showing how they establish the conflicts in interpretations of parenthood that forced the surrender of a child. In telling their stories birthparents assert their "real" parenthood against the "fiction" of adoption, displaying inconsistencies in a core cultural concept. Furthermore, birthparents link the relinquishment of a child to the loss of memories of having had that child. A concept of coercion, used metaphorically, organizes the narratives and· underlies the birthparent critique.

Adoption Reform

In 1976 a woman ran an advertisement in a Boston newspaper asking for responses from people who had relinquished a child for adoption. As a result, a small group of people met in her living room and established the foundation of Concerned United Birthparents (Campbell, 1979). Membership has grown from the original six to approximately three thousand people across the United States. CUB is part of an adoption reform movement, allied with adoptee groups like ALMA (Adoptees' Liberty Movement Association) and Orphan Voyage. Under the umbrella of the American Adoption Congress, these groups advocate change in the institution of adoption in American society.

This program for change focuses on the secrecy, anonymity, and closed records characteristic of American adoption, at least as conventionally practiced. Reform groups aim their criticism at "stranger" adoption: the stereotypical adoption of an infant or young child by people who had no previous relationship with the baby and will have no future contact with the baby's family of birth. The infant's tie with a birth family is also permanently severed, and the adoptee becomes a "full member" of the adoptive family, receiving a new birth certificate listing the adoptive parents as his parents. This policy, written into all state laws since the post–World War II period, is the target of reform. Remedies range from open adoption, in which birthparents and adoptive parents know one another and maintain contact, to permitting access to records to those who request it.

Dissatisfaction with traditional adoption policy has several sources, some related specifically to adoption and some to wider social and cultural developments. Within adoption, the disappearance of an available infant population in the mid-1970s meant a change in the adopted population from infants to older children, from American-born to foreign-born, and from healthy to "special needs." ("Special needs" includes physical and mental handicaps, sibling groups, and older children, with some variations depending upon region. These trends are fairly well documented; e.g., Benet, 1976; Feigelman and Silverman, 1983; CWLA, 1987.) These changes affected the prescribed secrecy and anonymity of adoption: older children know their biological family; interracial or transcultural adoptions cannot be hidden; special-needs children often bring an evident past. Individuals who had been part of an anonymous adoption began to demand equivalent information about themselves and a right to know their biological background. They were the founders of an adoption reform movement.

In formulating the case for change, adoption reformers borrowed rhetoric from the women's liberation and civil rights movements of the 1960s and 1970s. These movements, as well as an ideology that emphasized "roots" as a source of personal identity, provided symbolism and structure for the argument that secrecy and closed records were discriminatory (Modell, n.d.).

Not every birthparent I interviewed was involved in the adoption reform movement or was searching for a relinquished child. All were aware of searches and of controversies surrounding the anonymity and permanent separation characteristic of American adoption. Narrators drew on a rhetoric developed within the reform movement and popularized on television shows and in magazines and best-sellers. The adoption-reform movement granted birthparents a voice—even those who did not participate actively, had no desire to locate a child, and were satisfied with the decision they had made about adoption. The people I interviewed borrowed from the available rhetoric moral support and a framework in which to place their own experiences. With "performative and narrative resources," the experience became "storyable" (Bruner, 1986, 7).

I participated in and observed two support groups, one a branch of CUB and the other an adoptee support group. Each included members representing all sides of the triad: adoptee, adoptive parent(s), birthparent(s). Spouses, parents, and significant others, as well as social workers and professionals, also attended meetings. My research was welcomed and appreciated, as was my status as an adoptive parent. I drew my interviews of birthparents largely from members of the two groups, supplemented by references from agencies and from individuals I interviewed. In this way I gained informants who had not joined a support group and were not active in adoption reform.

Women were the majority in both support groups, though the inequality was less pronounced in the adoptee than in the birthparent group. The groups were racially homogeneous—mainly white, with a scattering of biracial adoptees.[2] Religious background was, predictably, primarily Protestant (of various denominations) and Catholic. The proportions were influenced by the location of each group. Age, education, and economic level varied. Members might be as young as fifteen or sixteen (generally adoptees) or as old as seventy-five or eighty (mainly birthmothers, though I did meet searching adoptees in their sixties and seventies whose hopes of finding a living birthparent were not totally unrealistic). The groups included high school dropouts and Ph.D.'s. The majority of people were middle or lower middle class, with a few visibly wealthier than that. The rhetoric shared by the group and utilized by individuals, however, portrayed adoption as an exploitative system in which the "rich and powerful" took advantage of the "poor and vulnerable." The class implications in this account were adjusted to the individual story.[3]

Meetings were based on story telling. As the CUB newsletter put it, "Each time you tell your story, remember that you make a difference for someone." After discussing objective issues—for instance, a summary of the progress of a proposed bill in the state legislature or a report on an agency's policy regarding open records—individuals were encouraged to talk. "Talk" consisted of accounts of relinquishment, of the discovery that one was adopted, of a decision to search for a "lost" relative, and so on. I did not use my tape recorder at meetings because for many participants these were private and painful confessions. I did tape-record individual interviews except when I was asked not to (three out of the seventeen birthparents I interviewed asked me not to tape). Birthparents included one birthfather; ages ranged from twenty to early sixties, with most people in their mid-thirties and forties. The time since relinquishment varied between two and thirty-five years; the average was about twenty years.[4] All material is confidential, names have been changed, and identifying information altered.

Interviews ordinarily lasted between two and four hours, enough time for a narrative strategy to emerge. It became apparent, when I listened and when I analyzed the material, that birthparents drew on a public rhetoric to express private experiences (Bruner, 1986, 19; Schwartzman, 1984, 84). Such intertwining was crucial to the content and purpose of story telling. Consequently, my analysis focused on the recurring themes, metaphors, and symbols that connected the individual story to the shared story composed at meetings and in newsletters (Sarbin, 1986; Agar, 1987; Martin, 1987; Rosaldo, 1986). The same narrative devices linked the birthparent story to the presumably "normal" experience of parenthood in American society.

Birthparents seemed unusually sensitive to language until I realized this was an effect of their status. Historically, terms for the relinquishing parent have reflected cultural values concerning sexuality, parenthood, and family. Recognizing this, the reform movement made terminology a central part of its agenda. The choice of *birthparent* marked a response to recent terms like *natural parent, real parent,* and *biological parent,* as well as to the negative labels that have faded from adoption literature but remain vigorous in the popular press: teen parent, unwed mother, out-of-wedlock birth, illegitimate birth (the last two refer to the parent through the child's status). A concern with terminology and its implications appeared in interviews with all birthparents, not just members of a support group.

The term *birthparent* is not neutral and is not meant to be. In birthparent literature, the designation intentionally draws on cultural interpretations of birth as a profound, unique, and memorable experience. Birthparents reject "biological parent" because it eliminates these culturally valued aspects of birth. "We are not baby-making machines," reads the rhetoric, or alternatively, the CUB *Communicator* told its readers "We are not brood-mares" (Dusky, 1979). "Parent by birth also has value vis-à-vis the adoptive parent, recalling as it does the (conventionally) natural and normal way of having a child and emphasizing the origin of "adoptive" in a social contract or option. Playing on the cultural resonances of birth, birthparents add a social element to the physiological tie they have with the child. In rejecting the designations "real" and "natural," birthparent narratives implicitly acknowledge adoptive parenthood and ask that "birth" and "blood" be made part of the contracted tie between adoptive parent and child.

Birthparent Narratives: Conflicting Cultural Imperatives

Birthparent narratives are autobiographical accounts detailing a sequence of personal events and establishing a path to maturity and self-esteem. They are also explanatory, justifying primarily the act of surrender and secondarily the act of having had a baby "at the wrong time." On a more abstract level, birthparent narratives portray "disharmonies" in cultural interpretations of parenthood (Ginsburg, 1987, 625). The narratives demonstrate inconsistencies in the cultural meanings of being a parent through descriptions of surrendering a child to adoption.

Each telling of this intensely personal experience contains a critique of the "cultural domain" of parenthood (cf. Schneider, 1980). "Stories of our concrete experiences, even anecdotes, can be insightful commentaries on the social order," writes Emily Martin, adding: "we must not make the mistake of hearing the particularistic, concrete stories of these and other women and assume that they are less likely than more universalistic, abstract discourse to contain an analysis of society" (Martin, 1987, 197, 201). People do not have to be self-conscious about the critique in order to accomplish it: some but not all of the birthparents I talked with recognized and accentuated the critical thrust of their story.

Criticism focused on the context of an adoption and the shift in values that permitted a natural parent to lose a child permanently, a birthparent to erase memories of the birth, and a parent to be considered childless. The inconsistencies portrayed in birthparent narratives are complex, involving at one level a contradiction within adoption between the values attached to parenthood and the negative connotation of those values when parenthood has not been planned. At another level, these narratives suggest a conflict in American cultural interpretations of parenthood between "blood" and "law," natural and social bonds.

Relinquishment was the central scene in birthparent narratives, at whatever point in the story it occurred. The words describing that event carried the meaning given the whole life story (Bertaux, 1981, 7). Relinquish, give up, give away, surrender: none conveyed a positive action, and all suggested an unwilling decision: "I had no choice." "Surrender" is the word preferred by birthparents. "Like the white-flag surrender of a losing nation in war, most birthparents surrendered not because they wanted to but because their situations gave them no other choice" (Anderson, n.d.). Every birthparent narrative was a story of being forced to relinquish.

Coercion was a key concept, used metaphorically to organize events birthparents had been told to forget. The metaphor drew upon the physical experience of being forced to communicate the feeling of giving up a child and an aspect of one's identity in a culture in which having a child is presumed to mean raising that child (Johnson, 1987; Blustein, 1982). "Coercion" was an apt rhetorical device, inasmuch as it emphasized conditions of surrender and the vulnerability that led an individual into giving up.

Whether or not a birthparent was literally forced to relinquish a child, coercion represented the "truth" of the birthparent experience. The metaphor explains the unnatural and uncultural phenomenon of giving away a child and eliminating a part of one's past. "I had kept my whole little past about being a birthmother all sewn up in a little box" (*Waterville* [Maine] *Sentinel* 3/9/83, 20). In narratives birthparents exerted their own force, reclaiming the child that accorded parenthood and restoring a lost episode to their histories.

"You may be able to numb your emotions . . . , but you cannot 'forget' forever" (CUB, 1981, 42).[5] This sentence from a CUB pamphlet suggests the response to coercion in the narratives: remembering and reclaiming the experience of having had a child. Scenes repeated from story to story established the imperatives that had forced the surrender: an invisible and simultaneously stigmatized pregnancy; a "false" birth and a child whose value was evident; an act of love that involved signing away a baby. The contradictions in these aspects of birthparent experience gave rise to the term *childless mother*.

Pregnancy: Invisible, stigmatized, discounted

"Then again it was like it [pregnancy] wasn't real and my family came to visit me and they didn't say, 'Gee, you're getting big, is the baby kicking? How do you feel?' It was like, 'so what's new,' you know." This woman, pregnant at sixteen, had been sent away from her hometown to be "invisible" to others. She was not invisible to her family, who visited, but her pregnancy was: her family acted as if it weren't there. This was not an uncommon experience; "our parenthood," a birthfather said, "vaporized."

Some birthparents created their own invisibility by hiding the pregnancy. Motivated by fear, uncertainty, or a decision to embrace the experience alone, hiding had the same effect: it deprived a person of an identity in the eyes of others. "So I didn't tell anybody I was pregnant partly because I didn't want my aunt to be caught trying to decide whether to give me shelter or throw me out, because if her husband's [second] wife found out, she could have made some trouble, giving her a hard time. And because also I just didn't want to be hassled by people. In spite of the fact that I realized that I was probably going to give the baby up for adoption, I was really enjoying being pregnant and I just didn't want people bugging me. So I didn't tell anybody and nobody ever guessed." (Pregnant in the late 1960s, this woman had considered abortion and decided it was too dangerous.) She lived with an aunt who "asked me once, after I got quite big, but you know, I didn't carry myself like a pregnant person. I didn't walk around sway-backed like people do. I don't know why they do that, there's no reason for it. I just looked like I was getting fat and I gained a little weight to cover it up. She asked me, 'Are you sure you're not pregnant?' I said, 'No.' And she really believed me."

Another birthparent, pregnant at fourteen, remembered not telling anyone. "I was petrified to approach my mother or my family at all. I told no one, and had been in ninth grade at the time, and continued going to school. I was sent home probably several times a week. I would black out at school and would have problems. They didn't figure it out either. To this day it amazes me that I went through seven months pregnant before anyone knew that I was pregnant." She explained how her mother happened to find out: "And the only way that happened was one day I just could not hide it any longer. I couldn't fit in any more clothes. I couldn't put gumbands [rubber bands] around the buttons of my pants any longer. I couldn't fit in any of my tops. We were going someplace and my mother said, 'Are you ready? Are you ready yet?' I just couldn't find anything to wear. She said, 'Boy, are you getting chubby or what? Boy, if I didn't know better, I would say you were pregnant.' And the next thing you know, I burst out crying and she said, 'Are you?' 'Yes.'"

When it was discovered, the pregnancy was severed from parenthood. Birthparents remembered being treated like children, not like potential mothers or fathers. In the stories, social workers communicated this even more definitively than parents. "She [social worker] passed down to me mostly just as a young person who didn't know anything and because she didn't know anything, what was best for herself, how could she know what was best for a baby, or she couldn't really know her own feelings either, she was just a kid. And I just remember being patronized a lot, patted on the head. I'd try to say something and she'd say, 'Oh, that isn't really how you feel. It's because of this or that and it will go away,' or 'That's natural.'" Though very young, she was expected to make an adult decision for the sake of her child.[6] One birthmother tried to resolve the paradox: "Someone should adopt the pregnant mother."

Parents did offer to take their child's child. But "there was no way I could have my mother raise a child the way she raised me, because I just couldn't deal with that. So I turned that alternative down, and that only left adoption open." "And then my mother, I think she was having a harder time with it [relinquishment] than I was, being that she was older, and up to the last minute that we were leaving [the hospital], she said, 'You know, if you really want to keep this baby, we'll manage, we'll think of something.' And I know she meant it, but I kept thinking that she would have really been the mother." One woman said, "To have my own child call me sister would have been unbearable." The reference to kin terms dramatized the loss of parental status that would come from a parent parenting one's child.

"Stigma" was another way birthparents talked about being both a nonparent and a parent in the eyes of others. By their accounts, pregnancy was simultaneously unnoticed and stigmatized, an insistent contradiction that constituted a powerful push toward surrender. "A lot of the people who I thought were close friends told me that their parents wouldn't let them—forbid them to see me. I guess they thought that it would rub off." "Everybody avoided me just when I needed their help the most." "It really bothered me that I was shunned by a lot of my friends. I had a whole bunch of friends when I was in high school, and then when I got pregnant, Tom [the father] and I both had a lot of friends, and when I got pregnant and we were going through all those problems, we had two—two good friends. And that killed me. That really hurt. It's like, 'Wait, I don't have a disease. I'm carrying a child, not I have gonorrhea or AIDS.'"

In their stories, birthparents were punished for an unexpected pregnancy, not for sexual behavior. Descriptions of being stigmatized suggested that values collided over parenthood. "How dare you say to me, 'Well, you're pregnant.' You fooled around just as much as I did. I got caught, you didn't. You didn't get caught, don't treat me that way." "And I think it was my mother who explained to me that that's what happens to nice girls. The bad girls know better and don't get caught."

The stories also tried to establish the "normalness" of a birthparent's sexual experience. "So then all of a sudden, years went by, two or three, you know, no date or anything. And I finally realized that if you want a date, if you want somebody, you've got to do what they say, I guess. If they want to, if they take you out for dinner and a movie, and you want to see them again, you've got to thank them the way they want to be thanked. And all of a sudden, after three months of that, I was pregnant. And I thought, now wait a minute, no, it took my mother all these years to get pregnant." "But I thought I was in love with him, but I don't think that's any reason to believe everything someone says, just because you're in love with him." "I was dating a seventeen-year-old guy, who I thought I was in love with. And he convinced me that he loved me and what we did was right."

By characterizing themselves as innocent and gullible, birthparents underlined the unfairness of the punishment—losing a baby. More to the point, they had been loving, and the narratives go on to imply that "greedy" social workers distorted the relationship between love and parenthood by focusing on sex. "And I mean, I came back and I was just stunned. I just, no wonder she [social worker] didn't want to help me, no wonder she had no counseling and no advice to me, she thought of me as slime of the gutter, slime of the earth. God forbid she would let me keep a child." Adoptive parents played a similar role: "They probably thought, This little whore, she just had this baby and didn't want to take care of her, and here we are, we are the saviors." Or, "But to them, what am I? Some tramp that got pregnant at fifteen years old?" And one birthmother asked, "If they think we're such trash, why do they take our babies?"

Birth: Having a child

"I remember my sister calling me once and I told her I was in labor and she said, 'How long have you been getting pains?' And I told her all day and she said, 'It must be false labor,' and you know, it was like you didn't even know if you should call anybody when you delivered." Pregnancy was invisible, parenthood an error, and as the symbolism of false labor prefigured, birth was "not real." "It had been two weeks prior to when I went into labor, which it turned out that I went into the hospital and it was false labor. So about two weeks later, about ten o'clock at night I was watching TV and I started labor, and being so naïve I thought I was having false labor again. I was in labor all night, I never slept the entire night, it was horrible. . . . And my mother got up and was getting ready for work, and I didn't say a word to her, and she was getting ready to leave and she went past my room and she came and said, 'Are you awake?' I said 'Yes.'" The birthparent recognized the reality of her labor, called her father, and went to the hospital.

In birthparent narratives, falseness extended from labor to a birth in which there was "no child" and culminated in the documents that denied the facts of birth. "And it's lies. The whole thing is lies. It says it was a spontaneous birth, it wasn't. I was in hard labor for a good twelve hours and in total labor twenty-eight hours. And they put down that my labor was like six hours or something, I can't remember what it was. But they lied about that and they said it was spontaneous and it wasn't. For four hours I was on the delivery table and they finally had to take forceps and pull her [baby] out." In contrast, giving birth represented the birthparent's truth, a physiological experience engraved in memory and a social experience incorporated in the reality of the parent-child relationship. The truth of having a child was conveyed through descriptions of the baby, of feelings associated with holding an infant, and of the significance of naming the child. Birth was remembered as the moment a birthparent began staking her claim to parenthood.

Birthfathers and birthmothers described their babies as beautiful, wonderful, perfect. "They [nurses] didn't tell other people that their babies were gorgeous. But she was gorgeous, though, and they would say, 'Your baby is so beautiful.' And she was. She was a really beautiful baby. . . . They were all raving about her." Descriptions did not individualize the baby but rather imposed his or her existence on those who had "not seen" the pregnancy. The beauty of the baby also redeemed the birthmother in her own eyes. "And once you see the baby you realize if there was any mistake, it certainly wasn't that—that beautiful baby was not the mistake. And because your baby is so beautiful it makes you feel better about yourself because you can see something so beautiful that you have produced. It shows that you are not a rotten person. Otherwise this baby would look rotten." Others felt "rewarded" and "justified" by the beauty of their child. "And I wanted her [own mother] to come down [to the hospital] and see. Cause it was the most beautiful baby—there were thirty-five babies in the nursery, in the big nursery, and there were about five newborns in the smaller nursery. And of all the babies mine was the prettiest. And that's just not my opinion."

One birthmother overheard the social worker describe her son as their "number one baby" and add, pointing to her, "because she's so smart." (The birthmother laughed then and said to me, "I wanted to say, 'If I'm so smart, why am I pregnant?'") The beauty of the baby lessened the negative aspects of the experience and, birthparents commented, increased the likelihood of adoption: "Because I also thought, 'What if she had never been adopted?' But I didn't think that would be the case because she was a beautiful baby. Anybody would have wanted her."

Giving birth also prompted a struggle against adoption, sometimes not recognized until the story was brought up from memory. "Yeah, you lose the little power you have [in relinquishing]. Yeah, so it was in fact like a little two-year-old, although I was so grateful that—because I thought I gave in really easy and I felt so guilty about giving in. If I had really given them a fight I may not have felt so bad, and I never thought I did. But here years later when my mother and I could finally talk about some things, she says, 'Oh, no, you gave us a real fight.'" In retrospect, the fight involved a demand to see and hold the baby. "Seeing and holding your baby will help to connect you with the reality of your experience" (CUB, 1981, 54).

"So when I wanted to see her, they [nurses and social workers] wouldn't let me see her through that night or the next day. I kept asking and they wouldn't let me see her, and I believe it was the second or third day after, and it was the day before I was going home and they had not allowed me to see her. . . . I kept telling them that I had to see her and I really felt that I could see her, that I couldn't go through with it without seeing her. It's strange, but that's how I felt. So they just kept trying to talk me out of it. I guess it was the next morning when Dr. King came in and we talked, and he felt the same way as they did. He acted more like a father with me, he said, 'I know what's best for you, and I know it's hard, but it will be easier if you don't see her.' I insisted, and he finally agreed with it and it was hours later when they finally brought her in to me. The nurse brought her in, and I held her, and the nurse was standing over me, wanting to take her back instantly. So I can't say I had her more than three minutes when they whisked her back away from me. And I thought they were doing me a big favor." "I begged to see her [the baby]. I stomped my feet and said, 'I won't go through with any of this, if you don't let me see her.'"

Even when it was policy for a birthmother to hold the baby, the event became an arena for struggle.[7] A birthmother who relinquished in the mid-1980s reported a nurse's objection to her unwrapping the baby from his blanket: "I said, 'So what? What are you going to do, not bring him to me? I'll complain. He's my baby.' I hated it when they used to . . . I had a wristband, and he had a wristband, and they would say, 'Is this your son? Let me check your wristband.' I mean, they would bring him to me four or five times a day, 'Let me check your wristband.' Well, wait a minute, of course he's mine, you just brought him in here three hours ago."

For birthparents, holding the baby normalized the birth and legitimated their parenthood. "He had these little, teeny weeny, skinny things [legs], about this big [hand gesture]. And the bottle was an ounce, maybe two, and he couldn't even drink half of that bottle. Maybe half." A woman who had twins recalled, "And after the first baby came I remember the doctors—and I heard the cry and I remember, my mother always said, 'Just so it's healthy, it has all its toes and all its fingers.' And so that's what I said, that's the right thing to say. Because I was laughing to myself, I said, 'That's your little baby' when I could hear its cry." These memories proved the baby was theirs and that the relationship was more than biological. "I was allowed to look at my son for three short minutes, very short, very short, and I was extremely attached to him." The permanence of this parent-child relationship was further conveyed by birthparents when they talked about naming their child.

Every birthparent I talked with had named the child, even though they knew the name was likely to be changed with adoption. In American culture a name confirms the baby's place in a social world and also places him or her in the birthfamily, establishes a connection with the birthparent, and accords the child a unique identity. Sometimes the name was fanciful: "I had always wanted to call her Kim. There was a little girl right next door to us with dark hair and big brown eyes. And she was always what I pictured my baby would look like. And her name was Kim. And that's what I wanted to call her [own baby]." Usually the name had a special meaning. "I named him Jayson William. With a y [in Jayson] because he was a special baby." There was more to the baby's name: "William was Tom's [father] middle name. And Jayson, it might have been because of my mother when my stepfather—he was dying—that this baby be named after him. So I gave him the name Jayson to make her happy, but I changed the spelling because I couldn't stand her husband. So, yes, he's special and he has the name Jayson, but it's not like my stepfather. And his name has a lot to do with every guy I ever went out with [using similar letters and so on]. . . . I put everything together in one cute little package." Occasionally the baby's father chose the name. "Actually he was the one that chose the name [Danielle Marie]. There was some movie, some French movie, I can't even remember what it was. He loves that name, Danielle. And Marie was his sister's name."

Names also prompted questions in a birthparent's narrative. Virtually everyone I interviewed wondered what the child was presently called and were pleased if they learned that a birthname had been kept by adoptive parents. "Yes, I named her Liza and her family kept her name, which I thought was really nice. I named her Liza Louise and they kept her first name. . . . So I thought that was very nice. I don't know whether the mother did it as sort of a gesture or just because she liked the name." Others were pleased if the name had the same first letter or was the same as a name in the birthfamily. A continuity of name symbolized the enduring bond that birth created but which, in these cases, had been "artificially severed" by adoption. For birthparents, the preservation of the same or a familiar name underlined the permanency of their bond with the child. The possibility of coincidence and chance did not make this any less persuasive: for some birthparents, the chance element proved how strong and unbreakable the tie of blood was. A continuity in name showed the persistence of a "natural" link.

Surrender: Signing away a baby

"I cannot remember being in the hospital. I cannot remember signing anything." This woman reported that she had "numbed" herself throughout the pregnancy, birth, and signing of surrender papers. Papers were a central symbol in all accounts, whether the birthparent remembered being numb, confused, or tricked into signing. "You know, I was crying so hard, they had me doped up because I was in horrible pain. It was only two days after I almost died from childbirth. And so they had me doped up, I had double the dose of sleeping pills that I was supposed to have because I couldn't get to sleep. And I had tons of pain pills in me plus all kinds of other things. And they got me up at midnight because this person from the county that moonlighted and would come and take care of the stuff at midnight, came for the surrender—for me to sign the surrender papers. And that was only two days after I had given birth. And so I had no idea what I was doing and they said the only—and I didn't want to sign it, I was crying and crying. And I have no idea what I signed. I did not get a copy of the surrender papers."

This woman was not the only one who remembered feeling confused, vulnerable, and literally or figuratively "doped up." Others who signed surrender papers in the hospital attributed their confusion to painkilling pills and the greed of social workers eager to get babies. Talking about her social worker, a birthmother generalized: "And we know once that paper was signed they wouldn't give us the time of day and we were nobody." She signed by pretending the babies weren't hers, "Because I know I would never give my babies away." "I next remember a lady coming in to see me with a paper in her hand. This woman in authority, she didn't care about me or my child, what I was feeling or what my child would feel later. . . . Her main concern was not my hurt at that point only my name on that contract. . . . Where were all the people who said they loved me?" (CUB *Communicator*, 2/83, 5).

Social workers were not the only villains. One woman remembered signing papers in the county courthouse, under a clerk's supervision. "And they took me downstairs and said, 'Sign this.'" She did not know, twenty years later, whether she had signed surrender papers or whether her child had been adopted. Her husband blamed the priest: "I cannot see how a man of the cloth would do this, would take someone's baby away." Another described the relinquishment with a sparse, "I signed her away in some attorney's office." One woman did not remember ever signing: "We left her [baby] and that was that."

Even for those who felt they had made the decision on their own, putting a signature on paper evoked the inevitability of an adoptive arrangement. This was the moment when the force of social pressure triumphed and, her vulnerability evident, the birthparent gave up. In narratives, surrender papers were a primary symbol of the tricks and inconsistencies through which parenthood was transferred. The idea of signing away a baby out of love epitomized the sense of deception that characterized the birthparent experience of adoption.

"We [birthparents] were told, 'If you love your baby . . . you'll give it away'" (*St. Paul* [Minnesota] *Pioneer Press,* 10/13/85, 1G). Birthparents reported the prescription with irony; signing away a baby out of love made no emotional, logical, or cultural sense. Their stories conveyed the deception in this view of parental love by stressing the lies they were told about adoptive families. "Then they came. 'Sign this paper.' I was told that he'd [baby] go to the perfect family, possibly professional people, and he'd have a mother and a father, a nice home, good care, and everything that you cannot give him" (cub *Communicator,* 2/85, 7).[8] A birthparent I interviewed remembered being asked, "'Don't you want to give her [baby] to two people that are economically sound and can provide everything for her and give her this joyous, wonderful home?' That's a joke." This same woman added: "I was told that the mother looked so much like me that she could be my sister. That couldn't be further from the truth than the sun and the moon. . . . I mean, obviously, I was told so many lies, and I was told the father had blond hair and that he was very, very similar to her father."

Adoptive parents turned out not to be what they were said to be; they were not professional, or stably married, or—a special theme in birthparent stories—permanently bound to the child. "Of course the baby gets a family, a mother and a father guaranteed for life, supposedly." "I was given the 'Hollywood version' of adoption, that they always work out." A woman who relinquished a five-year-old was promised pictures, but the adoptive parents stopped sending them. They "want to punish me for giving up a baby," she said, suggesting an inability to share and be generous. Through characterizations of the adoptive family, birthparents conveyed the conflict adoption revealed between loving a child "naturally" and being "socially prepared" to love a child. Zeroing in on adoption's paradox, they contrasted their "giving" with the adoptive parents' selfishness.

"If I could reach every adoptive parent through one sentence, I would say that no matter what papers you have in your possession, you cannot 'have an exclusive claim to any individual' . . . morally" (cub *Communicator,* 8/85, 4).[9] A version of the same point appeared in a *Communicator* editorial responding to a woman trying to decide about her untimely pregnancy: "She feels selfish for wanting her child, too naïve to realize how much more selfish it is to try to get someone else's" (cub *Communicator,* 11/86, 3). Just as signing a paper represented the birthparent's vulnerability, in birthparent narratives signing papers represented the adoptive parents' possessive appropriation of parenthood. A multivocal symbol, papers exhibited the cultural imperatives in adoption: the conflict between love and duty, feelings and qualifications, attachment to and ownership of a child.

The conflict was not always articulated. Yet the way birthparents told their stories—the falsification and deception in their experience of adoption—expressed their view that conflicts in interpretations of parenthood had pressed them into relinquishing a child. Their perception of a split between love and an ability to parent, between natural feelings and a "proper" environment, struck at the heart not only of adoption but also of assumptions about being a parent. "And I know these people have enough money, too, so he [baby] doesn't have to want for anything. I'm sure that they don't just give him everything so that he is a spoiled, rotten brat, but that he doesn't have to want. That was my biggest thing, that he would have to want for things if I kept him. . . . The only thing I could give more . . . was to be more loved. If people could live on love in this world, he would be the richest, happiest baby." This birthparent also knew she was supposed to forget her love for the child: "So I am standing there, calling him Jayson, and he lifted up his little head and he turned it over and looked and smiled and then he turned the other way."

Forgetting: Becoming a childless parent

Signing papers completed the birthparent story by symbolizing the prescription to forget the birth of a child. "My parents said I could come back home if I never mentioned the baby again." A young birthmother awkwardly negotiated the loss of childhood and the loss of an experience: "I am more of a kid than I am anything else. Now I have to be this grown-up person in this grown-up world that I am not ready for. I still want to be sixteen and seventeen years old and just start all over again. The part that I missed when I was pregnant. Of course I would have to grow up again, and that was rough." The birthparent was supposed to eliminate a scene in her life; she became a "childless mother" by reversing time.

Being told that time could disappear was a powerful lie for birthparents: "As if the *papers* could turn the clock back to before the conception" (Anderson, 1980, italics in original). For some, the possibility of turning back the clock provided the strongest pressure for relinquishing a child. "And I think, now I admit to it, at that time [of relinquishing], I was thinking that if I gave up this baby, I would still have a chance with Mike. I don't think I ever admitted that to anybody before but now I admit it." Later, the promise that a return to the past would constitute a step to the future seemed another contradictory message bombarding the birthparent. "But it was all a bunch of lies. 'You'll forget. You'll close this chapter in your life. You'll do all these wonderful things. This is not the end, it is the beginning.' And all that, you know, you don't forget." "Actually this is something that stays on a father's mind from the very moment it happens." In a culture where having a child was presumed to be a memorable and lasting experience, being told to forget was not only unnatural but also "uncultural."

Birthparents borrowed narrative strategies from stories told at meetings and in newsletters as a way of "unfreezing" memory and reclaiming parenthood. Surrender was the central scene in a birthparent story, but the pressure to forget was the dominant emotional and rhetorical moment. The play on natural/unnatural running through these narratives climaxed in the perceived contradiction contained in the notion that a loving parent can dismiss a child from memory. Asserting the unnaturalness of this, birthparent narratives argue that American adoption relies as much on the pressure to forget as on the force exerted by peers, parents, and professionals to relinquish parenthood. Birthparent narratives are about the imposed life story that permits an adoption to occur.

Giving Up: The Metaphor of Coercion in Birthparent Narratives

What is the meaning of stories told by birthparents who are reconsidering the basis of a decision made in the past? Is there broader significance to stories whose purpose is to justify that decision for the teller and an audience? How does one weigh the importance of accounts provided only by a small number of the people who ever made an adoption plan? The retrospective, justificatory, and minority aspects of these stories affect the "analysis of society" and, specifically, the interpretation of parenthood they convey through personal details. Birthparent narratives look back in order to justify an action that is individually difficult and socially unconventional: giving away a baby. And they accomplish this through a metaphor of coercion that also exposes inconsistencies in American cultural concepts of parenthood.

"The essence of metaphor is understanding and experiencing one kind of thing in terms of another" (Lakoff and Johnson, 1980, 5). Within a culture, metaphors are a way of understanding and communicating complicated, partially unshared experiences (ibid., 225). "Metaphors have entailments through which they highlight and make coherent certain aspects of our experience" (ibid., 156). Birthparents convey "coercion" through the words, phrases, and concepts they use to describe relinquishment; the metaphors shape their perceptions and narratives of the event (ibid., 4–5). The physical connotation of being forced against one's will—"I had no choice"—makes coherent and communicable an experience fraught with contradiction: being treated like a child in order to make an adult decision; giving away a child out of love for that child; being told to forget an experience otherwise deemed unforgettable in the cultural context. In birthparent narratives, "coercion" stands for being forced to give up a child and to forget the experience of having had that child.

Coercion is also a "metaphor of self" in birthparent narratives (Olney, 1972). "One of the most basic ways that the autobiographer has of ordering the experiences of that paradoxical, problematic, elusive entity he seeks is to choose a metaphor of the self and develop it in a narrative" (Landow, 1979, xxxiv, acknowledging the source in Olney). As a metaphor, coercion explains the individual's surrender to pressure and her assumption of an identity as childless parent. In the cultural context of these narratives, a parent does not "lovingly" give away a child; to do so, she must have been subject to forces beyond her control. Consequently, whatever the exact terms of relinquishment, every birthparent story is "really" about being forced into an action that would ordinarily be considered unnatural and unloving. The metaphor also emphasizes the revision of the past that this entails; by their own accounts, birthparents have been coerced into forgetting a part of their history. The imposed freezing of memory shapes the birthparent's self-image, in a retrospective but also in a constructive sense. The "thawing" of memory accomplished by sharing stories forms the basis for a new self-image that includes the child.

As a rhetorical device, coercion does more than organize a narrative. The metaphor calls experience out of memory and makes the past storyable (Bruner, 1986). "My memories began to thaw." Meetings, interviews, and newsletters give birthparents the resources for articulating a memory presumed to be nonexistent. In the process of reclaiming parenthood by describing pregnancy, birth, and a lasting attachment to the child, birthparent-narrators probed into the concept of parenthood and its components—permanency, responsibility, and love. As birthparents made their case, only coercion could explain the paradox by which the ordinarily valued and presumably unforgettable biological and social event of having a child became the basis for denying parental status.

"How do you introduce yourself as a childless mother?" (cub *Communicator*, 12/82, 13). The oxymoron epitomizes the contradictions in adoption and in the cultural interpretations that sanction the permanent transfer of a child from a natural to a social parent. In the birthparent version of adoption, a child has no biological parent and a parent who has given birth has no child. In this view, expressed from a distinct vantage point, adoption exploits a split between "nature" and "culture" in the concept of parent. Nature becomes a negative attribute for the purposes of granting social status to a parent. Adoptive arrangements take advantage of an inconsistency at the core of parent-child relationships.

Birthparents do not object to adoption as a way of having a child. They object to the conflicting imperatives that facilitate the transaction and demand a freezing of memory, a rewriting of the past. Their stories assert, too, that the imperatives in adoption stem from wider inconsistencies in assumptions about being a parent. The assumptions that birth grants parental status, love entails enduring commitment, and "blood" forms the basis of relatedness give way before a birth that is "nonexistent," a love that requires relinquishing contact, and a kinship based on contract or option. Birthparent narratives imply that the conflict evident in that contest has roots in cultural ambiguity about the role of birth in being a parent and of nature in being related. The concepts defining parenthood have a nonrational referent that renders them inadequate for according the status of parent, even while they strongly color the significance and behavior of being a parent. Birthparent narratives point out that creating an "artificial family" involves manipulating the concept of nature, a manipulation that reveals its situational meaning in the domain of kinship. The birthparent experience is that a natural (unplanned) parent is not the natural (right) parent for her child.

Birthparent narratives ask for consistency in the delegation of parenthood and in the constitution of parent-child relatedness. Culturally, having a child forms the basis for being a parent, and biological links are the core of kinship. From the birthparent point of view, acknowledging a birthparent's attachment to her child would harmonize the values surrounding parenthood and make sense of the components of kinship in an adoptive arrangement. A return of the child is figurative but no less significant: becoming a "childed" parent gives back to the birthparent a missing piece of her or his life story and restores the proper terms of relationship to adoptee and adoptive parents. Told at meetings, to themselves, and, increasingly, to the general public, birthparent narratives demand that memories of a birth be acknowledged in adoption and that their stories be added to the cultural narrative of parenthood, family, and kinship.

NOTES

1. *Birthparent* is the preferred term, replacing biological parent, real or natural parent, as well as unwed mother and pregnant teen.
2. The location of the CUB branch made this unsurprising; the area did not have a large minority population. The adoptee group existed in a more racially mixed area; nevertheless no blacks came to any meeting I attended.
3. There were patterns here. Birthparents tended to be lower middle class and adoptive parents to be middle or upper middle class. Adoptees came from diverse backgrounds. But the exceptions to this were many (Bachrach, 1985; Bonham, 1977).
4. Both groups discouraged birthparents from searching for minor children, which may explain the concentration on a twenty-year span since relinquishment.
5. *Choices, Chances, Changes* is a CUB pamphlet for individuals facing an "untimely pregnancy," ostensibly laying out the options but in effect opposing adoption. A decision not to abort is presumed.
6. Birthparent memories are supported by a literature that attributes irresponsibility to the unwed mother who keeps her child and maturity to those who surrender the child (e.g., Vincent, 1961).
7. Over the past ten years, the notion that not seeing the baby will help the birthparent forget has disappeared; currently, birthparents are encouraged to see and hold their babies in preparation for relinquishment.
8. In the 1950s, and 1960s adoption workers generally did assure a birthparent that her child was going into a "good, professional home" (Brenner, 1951; Witmer et al., 1963).
9. The perception of adoptive parent possessiveness in birthparent stories is supported by

adoption literature, especially of the 1960s, when adoptive parents were advised to develop a "sense of ownership" and "entitlement" to the child. Adoption, John Bowlby wrote, "means . . . taking possession for better or for worse of a human life" (Bowlby, 1963, 439).

REFERENCES

Agar, M. 1987. "Political Talk." In *Power through Discourse*. Edited by L. Kedar. Norwood, N.J.: Ablex.

Anderson, C. 1980. *The Social Worker's Role in Adoption*. Dover, N.H.: CUB.

————. n.d. *Are Adoptees Cutting Their Own Throats?* Dover, N.H.: CUB.

Bachrach, C. 1985. *Adoption Plans, Adopted Children, and Adoptive Mothers,* working paper 22. Hyattsville, Md.: National Center for Health Statistics.

Benet, M. K. 1976. *The Politics of Adoption*. New York: Free Press.

Bertaux, D. 1981. "Introduction." In *Biography and Society*. Edited by D. Bertaux. Beverly Hills, Calif.: Sage Publications.

Blustein, J. 1982. *Parents and Children*. New York: Oxford University Press.

Bonham, G. 1977. "Who Adopts." In *Journal of Marriage and the Family* 39(2):295–306.

Bowlby, J. 1963. "Substitute Families." In *Readings in Adoption*. Edited by E. Smith. New York: Philosophical Library.

Brenner, R. 1951. *Follow-Up Study of Adoptive Families*. New York: Child Adoption Research Committee.

Bruner, E. 1986. "Experience and Its Expressions." In *The Anthropology of Experience*. Edited by V. Turner and E. Bruner. Urbana: University of Illinois Press.

Campbell, L. 1979. "The Birthparent's Right to Know." In *Public Welfare* 37(3):22–27.

Child Welfare League of America (CWLA). 1987. *Report of the CWLA National Adoption Task Force*. Washington, D.C.: CWLA.

CUB *Communicator* (Newsletter of Concerned United Birthparents). Dover, N.H.: CUB.

CUB. 1981. *Choices, Chances, Changes*. Dover, N.H.: CUB.

Dusky, L. 1979. *Birthmark*. New York: M. Evans.

Feigelman, W., and A. R. Silverman. 1983. *Chosen Children*. New York: Praeger.

Fisher, F. 1973. *The Search for Anna Fisher*. New York: Arthur Fields.

Ginsburg, F. 1987. "Procreation Stories." In *American Ethnologist* 14(4):623–636.

Johnson, M. 1987. *The Body in the Mind*. Chicago: University of Chicago Press.

Lakoff, G., and M. Johnson. 1980. *Metaphors We Live By*. Chicago: University of Chicago Press.

Landow, G. 1979. *Approaches to Victorian Autobiography*. Athens: Ohio University Press.

Martin, E. 1987. *The Woman in the Body*. Boston: Beacon Press.

Modell, J. n.d. "Private to Public: The Effectiveness of Adoption Lobbying Groups." Unpublished paper.

Olney, J. 1972. *Metaphors of Self*. Princeton, N.J.: Princeton University Press.

Paton, J. 1968. *Orphan Voyage*. New York: Vantage Press.

Roberts, R. W. 1966. "A Theoretical Overview of the Unwed Mother." In *The Unwed Mother*. Edited by R. Roberts. Westport, Conn: Greenwood Press.

Rosaldo, R. 1986. "Ilongot Hunting as Story and Experience." In *The Anthropology of Experience*. Edited by V. Turner and E. Bruner. Urbana: University of Illinois Press.

St. Paul [Minnesota] *Pioneer Press* 10/13/85:1G.

Sarbin, T., ed. 1986. *Narrative Psychology*. New York: Praeger.

Schneider, D. 1980. *American Kinship*. Chicago: University of Chicago Press.

―――. 1984. *A Critique of the Study of Kinship*. Ann Arbor: University of Michigan Press.

Schwartzman, H. 1984. "Stories at Work." In *Text, Play, and Story*. Edited by E. Bruner. Washington, D.C.: American Ethnological Society.

Sorosky, A., A. Baran, and R. Pannor. 1979. *The Adoption Triangle*. New York: Anchor Books.

Vincent, C. 1961. *Unmarried Mothers*. New York: Free Press.

Waterville [Maine] *Sentinel* 3/9/83:20.

Witmer, H., et al. 1963. *Independent Adoptions*. New York: Russell Sage Foundation.

JEFFREY E. EVANS

5 Language and the Body: Communication and Identity Formation in Choreography

I n life as in art, there are "authors" and there are "audiences" the authors are attempting to reach. How to accomplish that communication is a problem each of us must solve anew. Formulas are of little help, although "open," "direct," or "clear" communication is often assumed to be universally helpful, therapeutic, or at least to the point. But as we know from rhetoric and body language, the clearest words are often too simple to convey what an author intends or what an audience is able maximally to receive. For the artist, artistry is rarely the shortest distance between two points. In art as in life, showing is often preferable to telling.

For authors, solving the problem of communication is more complex than just writing with grammatical or syntactical correctness, or even than putting on a good show, for the solution has psychological as well as pragmatic or aesthetic aims. It can be conceived as a mediation between competing forms of self-representation: maintaining privacy or going public; appearing mysterious and interesting or obvious and unsophisticated; fulfilling expectations or being full of surprises. In fact, opacity may convey more of what an author intends than clarity. How the author represents himself or herself depends on character, culture, and the meaning to the author of communicating in general and of the message in question. And those meanings are figured, in part, by who the audience is to the author.

The work of the artist illustrates these complexities of communication. Working within a particular medium, with its history and its techniques, the artist responds to trends of the day—styles taught by teachers or favored by colleagues, critics, or the public. But these are not simply lobbyists for their favorite styles; they are also persons whose significance is conditioned by the artist's life history. That is, the artist mediates between emotional as well as artistic demands, and the act of communication becomes not only a way of relating to others but also a choice of

This work was supported in part by a grant from the Horace H. Racham School of Graduate Studies at the University of Michigan.

aesthetic. A complex of subjective and aesthetic factors (the artist's needs and ideals) are harmonized in the artist's creative style, and the evolution of that harmony is the story of the artist's personal and professional development.

This chapter illustrates, through interviews with two modern dance choreographers, the interplay between personal development and ideas of successful communication. It demonstrates the influence of character and culture on means of self-expression and of self-representation.

I first present an artist for whom dance that is representational or narrative in structure has come to be a personally formative aesthetic worth pursuing. I then present, in greater detail, an artist whose interest is in producing a physical impact on the audience and for whom words (including our interviews) are dangerous, threatening the creative process. For her own (life-historical) reasons, each artist entertains ambivalence toward narrative clarity; the culture of modern dance supports that ambivalence by providing aesthetics and methods that stress ambiguity, indirection, and opacity.

Historical Overview

The history of Western dance can be viewed as evolving methods for reaching an audience.[1] Key dimensions of that evolution include the status of narrative and the representational as structures for dance; the status of physicality; the degree to which the body was constrained to the demands of a fixed movement vocabulary (or to the demands of propriety); and the degree to which artists felt encouraged to explore and create new forms.

Before this century, the only secular dance form to receive official sanction was European ballet, with its narratives and restrained and codified expression of physicality. Other forms of dance were considered entertainment and therefore corrupt. Early choreographic artists, such as Isadora Duncan, shared a desire to elevate such nonballetic dance from frivolous "show dancing" to a serious medium of expression. Duncan and her contemporaries chose music of "serious" composers and attempted to convey images and feelings to the audience by using their bodies to explore themes of nature, myth, and foreign cultures. Their focus was not on story telling, yet their intent was still representational.

Much as those forerunners of modern dance had rejected the frivolity of show dancing, the next historic generation felt that their predecessors had not been serious enough (McDonagh, 1970). The forerunners demonstrated that dance had more imaginative possibilities, but their solutions pandered to the popular taste for lyricism and the exotic. In time dance became independent of audience expectations. For the first time the term *modern dance* was used; it referred to a self-conscious movement of artists who wanted dance to be relevant to the social realities of post–World War I America and the human concerns and emotions of daily life.

The historic generation's concerns were largely thematic. They had stories to tell, like those of classical ballet, and they wanted to communicate their ideas clearly through fixed, but nonballetic movement vocabularies that audiences could understand. For Martha Graham that vocabulary was frankly percussive and designed to communicate emotion with force. Many of her dances were narratives, but her movements, though codified and largely predictable, were far from restrained.

In the post-Depression era, students of the historic generation stepped outside the bounds of single styles and frequently attended classes in several techniques, including ballet, which they often studied secretly. They also were influenced by jazz, dada, and surrealism, which brought elements of nonlinearity, absurdity, and deceptiveness of appearance into dance. Choreography became an occasion for the exploration of still wider possibilities, and as younger artists abandoned allegiance to established forms, narrative and representational forms were the most frequent casualties. Choreography became frequently obscure to all but the most avant-garde audiences.

In the posthistoric era, from the 1950s to the 1970s, more rules were broken. The number of choreographers swelled during this era, and none was more representative than Merce Cunningham. The signature of the era was the search for new forms, and a dancer's training seemed less important than the spirit to experiment with whatever tools were available. Inspired by dada and Zen Buddhism, the collaboration between Cunningham and musician John Cage led to such fundamental innovations as the abandonment of logical structures based on narrative, music, and character development, and the elevation of simultaneity, chance, and bodies simply moving through space. The attempt was to give audiences a sense of what those artists saw as undefined but all around us: the complexity and simultaneity of events in daily life ordered only by the mind's shifting focus of attention, and leading to a dance with as many meanings as audience members. As Merce Cunningham said in a 1977 interview: "Why not have this in dancing? Why not have different things at the same time, with music, dance, and the visual as significant and separate things?" (Kisselgoff, 1977). With this kind of "thick," nonlinear presentation, the choreographer was able to give up responsibility for the direction of the audience's attention and make the physical and the spatial his main concern.

Other than in New York City and a few other centers of dance, it was difficult in the 1970s, however, to cultivate audiences that would be interested in rather than confused by this kind of complexity. Gail, our first choreographer, found it difficult in college to reconcile her early training in narrative and representation forms with her teachers' and colleagues' interest in the more contemporary Cunningham. The importance of communicating with avant-garde teachers and colleagues versus an audience with more traditional tastes temporarily created conflicts, which eventually were reconciled as she achieved success in her professional life. Doing well professionally gave her the courage to create for her audience easily read dances that were designed to enlighten with their message.

Jan, our second interviewee, is not interested in a narrative reading of her work because she feels words cannot be trusted. Rather, she is interested in creating a style of movement that is so new and powerful that its sheer physical impact will cause the audience to resonate with her. For Jan, the audience must be hit hard with a message that cannot be put into words and therefore cannot be misinterpreted. In her life Jan has learned the frustrating ambiguity of language. Gail believes that the audience may misunderstand if her work is *not* translatable into words. From her life in school she remembers feeling confused before she was able to perceive "themes in novels" and now feels "responsible" to help her audience understand what her dances mean. Both artists are ambivalent toward narrative. Jan cannot trust words to carry her true meaning, despite their pragmatic social value in daily life. For Gail, narrative clarity was appreciated by audiences but not by her peers.

Gail

Gail is a university dance instructor in her late twenties. True to her early training in the style of Martha Graham, she feels the need to communicate an unambiguous message that can be put into words and thought about by the audience— "something to intellectualize about . . . rather than to sit back and see carving of space." In response to the influence of Merce Cunningham through her college dance instructors, however, she has not always formed her messages through a linear process. Rather, she has deciphered her messages from almost random sequencing of short movement phrases. She develops a number of ideas and then, with a reaction of surprise, senses their relationship to one another in a "subconscious organization." This moment of discovery, when Gail learns something about herself, is the personal satisfaction she waits for.

Though choreographing leads Gail to better self-understanding, her final product is dominated by the message, not by the process. In college she was in conflict about communicating a message through her work because this went against the preferred dance style of her peers and teachers. When choreographing in undergraduate school, she felt that Cunningham's style, though interesting as a medium, did not help her meet her responsibility to project an idea. She did not want to use that approach but neither did she want to look old fashioned by resorting to balletic means of expression. "That's when I sort of bogged down choreographically." Being "bogged down" expressed a conflict over serving two masters—her posthistoric teachers and her roots in the more narrative Graham style. As we shall see, these roots were influenced by her rather fastidious mother and were shaped, for example, by Gail trying to express meaning as precisely as possible in her themes in English class. In graduate school Gail's conflict lessened, and recently she has been trying to reach audiences by introducing "strongly recognizable elements," including humor, in her pieces. She feels able to do this because of increased autonomy since she has been out of school and working. She now feels free to include in her work what she formerly feared her teachers and peers would regard as "sophomoric."

Because a previous composition had been "fairly misunderstood," she tried to be "extremely literal" in a more recent dance.

> I didn't want it to have one specific meaning but to present a lot of images that would be just bound to touch at least one point in each person. . . . What is most important about that was that I was successful in what I wanted to do. I wanted to have people laugh at a certain time, and sure enough they did laugh exactly as I planned . . . which is probably very ingrained with the whole idea that I can live by myself, and I can have this good job and do a decent job of teaching and everything else.

The thrust of Gail's artistic development at this point is to exercise the "power to make it a little more specific." In the greater specificity and clarity of her self-expression, Gail communicates more effectively with audiences and sends a message to her colleagues and former teachers about her determination to be herself. She has proven that she can get a good job and take care of herself and feels less need to conform to others' standards.

Gail's style of communication is related to the formation of her identity as well as to her artistic development. This point is emphasized in Gail's comments about our interviews and the increased understanding and appreciation of herself resulting from them. "I feel really good about it [the interviews]; it's made me think a whole lot. I think it's been really good for me. . . . I am appreciating being on my own and I like it."

At this point she has a surprising association. Some months ago she awoke with a start to hear a burglar in her house. Ever since, she has been edgy at night—until this week. She offered the speculation that having come to feel more secure about herself, partly owing to these interviews, she no longer feels so strenuously that she has to strive and prove herself: "I've done OK . . . and if I'm snuffed out right now it's not going to matter because I am a little more happy . . . about what's happened to me."

Clarifying her artistic integrity has evidently helped Gail feel more secure about her bodily integrity. Despite her current interest in being more literal in her work, she reveals ambivalence toward narrative forms because producing them has been a struggle for a long time. Indeed, she describes choreographing as an "indulgence" after years of emphasis on correctness and precision.

> You get better grades on your themes if you write as precisely as you can, solve problems as correctly as you can. . . . I guess that's what I mean by precision, all that wanting to be right, accepted, and understood. . . . I've struggled for

this kind of precision all my life, and I just love to indulge myself in the safety of this kind of medium where if something goes wrong you can say, "But you just didn't see it right."

Gail has continued to feel as if she is in school, where being wrong threatens her "safety"; attempting to convey a literal message holds the danger of not saying it right. Dance, however, allowed an escape from that kind of pressure. Even before going to school, Gail recalls, she was subject to her mother's concern with order and correctness. When her mother expressed an opinion about what Gail should do, Gail accepted it as right, even when it contradicted her own wishes. She could not oppose mother for long: "I have more fear . . . fear isn't the word . . . I have more uneasiness toward my mother than toward my father."

As the oldest of three daughters, she patterned herself closely after her mother. Gail turned out to be the neatest, most punctual, and obedient—"not a trouble-maker by any means." But her entry into grade school involved submission to new rules. "I felt it was disorganized in a way . . . things didn't connect . . . trying to collect facts . . . was just memorization."

Gail's reaction to this confusion seems a precursor to her approach to dance and choreography. "From the time I was six to eleven or so, I'd go outside and just run, and I'd run around the backyard or through the fields in back of our house for maybe an hour or two at a time, just telling myself stories or looking at things, thinking about birds and trees and stuff like that. . . . I got away from everything in that way."

This retreat from disorder or from rules that didn't make sense was not, however, a retreat from the influence of other people. Gail's father modeled a playful and yet organized approach, which may have permitted her to "get away" when the pressure became too great.

> I can remember playing with my father a lot. Having him teach me things . . . he was interested in nature studies . . . things about white oaks and red oaks and how to tell the difference, stuff like that. I think basically that I connected having fun and doing things that I liked to do, playing outside or walking alone outside in the woods, with my father. I connect sort of the woman's passive, hard-working role with my mother.

School also became more comfortable for Gail as the emphasis shifted from memorization to the discovery and appreciation of themes. "I was very amazed and pleased to find in about tenth or eleventh grade that things really were related to each other. That you could find a theme in a novel in the same way that you could find a theme in a symphony. I was really happy to know that if you knew several large things you could kind of extrapolate and figure out from other things what was happening."

Gail's "extrapolations" continue today as she "reads" her own work to find out things about herself. However, those self-communications have been so private as to be opaque to audiences. Thus, Cunningham's and Graham's techniques were each only partly useful to Gail. Cunningham allowed her to escape the emphasis on precision associated with her mother and with writing themes for English class. But it confused audiences much as she had been confused when things seemed disorganized in grade school. Graham continued the burden of precision but elicited a satisfying audience response and allowed Gail to discharge her "responsibility" of delivering a message. Her compromise has been to introduce clearly identifiable elements into her dances in addition to her more personal explorations and extrapolations. The new ease of adding those elements has only come, however, with increased autonomy and success in her career. Previously, Gail had been overtly following the rules—at home, in school, and even in college. For most of her life, Gail's communicating with others was dominated by a concern for *security*. Now, as she feels more autonomous, she has found a compromise, which reduces her conflict over serving two masters.

Jan

Jan also wants to communicate—but in a quite different way. Gail wants words to have precision, risking error but maintaining order. As Jan sees it, words interrupt a more important communion—with instinct and the body.

For Jan, an independent choreographer in her thirties, choreographing a dance involves "making the audience feel" a certain way not because of what they think about or read into the dance as narrative but because of how the dance looks and feels in their bodies. She comments about one dance that worked in that way: "People just love this dance. They just get out of there and they feel high, strong, resolved, and independent. They don't look at it and say, 'The man did this, the woman did that and so I feel independent.' . . . They didn't get it from some story line of the dance, that's *how the dance makes them feel*. They have realized an experience; that's the object of my work."

What Jan communicates to the audience is direct and physical. The experiences she gives audiences are the result of her "meeting the challenge" to create new movement and ultimately a new dance style.

> When I make a dance I try to do it differently every time. Since I feel the only thing that interests me very much is challenge, I try to find a new problem for myself which interests me, and I am interested in doing better and doing better. . . . [For example] mostly in dance people do legs and they accent it with their top. Whereas I am doing the opposite, I am making portebra [arm motion] and accenting it with the legs, like you're flipped . . . which produces an entirely different sort of look from anything else, because some elastic deformation takes place, and it gets sort of distorted and simply looks like

something different that you have never seen before. . . . I want to make a new
technique and a new style.

In addition to solving a new problem in communication with the audience each
time she makes a dance, the problem in communication arises also in regard to
herself: she must come up with radically new ideas that are difficult to conceive
and difficult to hold on to but are rewarding in their realization.

When it's coming out in little threads is when I enjoy it the most. . . . They are
very, very fragile, they sort of seep up from somewhere. It's the little individual
mechanisms putting together all your information. . . . I get satisfaction out of
mentally solving a problem well, but it's not the same as when your whole body
is like an organism, and the whole body solves the problem, and the thoughts
sort of come out from underneath and it has birth. And it's just like giving birth
to something, it has a whole life of its own. And that's what making a dance is.

Jan instinctively feels, rather than thinks out, the solutions to her movement
problems. The feeling is like threads that come together in a birth. In order for this
delicate process to work, Jan must have silence and solitude. "When I make a
dance I can't bear to see anyone for sometimes two months. I won't see anyone,
not even my friends. I may not answer the phone for four or five days just because
my mind is putting things together."
She describes a time in the studio when one of her dancers distracted her by
talking.

I was in class the other day, and I had been dealing with this problem of how I
was going to put this dance together. And I was watching this woman do this
material, and just as this thread was coming out of my mind one of the other
dancers started to talk to me and it was gone, and I haven't been able to get it
back. Because they come out at a certain time. If the opening isn't there for
the thought to come out, you have a hole, which you have to solve intellectually. Your mind will do it for you in a sort of physical and instinctive way, and
if it doesn't get out, then you have to do it in a sort of very overt mental way.
Or *I* do.

Thus, others' talk carries the danger of interrupting Jan's communion with her
instincts and her body. The "hole" is a broken connection. Furthermore, Jan rarely
talks *about* her work herself, because even outside of the studio, talk has the
potential of disrupting her creativity. Our interviews made her feel increasingly
"antagonistic" toward me, although, because she had agreed to participate in the
project, she did not reveal her feelings until later. "I guess I don't like to talk about
it a lot because it makes a hole between me and my creating and then it takes me
awhile to get over that space so I can start creating again. And since I am in the

middle of making a dance I am not so anxious to make a hole. . . . I guess that's why I feel very antagonistic today."

At another time, she spoke ruefully about her self-disclosures:

Boy I am feeling violent tonight. I felt that I had led you in a real deep space. And I didn't know you very well, and I was surprised at that. And maybe I felt that something went away from me that was connected to my work, and it made me feel very antagonistic. I am still trying to be as honest with you as I was last time, but I don't feel as open, so the honesty doesn't go down as far . . . that space is mine, and I don't like to share it, I never share it with anyone. And I shared some of it with you and I'm feeling some antagonism with you. It's mine and it's hard to get to that space, it's one of the few things that are mine.

Communication with herself and with others is fraught with hazards, leading Jan to ambivalence about narrative. To avoid this danger to her creativity she communicates by using not words but physical action; it is "one thing, it is real, and it cannot be altered." That is, her communication and her success as a choreographer rest on her power with the nonverbal message, which simultaneously separates her from others and connects her with them.

But Jan's stake in communicating physically and nonverbally is not only artistic but biographical. It applies equally to her success in forming an identity.

Jan's mother has been influential in the interplay between her work and her identity. A physical scientist with whom Jan closely identified, her mother was both a model and a competitor, and she was the source of Jan's concern with challenges.

[When I was a child, mother] would sit down at the dinner table and say bizarre things like, "We aren't liars, we aren't weak, we are not cowards," and she'd have this list of liberal, good qualities that one wanted to be. And one of them was "we are not cowards," and she gave a long explanation of what that meant, and I remember saying, "well, *I'm* afraid," and she said, "well, it's not a problem of being afraid; I'm afraid all the time. It's simply a problem of you overcome it. The fear is not the cowardice; the not overcoming it is the cowardice." Somehow that is associated with challenges. I mean, she does not pick the secure way in her work. She picks her work because each job challenges her. She never stays with one company for twenty-five years to get a pension; in fact she moves all the time. As soon as she has completed one project, if they cannot come up with a challenging project she finds another one. And I feel exactly the same way. I mean I feel like her when those things come up. I identify with her, I not only identify with her I feel like I am her for that moment.

Jan, when she feels that she has not met the challenge, has a catastrophic reaction: "It feels like I'm drowning. It feels like I didn't put forth enough effort or care. It feels like I took the easy way out. That doesn't always mean I did that when I made the piece, that means that's what it feels like. (I can only be this candid with you because you can't print any of this unless I give my permission, you understand . . . I would never discuss this with the press or anything)."[2] Apparently Jan felt that she had communicated too much, that being careless and taking the easy way out invited a dissolution of the self. She followed this thought with an association:

> You know, I read this very bizarre thing in the *New Yorker* and I am only recounting it because it sort of struck a note. It was a poem and it was by a Jewish poet and he got to the end of his poem and he said that he would get great enough that they wouldn't kill him. . . . I was amused because it illuminated something in me, because it had struck a note that I had never dealt with. Sort of fear of purge or something, you know, dying, someone killing you for some weird abstract reason that you have nothing to do with. I can't help looking at a news serial and identifying, you know, I look at one and I say, Is that me? Could that be me someday?

Jan's identifications with her mother has made success in her work feel like a matter of life and death. With so much at stake, it is not surprising that she takes extreme measures to protect herself from distraction or intrusion. But how did the influence of others become so noxious to her work? Jan's protective maneuvers seem to be both a personal limitation and a condition of her creativity.

While Jan is susceptible to the distraction of people talking while she works, elements of her biography show that people can represent not simply distraction but *intrusion*. Nonetheless, she also seeks to communicate and to reach the audience. Jan has always been distrustful of words. "I am getting better . . . but it's nothing like physicality. I mean when you have a physical experience it's *one* thing, it's *real,* and it cannot be altered. And that is what interests me about making work—that I can produce that in an audience."

Aside from this mode of communication, Jan is seclusive and has very few friends. As she speaks of her mistrust of words, she recalls her mother's casual promises to her as a little girl, promises that usually went unfulfilled.

> [Her father] . . . was completely constant. If he said I am going to bring you home two erasers, a pencil, and a pad of paper from work on Friday, it would come home. And if my mother said she was going to do it, you probably would not get it. He was trustworthy as far as doing those kinds of obligations. She very rarely did what she said she was going to do, insofar as bringing you things or taking you somewhere. With him if he said you wait until Friday you'll get two of them, I'd wait. With her if she said if you wait until Friday you'll get two of them, I'd say, "no, I just really want one, and I'll take it right now."

If her mother's words were an uncertain guide to her intentions, her body language could be all the more pithy.

[Mother] never intersected my creative work . . . she's never told me while I was creating I should do this I should do that, she likes this or she likes that, she has never said a *word;* she always sort of goes . . . makes faces and walks out. If I ask her she'll tell me what she thinks of it, if I don't ask her she won't. She really tries to stay out of it, out of my aspect of it, she doesn't want to be in it. I think that's quite admirable.

Asked what she makes of this pattern, Jan speculates: "I think it's because she wants me to be my own person. She is very concerned that her children won't grow up whole because she is what she is and not a normal mommy who cleans house."

Jan's mother was a powerful mime. What she didn't say in words she conveyed in body language, leaving her daughter uncertain about which message to trust. Jan describes another instance in which her mother's actions belied her words. "Occasionally I felt like she competed with me for my father's affections when I was younger. It was never a big heavy deal. If one ever brought it up and said you're competing with me for my father's affection, she would say, 'Oh, no no no,' and walk off and leave me alone with him."

In the strain between her mother's words and actions, we see the foundation of Jan's central life concern—the relation between what is said and what is done. Yet her mother's messages are not always at odds. Recently Jan pleased her mother with a dance, and her mother's body and words were in unison, which produced a powerful feeling of pleasure for Jan.

In my last dance something very interesting happened to me, she was very pleased. You always want to please your mother, you always want to be on the good side, you always want to get the pat on the head. I feel I had totally done it. She was beaming ear to ear, strutting up and down the stage telling me what a fantastic dance I had made, definitely the best dance I had ever made. I had never satisfied her so completely. It was *orgasmic*. It was amazing to actually be in the position of feeling that you had achieved that. I really felt that it was perhaps the major reason why I did things, although I never thought of it in that context. But also, in many ways the main person that I compete with is my mother. . . . I can only say that having made this dance that really pleased her was a real high. It was like a total satisfaction; I felt I had really achieved something without any qualifications on it. It was a trip. It's a real physical thing; it was like the best audience in the world. And I don't necessarily agree with all her artistic presumptions. I mean I still considered it to be my best dance, but the fact that I had totally . . . she couldn't pick it apart because she couldn't see any flaws in it. It was perfect for her.

Jan's solution to her problem with other people is to create a physical experience in her audience that cannot be enhanced with words. Jan's dances let her feel "connected" to the world, and they solve her problem of isolation and mistrust. "I don't worry about it; I just make dances. Every time I feel a big hole I make a dance, I fill the hole up with the dance, and I feel fine. It's that thing, that hedonistic thing, I feel connected to everyone, and sharing the experience with other people . . . until I need another challenge and another dance. I told you I was addicted to creating."

Jan's "hole" is the gap between words and the body. Whereas Gail spans the gap through "strongly identifiable" narrative elements in her dances, elements that can be put into words and that the audience can take home with them, Jan appeals directly to the body through new movement that she believes makes the audience feel, for an instant, what she herself is feeling. Gail felt able to communicate in narrative only after she had achieved more autonomy in her professional life. Jan's sense of separateness is more ambiguous: when she is most apart she is creative but unhappy and not communicating. In her life, communicating means a type of fusion, producing an instant of physical connectedness that must eventually be renewed through another challenge and another dance.

Jan's and Gail's stories show the struggle of two artists to mediate and harmonize the forces in their lives—artistic, cultural, biographical. The interplay among those forces is evident in their *expressive* and *reflexive* processes.

The side of art making associated with self-expression is the finished work itself, which shows, directly or indirectly, something of the life that has created it. Equally expressive is the *use* to which that work is put in the shaping of the artist's identity, however, and of her relationships with others. Both Jan and Gail want to communicate, but both have reasons for not wanting to be clear. Jan is an innovator of penetrating new forms that isolate her from others but allow her to affect others deeply. Without words, she makes the audience feel. Gail produces subtle and various images, which reveal her to herself but speak to audiences only when she italicizes the dance with elements that are representational or narrative. Gail makes up to the audience for her indulgence in a less precise medium by including a clear message in her work that the audience can take home and think about.

In these interviews the artists reflect on their creative styles and on the relation between their lives and their work. Our conversations reassured Gail that she had done well enough in her career. Therefore, she could dare to insert a narrative message into her more avant-garde impressionism. For Gail, language finally clears things up, both for herself and for the audience, although her ambivalence is understandable given her attempts to satisfy contrasting tastes in her colleagues and her audience. But talk is the enemy of Jan's art because of its potential to destroy her communion with herself and thus her ability to connect with the audience. Her ambivalence is born of a need to communicate in the usual way, despite her experience of the intrusiveness and ambiguity of language. The ambivalence of these artists toward narrative clarity is well accommodated by the mores and methods of the contemporary culture of dance.

Both Jan and Gail try to communicate with the audience, but for complex reasons talk plays opposite roles in each life. Furthermore, their histories suggest that self-knowledge, traditionally understood as expressing oneself through words, need not proceed parallel with development. The "talking cure" notwithstanding, development proceeds with and without verbal self-understanding as persons clear a path to mediate the forces moving their lives.

NOTES

1. Material for this section was gathered principally from McDonagh 1970 and 1977.
2. Gail and Jan, whose identities have been disguised, kindly gave their permission for the publication of their interview transcripts.

REFERENCES

Kisselgoff, Anna. 1977. "A Dance Revolution on Broadway." *New York Times,* January 16.
McDonagh, Don. 1970. *The Rise and Fall and Rise of Modern Dance.* New York: New American Library.
———. 1977. *Don McDonagh's Complete Guide to Modern Dance.* New York: Doubleday.

RUTH BEHAR

6 A Life Story to Take
across the Border:
Notes on an Exchange

For the past five years I have been working on the life story of Esperanza Hernández, a Mexican woman who lives in a rural town a half-hour away from the city of San Luis Potosí. Esperanza is self-employed as a farmer, peddler, and occasional domestic servant. Our work together has developed in stages. The first stage involved the formation of our relationship as co-mothers (*comadres*), which did not occur immediately on my arrival in the town in 1982 but rather took until 1985 to develop, after which we became good friends. In the second stage of our work, after Esperanza initiated our relationship as *comadres*, we began to meet together for late-night kitchen conversations to produce an account of her life story. In the most recent stage, we have been exploring the possibilities and contradictions of the work itself and of our own relationship.

This chapter is about the most recent stage of mutual questioning, which has thrown into relief the cleavages of privilege and class that separate us. Earlier feminist thinking sought to assert claims of sisterhood among distant women. Marjorie Shostak (1981) described Nisa, the !Kung woman whose life history becomes an allegory of female sexual liberation, as a "distant sister." But as the dubiousness of such sisterhood began to be exposed, many feminist researchers began to worry, as did Judith Stacey (1988), that there could be no fully feminist ethnography amid the many unresolvable separations between the women doing the research and the women being researched. More recently, feminist ethnographers have been looking for ways to write ethnography in such a way that the differences among women can be spoken about without signaling the impossibility of mutual understanding (Visweswaran, 1992). I locate this study within this newly emerging perspective, as an ongoing set of "notes on an exchange" between two very differently situated women who have come together for very different reasons to produce a hybrid text.

Before I knew her, I had learned from various other women that Esperanza had

I would like to thank the Harry Frank Guggenheim Foundation and the MacArthur Foundation for their support. I am grateful to George C. Rosenwald for his thoughtful reading and encouragement.

bewitched her former husband, Julio, after he left her and returned to town with another woman and their children. During their marriage, he had abused and beaten her. Cursing him, according to one story, with the words "So that you will never again see women," she had caused him, possibly by using magical powers, to go suddenly blind. That women have supernatural powers to hurt the men who wrong them is a long-standing cultural theme in Mexican society, so the assertion that Esperanza had bewitched Julio need not have reflected badly on her. But Esperanza, I was told, was a bad-tempered, sharp-tongued, combative woman whom one had to take care not to offend. Both she and her mother were reputed to be witches. It was clear that class divisions in the town also informed this portrait. Esperanza is from the lowest rung in the social ladder, a single mother and a working woman. What is particularly offensive about her, I suspect, is that she does not act like a woman of her class: she is neither demure nor defeated.

Without my fully realizing it, the rumors I had heard about her had affected me. I did not seek her out as I did some other women. Nor did I run into her much in my daily walks through the town. Esperanza deliberately restricts her movements, leaving her house only to work her plot of land and on her thrice-weekly trips to the city to sell vegetables, fruits, and flowers door-to-door. In part this is because of the cultural practice of restricting women to the domestic space of the home, which Esperanza has interpreted strictly, but it is also the result of her sense that she is a marginal person and not fully an occupant of those town streets, in which she refuses to be seen except when absolutely necessary. Our talks together were always conducted in the secrecy of night, and when Esperanza would leave, she always covered her face with her shawl.

My first encounter with Esperanza took place on the Day of the Dead in 1983, in the cemetery, where I had spent the day taking photographs. Holding a bouquet of calla lilies, she looked striking, almost like something out of one of Diego Rivera's Indian nativist canvases. As I drew closer I asked if I might photograph her. She looked at me haughtily and asked me in turn, with a brusqueness I had not encountered before among local women, *why* I wanted to take her picture. I made some weak reply, and she let me photograph her, though I was so nervous that I snapped the last picture in the roll (which didn't come out) and moved on, certain that I would have little to do with her.

I think that many of the contradictions of my work with Esperanza were already evident in that first encounter. I had fastened on her as an alluring image of Mexican womanhood, ready to do my own upper-class, exoticizing portrait of her; but the image had spoken back to me, questioning my project and making it impossible for me to carry it out.

I did not speak to her again until December of the following year, when I saw her in church on the festival day for the Virgin of Guadalupe. I had been away from the town for a few months and, excited to be back, was offering greetings with greater cheer than usual. I found the nerve to greet Esperanza and chat with her briefly, and she clearly took this as a sign of my readiness to initiate a relationship. Later that week she knocked at our door to ask if my husband and I would be godparents for the cake for her daughter's coming-of-age party (*quinceañera*), to which we agreed. Several days later she came and asked us to become the godparents of her Christ child, a doll that is used in the yearly home Christmas festivities. These requests seemed to me at the time to come out of the blue. Only later did I learn that she had been observing us carefully, noting the way—unlike town elites—we spoke to everyone, rich and poor alike. And she had learned that we had become the godparents of a little girl born to a poor single mother in the town; she had been moved to see me caress the child one day as I met her on the street. Her observations had led her to think that we were good people and would not shun her efforts to initiate a relationship.

By agreeing to these requests, my husband and I became *compadres,* spiritual coparents of her daughter and her Christ child. She and I would from then on address each other as comadre and participate in the particular form of close but respectful friendship and mixture of patronage and reciprocity that goes with being compadres. A *compadrazgo* relation in rural Mexico is typically forged between persons of high and low economic standing; as the better-off person in my relation with Esperanza, I would be expected to offer financial or other assistance if she requested it. At the same time, she would be expected to offer me small gifts from time to time—say, of produce from her field—and to act with extreme courtesy whenever we met.

Yet initially I was not quite sure how to interpret Esperanza's actions. When she asked us to serve as godparents to her Christ child I felt suspicious, uncertain of this assertive "informant" who seemed to demand rather than request favors. She told us, for example, that her Christ child had fallen from the altar several times because he was upset at not having had his *acostada* ritual; therefore, could we perform the ritual immediately? Both requests represented significant outlays of money from my husband and me. Obviously we could afford it, but we were still strangers to her. Why had she suddenly taken a liking to us? What other requests would follow? Had she just discovered that we were an easy source of funds? Where was the reciprocity in this relationship? When we performed the ritual for her Christ child we felt suspicious enough that we bought only the minimum—the crocheted outfit for the doll and some treats for the guests—but skimped on the oranges and did not bring a piñata. I remember feeling the sense of disappointment; the gringos, merely students yet richer than anyone there, had been cheap.

Later, of course, I regretted my actions. I had no idea then of the story Esperanza had to tell of her life or of the work we would do together. I had not yet gone beyond the twin images I had of her: the romantic image of the intense Indian woman with the calla lilies versus the "uncooperative informant" and pushy, witchy woman I had been warned to stay away from. Only as I got to know Esperanza did I realize that our becoming comadres had allowed us, as differently situated women, to forge a relationship of mutual caring, reciprocity, and trust. This relationship made it possible for us to transcend our situatedness as *gringa* and *mexicana* and relate to each other as equals of a sort. Esperanza's deference to me could thus be that of a comadre rather than that simply of a woman of a rural working-class background; and it meant that I too could be, had to be, deferential, offering the kind of formal respect—addressing her in the formal "you," shaking hands softly at every encounter—expected from me, in turn, as a comadre. By asking me to become her comadre Esperanza had opened up a terrain for our exchange.

After our participation in the two ritual events we began to see more of Esperanza. In her small, unlit cinder-block room she would tell me about herself and also tell gripping stories about encounters with the devil and other spirits. Even before I thought to tape-record her life story, she had told me, in compressed form, much of what would later find its way into the tapes. When I told Esperanza that I thought her life narrative would make a very good book, she completely agreed and took a certain pride in thinking that she alone of all the women in the town had a life worth turning into a text. Why? The answer, in her mind, was obvious: she had suffered. Suffering gave a woman the right, and the need, to write a text. Within her Catholic worldview and sense of narrative, it is by suffering and surviving, laughing through the tears, that a woman earns the privilege of telling her life. In her mind her living had earned her the right of telling—of inscribing her life.

In July 1985, when she came to our house in town for an evening chat, I asked if we could tape her story. I began by saying, "Comadre, I'd like you to tell me about your life. From your first memory." She was accompanied that night by her son and younger daughter, as she was for almost all our conversations. I had barely finished asking my question when Esperanza broke out in torrents of laughter. Her children laughed with her, amused by the hilarity I had provoked.

As the laughter died down Esperanza said, "Comadre, what a life, what a life I've had. No, my life is a very long history."

The persistent ethnographer, I replied, "No, well, tell me your history."

Esperanza laughed again. "Ay, comadre. Ay, the chewing gum is falling out of my mouth! No, my life has been very sad. Sad. Dark, dark. Like my mother's life. Look, do you want me to tell you from the time I was born?"

Unaware that this was a joke, I responded, "Yes."

There was more laughter. "I'm very scandalous about laughing, talking. My sister says to me, 'Ay, woman, what do you say? Laugh calmly. Laugh seriously. Calm down. You get too excited.' 'That's the way I am. You because you're bitter. Not me.' Despite the fact that I've had some dark times in my life."

The swallows that had built nests in the rafters of the courtyard suddenly flew around noisily. We stopped to listen. In the meantime I passed around sodas and cookies (as I would do at all later talks). After a pause Esperanza turned to me, suddenly serious. "Look, comadre, why would you like me to tell you about my life since childhood?"

I said, hoping to sound convincing, "It seems very interesting."

Esperanza was laughing again.

I added, encouragingly, "And you speak very well," and after a pause, "I like to hear you tell stories."

She still found this all quite funny. But she soon became serious and started. "Well, look. Since I was born, well, God knows. My mother says that I was born at three in the afternoon, behind the grinding stone. When my mother was— Because my mother went with my father to a ranch, there in La Campana."

With these words and what seemed an unpromising beginning we embarked on a series of conversations over several evenings in which Esperanza told the "long history" of her life, episode by episode. As this extract from our first conversation shows, Esperanza found humorous my sincere and determined efforts to get her to tell her story; though she wanted to tell me her story and had, in her perception, a sad story to tell, she refused—and still refuses—to approach her life with any-thing less than a burst of Rabelaisian humor. This laughter is, in a sense, her critique, too, of my academic pretensions: the way in which I find things "interest-ing" and cajole her and pounce on her so that she will talk and tell me more. That I should want to take her life seriously strikes her as comical in terms of the inversions of social position and hierarchy that it also suggests: an educated, obviously middle-class gringa asking an unschooled Mexican woman of the rural working class to tell her life story. Within the strict hierarchy of race and class in Mexico, and from Esperanza's perspective as someone on the lower fringes of the hierarchy, our interaction continues to amuse and amaze her, seeming somewhat unreal. So embedded is her sense of racial and class domination that she has asked me if I am not embarrassed to be seen with her. Our relationship as comadres cannot totally erase the fundamental ironies and contradictions of our work to-gether.

As she told me her story, pushing it into my hands and stuffing it into my ears so I could take it back across the border, I began to realize that she wanted me to vindicate her life in a way that no one else, except a priest with thirty hours to spare, could: by listening to her version of her story and passing it on so that eventually it might be heard in the court of divine justice. She presented herself as a woman who was wronged and whom God, judging well and knowing her faith, has helped to find some degree of justice and triumph. Indeed, Esperanza de-scribes her story, at the end of our conversations in 1985, as a confession that she has made to me, her comadre, rather than to the priest, and tells me that my task is to get rid of the sins that she has burdened me with by passing on her story to someone else, in the same endless discursivity with which priests confess people, bishops confess priests, archbishops confess bishops, and all the way on up to God. As she put it, "I have made a confession. . . . Now I should confess with the priest. . . . Now you carry my sins . . . because it is as if I have been confessing with my comadre, instead of with the priest. You will carry my sins now, because you carry them in your head. Priests confess people, right? . . . Then they confess to the bishops . . . And the bishops, with whom? With the archbishops. And the archbishops, with whom? With God! Now you, comadre, who are you going to get rid of them with? You tell them somewhere ahead so someone else can carry the burden."

The dialogic construction of her life story has become for her a means of mending the splits in her public and private selves. In Mexquitic, she knows she will always be an outcast, an angry woman abandoned by her husband, whose rage exploded in witchcraft; and she will always be a woman of her class, a poor working woman, marketing on the fringes of the capitalist economy, and a fallen woman who has alone raised three children out of wedlock. But who in Mexquitic knows or cares to know the spiritual chronicle of her soul's journey? To whom can she confess but to a stranger? In small village parishes it has long been customary for foreign priests to hear confessions at Easter; they have less at stake than the parish priest and, having confessed you, they leave. Esperanza has placed me in the position of the visiting priest. Telling me her life story becomes a means of seeking absolution. Giving me her story to take back across the border to the mysterious and powerful "other side" (*el otro lado,* as the United States are referred to by working-class Mexicans) offers the possibility not only of sending her "sins" forward but also of a rebirth in this life: a rebirth in the text about her life that strangers in a strange country will read.

Her narrative, as she herself defines it, is ultimately an examination of the Christian soul through its inscription in one of the oldest forms of autobiography: the confession. While she has not, in fact, confessed to a priest nor taken communion since her marriage in 1949, she has told me her "sins" so that I might free her of this "burden" in that other world across the border, a spatial divide that is as vivid for rural Mexicans as that separating this life and the next.

On the basis of the first conversations from 1985 and some briefer conversations from 1987, I wrote an essay detailing the key themes in Esperanza's life story as she presented it (Behar, 1990). Thus I became, as she foresaw, a storyteller myself, selecting the parts of her story I would highlight, finding the places where I needed to interrupt the text to interpret a point for my academic readers, and honing the different, but sometimes meshing, tones of her voice and mine. When I returned to Mexquitic in the summer of 1988 I found myself in the interesting situation of retelling Esperanza's story to her as I tried to explain how I was organizing the book that by then I had planned to write based on our conversations. I wanted very much to hear her comments on what I was doing and get some sense of whether she approved of the project. This more recent stage of our work together—the talking about the work we have done and the uses to which it will be put—is what I want to focus on here. Thus I will discuss Esperanza's life story only indirectly, turning my attention instead to what could be called the terms of the exchange by which I have obtained the story in the first place.

Curled around the kitchen table, where we had just been talking about a sexual joke she had told me that I had pleaded with her to repeat into the tape, she paused and said, quizzically, "My comadre [speaking of me] says this is very interesting. Does this seem very interesting to you?"

"Yes," I answered.

"And you're going to write this down and turn it into a history?"

"Well, not all of it, some parts. Would you like to see how I'm writing it?"

"Let's see."

I turned to my husband, David, and asked in English, "Can you bring what I have in the— It's in the study room. On my desk. The outline and the—"

As we waited for David to return, Esperanza said cryptically, "I just want to see how you're writing it, but don't tell me."

"No, I'll show it to you," I replied. "Because you said that in the book you want me to call you Esperanza, right? Isn't that true? Didn't you say not to use your real name, but use Esperanza, which is your second name?"

"My second name. I am Benigno and Esperanza."

"Esperanza," I repeated softly.

Laughing, she said, "The only *esperanza* [hope]. Ay, ay, ay! No, comadre, how are you going to do it? How are you going to do that history?"

"I'll show you. So far I have not used your other name, but when I write it to publish it, I can use that name instead, if you like."

"Comadre, and that? You are going to put it together over there, or you're putting it together here? And are you going to go around with all the women here in Mexquitic and talk?"

"No, no, no, let me show you."

"Well, no, that's why I said, no. Here they'll make fun of me."

"They wouldn't make fun. Why?"

"No, yes they would, if you were to go around talking to them. Well, that lady who is my comadre, that this and that and the other. Ay!"

"Well, no, whatever you say, I won't talk to them. If you don't want me to say anything to them, I won't. I won't say anything.

"No, nothing."

"Only there, where it will be published in English."

"Well that's up to all of you there. It's up to all of you, after all."

"For the people on the other side."

Laughing, she replied, "The other side. Here we say 'the other side of what?' The other side of the river! Well, yes, the other side of the river, don't you see that there's a river there?"

"And what do you think, does it seem all right to you that people on the other side read your history? Does that seem all right to you?"

"Well, I don't know. Over there I don't know them and they don't know me. Well, if you tell them: this, that, and the other. And will they like that? They won't, will they?"

"No, why not?"

"I say that they won't. That life isn't right— It's a life that's very, very— What do I want to say? Well, sad, very, yes—or very ridiculous!"

"No, comadre."

"I don't know what. Eh? There's a saying, eyes that don't see, heart that doesn't feel. What do you think?" And after a pause, "And this book, you're going to give it to people there to read, or what?"

"Well, first, when it's written, after it's published, we'll see if people are interested in reading it. This is what we don't know, if anyone will be interested or not. It's chancy. But I think so."

"Ay, comadre, why are you using up your life on this?" She laughed. "Wracking your brain and struggling doing this. Well, if you think that this might be worth it for you over there, well then it's up to you. Right? But I say that here, no. No, here, no."

"Not here. And not in Mexico City, either, right? There, far away, in the city?"

"And then what if they bring the books here? You see how that lady showed me that about the young man who ended up in prison. He ended up in prison, and she says that his histories are now sold in San Luis. But that they happened in Mexico City.

"That young man, he entered as a young man and came out when he was sixty years old. He did his history. And he's in photographs, too. There he is in the book—like in a caricature, and very, very ugly. And I said to the lady, 'Well, but he did it.' And she says, 'Yes, he did it himself. About his life, what he went through.' And she says, 'It's interesting. It's nice. I'd lend it to you, but it's old.' And she showed it to me like that. The binding was already breaking. It's that thick. And I said to her, 'And where is he from?' 'From Mexico City.' That's where it happened to that young man. And he came out when he was sixty, an old man. An old man, because he's already sixty. And I'm entering my sixtieth year. Next year I'll be sixty."

That such a life story could be turned into a book had evidently impressed Esperanza and led her to wonder about the book I would produce about her. I realized that in this conversation we were negotiating both the terms by which I would be able to use her story and the terrain on which it could be made public: who should hear it, who should not, and where and why. She has given me her story on the condition that it remain secret in Mexquitic and in Mexico generally, for fear of the gossip she feels certain would ensue if others—especially other women—saw her story in a book. She means for her story to be told elsewhere, where no one knows her; at home, where people maintain closely guarded boundaries around their private identities and domestic space, she would be ridiculed for indulging in such a "confession" with her gringa comadre. Just as rural Mexican laborers export their bodies to work on American soil, Esperanza has given me her story for export only.

I said, "Then you'd like only for people in the United States to read it—your history? Here in Mexico no one should know of it?"

"No. Because from there they'll send some here. Or those histories that they turn into books, those are the ones they send us here, or do they come from far away? I don't know. Like all those books they sell in San Luis, there are many of them, histories, who knows what."

"Yes."

"That's right. And then you, what will you do? How will you do it in Mexico City? From there I think they'll send them here. No, comadre, no, no!"

"I'm going to write it in English. And this way we'll publish it there. For people on the other side to learn about your life."

"Ay, yes. So is it going to be like that man's, that young man's? Is that what it's going to be?"

"Something like that, but it will be told in your words. Because you've been telling it to me."

"Yes, like that young man. Because the lady said, 'Look, here it says everything.' And I said, 'What does it say?' 'What he did, what he went through in life and everything. He wrote all of that, he did his history.' I say that's what this might be, or will be." Pointing to the stack of papers in my hand, which David had brought in from the next room, she asked, "And what's that you have there?"

Showing her my book outline, I said, "Well, this is an idea of what I'm going to write. The first chapter will be like an introduction. About the way I am reading your history, the way I understand it. I'm going to explain how we met, and the way you used to come to the house to tell your history. In other words, the way I came to have this history."

"Yes, yes."

"And then, the second chapter, I'm going to explain a little bit what you say at the beginning about the way you lived the same life as your mother. That's what you told me at the beginning. That you saw what your mother suffered and then you lived the same life. [She left an abusive husband just as Esperanza did, raising her children alone.] Then the third chapter will be about your life as a worker. In other words, the way you went to work in the cotton harvest, which you told me about."

"That was a lot of suffering."

"And then the way you started to work in San Luis."

"When my father took me to the Lagunera fields. I remember. Oh, what suffering. On the way there, really. He took me there twice. Then he no longer took us there. And then afterward my mother and us left my father because my father was going to kill my mother. My mother tried to get away that night. And that was the history of that. . . . A lady in San Luis said to me, 'It's that your life is like a history.' And I said, 'Yes, that's right. I never finish. I never finish telling it.'"

"And then about the way you worked in San Luis also [as a domestic servant]. And the next chapter I call, 'The Cross of the White Wedding Dress.'"

"Yes, that I got married."

"When you got married. And the next one is about *coraje* [anger], it's about corajes."

Laughing a bit, "Because of my children."

"And your husband. You talked about how a little girl or boy of yours died from a coraje that you suffered." [Her anger suffused her breast milk, turning it into a deadly potion.]

"Almost all of them died, I don't know if because of coraje. Yes, they died. But all were badly taken care of, they would get sick and with my corajes— And this isn't even everything I have to tell. The parts I forgot. A lot. During sixteen years."

"And then about the time your mother became ill. The evil illness. [She was bewitched by Esperanza's mother-in-law after she took in Esperanza and her children.] Then another chapter called '*Marchanta*,' about the way you became a *marchanta* [marketing woman]."

"Ay, about the way I went to sell."

"Then 'Sons and Daughters.' It's about your sons and daughters. And the next one, that's complicated, it's about money cancer, justice. You've sometimes said that 'you pay for everything in this life.' I try to explain that too, that idea."

Esperanza starts laughing. "Don't tell me they don't know that there!" Her children laugh, too. "How are they not going to know that there?"

"They don't know that there," I say.

"Don't tell me they don't know how to swear? They don't even know how to swear or curse?"

"Yes, of course."

"Well, then, I think that this, too, those jokes they also know. A joke meaning that here one knows that you pay for everything in life. Sooner or later you pay for everything. If you believe— Let's suppose that one believes in God, right? Well, one says why do anything more, let's leave those things to God and he'll know how. Sooner or later one pays. For one thing or another, and that's it. That's the saying we have."

"That you pay for everything, or that God is the one who makes everyone—"

"Well, of course. As I told you, that lady, that Santos, told me to do that harm [witchcraft] to Julio [her former husband]. Because she knew how, right? And she'd show me. And I said, 'No, why?' I said, 'The only thing is that sooner or later he'll have to pay, and with God's help those sins will be well paid for, sooner or later. Why should I do harm to him?' Then when she said to me, 'Hum, from now until God decides—' No, why should I try to do it? If I say yes, do the evil for me, why? If I do harm to him, then I too, what salvation can I expect from God? What I do say, softly, sooner or later he has to pay. That's for sure. Eh? Things left to God will be well paid. Eh? Easy. It didn't take long. He's already blind. Eh? That's why I say so. It's said that in this life you pay for everything, and what isn't paid is charged to your account." Esperanza laughs.

"And you pay in the next life?"

"Of course."

The economic discourse here—of accountability, of God as accountant and judge making sure we "pay" for sins—permeates Esperanza's thinking so thoroughly that she can't imagine this isn't an obvious fact. Thus I invoke exchange in this essay as part of the way Esperanza, who markets in the penny capitalism of a woman on the margins, sizes up the world. Given the opportunity to bewitch her husband by Doua Santos, a dealer in black magic, she refuses because she knows that God will take care of him, as indeed her husband's sudden blindness showed in its profound poetic justice—for he had been an incorrigible lecher, constantly eyeing women, eating them with his eyes. But, in her view, everyone must measure up before God. Esperanza went on to note that even *angelitos* (dead children) take some sins with them to the next world because of the corajes (anger) they have felt upon crying. "They, too, have to dip a foot in purgatory."

Our conversation having turned to the afterlife, I asked Esperanza, "Then you're not afraid of death?"

She answered immediately. "No, why? If it's destined, then why? Why should I say, 'Oh that I shouldn't have to die!' If God says, 'Let's go now,' I say, 'Let's go!'" She laughs. "They say that with a long life, long account. Think about it. Whoever lives more, sees more and knows more. Right? That's why they say, short life, short account. Long life, long account." There was a pause as she laughed again. "Well, what do you think, comadre? Just lies I'm telling you, right? You must think, that woman's stories are real lies."

Unable to respond to this comment, I asked, "And what did you think of my outline, the plan I've got?"

"It's just fine."

"It is? What would you like to add to it? Do you want to add anything to those chapters? Something I forgot, some part that—"

"No, it's going well."

Half-embarrassed, I ask a question that feels dumb as I say it. "And what would you like people in the United States to think when they read your story? What would you like them to think?"

"They're not going to believe it."

"They're not going to believe it," I mimic.

And David, almost asleep in his seat as the clock passes midnight, chimes, "I don't think so."

Esperanza breaks the nighttime stillness with a howl of laughter. "I don't think so," she repeats. We all start laughing. "How is it possible? I say that they won't believe it."

The view that her story will seem unbelievable to her unknown and unknowable potential American readers, and the subtle intimation that she has been telling me lies, not the true story of her life in any sense, are interesting insights into the production of life history texts. I think it significant that Esperanza should focus on the unbelievability of the text we have produced together. She doesn't seem to believe totally that absolution is possible, that her clean comadre from clean America will truly be able to launder her story. Like the comic book novels about miracles that are so popular in working-class Mexico, and to which Esperanza is especially attached, there is almost a comic book miraculousness about the inducement that I, as redemptive ethnographer-priest, have offered in promising to produce a book about the unfolding story of her life.

Do I believe her story? Will other gringos believe it, too? With my power and privilege as an academic woman who can write and publish a book, I can set things right—but will I? Is this all too good to be true? To me, the ethnographer and stranger, Esperanza could offer a different story about herself than she could townspeople in Mexquitic. Yet this is a story that she firmly does not want townspeople to know. It is for export, intended for use far from its native land, where it will be translated and read in English, that impossible foreign tongue. Her narrative is unreal because it presents a private suffering and struggling self that clashes with the public self of the combative woman who doesn't know her place. Certainly no one would believe her version of her life story in Mexquitic. But will people believe her in the United States?

It is not just the text that is unreal in the sense of it being a construction, an imaginative reconstruction, a story imagining how a closely guarded inner life has been lived. My ability and privilege to duck in and out of my various identities, moving from one location to another as needed for my research, have lent an unreal quality to the fieldwork itself. Ethnographers have always voyaged out to find their subjects; what makes the "postmodern condition" different is the way one can voyage in and out of the fieldwork situation *during* the fieldwork. The fieldwork "site" ceases to be a unitary place; it is fragmented by the ethnographer's crosscutting movements. So too are the stories we derive from such fieldwork. To offer a representation of those stories it would seem we need to interrupt them, to keep them from becoming seamless, so as to render visible and audible the conditions of their making as the product of a relationship between differently situated tellers and listeners.

Four days before my conversation with Esperanza, I had gone to Sanborn's, a luxury department store for tourists and local elites, located in a new shopping mall at the edge of the city, in search of newspapers and magazines. I ended up spending 90,000 pesos (about forty-five dollars) on recently published books about Mexican women, history, and religion.

The next day I went marketing with Esperanza. From her garden she brought zucchini, garlic, chayotes, and peaches, and we took the bus into the city. Because she needs more vegetables to sell than just the ones she brings from her garden we stopped at the market to buy lettuce, cucumbers, zucchini, carrots, and chili peppers. She carried a large plastic shopping bag on her head and a heavy pail on her arm. We made our journey through the city, stopping at one door and another, selling small amounts of her produce, sometimes on credit, to her regular clients, middle-class women who inevitably answered the door in their bathrobes. One of the women instructed her to return later and then gave her a bag of day-old tortillas and some *masa* (corn flour dough). Though not lacking for food, Esperanza took it gracefully. After walking from one end of the city to the other for an entire day, I figured that Esperanza had made about 5,000 pesos (just over two dollars); she said that if she had sold everything she would have made 8,000 pesos. The round-trip bus ride cost 1,000 pesos from these earnings. She is working to make two, three, or four dollars a day, I thought, and there I had just spent a minor fortune on some books in a store that would probably cast out Esperanza if she miraculously found her way there and even conceived of entering.

At every house we stopped, Esperanza would introduce me. "Today I come with someone. She's a comadre. She's from the United States. She's not from here. She wanted to come with me to see how I sell. She says it's good exercise for her." Some of the women seemed surprised, others suspicious, others not terribly interested. Esperanza said that people were staring at us as we walked down the street next to each other. "They see me as very *ranchera* [a ranch woman] and you, comadre, a *güera* [a fair-skinned woman] from the United States, following me." Rounding a corner she said that some men delivering bread could not take their eyes off us. "They were simply amazed."

At one house where Esperanza had a comadre whose family was from the Mexquitic area, we stopped to talk for two hours and were served *gorditas* (filled tortillas). Enedina, our host, had a lively wit, and she said that when she saw the latest film sequel to the Indian María series she had thought of us and Esperanza. The film is about a gringo couple who brings Maria to the United States to be their domestic servant; Maria's exploits made for hilarious comedy. Enedina remarked, "Imagine you and your husband taking your comadre back, it was like that." I was struck by the irony of the remark and what it suggested about my work with Esperanza: that her life story could cross the border with me, her American comadre, but that she could not make the crossing except as an undocumented domestic servant. She was making her crossing vicariously by allowing me to take her story back.

Later in the conversation Esperanza remarked that people liked us in Mexquitic. Enedina nodded, unsurprised. "In Mexquitic they don't say anything to you. You know, there are places where they don't want you. But not Mexquitic. No one says to you, Why are you here, what are you doing here?"

"You see," said Esperanza, "they [Mexicans] go to the other side. There they throw them out, treat them badly. They don't let them cross. They beat them or kill them. And all they want is to work."

"For you it's easy to cross, isn't it?" inquired Enedina.

This question was asked so often of us in Mexico that I was never able to forget the fact of that fundamental asymmetry—determining who could cross easily with a few dollars tip, as we did, and who had to put their life on the line simply to find a little back-breaking work. The asymmetry had to do not only with our position as American and theirs as Mexican but also with the disjuncture in our socioeconomic positions. Fieldwork in Mexico was for me about the way class intersected with, and intercepted, cultural understanding.

"All of us inhabit an interdependent late-twentieth-century world marked by borrowing and lending across porous national and cultural boundaries that are saturated with inequality, power, and domination," writes Renato Rosaldo (1989, 217). What happens when we bring such an insight to the production of life-history texts? I have tried to begin to answer that question here by presenting, dialogically, the ways in which Esperanza and I have sought to negotiate the transfers from our different locations. As Daphne Patai points out, the researcher who works on life-history texts plays the role of both capitalist and laborer. In the capitalist image, the entrepreneurial researcher seeks raw material from a "native informant" in order to produce a text. "It is the researcher who owns or has access to the means of production capable of transforming the spoken words into a commodity" (1988, 7). Yet, as Patai points out, the analogy is muddy because the researcher's labor creates the text by "turning spoken words into written ones, editing, translating if necessary, or studying and interpreting the stories" (ibid.). From this double-edged position, she suggests that life histories be collected and produced in such a way that they at least challenge rather than simply re-create "the structures of inequality that make other women serve as the subjects of our books" (ibid.).

As capitalist and laborer, I have both eagerly sought out Esperanza's story and turned it into a source of work for myself. As Esperanza remarks, I am "using up" my own life doing this work, but as she also recognizes this must somehow be worth it to me. And, as I have tried to suggest, this work is, in different and maybe more uncertain but also important ways, worth it to her. At this critical juncture, as Rosaldo and Patai among others urge, we need to start making the power relations that inform ethnographic work more central in our thinking and writing. Certainly, there is no escaping the fact that I will be composing the book about Esperanza's life and that this is a privilege and power—given her gender, color, class, and nationality—quite beyond her reach. But as the selections from our conversations suggest, even in situations of obvious inequality there is much to negotiate. Esperanza has the last word about how her story may be used and who may hear it, and she will be the one to decide what she wants and expects from our exchange. None of this can undo the structures of inequality that situate us differently. But by making the process of exchange through which we obtain stories of others across borders a key part of life-history writing, it may open up to us other ways of thinking about the contradictions that separate us from the subjects of our essays and books. If the contradictions become, from this new perspective, glaringly obvious and absurd, perhaps we will also begin to think of how to mediate them. Life history, a venerable but as yet little theorized genre of ethnographic writing, offers a challenging form for working through the contradictions of cultural exchange at a moment when the fences of privilege are reaching Babelesque proportions, and borders, like that separating Mexico and the United States, are getting harder to cross from the "wrong" side.

In the space, then, of a couple of days in July 1988, I spent, by rural Mexican standards, a fortune on books at a luxury store, then accompanied Esperanza on her selling route through the city, where she sold handfuls of produce for pennies, and had, finally, a talk with her—which I inscribed on tape—negotiating the terms of the book I had yet to write about her life. I had crossed in and out of borders, buying books, talking about books, entering and exiting from different cultural-economic production zones at a speed that made things seem surreal. In the process I had learned from Esperanza that she had a double-sided view of what allowing her story to cross the border meant. On the one hand, she clearly sees the border as a liberating site for the construction and realization of a new, more positive, identity on "the other side," where people might view her sympathetically in light of her suffering and quest for justice and redemption. But, on the other hand, her remarks during the visit to her comadre in San Luis also showed that she thinks of the "other side" as a site for the political and psychological repression of Mexicans who seek nothing more than honest work. Crossing the border by means of her story offers a hope of liberation—the remaking of her self in her own image—but that hope is embedded in the understanding that the bodies of real Mexicans are treated harshly and cruelly in that same place where her other self can unfold. The terms of exchange, then, are not transparent nor easy for Esperanza, and they are not for me, either. And these terms of exchange are sedimented in the story itself, not only in what Esperanza has told me but in the very fact that what she has told me will be heard across the border.

I would be misrepresenting the terms of our exchange if I failed to say that Esperanza's textual border crossing, like that of Mexican laborers, also carries with it the hope of obtaining more prosaic things from "the other side." After our conversations in 1987 she asked me for a radio-tape recorder, and her youngest son wrote me several letters to remind me. When I gave it to her in 1987, she turned happily to her son and said, "Se nos concedió!" (We got our wish!); I felt like a fairy godmother. She wrapped up the recorder in her shawl, as though it were a baby, and promised not to let anyone know she had gotten it from me, for if the word got around there would surely be bad feelings among our other friends in the town. The following year her son wrote us to say that they would soon have electricity and that my comadre would like a television set. When I gave Esperanza the television set, she reacted in the same way she had before: "We got our wish!" And now the set sits on a small table in her bedroom next to her altar of religious images, protected from dust by a white crocheted cloth. In recent months her son has written to let us know my comadre needs a motor to irrigate her field and that it costs over a million pesos; could we bring it in our car, he wants to know, on our next visit? These too are part of the things being exchanged in our work and in my crossings back and forth from my academic production plant to the terrain of storytelling and wishing across the border.

REFERENCES

Behar, Ruth. 1990. "Rage and Redemption: Reading the Life Story of a Mexican Marketing Woman." *Feminist Studies* 16(2):223–258.

Patai, Daphne. 1988. *Brazilian Women Speak: Contemporary Life Histories*. New Brunswick, N.J.: Rutgers University Press.

Rosaldo, Renato. 1989. *Culture and Truth: The Remaking of Social Analysis*. Boston: Beacon Press.

Shostak, Marjorie. 1981. *Nisa: The Life and Words of a !Kung Woman*. Cambridge, Mass.: Harvard University Press.

Stacey, Judith. 1988. "Can There Be a Feminist Ethnography?" *Women's Studies International Forum* 11(1):21–27.

Visweswaran, Kamala. 1992. "Betrayal: An Analysis in Three Acts." In *Postmodernism and Transnational Feminist Practice*. Edited by Inderpal Grewal and Caren Kaplan. Minneapolis: University of Minnesota Press.

II

Cultural Politics and the
Constraint of Narrative Identity

7 Life Stories:
Pieces of a Dream

Mermaids' Songs

"I have heard the mermaids singing, each to each." —T. S. Eliot

The songs of mermaids are not like other songs. Mermaids' voices sing beyond the human range—notes not heard, forms not tolerated, and each to each, not one to many, one above all. If we imagine the mermaids, we might almost hear them singing. Their voices blending, so that each, in its own special timbre, lends to the harmony of the whole. So it might be as one writes—a voice in a choir at the threshold of sensibility. My voice shall be only one of many to be heard.

When you hear one voice it is the voice of authority, the father's voice. One voice belongs to an androcentric order.

Will our singing mute the single voice before we drown?

"We need to learn how to see our theorizing projects as . . . 'riffing' between and over the beats of patriarchal theories" (Sandra Harding, 1986, 649).

This is an interwoven etude about life stories; it seeks to disrupt the usual narrative line, the rules of patriarchal form. I wish to escape the culturally contoured modes of discourse. Yet I, too, am mired in convention. If I write in all the acceptable ways, I shall only recapitulate the patriarchal forms. Yet, if I violate expectations too grievously, my words will become nonsense. Still, the mermaids sing.

"Finding voices authentic to women's experience is appallingly difficult. Not only

Besides the many voices within the text, many others added their notes to this composition, in particular my colleague at Penn State Carol Kessler, and Peter Maier, Walter Heinz, and Wojciech Sadurski, my hallmates at the Netherlands Institute for Advanced Study, who directed my readings and cheered me on. Representatives of both institutions have also generously granted me the support and time to work on this piece. I wish to thank them, as well as George Rosenwald and Richard Ochberg, who took their editing tasks seriously and did them well. Last I wish to express my gratitude to Kenneth Gergen, my trusty dolphin, who saved me many times from floundering in this tide of words.

*are the languages and concepts we have . . . male oriented, but historically
women's experiences have been interpreted for us by men and male norms" (Kathryn Rabuzzi, 1988, 12).*

We play at the shores of understanding. If you assent to the bending of traditional forms, then perhaps our collective act may jostle the sand castles of the ordered kingdom. We need one another, even if we do not always agree.

"If we do our work well, 'reality' will appear even more unstable, complex, and disorderly than it does now" (Jane Flax, 1987, 643).

The Paradox of the Private: Our Public Secrets

When we tell one another our deepest secrets we use a public language. The nuances of consciousness, emotions both subtle and profound, inner yearnings, the whispering of conscience—all of these are created in the matrix of this language. The words form and deform around us as we speak and listen. We swim in a sea of words. Only that which is public can be private. We dwell in a paradox.

"Individual consciousness is a socio-ideological fact. If you cannot talk about an experience, at least to yourself, you did not have it" (Caryl Emerson, 1983, 10).

Our cultures provide models not only for the contents of what we say but also for the forms. We use these forms unwittingly; they create the means by which we interpret our lives. We know ourselves via the mediating forms of our cultures, through telling, and through listening.

"What created humanity is narration" (Pierre Janet, 1928, 42).

"Know thyself," a seemingly timeless motto, loses clarity when we hold that our forms of self-understanding are the creation of the unknown multitudes who have gone before us. We have become, we are becoming because "they" have set out the linguistic forestructures of intelligibility. What then does a personal identity amount to?

"Every text is an articulation of the relations between texts, a product of intertextuality, a weaving together of what has already been produced elsewhere in discontinuous form; every subject, every author, every self is the articulation of an intersubjectivity structured within and around the discourses available to it at any moment in time" (Michael Sprinker, 1980, 325).

If self-understanding is derived from our cultures, and the stories we can tell about ourselves are prototypically performed, what implications does this have for our life affairs? The reverberations of this question will ring in our ears.

"Every version of an 'other' . . . is also the construction of a 'self'" (*James Clifford, 1986, 23*).
And, I add, every version of a self must be a construction of the other.

Our first mark of identity is by gender. We are called "boy" or "girl" in our first moment of life. Our personal identities are always genderized, then so must life stories be. I am concerned with the gendered nature of our life stories. What are manstories and womanstories? How do they differ? And what difference do these differences make?

"The literary construction of gender is always artificial . . . one can never unveil the essence *of masculinity or femininity. Instead, all one exposes are other representations" (Linda Kauffman, 1986, 314).*

This overture suggests the major themes. Countertones may resist articulation. You may not find what you want. The voices mingle and collide. Only in the confluence will the totality be fixed . . . temporarily.

Defining Powers: Doubts about the Structure

What do I mean by the narratives or stories of our lives? When we began our work on the traditional narrative, Kenneth Gergen and I described it as being composed of a valued end point; events relevant to this end point; the temporal ordering of these events toward the endpoint; the causal linkages between events (see also Gergen and Gergen, 1983; 1984; 1988).

Now I become uneasy. I wonder why this definition must be as it is. Doesn't a definition defend an order of discourse, an order of life? Whose lives are advantaged by this form and whose disadvantaged? Should we ask?

What are the forms of our life stories? We recognize them—a comedy, a tragedy, a romance, a satire. We know them as they are told. Their plots are implicated in their structures. A climax is a matter of form as well as content. Though separating form and content may be desirable from an analytic point of view, it is also arbitrary. (What are the forms of a womanstory and a manstory? How do they differ?)

"The dramatic structure of conversion . . . where the self is presented as the stage for a battle of opposing forces and where a climactic victory for one force— spirit defeating flesh—completes the drama of the self, simply does not accord with the deepest realities of women's experience and so is inappropriate as a model for women's life-writing" (Mary G. Mason, 1980, 210).

Should we question the ways in which patriarchal authority has controlled the narrative forms? We would be in good company. Many feminist literary critics have expanded this perspective (see also Shari Benstock, 1986; Rachel Duplessis,

1985; Sidonie Smith, 1987). Such writers as Virginia Woolf (1957, 1958) have also struggled with how male domination in literary forms has made some works great and others trivial, some worthy and some not. What has been judged by the figures of authority as correct has been granted publication, critical acclaim, and respect; the rest has often been ignored or abused.

". . . both in life and in art, the values of a woman are not the values of a man. Thus, when a woman comes to write a novel, she will find that she is perpetually wishing to alter the established values—to make serious what appears insignificant to a man and trivial what is to him important" (Virginia Woolf, 1958, 81).

Although androcentric control over literary forms is a serious matter, how much graver is the accusation that the forms of our personal narratives are also under such control? The relation between one and the other is strong, but the more pervasive nature and consequence of male-dominated life stories is certainly more threatening to me.

"Narrative in the most general terms is a version of, or a special expression of, ideology; representations by which we construct and accept values and institutions" (Rachel DuPlessis, 1985, x).
I would add, construct and accept ourselves!

Thus, I become increasingly skeptical of our classical definitions of the narrative. Judgments of what constitutes a proper telling are suspect on the grounds that what seem to be simple canons of good judgment, aesthetic taste, or even familiar custom may also be unquestioned expressions of patriarchal power. Under the seemingly innocent guise of telling a true story, one's life story validates the status quo.

Genderizing: Tenderizing the monomyth

Myths have carried the form and content of narratives throughout the centuries. They tell us how great events occur as well as how stories are made. Joseph Campbell (1956) has analyzed these ancient myths. He proposes that there is one fundamental myth—the "monomyth." This myth begins as the hero, having been dedicated to a quest, ventures forth from the everyday world. He goes into the region of the supernatural, where he encounters strange, dangerous, and powerful forces, which he must vanquish. Then the victorious hero returns and is rewarded for his great deeds. The monomyth is the hero's myth and the major manstory. (Where is the woman in this story? She is only to be found as a snare, an obstacle, a magic power, or a prize.)

"The whole ideology of representational significance is an ideology of power" (Stephen Tyler, 1986, 131).

This monomyth is not just a historical curiosity. It is the basic model for the stories of achievement in everyday lives. Life stories are often about quests; they, like the monomyth, are stories of achievement. The story hangs on the end point—will the goal be achieved or not? In such stories all is subsumed by the goal. The heroic character must not allow anything to interfere with the quest.

Do you assume that a heroine is the same as a hero, except for gender? Some might say that narratives of heroes are equally available to women. I doubt this is so. Cultural expectations about how the two genders should express their heroism are clearly divergent.

Consider the central characters and the major plots of life stories codified in literature, history, or personal narrative; we could easily conclude that women do not belong, at least in the starring role. The adventures of the hero of the monomyth would make rather strange sense if he were a woman. If He is the subject of the story, She must be the object. In the System opposites cannot occupy the same position. The woman represents the totality of what is to be known. The hero is the knower. She is life; he is the master of life. He is the main character; she is a supporting actress. He is the actor; she is acted upon.

"Although theoretically the hero was meant generically to stand for individuals of both sexes, actually, like so-called 'generic man,' the hero is a thoroughly androcentric construction" (Kathryn Rabuzzi, 1988, 10).

In general, the cultural repertoire of heroic stories requires different qualities for each gender. The contrast of the ideal narrative line pits the autonomous ego-enhancing hero single-handedly and single-heartedly progressing toward a goal versus the long-suffering, selfless, socially embedded heroine, being moved in many directions, lacking the tenacious loyalty demanded of a quest.

"Culture is male, our literary myths are for heroes, not heroines" (Joanne Russ, 1972, 18).

The differences in our stories are not generally recognized in our culture. In a democratic society, with equal opportunity for all, we do not consider the absence of narrative lines as relevant to unequal representation of people in public positions of power. We do not turn to our biographies to help explain, for example, why so few women are the heads of organizations, climb mountains, or teach math classes, or why so few men are primary caretakers of children. Even when women are leaders in their professions, or exceptional in some arena of life, they find it difficult to tell their personal narratives in the forms that would be suitable to their male colleagues. They are in a cultural hiatus, with a paucity of stories to tell. (How does one become when no story can be found?)

"The emphasis by women on the personal, especially on other people, rather than on their work life, their professional success, or their connectedness to

*current political or intellectual history clearly contradicts the established crite-
rion about the content of autobiography" (Estelle Jelinek, 1980, 10).*

Feminist Theories and Gender Differences

Various feminist theorists have emphasized the underlying family dynamics that
may sustain our gendered stories. As Nancy Chodorow (1978), Dorothy Dinnerstein (1976), Jane Flax (1983), Carol Gilligan (1982), Evelyn Fox Keller (1983),
and others have suggested, boys and girls are raised to regard their life trajectories
differently. All children have as their first love object their mothering figure.
However, boys are reared to separate from their mothers, and they learn to replace
their attachment to mother with pride in masculine achievements and to derogate
women and their relationships with them. Girls are not cut away from their
mothers and forced to reidentify themselves. They remain embedded in their
relations and do not learn the solitary hero role. But they must bear the burden of
shame that the androcentered culture assigns to their gender.

This, then, is my theme: each gender acquires for personal use a repertoire of
potential life stories relevant to their own gender. Understanding one's past,
interpreting one's actions, evaluating future possibilities—each is filtered through
these stories. Events "make sense" as they are placed in the correct story form. If
certain story forms are absent, events cannot take on the same meaning.

"We assume that life produces *the autobiography, as an act produces its consequence, but can we not suggest, with equal justice, that the autobiography project
may itself produce and determine life" (Paul de Man, 1979, 920).*

Autobiographies as the Gendered Stories of Lives

I have been studying the popular autobiographies of men and women. Of interest
to me is not what is there, in the story lines, but what is missing. What is it that
each gender cannot talk about—and thus cannot integrate into life stories and life
plans? What can a manstory tell that a womanstory cannot, and vice versa?

*"What appears as 'real' in history, the social sciences, the arts, even in common
sense, is always analyzable as a restrictive and expressive set of social codes and
conventions" (James Clifford, 1986, 10).*

In critical works concerning autobiography, women's narratives have been almost totally neglected (cf. Sayre, 1980; Olney, 1980; Smith, 1974). Women's
writings have usually been exempted because they did not fit the proper formal
mold. Their work has been more fragmentary, multidimensional, understated, and
temporally disjunctive. "Insignificant" has been the predominant critical judgment toward women's autobiographies (and their lives) (Estelle Jelinek, 1980).

*"When a woman writes or speaks herself into existence, she is forced to speak in
something like a foreign tongue" (Carolyn Burke, 1978, 844).*

Interpreting the Stories

I look into autobiographies to discover the forms we use to tell a manstory, a
womanstory. What story can I tell?

*"Autobiography reveals the impossibility of its own dream: What begins on the
presumption of self-knowledge ends in the creation of a fiction that covers over the
premises of its construction" (Shari Benstock, 1988, 11).*

My materials are taken from many biographies. This chapter concentrates on but
a few. In this way a sense of life may perhaps be felt. The quotations I have drawn
from these texts are hardly proof of my conclusions; they are better viewed as
illustrations to vivify my interpretations. Other interpretations can and should be
made.

Seeking the Quest

Traditional narratives demand an end point, a goal. Certain rhetorical moves are
required by custom—concentrating on the goal, moving toward the point, putting
events in a sequence, building the case (no tangents, please). Classical autobiographies delineate the life of cultural heroes—those who have achieved greatness
through their accomplishments. We expect those who write their biographies must
be such heroes.

*"Men tend to idealize their lives or to cast them into heroic molds to project their
universal import" (Estelle Jelinek, 1980, 14).*

How single-minded are these heroes in pursuit of their goals? How committed
are the women who write their biographies? Does their story also fit the classic
mold?

Listen to some of their voices.

Lee Iacocca's best-selling autobiography focused on his automotive career. His
family life, in contrast, received scant attention. Iacocca's wife, Mary, was a
diabetic. Her condition worsened over the years; after two heart attacks, one in
1978 and the other in 1980, she died in 1983 at the age of fifty-seven. According to
Iacocca, each heart attack came after a crisis period in his career at Ford or
Chrysler.

Iacocca wrote: "Above all, a person with diabetes has to avoid stress. Unfortunately, with the path I had chosen to follow, this was virtually impossible" (Lee
Iacocca, 301).

Iacocca's description of his wife's death was not intended to expose his cruelty. It is a conventional narrative report—appropriate to his gender. The book (and his life) are dedicated to his career. Iacocca seems to have found it unimaginable that he could have ended his career in order to reduce his wife's ill health. As a manstory, the passage is not condemning; however, if we reverse the sexes, as a wife's description of the death of her husband or child, the story would appear callous, to say the least. Unlike Iacocca, a woman who would do such a thing would not be considered an outstanding folk hero.

Yeager is the autobiography of the quintessential American hero, the man with the "right stuff." His story is intensively focused on his career as a pilot in the air force. He was the father of four children born in quick succession, and his wife became gravely ill during her last pregnancy. Nothing, however, stopped him from flying. Constantly moving around the globe, always seeking the most dangerous missions, he openly states: "Whenever Glennis needed me over the years, I was usually off in the wild blue yonder" (Chuck Yeager and Leo James, 103).

America's favorite hero would be considered an abusive parent were his story regendered.

Richard Feynman, autobiographer and Nobel prize–winning physicist, was married to a woman who had been stricken with tuberculosis for seven years. During World War II, he moved to Los Alamos to work on the Manhattan Project developing the atomic bomb, and she was several hours away in a hospital in Albuquerque. The day she was dying he borrowed a car to go to her bedside.

He reports: "When I got back (yet another tire went flat on the way), they asked me what happened. 'She's dead. And how's the program going?' They caught on right away that I didn't want to moon over it" (Richard Feynman, 113).

Manstories tend to follow the traditional narrative pattern: becoming their own heroes, facing crises, following their quests, and ultimately achieving victory. Their careers provide them their central lines of narrative structuring, and personal commitments, external to their careers, are relegated to insignificant subplots.

What does one find among women authors?

"There is virtually only one occupation for a female protagonist—love, of course—which our culture uses to absorb all possible Bildung, *success/failure, learning, education, and transition to adulthood" (Rachel DuPlessis, 1985, 182).*

Beverly Sills, who became a star at the New York City Opera, all but gave up her singing career for two years to live in Cleveland because this was where her husband worked. She describes her thoughts: "Peter had spent all of his professional life working for the *Plain Dealer,* and he had every intention of eventually becoming the newspaper's editor-in-chief. I was just going to have to get used to Cleveland. My only alternative was to ask Peter to scuttle the goal he'd been working toward for almost twenty-five years. If I did that, I didn't deserve to be his wife. Not coincidentally, I began reevaluating whether or not I truly wanted a career as an opera singer. I decided I didn't. . . . I was twenty-eight years old, and I wanted to have a baby" (Beverly Sills and Lawrence Linderman, 120).

The only businesswoman in my sample, Sydney Biddle Barrows, also known by the title of her autobiography, *Mayflower Madam,* shows second thoughts about maintaining a then extremely successful business when it clashed with private goals:

"By early 1984 . . . I realized that I couldn't spend the rest of my life in the escort business. I was now in my early thirties and starting to think more practically about my future—which would, I hoped, include marriage. As much as I loved my job, I had to acknowledge that the kind of man I was likely to fall in love with would never marry the owner of an escort service. . . . If I didn't want to remain single forever, I would sooner or later have to return to a more conventional line of work" (Sydney Biddle Barrows, 205).

Martina Navratilova discusses her feelings about going skiing after many years of foregoing this dangerous sport: "I made a decision in my teens to not risk my tennis career on the slopes, but in recent years I've wanted to feel the wind on my face again . . . I wasn't willing to wait God-knows-how-many-years to stop playing and start living" (Martina Navratilova, 320).

Nien Cheng's *Life and Death in Shanghai* details her survival during years of imprisonment in China. Although her own survival might be seen as the major goal of her story, this focus is deeply compromised by her concerns with her daughter's welfare. "I hoped my removal to the detention house would free her from any further pressure to denounce me. If that were indeed the case . . . , I would be prepared to put up with anything" (Nien Cheng, 132).

Discovering that her daughter is dead greatly disturbs her own will to go on. "Now there was nothing left. It would have been less painful if I had died in prison and never known that Meiping was dead. My struggle to keep alive . . . suddenly seemed meaningless" (ibid., 360).

For the women, the career line was important, but it was not an ultimate end point. Whereas men seemed to sacrifice their lives to careers, women seemed to tell the story in reverse. This is not to say that women avoided achieving goals. They, too, yearn for the joy of success. But men and women do not describe their feelings in the same way. Let us listen.

Lee Iacocca: "My years as general manager of the Ford Division were the happiest period of my life. For my colleagues and me, this was fire-in-the-belly time. We were high from smoking our own brand—a combination of hard work and big dreams" (Lee Iacocca, 65).

Chuck Yeager: "I don't recommend going to war as a way of testing character, but by the time our tour ended we felt damned good about ourselves and what we had accomplished. Whatever the future held, we knew our skills as pilots, our ability to handle stress and danger, and our reliability in tight spots. It was the difference between thinking you're pretty good, and proving it" (Chuck Yeager and Leo James, 88).

Edward Koch: "I am the Mayor of a city that has more Jews than live in Jerusalem, more Italians than live in Rome . . . and more Puerto Ricans than live in San Juan. . . . It is a tremendous responsibility, but there is no other job in the world that compares with it . . . Every day has the possibility of accomplishing some major success" (Edward Koch, 359).

When John Paul Getty drilled his first great oil well, he was overjoyed: "The sense of elation and triumph was-and-is always there. It stems from knowing that one has beaten nature's incalculable odds by finding and capturing a most elusive (and often a dangerous and malevolent) prey" (John Paul Getty, 28).

Male voices often have a tone of hostility, aggression, or domination. Their celebration of achievement seems to be the result of what is fundamentally an antagonistic encounter.

The ways that women's voices speak of achievements take a rather different slant.

Martina Navratilova: "For the first time I was a Wimbledon champion, fulfilling the dream of my father many years before. . . . I could feel Chris patting me on the back, smiling and congratulating me. . . . Four days later, the Women's Tennis Association computer ranked me number 1 in the world, breaking Chris's four-year domination. I felt I was on top of the world" (Martina Navratilova, 190).

Beverly Sills: "I think 'se pieta' was the single most extraordinary piece of singing I ever did. I know I had never heard myself sing that way before . . . the curtain began coming down very slowly . . . and then a roar went through that house the likes of which I'd never heard. I was a little stunned by it: the audience wouldn't stop applauding" (Beverly Sills and Lawrence Linderman, 172).

Sydney Biddle Barrows: "I was motivated by the challenge of doing something better than everyone else . . . I was determined to create a business that would appeal to . . . men, who constituted the high end of the market . . . I was sure we could turn our agency into one hell of an operation—successful, elegant, honest, and fun" (Sydney Biddle Barrows, 48–49).

In the womanstories, the love of the audience response, the affection of the opponent, and the satisfaction of customers are the significant factors in their descriptions. The womanstory emphasizes continuity with others' goals, not opposition to them. In fact, one's opponent can be seen as a necessary part of one's success:

"You're totally out for yourself, to win a match, yet you're dependent on your opponent to some degree for the type of match it is and how well you play. You need the opponent; without her you do not exist" (Martina Navaratilova, 162).

Emotional Interdependency

What do these stories say about emotion interdependency—being with others and needing reciprocal affections? Here the manstory may be rather thin. Sticking to the narrative line may cut short their emotional lives, at least in print. But this is too black and white a message. Men have their buddies, their sidekicks, their intimate rivals, and compatriots. Perhaps the difference is that together they look outward, rather than at one another.

Let us look at how manstories allowed for the expression of relatedness and emotionality.

Ed Koch, reporting a conversation: "I've been Mayor for close to three years . . . I get involved in a lot of controversies and I make a lot of people mad at me, and so maybe at the end of these four years they'll say, 'he's too controversial and we don't want him!' And maybe they'll throw me out. That's okay with me. I'll get a better job, and you won't get a better Mayor" (Edward Koch, 227).

Chuck Yeager: "Often at the end of a hard day, the choice was going home to a wife who really didn't understand what you were talking about . . . or gathering around the bar with guys who had also spent the day in a cockpit. Talking flying was the next best thing to flying itself. And after we had a few drinks in us, we'd get happy or belligerent and raise some hell. Flying and hell-raising—one fueled the other" (Chuck Yeager and Leo James, 173).

John Paul Getty: "For some reason, I have always been much freer in recording my emotions and feelings in my diaries. . . . Taken as a whole, they might serve to provide insight into a father's true feeling about his sons.

1939
Los Angeles, California:
May 20: Saw George, a remarkable boy rapidly becoming a man. He is 5'9" tall and weighs 145 pounds.
Genève, Switzerland:
July 9: Drove to Ronny's school . . . Ronny is well, happy, and likes his school. His teachers give him a good report. He is intelligent and has good character, they say. Took Ronny and Fini to the Bergues Hotel for lunch and then to Chamonix. . . .
Los Angeles:
December 10: Went to Ann's house (Ann Rork, my fourth wife who divorced me in 1935) and saw Pabby and Gordon, bless them. They are both fine boys" (John Paul Getty, 11).

Manstories seem to celebrate the song of the self. Emotional ties are mentioned as "facts" where necessary, but the author does not try to re-create in the reader emphatic emotional responses. The willingness to play the role of the "bastard" is seen in manstories, for example in Koch's remarks above, but women do not take this stance in their stories.

And about our heroines? What do their stories tell about their emotional interdependencies? How important are relationships to their life courses? Is there a womanstory, too?

Let us listen.

Beverly Sills: "One of the things I always loved best about being an opera singer was the chance to make new friends every time I went into a new production" (Beverly Sills and Lawrence Linderman, 229).

She wrote about how she and Carol Burnett had cried after finishing a television show together. "We knew we'd have nobody to play with the next day. After that we telephoned each other three times a day" (ibid., 280).

Martina Navratilova: "I've never been able to treat my opponent as the enemy, particularly Pam Shriver, my doubles partner and one of my best friends" (Martina Navratilova, 167).

Sydney Biddle Barrows emphasized in her book her ladylike upbringing, sensitive manners, and appreciation of the finer things of life. Her style of living was obviously challenged when she was arrested and thrown in jail.

On leaving a group of street-walking prostitutes with whom she had been jailed she wrote: "As I left the cell, everybody started shouting and cheering me on. 'Go get' em, girlfren!' I left with mixed emotions. These girls had been so nice to me, and so open and interesting, that my brief experience in jail was far more positive than I could have imagined" (Sydney Biddle Barrows, 284).

The necessity of relating to others in a womanstory is especially crucial in Nien Cheng's narrative about solitary confinement. To avoid the bitter loneliness she adopted a small spider as a friend. She describes her concern for this spider: "My small friend seemed rather weak. It stumbled and stopped every few steps. Could a spider get sick, or was it merely cold? . . . It made a tiny web . . . forming something rather like a cocoon . . . when I had to use the toilet, I carefully sat well to one side so that I did not disturb it" (Nien Cheng, 155).

Though many other examples might be given, these illustrate the major differences I have found between the relatively more profound emotional interdependency and intimacy requirement of women, in the telling of their stories, and those of men. The important aspects of women's autobiographies depend heavily on their affiliative relationships with others. They seem to focus on these ties without drawing strong demarcations between their public world and "private" life. Their stories highlight the interdependent nature of their involvements and the centrality of emotional well-being to all facets of life much more vividly than men's stories do.

Voices as Verses: Forms and Foam

As stories are told, forms are re-created. The content belongs to the forms, and the forms control the content. Let us look at the forms more closely.

"Individuals have characteristic ways of navigating their lives. What is characteristic—the signature we need across episodes—exists at the level of narrative structure. We can analyze the structure of a life plot as symbolic in its own right" (Richard Ochberg, 1988, 172).

Popular autobiographies of men are very similar in form. Their narrative lines tend to be linear (that is, strongly related to an explicit goal state, the career or quest) and progressive (the action moves toward this goal). Manstories also tend to be characterized by one or more major climaxes, usually related to career trajectories. The emphasis of a manstory on the single narrative line is evident from the beginning of the book. Edward Koch's autobiography, *Mayor,* for example, is totally devoted to his political career, especially as it "mirrors" the life of New York City from the mayor's office. Chapter 1, entitled "A Child of the City," begins not with a biological childhood but with his political youth: "In March of 1975, when I was a U.S. Congressman from New York." Koch begins at a crisis point for the book's long-suffering heroine—not a flesh and blood woman, but New York City.

Chuck Yeager's book about his life as a pilot begins with a crash landing. Getty initiates his book with a sentence indicating that he was born in 1892 "and an active businessman since 1914" (John Paul Getty, vii). Physicist Feynman starts, "When I was about eleven or twelve I set up a lab in my house" (Richard Feynman, 3). Iacocca states, "You're about to read the history of a man who's had more than his share of successes." (Lee Iacocca, xiv).

"The autobiographer confronts personally her culture's stories of male and female desire, insinuating the lines of her story through the lines of the patriarchal story that has been autobiography" (Sidonie Smith, 1987, 19).

Womanstories also contain a progressive theme related to achievement goals, but often the text emphasizes another facet of personal identity and deviates from one clear narrative line associated with career. Beverly Sills's first chapter recalls the last night she sang at the New York State Theater—a gala charity performance. The event was not presented as a career triumph but as an emotionally significant "swan song." Sydney Biddle Barrows commences with a description of the annual meeting of the Society of Mayflower Descendants, of which she is a member, thus complexifying the question of how she became the owner of an escort service. Nien Cheng recalls her old home in Shanghai, her daughter asleep in her room. The importance of her daughter's activities plays a strong counterpoint to her own issues of existence. "Apple Trees" is the title of Martina Navratilova's first chapter; she begins: "I was three years old when my mother and father divorced" (Martina Navratilova, 1).

For female authors, the story forms available to them are much fuller (and more multiple in perspective) than for the men. Career successes and failures are mingled with other issues of great personal importance. Thus the story line becomes less clearly demarcated. The narrative threads are more complexly woven by the women. The story is about a person who is embedded in a variety of relationships, which all have some priority in the telling of the life. Ambiguity about any outcome complexifies the task of giving value to any particular event.

Can Stories and Lives Be Changed?

Throughout this composition I have illustrated how personal identities are construed through the gendered stories of lives. Autobiographies exemplify the repertoire of life-story forms by which "significant" members of a culture define themselves. Less important people, those who merely tell their stories to themselves and their private audiences, also use these forms. We all know ourselves, define our pasts, and project our futures as they fit into the acculturated story forms. But the forms for each gender are restrictive, and in many critical areas, such as achievement strivings and intimate relationships, men and women are inhibited from formulating selves that would allow for a different range of expressions and actions. Neither a man nor a woman can easily swap roles without the loss of social approval.

> *"The structure of autobiography, a story that is at once by and about the same individual, echoes and reinforces a structure already implicit in our language, a structure that is also (not accidentally) very like what we usually take to be the structure of self-consciousness itself: the capacity to know and simultaneously be that which one knows" (Elizabeth W. Bruss, 1980, 301).*

I began this work with a special sensitivity to the losses that women have endured because they have been absent from the public sphere. I saw that because the story lines that lead a woman from childhood to maturity did not show the path by which strong achievement strivings could be satisfied without great personal sacrifice, women could not become all they had the potential to be.

As I read the autobiographies of our "great" men, I confronted anew what many social critics, especially feminists, have frequently claimed: the goals, values, and methods that sustain men's lives are antagonistic to other social values, those associated with women's narratives and lives. Particularly in re-visioning these stories, I saw the basic values of each clustering around themes of power versus themes of love.

Increasingly, as I read, what most needed change seemed to be not women's narratives, for them to become more like men's, but the reverse. Men, perhaps even more than women, needed new story lines, lines that were more multiplex, relational, and "messy." Both seemed imprisoned by their stories; both bound to separate pieces of the world, which if somehow put together would create new possibilities—ones in which each could share the other's dreams.

But how can we escape our story lines, our prisons made of words?

"Plots are dramatic embodiments of what a culture believes to be true . . . of all the possible actions people can do in fiction, very few can be done by women" (Joanne Russ, 1972, 4).

Language: Source and Sorceress

Language seems almost magical. Only through its powers to name can we identify our experiences and our persons. There are no social structures that bear upon us beyond this linguistic order. All that exists is within it. If we want to change our lives, we need to change our patterns of discourse. The "language games" constitute what there is to change.

Can we lift ourselves by our shoestrings?

"Individuals construct themselves as subjects through language, but individual subjects—rather than being the source of their own self-generated and self-expressive meaning—adopt positions available within the language at a given moment" (Felicity Nussbaum, 1988, 149).

Our narrative forms, our metaphors, our ways of communicating do not emerge from nothingness. They are embedded in the foundations of society. Stories and their structural instantiations reverberate against and with one another. Are we prisoners of our father tongue? Yes . . . , mostly . . . , maybe . . . , sometimes . . . , no. Perhaps we can at least wiggle a bit.

"In altering the images and narrative structures through which we compose the stories of our lives, we may hope to alter the very experiences of those lives as well" (Annette Kolodny, 1980, 258).

Many voices singing different tunes can sound noisy. Do you feel drowned out? We must sing like mermaids—and hope that a melody or two will be carried on the wind.

"Subversively, she rearranges the dominant discourse and the dominant ideology of gender, seizing the language and its power to turn cultural fictions into her very own story" (Sidonie Smith, 1987, 175).

How do we rearrange the melodies of talk? I will suggest some ways. Let us listen carefully as our words divide us and emphasize power differences among us. Let us resist these discordant tunes. (This will be less appealing at first to those whose words have been on everyone's lips.) Let us note, for example, that we call ourselves for some man long since dead. In a sense we belong to him. Let our names hang lightly in the air, or blow them away, if we wish.

"For a symbolic order that equates the ideas of the author with a phallic pen transmitted from father to son places the female writer in contradiction to the dominant definition of woman and casts her as the usurper of male prerogatives" (Domna Stanton, 1984, 13).

Let us listen to the metaphors we carry with us. Let us choose them carefully. Do we mimic our brothers who scoff at "soft" sciences and who love "hard" data? Do we feel the grasp of "sexual politics" at our throats?

"To change a story signals a dissent from social norms as well as narrative forms" (Rachel DuPlessis, 1985, 20).

Let us play with story lines. Let us not always conform to androcentric styles. Let us demure. Maybe stories don't need lines. Perhaps they need to step out of the queue and refuse to march in orderly progression. Let us not stick to the point. Let us improvise! (see also Gergen, 1990).

"The construction is nothing more than an improvisation" (George Rosenwald, 1988, 256).

Let us claim the tentative and fuzzy nature of all our linguistic formulations. Let us shake the tree of knowledge, unashamed. Let us eat the apple to the core and spit out "truth." Let us grant ourselves the pleasures of making and changing languages, as they transform us. Let us sing songs that will free us from the past and hum sweet dirges for androcentric systems as they drown.

AUTOBIOGRAPHICAL REFERENCES

Barrows, Sydney Biddle, with William Novak. 1986. *Mayflower Madam*. New York: Arbor House.
Cheng, Nien. 1986. *Life and Death in Shanghai*. New York: Penguin.
Feynman, Richard P. 1986. *"Surely You're Joking, Mr. Feynman!"* New York: Bantam Books.
Getty, J. Paul. [1976] 1986. *As I See It: An Autobiography of J. Paul Getty*. New York: Berkley.
Iacocca, Lee, with William Novak. 1984. *Iacocca: An Autobiography*. New York: Bantam Books.
Koch, Edward I., with William Rauch. 1986. *Mayor*. New York: Warner Books.
Navratilova, Martina, with George Vecsey. 1985. *Martina*. New York: Fawcett Crest.

Sills, Beverly, and Lawrence Linderman. 1987. *Beverly*. New York: Bantam Books.
Yeager, General Chuck, and Leo James. 1985. *Yeager: An Autobiography*. New York: Bantam Books.

GENERAL REFERENCES

Benstock, Shari. 1988. "Authorizing the Autobiography." In *The Private Self: Theory and Practice in Women's Autobiographical Writings*. Edited by S. Benstock. London: Routledge.

Bruss, Elizabeth W. 1980. "Eye for I: Making and Unmaking Autobiography in Film." In *Autobiography: Essays, Theoretical and Critical*. Edited by J. Olney. Princeton, N.J.: Princeton University Press.

Burke, Carolyn G. 1978. "Report from Paris: Women's Writing and the Women's Movement." *Signs, Journal of Women in Culture and Society* 3:844.

Campbell, Joseph. 1956. *The Hero with One Thousand Faces*. New York: Bollingen.

Chodorow, Nancy. 1978. *The Reproduction of Mothering: Psychoanalysis and the Sociology of Gender*. Berkeley: University of California Press.

Clifford, James. 1986. "Introduction: Partial Truths." In *Writing Culture*. Edited by J. Clifford and G. Marcus. Berkeley: University of California Press.

de Man, Paul. 1979. "Autobiography as De-Facement." *Modern Language Notes* 94:920.

Dinnerstein, Dorothy. 1976. *The Mermaid and the Minotaur: Sexual Arrangements and the Human Malaise*. New York: Harper and Row.

DuPlessis, Rachel Blau. 1985. *Writing Beyond the Ending*. Bloomington: Indiana University Press.

Eliot, T. S. 1963. "The Love Song of J. Alfred Prufrock." In *Collected Poems, 1909–1962*. London: Faber and Faber.

Emerson, Caryl. 1983. "The Outer Word and Inner Speech: Bakhtin, Vygotsky, and the Internalization of Language." *Critical Inquiry* 10:245–264.

Flax, Jane. 1987. "Postmodernism and Gender Relations in Feminist Theory." *Signs, Journal of Women in Culture and Society* 12:621–643.

———. 1983. "Political Philosophy and the Patriarchal Unconscious: A Psychoanalytic Perspective on Epistemology and Metaphysics." In *Discovering Reality: Feminist Perspectives on Epistemology, Metaphysics, Methodology, and Philosophy of Science*. Edited by S. Harding and M. B. Hintikka. Dordrecht, Holland: D. Reidel.

Gergen, Kenneth J., and Mary M. Gergen. 1988. "Narrative and the Self as Relationship." In *Advances in Experimental Social Psychology*, vol. 21. Edited by L. Berkowitz. San Diego: Academic Press.

———. 1983. "Narrative of the Self." In *Studies in Social Identity*. Edited by K. Schiebe and T. Sarbin. New York: Praeger.

Gergen, Mary M. 1990. "A Feminist Psychologist's Postmod Critique of Postmodernism." *Humanistic Psychologist* 18:95–104.

Gergen, Mary M., and Kenneth J. Gergen. 1984. "Narrative Structures and Their Social Construction." In *Historical Social Psychology*. Edited by K. Gergen and M. Gergen. Hillsdale, N.J.: Erlbaum.

Gilligan, Carol. 1982. *In a Different Voice*. Cambridge, Mass.: Harvard University Press.

Harding, Sandra. 1986. "The Instability of the Analytical Categories of Feminist Theory." *Signs, Journal of Women in Culture and Society* 11:645–664.

Janet, Pierre. 1928. *L'Evolution de la memoire et la notion du temps.* Paris: L. Alcan.

Jelinek, Estelle C. 1980. *Women's Autobiography: Essays in Criticism.* Bloomington: Indiana University Press.

Kauffman, Linda S. 1986. *Discourses of Desire: Gender, Genre, and Epistolary Fictions.* Ithaca, N.Y.: Cornell University Press.

Keller, Evelyn Fox. 1983. "Gender and Science." In *Discovering Reality: Feminist Perspectives on Epistemology, Metaphysics, Methodology, and Philosophy of Science.* Edited by S. Harding and M. B. Hintikka. Dordrecht, Holland: D. Reidel.

Kolodny, Annette. 1980. "The Lady's Not for Spurning: Kate Millett and the Critics." In *Women's Autobiography: Essays in Criticism.* Edited by E. Jelinek. Bloomington: Indiana University Press.

Mason, Mary G. 1980. "Autobiographies of Women Writers." In *Autobiography, Essays Theoretical and Critical.* Edited by J. Olney. Princeton, N.J.: Princeton University Press.

Nussbaum, Felicity. 1988. "Eighteenth-Century Women's Autobiographical Commonplaces." In *The Private Self.* Edited by S. Benstock. London: Routledge.

Ochberg, Richard L. 1988. "Life Stories and the Psychosocial Construction of Careers." *Journal of Personality* 56:171–202.

Olney, James. 1980. *Autobiography: Essays Theoretical and Critical.* Princeton, N.J.: Princeton University Press.

Rabuzzi, Kathryn Allen. 1988. *Motherself: A Mythic Analysis of Motherhood.* Bloomington: Indiana University Press.

Rosenwald, George C. 1988. "A Theory of Multiple-Case Research." *Journal of Personality* 56:239–264.

Russ, Joanna. 1972. "What Can a Heroine Do? Or Why Women Can't Write." In *Images of Women in Fiction.* Edited by S. Koppelman Cornillon. Bowling Green, Ohio: University Popular Press.

Sayre, Robert F. 1980. "Autobiography and the Making of America." In *Autobiography, Essays Theoretical and Critical.* Edited by J. Olney. Princeton, N.J.: Princeton University Press.

Smith, Sidonie A. 1974. *Where I'm Bound: Patterns of Slavery and Freedom in Black American Autobiography.* Westport, Conn.: Greenwood Press.

———. 1987. *A Poetics of Women's Autobiography. Marginality and the Functions of Self-Representation.* Bloomington: Indiana University Press.

Sprinker, Michael. 1980. "Fictions of the Self: The End of Autobiography." In *Autobiography: Essays Theoretical and Critical.* Edited by J. Olney. Princeton, N.J.: Princeton University Press.

Stanton, Domna. 1984. *The Female Autograph.* Chicago: University of Chicago Press.

Tyler, Stephen. 1986. "Post-Modern Ethnography: From Document of the Occult to Occult Documents." In *Writing Culture.* Edited by J. Clifford and G. Marcus. Berkeley: University of California Press.

Woolf, Virginia. [1929] 1957. *A Room of One's Own.* New York: Harcourt, Brace, Jovanovich.

———. 1958. *Granite and Rainbow.* New York: Harcourt, Brace, Jovanovich.

8 Lives as Texts: Symptoms as Modes of Recounting in the Life Histories of Holocaust Survivors

Symptoms as Recountable

The purpose of this chapter is to explicate a concept first discussed in a much longer study on how Holocaust survivors retell their traumatic memories. That concept is that much of what we usually interpret as psychiatric symptoms among survivors can be understood more productively as modes of recounting. Summarizing this idea in the earlier study, I stated:

> This study explores the efforts of seven Holocaust survivors to recount the destruction they remember. In the terms of one survivor interviewed, the focus is on how survivors "make a story" of what is "*not* a story." "Recounting" is defined more broadly than is conventionally the case. Even what are usually understood as "symptoms"—for example, survivors' expressions of guilt— are here considered to be a part of their recounting. For stories of self-recrimination *are* recountable stories. Even at their most agonized, they only suggest deaths far more encompassing than anything communicable through the narratives of individual lives and hearts. (Greenspan, 1986, abstract)

I argue, then, that survivors' recounting should be understood to include accounts of guilt, rage, or despair *now* no less than accounts of terror *then*. For all such accounts are based on the attempt to give comprehensible, communicable form to memories that for survivors live on as the negation of comprehensible and communicable form. Set against those memories, all such accounts are attempts to "make a story" of what is "not a story."

Leon, the survivor who contributed the idea of "making a story" of what is "not a story," further reflected that the Holocaust "has to be described in human terms, it cannot *be* described otherwise." Expressions of guilt or despair, as agonized as they may be, remain communicative "human terms." They are cries of individual hearts that only hint at a world in which all such cries were silenced. Recalling one scene from that world, returning to a ghetto that had been liquidated only hours before, Leon continued:

the scene coming back from the arms factory into the ghetto. And the grayness
of the morning. And those dozens of bodies wherever you turned. . . .

You're *supposed* to react! You're supposed to run up! And race! Yell!
Scream! Utter! Emote! Show *anything* about it! Anything, whether it is—. . .

Entering the ghetto in a dead silence. Those columns marching in. . . .
Maybe a poet can evoke something approaching it, but even sound would be
out of place. There's no sound actually. There is no sound. It would have to be a
silent poem.

Survivors' symptoms—whatever can be shown, uttered, emoted now—are one
way survivors give voice to the traumatic silence they remember. Similarly,
Leon's explosion of words about the death of words is itself a responsive cry of the
sort that was suffocated at the time. But the scene itself, devoid of sound or human
emotion, remains irreducibly alien to such attempts to evoke it. "A landscape of
death," Leon concluded, "where, in effect, no one beholds it."

Along with expressing their particular pain, survivors' symptoms give partial
and provisional form to this greater desolation.[1] They function in recounting as
analogies, providing human terms for landscapes in which even screams were
muzzled. And therefore the stories symptoms tell—accounts of personal recrimination or devastation—are significant, in part, because of the "not story"
they only dimly suggest.

In the recounting perspective, then, symptoms are approached not in terms of
what they result from but rather in terms of what they point toward. This is in
marked contrast to conventional psychiatric approaches to survivors' symptoms.
In those approaches, survivors' guilts or depressions, for example, are typically
viewed as the sequelae of traumatic experience: the results to be explained. Once
such explanations are accomplished, the work of interpretation is complete.
Viewed as modes of recounting, by contrast, symptoms stand at the beginning of
our attempts to understand. For their own (relatively speaking) comprehensible
pain always directs us toward what *cannot* be comprehensibly retold.

Further on I shall present two survivors, Reuben and Victor, whose accounts
seem to lend themselves especially well to traditional psychiatric interpretations.
Indeed, Reuben and Victor not only speak of terrible guilts and rages but also
dramatically enact those emotions in their everyday choices and behavior. I shall
argue that even such enacted symptoms can be understood as modes of recounting:
in these instances, modes in which survivors' whole lives become their texts.
More particularly, I shall also suggest that lives become texts to this extent by
default—when survivors, driven to retell, are convinced of the futility of other
ways to give form to what they remember.

To follow these instances of lives as texts, a more general understanding of the
vicissitudes of recounting is needed. I turn, therefore, to a consideration of what is

always at issue for survivors when they attempt to communicate their memories and what are the constraints, inner and outer, that condition their efforts to do so.

The Vicissitudes of Recounting

Words for silence

Ideally, a study of survivors' recounting should begin with survivors actually recounting: if possible, face-to-face; if not, then at least through audiotape or videotape. Within the immediacy of actual recounting, we can directly follow as survivors' stories break against the "not story" that they try to convey but cannot. We listen as survivors' narratives dissolve into a flood of disparate images—all present, all demanding articulation. The abstract "search for communicable meanings" becomes *someone's* struggle for words, and someone's failure to find them. Elie Wiesel has said of survivors' memoirs: "Their sentences are terse, sharp, etched into stone. Every word contains a hundred, and the silence between the words strikes us as hard as the words themselves. They wrote not with words but against them" (Wiesel, 1978, 200). If the silence between the words strikes us in survivors' written memoirs, where only space on a page marks its presence, it strikes harder when we can hear that silence as an abrupt halt, a gasp for breath, the agonized deliberation that may surround the choice of a single word. In embodied speech, the silence between the words becomes a fully palpable, sometimes consuming, presence. We more easily grasp, as Wiesel implies, that survivors' words are themselves survivors of a struggle between a hundred other words and no words at all.

In face-to-face recounting, we are also more likely to recognize the urgency that survivors bring to their retelling. Much of this is implicit, reflected in the intensity of survivors' efforts, their persistence in spite of futility simultaneously voiced, their persistence in spite of futility obviously lived. Additionally, of course, survivors may speak explicitly about their purposes in recounting: to warn or to indict or to remember the world that was destroyed. As earlier suggested, recounting may also be a way of countering traumatic silence with active, and activating, speech. Whatever the specific purposes, many survivors recall a period immediately after liberation when they were simply compelled to speak about what they had witnessed and survived. Thus Paula, a survivor of Auschwitz-Birkenau, confided to her journal on her first day of liberation: "Up until the last minute, the crematorium is our nightmare. We are telling everybody about this, whether we want to or not. Our stories are only about the crematorium, whether we want to or not." In these first days of freedom, retelling the nightmare was less a decision than a necessity. As we shall hear, Paula soon learned to be more selective about both the contents and contexts of her recounting. But even now the drive to communicate the destruction can regain all its original intensity. Indeed, for survivors like Reuben and Victor, the drive to retell can become fully consuming. That is part of why, as I have suggested, they turn their lives into their texts.

Survivors are compelled to recount what they remember. But part of what they remember remains irreducibly alien and other, persisting not only "between the words" but also, as Wiesel said, "against them." How does this struggle affect the actual practice of recounting?

In fact, the conflict between meaning and memory overlies a more profound duality with which survivors must contend, a duality at the heart of their survival itself. For survivors, Wiesel has written, "The problem is not: to be or not to be, but rather: to be *and* not to be" (Wiesel, 1982a, 54, emphasis added). Other survivors similarly speak both of having died during the Holocaust yet continuing to live, both of creating a life after the destruction yet never having left it.[2] As contrary as it is to our usual logic and experience, this simultaneity of being and not-being should be understood literally. The copresence of ongoing death and ongoing life—without resolution or higher synthesis—is, for survivors, embodied reality. Thus Wiesel wrote of one of his survivor-protagonists: "Michael felt suddenly that someone was standing behind him. He turned abruptly: no one. And yet he felt a presence in the room, even an odor, an awareness. Only then did he understand that death is something other, something more, than the simple absence of life. Life may quit a body, a consciousness, but death does not necessarily follow. Just as death may invade a creature, though life has not yet departed" (Wiesel, 1982b, 91). The personification of death as an "other" is older than literature itself. But here that metaphor is transformed. Someone becomes something. The language becomes increasingly sensory and organic—a presence, an odor, an awareness. Death is no longer the inheritor of life or simply life's absence but an independent presence palpable at life's core.[3]

When survivors recount, part of what they must retell is the death that lives on in their awareness. No wonder, then, that any other pain to which they give voice— guilt, outrage, or despair—can only be analogous. Indeed, measured against the death survivors know, expressions of guilt or outrage must be considered affirmations of ongoing life. With guilt, for example, there is still hope—the possibility of atonement and reconciliation. Outrage implies still-imaginable and meaningful justice or vengeance. Relatively speaking, these kinds of pain remain communicable "human terms," drawn from experiences and memories of experiences that are *not* unqualifiably terminal.

Such "human terms" remain vulnerable. The death survivors know lives on, inhabiting the silence and pulling against whatever forms and meanings survivors may find to represent it. Indeed, recounting may begin to reactivate the experience of not-being itself, as Paula described: "You don't want to get into it to a deepness that you feel you cannot get out. There's a way to get out of it. You have to have that inner force. . . . But the more you pull yourself into nonexistence, just, like being in midair, you don't always have the inner strength."

In a diary entry written one year after liberation, Paula described the "deepness" more fully. Waking from an Auschwitz nightmare, she wrote:

> God, You took my mother away. And my little brother. Where did you take them? To the fire? I'm looking into the fire. And I think I would go completely crazy if I thought that You, God in Heaven, You are looking upon all of this. And You have not gone crazy. . . .
>
> *This* cannot be true. That I am here, on this earth, all by myself. That there is fire. That there are people. That there are bones. That there are the suffocated innocents. This is impossible! That ours, that mine, are there. . . .
>
> My pen wants to go on and on by itself. It is sliding from my hand. At times like this my strength leaves me. It leaves me when I see it all again. When I see the truth once more.

In the grasp of her memories, Paula would like to "go on and on." If it were possible, she would continue to recount terminal images of the destruction: fire, people, bones, suffocated children. But pulled too far into the "deepness," her pen slides from her hand as her strength slides from her body.

Paula's burst of discrete images, all immediately present ("there are . . . there are . . . there are"), is characteristic of survivors' recounting in a state of rising extremity. At such times narrative unfolding stops, and instead of a plot's trajectory through foreground and background, we hear a staccato of snapshot images, each present and surrounding. While this way of recounting is, like the story mode, also a mediating form, it is *as though* memories start to retell themselves at these times. Crowding in at a faster pace than the recounter can speak them, it is as though these memories each make their own claim and, together, start to *re*claim the recounter.

The dissolution of narrative in survivors' recounting, then, tends to signal a rekindling of the recounter's personal dissolution, of a slide back toward the "deepness." But even narrative and personal dissolution taken together only point to a wider circle of remembered destruction. Thus Leon asserts but does not describe the "landscape of death," trying to indicate what remains outside all his words and stories and even outside their collapse. Elie Wiesel likewise asserts that even at its most inclusive, no act of recounting can be more than the cry of one particular recounter, voiced at one terrible moment of extremity. Survivors' efforts to retell, writes Wiesel, "are feeble, stammering, unfinished, incoherent attempts to describe a single moment of being painfully, excruciatingly alive—the closing in of darkness for one particular individual, nothing more and perhaps much less" (Wiesel, 1978, 198). Beyond the "closing in of darkness" for that individual, a whole world of darkness persists, remembered but not recounted.

This is another reason why survivors' symptoms, as modes of recounting, can only be analogies, now doubly so. Just as their own pain only begins to suggest a more terminal agony, so that individual agony itself only begins to suggest a whole landscape of death. In this way, survivors' symptoms become analogies for deaths which, in a terrible sense, are themselves analogies.

Private nightmares

Such, then, are some of the intrinsic vicissitudes of survivors' recounting. Survivors have had to accept that at the center of their memories there are deaths that are not communicable. At most, those deaths could be pointed toward, suggested but never grasped in their retelling. But this acceptance has not reduced survivors' drive to recount what *might* be conveyed, however "feeble, stammering, unfinished." Thus Paula did want to "go on and on" in her journal; Leon searches for "human terms" and for ways to compose a "silent poem."

From the point of view of sharing what *could* be conveyed, the problem has been that the inner silence survivors know has been matched by an outward one: the limits of their words has been matched by an absence of listeners. Describing the isolation survivors have experienced since liberation, Wiesel writes:

> The disappointment came almost at once. As they reentered the world, they found themselves in another kind of exile, another kind of prison. . . . They were disturbing misfits who deserved charity, but nothing else. . . .
>   In the beginning they tried to raise their voices—however shyly, however clumsily. In vain. People turned away. . . . And so they began to feel superfluous in a society that continued to repudiate them, thus forcing them into cynicism or despair. (Wiesel, 1978, 193–194)

Like many survivors, Paula remembers the repudiation. "Hush up your bad dreams," she recalls being told, "it's not going to happen, hush it away." Further, she describes the relationship between ongoing "exile" and *not* "hushing it up." She continued:

> Also, we were ashamed. We were made to feel ashamed. Because we had to survive again. . . . Would you have been friends with me if I would be morbid? . . .
>   So I covered up. "I'm fine, Joe. *That's* not *me*! How are *you*?"

Not only were survivors not heard, but the very act of recounting risked stigma. "We wouldn't talk about it because we didn't want to be different," Paula summarized. "We didn't want to be pointed to as the 'abnormal people.' . . . We tried to get along, you know, 'I'm an American too!' "

It is significant that these reflections do not apply to Paula's experience immediately after liberation. Discussing what she calls her "first steps back to life," Paula remembers with the greatest possible fondness the group of former prisoners of war with whom she happened to be liberated. They conveyed a care and a feeling of solidarity that were scarcely conceivable after the degradation she had so recently endured. In particular, shocked themselves by the first reports coming back from the liberated death camps, these men desperately wanted to hear survivors' own accounts. Thus at the same moment that Paula herself could speak only of the nightmare—"telling everybody," as she wrote, "whether we want to or not"—she had listeners who genuinely wanted to hear.

Only after this initial period, then, did Paula learn to "hush up" her recounting. The process of suppression emerges clearly in her diary, which itself became an increasingly important private context of recounting as she experienced growing isolation. Thus two years after liberation, now far from the group with whom she first found freedom, Paula confided to her journal: "God, what's wrong with me? I'm choked with my own cry. I'd like to cry but I can't. Today I came home all angered, for no reason."

In a nearby entry, Paula seemed to know why she had choked her own cry and why she was so angry. "It's hard to be smart," she noted, "but it's harder yet, with a smart head, to live as though ignorant." Three years later, Paula was in greater conflict about what she had and had not done with her "smart head." What was most clear was the pain of having to remember in isolation. Thus in 1950, writing on the fifth anniversary of her liberation, she reflected:

Five years is like half a century when you live your life with bitterness and reminiscing. Even when you are at a party, and you are in a good mood, later you realize your guilt. Is this anger? Is this conscience? Is this self-consciousness or self-criticism?

But why? What do you want, my soul, if I can call you that? Five years. It's not long to write it down, and it's very easy to pronounce it. But, when I remember, I am carried back even clearer than anytime before. But why?

I don't know what I am. I don't know when I'm doing right or wrong. Am I right when I am thinking? And *for what* I am thinking? Many times, I think I was just born for trouble. To be a burden and sorrow to everybody, because I cannot laugh. They say, "If you laugh, everybody laughs with you. And if you cry, you cry alone."

Yes, my diary, I am here in America. . . . But nobody's right and nobody's wrong. Only the truth is right. But that is so rare. Now I'm pushing the years back. For me, that's like putting the clock back a few minutes. Time elapses, but the impossible does not fade from my eyes.

As remains characteristic of her, Paula questions herself in this entry as much as those around her. Is she angry or guilty? Right for what she is thinking or wrong? She only knows that "the truth is right," and the truth is an impossible that would not fade from her eyes.

Looking back (for the first time) at these entries more than thirty years after writing them, Paula had mixed feelings. "It scares me to think how angry I was then," she noted, "how desperate and how frustrated." But she was also still attached to the young woman she had been and relieved to rediscover the intensity of her feelings *against* the deaths and silences she had endured: "Now I look back. It's frightening. But I am able to realize that I still had feelings. I wasn't dead altogether. There was still a soul deep down that wanted to come to the surface. But, you know, at the time I didn't realize it." It was also in the context of remembering these feelings that Paula first spoke of the general isolation of survivors. She recalled:

> What irked me at the time, as I think back, I felt I was the only one who felt that way. Everybody's normal! They didn't see my principles. . . .
> So I had to really suppress it. . . . Because everybody lived, "This is to forget!" . . . Maybe other people did the same thing I did. I don't know. To me, I was the only one.

Actually, Paula did not feel quite the only one. Along with having her journal, she had a small group of correspondents who did share her principles. She continued: "I decided, well, I can still do it for myself. I don't have to do it for anybody else. And it was helpful. I always had close people in my life that I could really write to. . . . I had close people that I could communicate with. And that was very helpful to me. For many years, instead of scribbling to myself, I scribbled to them." Paula thus sustained her recounting within this more private, limited sphere. As she often says, she learned to focus on what she could accomplish rather than dwell on what she could not. But clearly "doing it for herself" was far from Paula's original goal.

Leon, too, has had to accept more limited possibilities. As we have heard, he often emphasizes the inherent limits of recounting to explain his frustration. Thus he exclaims:

> Will it ever come out? That someone else will understand? I wouldn't mind if I could paint it. I wouldn't mind if I could do it in any fashion at all. Because I'm living almost in a—, my bitterness is that the Holocaust, the lesson of the Holocaust, will never be learned. . . .
> And therefore the illusions under which we labored—that learning the reality of the Holocaust will maybe prevent another one from happening, will maybe cure mankind of this madness—I think it doesn't come to pass. . . . It is not likely to come to a realization. Because no words are adequate to acquaint the people with the reality of the Holocaust.

The Holocaust cannot be communicated, says Leon, because there are no adequate words. Along with the inner silence, however, Leon also speaks of the outward one. He continues: "No words are adequate to acquaint the people with the reality of the Holocaust. But, then, another thought comes in. Supposing they do. Isn't there going to be a certain reluctance to submerge yourself in it? Who, on his own volition, will want to absorb the horror of it all?" Leon has answers to these questions. Indeed, he expects to find responsive listeners as little as he expects to find adequate words, and the problem goes beyond "a certain reluctance." "Deeply ingrained within me," said Leon, "is the conviction that the world didn't learn anything from the Holocaust and definitely doesn't regret anything about the Holocaust." Like Paula, he once had greater hopes. During the period immediately after liberation, he recalls being "young and naïve" enough to believe that "the whole world" was going to be changed by knowledge of the destruction. Leon himself was going to write about his experiences. Yet he now concludes:

> But it is a good indication of advanced age—of being jaded and cynical and maybe realism—that I feel defeated before I start. The world just doesn't care. My goal would be more modest: to impress Jewish generations to come on the Holocaust. . . . Do I hope thereby to avoid a repetition of it? This is all futile! At least, at least, they will not be caught unaware . . . as we were, when the Holocaust caught up with us.

Leon thus also finds a more constricted circle for his recounting: future Jewish generations and, in particular, his own children. But this is a far more "modest" circle than the one he had anticipated, and it is surrounded by a far more terrible futility. Perhaps for that reason, Leon only rarely does speak of his memories, either with his children or anyone else. Likewise, if recounting to his children is now Leon's "legacy"—as such recounting is often celebrated in contemporary rhetoric—it is clearly a legacy by default. It is the result of Leon not finding listeners anywhere else.

Leon's own term for the result is "private nightmares": memories that grow in horror exactly because they *are* private—in his phrase, "outside the public domain." When referring to such memories, Leon drew on an analogy to the silencing usually known *only* in nightmares. He commented: "Some individual horror stories—, it becomes almost, I don't know if you—, I remember reading somewhere about somebody having a nightmare. And he feels like screaming, and no words come out. You know, this horrible feeling—if only I could scream and call for help! I'd be all right! But no words come out. And somehow you feel the same way." Memories that are "private nightmares" are doubly unspeakable: first, because the nightmare itself muffles words; second, because that horror is relived in isolation. The forms of survivors' recounting are conditioned by both kinds of silencing.

Lives as Texts

What is it like to have lived a nightmare and not be able to retell it? If it were possible, Paula's pen would "go on and on by itself." Leon would "paint it" or "do it in any fashion at all." But constrained by both an inner and outer silence, their goals become more "modest." Survivors like Paula and Leon find more private, limited contexts of recounting. They retell what stories they can, choose the most promising situations for their recounting being heard, and bide their time. At times they wonder, as Leon put it, whether they have "learned to cope forever or whether, at a certain point, the past takes the upper hand."

Survivors like Reuben and Victor cannot bide their time. Earlier in their lives, they too accepted more "modest" goals. But being older and feeling close to the ends of their lives, both Reuben and Victor now feel they are out of time. For them, it appears that the past *has* taken the upper hand, and what the past demands is to be retold.

Paradoxically, this renewed urgency leads Reuben and Victor to contexts of recounting that are even more constricted than Paula's diary or Leon's occasional conversations with his children. Feeling that urgency in isolation, Reuben and Victor now draw on the medium of their lives to represent what they remember. Their recounting consists in large part of everyday enactment. Meanwhile their listeners become whoever would recognize that Reuben's and Victor's lives *have* become texts—individually constructed and privately performed dramas of remembrance.

It is important to emphasize that the dramas that Reuben and Victor do enact— one about guilt, the other about outrage—remain analogic. The stories that survivors live, no less than the stories survivors tell, only hint at deaths that remain unrecounted in *any* mode. At the same time, when survivors must draw on their lives to give form to those deaths, when actions and not only sentences must become "stammering" or "unfinished," lives are necessarily *de*formed in the attempt. In different terms, the deaths and the "deepness" survivors know pull most palpably when they must be most palpably represented.

How can single individuals convey the destruction of entire communities? How can they give voice to all those other voices, and to their silencing, without their own speech becoming shrill and distorted? How can they give form to whole worlds they carry in "invisible cemeteries" (Wiesel, 1978, 200) without turning themselves into perpetually wandering ghosts?

Reuben does try to convey a world that has been destroyed. Recurrently he speaks of the "whole life," the "complete culture and ethnic group" of prewar Polish Jewry, and attempts to describe that life's diversity and unity:

The whole variety of the Jewish people—you know, we had, within the Ortho-dox, we had Hasidic Jews. And we also had the Misnagadim, who didn't believe in the Hasidic rabbis. . . .

And then, even between those two groups, within them, you had some who were pro-Israel before the war. And some who were against Israel before the war. . . .

Then you had the other Jews. They were not Orthodox. You had the Zionists and the Bund—they were socialists, you know—and then you had the Communists . . . the whole thing.

And then you had, in those two, you had the intellectuals and among the non-Orthodox, too, you had the intellectuals. And you had, in both, the regular workers who were not intellectuals. . . .

I'm just saying, you had a complete—, the whole thing . . . so many different characters, good and bad, the whole range.

Thus Reuben begins to enumerate the opposing and overlapping circles that made up the world he remembers. Each time he does so, he ends with that world's fate: "Good and bad, you know. The whole range. It's—, you don't see it anymore. The whole range. It's all disappeared."

As one whose life was enmeshed in that world, Reuben tells us that he too has disappeared. He has become in fact a wandering ghost, more and more lost as the years have passed.

Like the Destruction of the Temple, the Diaspora of the Jewish people—as years went by, they felt it more and more. I mean, the same thing is with this. . . . The same thing, even a parent who loses a child—I mean, normal conditions—sometimes they never forget it. Everyday they go around, you know, they never forget it. That's normal conditions.

This is something terrible. Something more terrible. This was not normal conditions. They cut you off completely from *shoresh,* from your roots. You're uprooted completely. You're lost, completely. Everything. . . .

I'm lost too. I'm like a *gilgul.* You know what a *gilgul* is? A *gilgul* is, you know, the Jewish people believe, especially the Hasidim or the mystic Cabalists, they believe that the *shmos,* the soul, that the soul sometimes comes back. The same way the Hindus believe, the Jewish mystics believe too. So they say, sometimes a soul isn't that lucky. It doesn't go back into a human being. It just wanders around. It can't get in. So he's lost. And they call it a *gilgul.* He's lost. That's what I'm saying. I'm a lost soul.

Reuben's death, for that is what he describes, is further confirmed by an even more intimate dissolution than the loss of his roots. Recalling the "closing in of darkness" within the destruction, Reuben said:

It's very hard, you know what I mean. 'Til this day, I don't know. You see, they got you down. First, you're weak, you were half-dead. You didn't have no, no strength anymore. No desire to fight. Even to live anymore, you know what I mean. You had no desire, no strength, nothing. You lost your courage. You lost everything. . . .

It's very hard. Like someone who has a terminal illness, who is sick, who is dying. . . . He doesn't care anymore, you know what I mean. The same thing is with this, you know.

Such memories of an inner and outer death pervade Reuben's reflections. Drawing on analogies from "normal conditions"—a terminal illness, the death of a child, even the lostness of a gilgul—he tries to convey a still more encompassing destruction.

Of course, Reuben is not a disembodied spirit without substance or locale. The death he knows persists alongside ongoing life. The very culture that has been destroyed continues to provide ways to describe the experience of that loss: *as* a gilgul or one without shoresh. Through such terms, in part, Reuben retells and lives the story of his bereavement.

The new world has also provided imagery within which Reuben can situate his memories and give them communicable form. In this case, he "situates" literally—for the images are of an actual place: the abandoned, inner city neighborhood where Reuben has maintained his store. He reflected:

Sometimes, you know, I feel, I'm in a bad, my store is in a bad section of the city. Sometimes I, maybe if I would have wanted I could have moved out years back. But sometimes I just feel, I don't know—, it reminds me sometimes like, the buildings, you know, all boarded up, you know, sometimes it reminds me like, like the ghetto. . . .

Sometimes, I was thinking to myself, you know, unconsciously, maybe I didn't want to move out. I could have moved out . . . because over there it's very depressed, you know, the boarded-up buildings. From the riots in the city. After the riots in the city, you know, they never did nothing to it after, in those parts of the city. I don't know. It reminds me sometimes of the ghetto. The ghetto—, everything like, it's a lot like in the ghetto. Everything was boarded up. And ruined. You know what I mean. Maybe, maybe I'm punishing myself. I don't know. It could be. I don't know.

Here, then, Reuben gives form to his memories through the media of bricks and decaying storefronts—and through his self-punishing decision not to leave.

Like Reuben, Victor also is consumed by loss. He returns constantly to images of generations cut off from the future and erased from history itself. But Victor does not speak as a ghostly remnant of the past but as its interrogator. In Victor's own expression, he speaks as "the prosecutor": "Some Jews went ahead. They continue it, to marry again. And they were lucky that they were saved. I said, 'No, I am *not* lucky.' I am not satisfied with this. *They*! The six million that was killed. Because of this I am not satisfied that I survived. I don't call it a miracle. . . . So I became the prosecutor. And I am still the prosecutor." Contrasting himself with those who simply "went ahead" to "continue it," Victor takes the role of the six million left behind. He looks back and prosecutes for them.

The object of Victor's prosecution, however, is not other survivors or even the rest of the world that has "gone ahead" since the Holocaust. Rather Victor takes God as his accused and the Bible as his source of evidence. In fact, critically reading the Bible had become an obsession for Victor, and being the prosecutor specifically meant this now all-consuming study. Victor explained:

> I read it over twelve times, the Old Testament . . . I feel that when I sit down at the Bible I am a prosecutor. And the Bible is the material that I am trying to find something to criticize it. To criticize it. . . .
>
> I was still interested in my background. But besides this, I say, "God, where are you? Are you dumb? Are you deaf? You don't see nothing! Are you blind? Or are you *not at all?*"
>
> So why does these people fool me? Why so many thousands of generations want to put down the knowledge of religion, the authority of God, and the knowledge of everything in the way to live? Why the Ten Commandments? Why *everything?* Why was this bluffing going on?

In Victor's scheme, then, it is God's survival and religious tradition as such that must be questioned. The "bluffing" had to be criticized and unmasked.

Seeing *through* God and tradition is in fact the essence of Victor's critical method. Prosecuting means getting underneath the text and getting behind it. Said Victor:

> Religion is built one way. It was put away rough. Then the words were polished up, and the means was polished up, to suit better the sanctity and the purpose.
>
> King Solomon says, "Keep off your feet from God's house." Why? Where one can touch it, where one can go in, it loses the flavor of sanctity. It isn't that much at all. But if the Jews have to stay *outside* they hear only the crying from the calves, from the sheep, from the High Priest. They give it more reverence. . . .
>
> In their time, people was blind. They worshipped something far away . . . *I* want to see it closer.

What does the prosecutor see beneath the "polished words"? Most centrally, he insists that there are people beneath the words, whole generations behind the text, who have been left out and left behind. In particular, Victor focuses on the generations of Cain, who disappear from the biblical narrative without even a marker of their passage.

> The generations of Cain, after he married, he went over to the city of Nod and he married over there. They are not now nothing. . . . There was nobody to bother with it. And even Moses didn't bother with it. Because he didn't write it in. . . .
>
> From Cain, nobody give it over from generation to generation. And they

disappear in the Flood. From Adam, after his marriage, they give it over. There was a scripture, and they give it over. And Moses put everything on paper. Everything.

Clearly, Moses did *not* put everything on paper. Some generations "even Moses didn't bother with." Charging Moses with that omission, Victor spends his retirement prosecuting stories that leave out too many and too much.

What, then, should we make of *these* stories of Reuben and of Victor? Reuben himself suggests a psychiatric approach—that he "unconsciously didn't want to move out" because of unconscious self-punishment—and certainly we typically would interpret Reuben's behavior in terms of "survivor guilt" or "aggression turned inward." Similarly, we might view Victor's prosecution as an externalizing defense against guilt—*they* are the ones who abandon the dead—and perhaps also as an "identification with the aggressor" in becoming "the prosecutor."

In fact, Reuben and Victor each offer further support for such interpretations. When Reuben spoke about not moving his store, he contrasted himself with survivors who are "angry all the time, angry at the whole world." "I'm the other way around maybe," he added, suggesting that his self-punishment could indeed be his way of managing a potentially endless rage. Conversely, Victor interprets his aggressive prosecuting as his way of managing guilt, most specifically his guilt for having married a Catholic and thus, as he now experiences it, having betrayed the past. He explains: "I am trying to justify myself. In order not to let the sorrow grow higher. To keep down the pain, the misgiving against myself. . . . With this, I can go ahead. I calm my pain. When I say, 'It's *him*! *He* is guilty.' Not *I* am guilty." Becoming the prosecutor, Victor says, gives *himself* a way of "going ahead," whatever misgivings he (as Cain) might have.

No doubt Reuben and Victor are correct about these dynamic relationships between their anger and their guilt. In themselves, these affects persist for Reuben and Victor *in exactly the same way as they do for all the rest of us*. Anger or guilt or both, they are part of what Reuben would call "normal conditions."

The point, from a recounting point of view, is that part of what these emotions also do, for survivors, is to give comprehensible and communicable form to memories that are *not* from "normal conditions." Enacted or retold, they function once again as analogies: ways of finding "human terms" or "making a story" of what is "not a story." In Victor's own terms, the stories of one man's prosecution or another's self-punishment are like religion's "polished words." Relative to the Holocaust, such dramas sustain, even enable, faith.

As earlier noted, Reuben draws on analogies from "normal conditions" throughout his recounting. Thus he says his experience is "like a gilgul" or "like someone who has a terminal illness" or "like the Destruction of the Temple," even while suggesting, often enough, that the deaths he knows are not really like any of these other circumstances. Similarly, though the ruins Reuben does not leave "remind" him of the ghetto and are even "a lot like in the ghetto," the inner city is *not* the ghetto he remembers. However "unconscious" the forces that hold him, he now remains by choice: "I could have moved out," "Maybe I didn't want to move out." No such choice characterized his original imprisonment. Indeed, the very capacity to "want" was then destroyed, as Reuben often repeated: "You didn't have no strength anymore. No desire to fight. Even to *live* anymore. . . . You had no desire, no strength, nothing."

Emerging from such devastation, Reuben's not moving his store is an act of will—of want and of choice—*against* the terminal despair. More specifically, it is an act of intended remembrance that Reuben situates not only within the inner city but also within another story of recurrent returns to a grave. Thus Reuben cites as antecedent for his own story the following traditional legend:

Have you heard of Rabbi Nahman of Bratslav? He was the only Hasidic rabbi, the grandson of the Baal Shem Tov. He was buried in Uman. Uman, that's in Russia, you know. So his Hasidim, they used to call them *Teute Hasidim*. You know what *teute* means? Dead. The Dead Hasidim. After he died, maybe two hundred fifty years ago, the Hasidim never named another rabbi. Usually, the Hasidim, if a rabbi dies, they name his son, or grandson, or somebody as a rabbi, somebody as the leader. After Reb Nahman of Bratslav died, they never named another rabbi after him. They used to go only to the grave. That's why they call them *Teute Hasidim*, because they have a dead rabbi. They used to have a song. In Yiddish it rhymes, "Why should we worry what's going to be tomorrow? Let's worry what we did wrong yesterday." Maybe we can do right, what we did wrong yesterday. Maybe we can do right about it.

However compromised the analogy, there have been other unprecedented losses, leading to precedented refusals to move on or to "move out."

In fact, the analogy *is* highly compromised. Within the story of the Dead Hasidim, guilt and self-questioning retain their meaning: "Maybe we can do right what we did wrong yesterday, we can do right about it." Turning back to the Holocaust, Reuben first asserts that there, too, one can learn from the past. Soon, however, he loses his way within the ending that past contains.

The past is very important. You may have a bad past, but still you may correct certain things. . . . So it's very important for the Jewish people, for years to come, to have it written down what happened, how did it happen.

There's a lot of pro and con. What they could do and what they could not do. But I'm just saying—, you see, I don't think so. The people of Europe, the Jewish people, it's never going to be like it was anymore, you know. I'm just saying, they were a good people. They had their own, we had our own culture, our own writers, our own poets. A complete ethnic group, you know what I mean. It's lost. It's never going to be anymore.

Deriving lessons from the past implies continuity: the capacity to "correct certain things" and move on. In the wake of the extinction that Reuben recalls, there is *no* moving on. Whatever may be learned from the past is superseded by the fact of its destruction.

The story Reuben lives thus remains fragile and provisional. Still, framed by his guilt, his ghetto, and the legend of the Dead Hasidim, it *is* a communicable story. The irreducible deaths that Reuben knows are translated into a pain, self-punishment, that *can* be given voice. Terminal despair becomes a choice to stay and to remember. One set of ruins, demonstrable and present, stands for another. A single grave in Russia represents millions of graves that exist nowhere. Within these substitutions, Reuben can remember the Dead Hasidim and join with the Dead Hasidim, as though they were still alive.

For all its own pain, the process by which Victor "makes a story" of the "not story" may be even more clear. Indeed, the whole drama of prosecuting God has the quality of allegory, most obviously because it *is* God whom Victor prosecutes. Within that frame, all the anonymous enemies and opponents are condensed into a single One. Victor's relationship with that One is characterized by an ambivalence—indeed, a depth of relationship itself—totally absent from the anonymous extermination he remembers. Above all, because God does remain an ultimate mystery—even after a prosecutor's most determined efforts to "see it closer"—the possibility of some eventual reconciliation or redeeming revelation can still be imagined. In fact, Victor seems to give God the best possible chance. For it is not, directly, the facts of the Holocaust with which he indicts the Creator but rather the far more ambiguous claims of those like Cain or Cain's descendants. It remains up to others to decide what else the Flood, and who else such forgotten generations, might represent. Victor himself does no deconstructing: he stays within his chosen text.

The drama of prosecuting God may also strike us as allegorical because it is a familiar, traditional story. Many others have questioned the loyalty and existence of the other partner in the Covenant. Victor finds his own primary antecedent in Maimonides, another "revealer of secrets." Said Victor: "When Maimonides wrote his books, he revealed a lot of things that Jewish geniuses—ones before—did not reveal. But Maimonides said, 'Since no one before me revealed it, and I know it, if I will not reveal it, maybe I will die with a heavy heart, that I didn't reveal it. So I take it upon my body, and my soul, the sin. And I will open the secrets now. And put it in print.'" As Reuben situated his story in the tradition of those who question themselves, Victor draws on the tradition of those who question outwardly. Following Maimonides, his story becomes an experiment in how much fact can be revealed and fidelity remain intact. More particularly, it is an experiment in how much death can be revealed and the story itself survive.

The answer is only so much. In the grasp of his memories, the images Victor sees do their own "unmasking." Now, as during the destruction, they provide *too* much "revelation." Thus Victor recalls a moment near the darkest center of the slaughter—the gas chambers and burial trenches of Treblinka:

> I saw the smoke. I heard the motor. At the time, I didn't realize—, I was thinking the motor was digging the graves, not producing carbon monoxide. . . .
>
> I was feeling like a sheep that's tied up in the slaughterhouse. And an animal *knows*. When they let them loose, behind the fence in the stockyard, they feel the death. . . . Man *doesn't* know that here is a danger. If he doesn't see nothing, he doesn't know.
>
> After, I hear the cries of the people: "АНННН!" and finished. "АНННН!" and finished. And I see the smoke, the black smoke. And all the Ukrainians with the guns, guarding . . . and here people undress.
>
> I say, "What is this?" I asked once. I was working close to the gas chamber. So I looked down. And I asked somebody, "What do they do with those people over there?" He answered me, "They send them to Heaven."
>
> So I was sure. They was killed. I didn't want to believe. I wanted to believe only what I and my eyes see.

In the immediate presence of the killing, Victor does *not* want to "see it closer." Even knowing, he does not want to believe, and hearing the cries from these sacrificed "lambs and calves," Victor would restore the "secrets."

Paradoxically, then, by becoming the prosecutor Victor actually *adds* mystery and "polish." Within that role, his revelations are indirect, quite unlike the revelations he endured. Likewise, the unmasking the prosecutor does is strictly limited by his choice of text, evidence, and accused—all of which keep the Holocaust itself at one remove. Only gradually does the story Victor lives, and the relentless persistence with which he lives it, begin to suggest the obliteration of stories he remembers.

Elie Wiesel has written that "the essence of a Hasidic legend" is "an attempt to humanize fate" (Wiesel, 1972, 257). So the stories that Reuben and Victor live, part traditional legend and part personal construction, "humanize" their own fates and make those fates communicable. Still, when survivors must enact their remembrance, there is no cause for celebration. Whatever may be "humanized" in the process, the lives of individual recounters are burdened and reduced by the deaths they must convey.

This process of reduction is particularly evident in Reuben's experience. Originally, he sought to recount through actual texts, accounts written rather than lived. Like Paula and Leon, Reuben remembered his initial drive to recount and recalled the articles he submitted to a Yiddish newspaper. "I was young at the time, soon after the war. . . . This was not stories. It was more like hopeful letters, hopeful articles, you know what I mean. About the survival. Like giving hope in the survival, that the Jewish people survived. Like in Hebrew they say, 'The eternity of the Jewish people is not a lie.' It's not a lie. It's actually a true thing." Looking back from out of his present grief, Reuben found it an effort even to repeat the messages of hope he had once written. Clearly, only after this period did he begin to live the story of his loss.

During the intervening years in fact Reuben several times attempted to write again. Now it *was* "stories" he intended—specifically, a novel in which he hoped to contextualize the Holocaust within the "whole life" of Jewish culture before the war. Reuben explained: "I tried to write a few times. Not a history, or documents. But I tried to write a novel around it, *around* it. . . . I tried to write a novel, not about the Holocaust, but about the whole life, the *whole life* before the Holocaust, with the Holocaust included. You know what I mean, the whole life. How it was . . . a novel around different characters. How it was." This was the point in our conversations at which Reuben started to describe "how it was"—the "whole range" of groups that he remembered. The stories of these groups and of various characters within them were to be the "human terms" that framed the destruction. Simultaneously, those stories would commemorate the life and lives that were destroyed. Reuben continued: "To me, writing the story would be like a monument to the Jewish people. The way they lived and the way they worked and the way they dealt with people. I mean, how it was—, how happy they were, and sad they were, at different times."

Reuben never completed his novel. In part, he said, he stopped because of the pure pain of trying to remember: "You have to live it through, back again. You have to concentrate, and go back in again." He also suggested that he stopped because of the negative reaction his writing might evoke. "Who knows what goes on in people's minds?" Reuben asked—but he did not hesitate to list pity, indifference, disbelief, and outright rejection as responses he had anticipated.

Between the depths of an inner silence and the expectation of an outward one, Reuben's pages thus lay unfinished. But his effort to recount did not end. I have been suggesting, rather, he eventually turned to his *individual* "whole life" to give form to his memories. The story he *lives* became his monument to the world he recalls, and to its destruction. As I have emphasized, in transforming his life into his text, he has found "human terms" and "made a story" of what is "not a story." But the story he lives is also more private, more obscure, and certainly more personally disfiguring, than the one he might have written.

The Silence of Enactment

The stories of Reuben and Victor call our attention to a third kind of silence critical to our understanding the recounting of Holocaust survivors. Along with the traumatic silence of memory and the extended silence of absent listeners there is also the silence of enactment: a silence derived from some survivors having been driven to live rather than to speak their retelling. The result is a mode of recounting even further from the "public domain" than the privatization of memory because of survivors' conscious decisions (in response to outward sanctions) to constrict or suppress their retelling. The result is also a mode of recounting that severely reduces the lives of recounters.

The purpose of this chapter has been, first, to aid our recognition of survivors' lived stories *as* recounting. We conventionally view such enactments in only psychiatric terms, as symptoms, and thus reinforce their muteness as memory. To work against that muteness through the recounting perspective provided here is the second purpose. Most ideally, as we are able to receive what survivors are attempting to convey, the process of privatization would be reversed. The more obscure language of symptoms and enactments would evolve back to spoken remembrance. To whatever degree, silence would yield to words or perhaps to a silence that is now experienced as shared.

NOTES

1. The phrase "partial and provisional form" comes from Alvin Rosenfeld (1980), who used it to describe the limits of literary attempts to communicate the Holocaust. Of the various studies on Holocaust literature, those that I have found particularly helpful in interpreting survivors' spoken recounting include Rosenfeld (1980), Ezrahi (1980), Fine (1978), Langer (1982), and the writing of Elie Wiesel.
2. Among published memoirs, see Livia Bitton-Jackson (1980, 247) or Kitty Hart (1982, 24–25). Regarding the duality of ongoing life and ongoing death in Wiesel's writing in particular, see Lawrence Langer's (1982) excellent discussion.
3. The best scientific discussion of the relations between massive psychic trauma, inner surrender, and death comes in Krystal's recent collection (1988, 137–169).

REFERENCES

Bitton-Jackson, Livia. 1980. *Elli: Coming of Age in the Holocaust.* New York: Quadrangle, Times Books.

Ezrahi, Sidra Dekoven. 1980. *By Words Alone: The Holocaust in Literature.* Chicago: University of Chicago Press.

Fine, Ellen S. 1978. *Legacy of Night: The Literary Universe of Elie Wiesel.* Albany: State University of New York Press.

Greenspan, Henry. 1986. "Who Can Retell: On the Recounting of Life History by Holocaust Survivors." Ph.D. diss., Brandeis University.

Hart, Kitty. 1982. *Return to Auschwitz.* New York: Atheneum.

Krystal, Henry. 1988. *Integration and Self-Healing: Affect, Trauma, Alexithymia*. Hillsdale, N.J.: Analytic Press.

Langer, Lawrence. 1982. *Versions of Survival*. Albany: State University of New York Press.

Rosenfeld, Alvin. 1980. *A Double Dying: Reflections on Holocaust Literature*. Bloomington: Indiana University Press.

Wiesel, Elie. 1972. *Souls on Fire*. Translated by Marion Wiesel. New York: Summit Books.

———. 1978. "A Plea for the Survivors." In *A Jew Today*. Translated by Marion Wiesel. New York: Random House.

———. 1982a. *The Accident*. Translated by Anne Borchardt. New York: Bantam Books.

———. 1982b. *The Town beyond the Wall*. Translated by Stephen Becker. New York: Schocken.

9 African-Americans and the Pursuit of Wider Identities: Self-Other Understandings in Black Female Narratives

D uring the Middle Passage—the journey from Africa to the Americas—
more than eleven million Africans died in chains. Those who survived
the journey were both strong and lucky. But their survival in the new
world would require more than luck and stamina. Driven by fear and mutual care,
these transplanted Africans, originating in different tribes, adopted one another.
Children whose parents had been killed in the struggle against enslavement found
new families that gave them love, understanding, and support in a new and hostile
world. African-American unity began with the Middle Passage.

Over the centuries these bonds of kinship have endured because of racism and
segregation. The newer trend toward increased racial and ethnic tolerance, however, has stimulated changes in the traditional unity of African-Americans. The
increase in interracial intimacy and marriage, the topic of this chapter, is only one
index of a more general process preoccupying many African-Americans—the
process of renegotiating self-identity.

Whereas once it was clear that anyone with any African ancestry was de facto
and de jure black, today many African-Americans choose to define themselves in
other terms. An apparent increase in racial tolerance has enabled many to claim an
enlarged self-identity. For example, Julius Lester, a noted black novelist who has
repeatedly come under criticism from members of the black community, asserted
that blacks are guilty of "black anti-Semitism" and has shown a preference for
white women in his private life. Responding to one black critic of his book *All Is
Well,* Lester counters by saying that

> the reader is asked to confront the many facets of identity as they exist in one
> person. I am black, but blackness is not the totality of my identity. *It is not even
> the core of my identity.* . . . I have the freedom to define myself as I think best
> (after all, who's living my life?) and if I have to fight white and black America
> to retain that freedom, so be it. Blackness is not my identity but an aspect only,

which I do not denigrate in racial self-hatred, nor elevate in panegyrics of narcissistic racial self-love. To do either would be childish. [*All Is Well* is] . . . the first autobiographical statement by a black mystic. . . . The mystical experience is as incomprehensible to the non-mystic as the black experience is to non-blacks. *All Is Well* is the story of a black man living with and mediating the tension between the racial reality and the mystical reality where always and forever, all is, indeed, quite well (Lester, 1982, pp. 84–85, emphasis added).

Lester seems to experience black and white critics as equally oppressive. He does not acknowledge that satisfying one's compelling personal needs does not also automatically change the social reality and may indeed do damage to collective liberation. What is problematic in Lester, as in those blacks who pimp black women and destroy black youth through drugs, is the suggestion that we are monads, racially unconnected except in an historical sense; that we are thus free to choose against within-group cohesion; and that this choice has no consequences for racial survival.

Living in this society, African-Americans must develop a greater tolerance for divergent value orientations. But this must be accompanied by a reduction in racism and other forms of oppression in the rest of the culture. Until then, individual African-Americans who pursue nontraditional interracial intimacy will have to struggle with the tensions such choices create.

Black America has never had the power of whites to enforce its sanctions against blacks who deviate from racial solidarity. Thus Lester is misguided in equating his black critics with white racists. Regrettably, the personal injury and alienation felt by Lester and others are often discounted by critics merely because these sentiments have often clashed with the group's demands for personal sacrifice. They must not be discounted.

This chapter seeks to clarify how personal choice detached from a regard for social realities may founder in a sea of self-misunderstanding. (The phenomenon under discussion is far from rare and perhaps increasingly common.) I begin with a brief elaboration of the singular predicament of the African-American within a racist society. I then cite case material to illustrate how current changes in American society may interact with African-Americans' own racial ambivalence.

American Contradiction and African-American Ambivalence

A contradiction lies embedded within racism that has resulted in ambivalent tendencies among whites. Frederick Douglass's owner once said: "I may be a Christian, but I am not a fool; I am not giving up my slaves." Blacks sometimes experienced kindness from whites, sometimes extreme brutality. Individual blacks' views of whites varied accordingly. But collectively blacks were isolated from and oppressed by white people, and the dominant view was that (1) whites are evil; (2) blacks are Christ-like victims; and (3) black racial self-love and loyalty are the highest goals. The deviant view—whites are essentially good; blacks are not morally or spiritually superior; racial integration is the highest goal—was usually held by those few blacks who had a particularly kind slave owner or escaped in some other way from white brutality.

DuBois (1903) referred to this ambivalence by the term *twoness*, blacks' simultaneous desire to be identified as American and as African-American. This ambivalence is aggravated by the premium Americans place on rugged individualism because survival for African-Americans has always depended upon group solidarity. In some instances the effort to fuse these contradictory values has resulted in privatized self-understandings.

Below are excerpts from interviews with two black women that illustrate their privatized integration of the American contradiction in the rationales they offer for mixed racial intimacy. Marcia's narrative reveals the failure of her "white experience" and her escape back to the "traditional view" that most white men value white women more highly than black women. She believes that white men generally view black women as sexually desirable but less than civilized (and human). Janice's narrative, on the other hand, reflects the failure of the "black experience." She sees black men as less than adequate: they fear and abandon their women and children. She escapes into a "mystical" stance. While Lester calls himself a "mystic," Janice calls herself an "earthling."

I shall show how each of these women (1) reflects the core contradiction; (2) rationalizes her break with traditional racial values; and (3) becomes reengulfed by the reality of racism.

The core contradiction is white racism—the conviction that blacks are not fully human combined with actions designed to prevent blacks from demonstrating their full membership in the species. This contradiction was illustrated during the time of slavery by the belief that blacks could not learn even though teaching them to read was illegal.

Marcia and Janice provide graphic illustrations of the corresponding black conflict. They want to go beyond the constraints of traditional African-American unity by becoming intimate with white men, but they continue to ask for the support of traditional African-American unity. When their rationales for breaking with the traditional expectations are compromised by their need to remain attached to the race, they come face-to-face with their paradoxical predicament. I begin with a brief introduction of the women and follow with an exposition of the form the contradiction and the rationalization takes in each case.

Marcia

I first met Marcia in 1988 when she was taking a class with me at the state university. An attractive, well-dressed woman, she comes from a rural region that has a relatively large black population and whose history goes back to the Underground Railroad and the Civil War. Marcia is the youngest of four females and three males. At thirty-three she is somewhat older and more mature than most of the students in her teacher education program. Nonetheless, she gets along well with them and attributes this to the size and closeness of her family. Marcia is a leader in her home community—she teaches Sunday school and serves as a spokesperson in the public housing complex where she resides with her son while she attends school full-time.

Though I knew that Marcia had a seven-year-old son, I learned only later that his father was white. Few black women readily volunteer that they are intimate with white men, and Marcia was no exception. She told me about her child's father only after we had become good friends and she knew I was tolerant of miscegenation. We see the first evidence of the core contradiction's effects in her description of her entrance into motherhood.

The core contradiction

Marcia: I once fell in love with someone, and I did not look at whether he was black or white. I was in love with him and unfortunately he was white. I don't want it said that my preference was not for a black man. It was assumed I would have one [a black male]. I think that it was a rebound situation. I can't explain it—it happened. I was seventeen and he was sixteen . . . very young . . . he was my first everything . . . how could I find this blue-eyed thing (laugh) . . .
ADG: How did your family and friends react?
Marcia: My family and friends were accepting of him . . . this was not uncommon in the community. . . . Well, there were some black families that saw this as the ultimate taboo. . . . It was as if they said: "With so many black men, how could you?"

Untraditional as Marcia's choice was, she could accept the idea that "she just fell in love" as long as things went well. Misfortune struck when Marcia came home one day to find her fiancé in bed with her best friend. Now she refuses to date white men and associates exclusively with black males, although she knows white men who are interested in her. Marcia stresses that her fiancé always treated her respectfully and that her outlook on interracial intimacy changed only because "of the trust factor falling through, the infidelity."

ADG: Do you think that his behavior was related to this attraction you say white men have to black women?
Marcia: The mystique with black women? Yes, because the situation creating the infidelity was not with a white woman. It was a situation where he seemed to say: "Gee! I had this one. I could probably do it again." And it worked.

Marcia had made a choice to break with traditional expectations of black women. She considers this a naturally unfolding, unpremeditated process. But her denial of racism and of the need for black within-group intimacy was shattered by the white male's infidelity. Further, she generalized her intolerance beyond her fiancé to all white males. Although this seems irrational, in historical perspective it is sensible. This white male's behavior has exploded not only Marcia's private myth—that she has been lucky enough to escape her blackness—but also the collective one—that whites have changed dramatically in their attitudes toward African-Americans. She now wants a black mate.

Marcia: I have been hurt by a white guy. I feel that my relationship was a lie with this guy. It was mystique for him. Unfortunately, the pregnancy happened. I feel that even though we were planning to be married . . . the mystique was continuous. It was me, it was her, it took place even before the wedding and even unto today; it is other black women who are his preference.

Single and pregnant, Marcia called off her wedding and returned home from the big city. She experienced a double disappointment: the infidelity itself and the discovery that her mate had a preference for black women. Indeed, the infidelity was tolerable; she tried to live with it. But her fiancé's preference for black women in general deeply affected Marcia. She introduced the concept of black woman as "mystique" to refer to this collective attraction. By "mystique" Marcia meant that women of color are seen as exciting but unfamiliar and exotic sexual beings. Her mate's repeated choice of black women explodes the myth that race and racism have been overcome. This is why she now mistrusts whites' ability to transcend racial stereotypes rather than their capacity for sexual fidelity.

Marcia wants black men to value her as a traditional black woman despite her earlier untraditional choice. When she was asked whether her past would affect her chances of finding a black man, she replied:

Marcia: Yes, because I have encountered black males who cannot deal with the fact that I have a biracial child. The ones I have dealt with have had relationships with black and white women, but they have not had a child through the relationship, so they can't deal with it. They find it hard to be a father to a child by a white man because of the identity problem. They seem to be asking: "What color is this kid?" And it bothers me because I feel that they can't look beyond the fact of color and see that he is a little boy.

Marcia herself does not consider this child merely a little boy. During the interview, she once called him a "special breed." After returning home, she had to deal with the other side of the core contradiction: outside her own family, African-American unity cannot easily tolerate the consequences of intimacy between a black woman and white man. But Marcia wishes to protect a privatized vision of reality: racism has been defeated and individual choices are free.

Marcia frequently alludes to the ways in which black men mistreat white women. This suggests that she did not simply "fall in love with" a man who happened to be white. Rather, she turned away from black men.

The privatized reality

Marcia seeks a black male who can be a father to her biracial child whom she declines to see as black. But the search for such a mate appears itself as paradoxical when Marcia describes her view of black men.

Marcia: I have known white men who treat black women as their equals, their partners. They show them the utmost respect. She is not docile, she is not a servant. She is someone whom he truly cares about. But on the other side of the coin is black men. I don't know. Maybe their way of treating the white woman as partner, as equal, is to mistreat her. Maybe I am wrong to judge him, but personally I . . . don't want to be treated like that. If I should choose to marry a black man, I feel that that man first of all must respect and understand my position that this child should have both a black and white culture because his father is white. If I choose to marry, he should be supportive of that notion, because, let's face it, we are talking two cultures. And although I may want to assimilate him into a black culture and say "this is what you are and this is what you will do, this is a part of you," he is gong to find the other culture anyway. He is going to seek the other side of himself. And I feel that it should be assimilated into his life-style, his very being at an early age.

Historically blacks have accepted all children with some "black blood" as black. The emergence of blacks with mixed racial parentage and the persistence of the "law" that any "black blood" made one black required this acceptance of "all colors" as black. An unstated racial chauvinist assumption lay behind this: one showed a preference for "blackness" by deemphasizing the presence of "white features"—hair, skin color, nose, and lips.[1] To be called "white" therefore often represented a provocation to violence. Accordingly, light-skinned females generally preferred dark-skinned black men, and light-skinned males reacted violently toward those who denied their "blackness."[2] Perhaps these tendencies were reaction formations or overcompensations. Still, they showed a defense of homogeneity in the interest of racial survival and mutual protection.

Marcia seemed to want something new. She did not, moreover, understand that "biraciality," this new racial value, was problematic. She wanted to give her son the "legacy of choice" so he could choose whether to be white, black, or himself. But this is not possible. Most whites judge a mulatto to be black. Most mulattoes must therefore find social and cultural support within mixed-racial and/or black communities. Few are fortunate enough to choose and sustain a separate identity as white or nonblack.

What then does one in Marcia's predicament do? She has suffered the consequences of her choice and must now find a community within which to forge a life for herself and her son. I offered support by pointing out that some mulattoes identify themselves as a separate group: "brown people" (Gresson, 1987).

ADG: Would you be supportive of this concept?

Marcia: Ah, definitely! Definitely! Because, let's face it, these children who may be seeking identity somewhere—maybe they don't want to be black; maybe they don't want to be white. And maybe they want to be brown . . . in their own way. They have a right to choose. If they choose to be brown, then that is their race, it's their right to choose.

African-Americans seeking to go beyond the limitations placed on their self-identity are within their rights. The "lies" inherent in ethnic chauvinism must ultimately be challenged regardless of the collective good they have promoted. But this cannot take place within a vacuum. The risk for the vanguard pursuing these newer identities is loss of any dependable associations. The tolerance of one's family and friends may help one endure the break with old values. But support of this kind does not address the collective political challenge.

This point is made powerfully by a story told by the well-known black psychiatrist Alvin Poussaint: during the Freedom marches of the 1960s he and a group of other black marchers were stopped by a southern sheriff. The sheriff called Poussaint: "Hey, boy!" Poussaint replied, "Are you addressing me? My name is Dr. Alvin Poussaint." The sheriff, brandishing his nightstick, repeated: "I said, boy, come here!" Poussaint confesses to his audience: "I looked at the black women and then at the stick and then I went to him." The point is that a newly chosen identity that goes beyond the traditional stereotypes is no more sound or permanent than the abandoned one until the conditions which brought forth the original identity have truly been changed.

Being an intelligent and courageous woman, Marcia returned home with a minimum of internal conflict. Her choice, however, thrust her back into a world that a successful interracial relationship might have helped her ignore. Conversations I have had with her since the interview reflect her appreciation of this irony. Indeed, even during the interview she was able to admit: "I would not do it this way if I had it to do over. Single parenthood and raising a biracial child by oneself in this society is very hard." But not everyone understands these social-psychological dynamics. Janice, introduced next, has not yet grasped them: like Marcia she pursues the enlargement of racial identity and creates similar misunderstandings.

Janice

I met Janice through her mother, also named Janice, with whom I worked. Janice's mother had participated in a black female study begun in 1982 from which the present illustrations are taken. The mother of six, four daughters and two sons, Janice, Sr., was a vibrant, active, life-affirming matriarch of fifty-five. She had struggled to raise her children alone after her estranged husband, a talented artist, had moved to the Midwest. A high school graduate, she had worked her way up to a paraprofessional social service position. She was well-liked and very well connected in her community. Like many other African-Americans in New England, she believed in success, hard work, and racial integration. Janice, Sr., had told me that she once dated a white man but did not feel comfortable in inter-racially intimate situations. She asked me to consider interviewing her daughter, Janice, describing her as "a very interesting girl [of twenty-three], very talented, but lately I've been worried about her: she is dating only white and Puerto Rican guys. Her cousin Margie is also dating a white guy—they plan to marry after graduation from the university. I'd be interested in what you think of Janice."

Children rarely are named for their mothers in our society. At the very least, it suggests that mother and child have been publicly identified with each other in a special way. In the present case, I think this shared name made Janice feel she had a special relationship and obligation to her mother. This obligation, however, was not to follow in her mother's footsteps. Rather, it was to become somebody special, to go beyond her mother's achievements. We get a clue to this interpretation when she recounts her childhood feelings regarding her name.

Janice's real name is similar to that of a comic book character. When Janice complained about the teasing she had to tolerate from fellow students in public school, her mother said, "You can always change it if you want to." The implication was that Janice was free to do as she wished. More significantly, the mother was telling the daughter that she was free to break with family and group tradition. Though Janice takes the credit for her independent spirit, there are numerous indications that the mother was living through Janice and that she sought to "free" her of the bondage of "traditional" black womanhood. Janice reveals this influence through her reflection on her sisters and how she differed from them.

Janice: When [mother] was bringing me up she was more financially stable than when she was bringing my other sisters up. So, my other sisters saw me as being spoiled because I got more things than they did, simply because my mother had more to give. I think that a lot of it had to do with I was the last girl in the house, so she focused on me more. I am the only daughter that can really express anything to my mother. I can talk about sex, I can talk about drugs, I can talk about anything, where my other sisters would be a little more frightened to talk about them-selves. . . . See, I express myself right down to details sometimes, where they would probably generalize. . . . I gave my mother a hard time, too, I took advantage of her. . . . I am so much different than my sisters. I am not a conventional person at all . . . I deliberately go against the grain . . . at least I used to. It was like a challenge to me.

One gets the picture of a young woman whose experience as the baby in the family took her along paths that converged on a core contradiction: transcendence of blackness is possible in a race-conscious world.

The core contradiction

Once I visited Janice's family during a crisis. A sister was fleeing her violent husband with their two small children. The family was thrust back into memories of another sister, whose husband had killed her some years ago. At one point, I was alone with Janice and her eldest sister, a married woman with two teenaged sons. The sister remarked that she was tired of being the one to shoulder all of the family's burdens and alluded to Janice's noninvolvement in family crises. Janice, also drawn into the passions of the family crisis, retorted: "I care about the family. I remember Sue's death. It hurt me, too." Janice had in fact talked to me about the murder. She was not only still grieving the loss of this sister but also felt very alienated from black men because of it. For example, she related to me that her first black male friend once attempted to beat her with his belt and that she threatened to kill him. "He said I was crazy. But I wasn't going to let no man beat me with his belt after what happened to my sister. I would just have to go to jail."

When blacks first began dating and marrying whites in large numbers, the rationale often offered was that whites were nicer to them and made them happier. Such negative experiences, whether or not they actually precede a given person's break with racial identification, are often suggested as a rationale for the break. We recall that Marcia implied a similar explanation. Janice felt betrayed by her father and one of her brothers, and these experiences seem to underlie her view of black men in general. I asked her about her own father.

Janice: Yeah, he's afraid of black women . . . he deals with nonblack women. I think that he is afraid of black women; they are too powerful for him. I don't look at people in categories . . . because everyone is an individual. As far as statistics go in this country with black men, I just see a lot of unhappy black men and they need . . . (sigh) help, support, understanding of themselves . . . as individuals.

Janice denied any ill feelings toward black males or any connection between her own familial and racial biography and her relations with white men. But throughout the discussion, she conveyed disdain for black males. Nor did Janice admit that she felt there were no black men available as mates. Admitting this might have meant acknowledging her father's failure toward her and the family. She could not reject her father outright or directly state a preference for white men. Unable to rebut her critics, she retreated into her private world.

The privatized reality

Janice's privatized reality features race as an obstacle she has transcended by force of her own personality. She believes she has risen above her friends and family. When reminded that her mother was also open to transracial relations, Janice replied:

Janice: Yes, well, because color is such an obstacle. When you start thinking about people because of their color, you lose so much . . . knowledge. I have gone out with every nationality there is . . . that's me, I guess. I'm a universal person I guess. I attract a lot of foreigners. I attract all kinds of colors. I think that [black resistance to marrying outside of the race] is their own security [issue] and something that they have to deal with . . . cause we are all earthlings . . . goddamn it, we are all on the same goddamn planet. Why can't we live on this planet?
ADG: How do you deal with the fact that there are people who want to control it . . . I mean white men in particular.
Janice: Okay, I'll tell you an experience. I went to this club . . . I mean it was an all white club and this black guy came up to me and said, "You've got a nerve being here." He said, "The white men were just looking at you like you were a piece of meat." This is what he told me. That they just want to pick up a piece of ass or something. So, I said, "Number one, I am not here for display or business, you know; number two, I don't look at people that way, so therefore I don't expect to be looked at in that way, and if I am, that is their problem." I didn't have to explain myself to him, but I felt it was necessary to give him some information.

Janice felt vulnerable to this black man because racism persists, and she cannot merely wish it away. She must respond to him but is angry at him because of his personal duplicity: he associates with white women himself. Is he also "meat" for them? His dishonesty offends her as a black woman. Perhaps he reminds her of her father, who wants to follow his own bent without being held accountable but expects the rest of the family to stay in line and to continue loving and respecting him as the self-sacrificing protector of family and race.

In justifying her cross-racial dating, Janice presents herself as an earthling, a universalist. Thus she denies the racist history that led African-Americans to insist on within-group mating. Further, she denies white racism by representing racism only as the result of the paranoia of black people. This denial of racism leads Janice to isolate herself from the black community, which daily struggles against racism. This isolation is illustrated when she misunderstands a friend's warning against interracial intimacy, believing that it stems from the friend's "personal insecurity."

Understandably, individuals like Janice experience peers as oppressive and limited because they cling to the traditional racial beliefs and values. To adopt an alternative set of values, one must discount the traditional ones. The danger is that one distorts one's own experience to the extent that it conflicts with the old values. Janice's encounter with a white woman is especially characteristic of the risk to self-understanding.

Janice: Let me tell you what this white woman said to me. She is supposed to be a regressor, she is supposed to regress people to their past life—which I believe is full of shit. I asked her if she would regress me. She goes through this whole trip: she tells you where you came from in your past life. And she tried to tell me, "You want to be white." She said that I was a white woman in my past life and I want to be a white woman today in this life. . . . To *me* I wasn't a stereotype black person but I was to *her.* And I said to her, "I don't want to be any color. I want to be me. I am me. I am female. I realize that I have brown skin. I enjoy having brown skin." I am thankful to have this color when we talk about visual effects.

Janice's pursuit of a wider identity lacks an established collective basis despite the rhetoric of diversity and global oneness. This is so because she does not confine her interactions to the community that shares her view. She is trying to be something of a "secular" mystic or communalist—but in a self-contradictory fashion. Mystics and communalists typically "leave the world" in order to validate their identity shifts. Janice tries to remain within the world and redefine it to meet her "mystical" vision. She actually wants to "leave the world" in a quite different way from the one she intends. Janice does not realize that she wants to have freedom of choice without having to accept the definitions and constraints.

She does not make connections, see contradictions, or acknowledge the historical and contemporary basis for others' views of her behavior and worldview. She envisions a privatized reality by representing race as a matter of skin pigment only. She wants to be "artistically" colored. This is comparable to Julius Lester's statement: "Blackness is not my core, it is only an aspect." Both Janice and Lester seek to escape not only the constraints of racism but also the sense of collective plight and mutual aid that led African slaves to become African-Americans with a shared fate. Janice's efforts lead her to a pathetic position.

Janice: I like my color, you know. I am proud of it. Artistically speaking, if I had a choice, I would keep this color cause I think it is much more attractive. But that doesn't have anything to do with race.
ADG: What does it have to do with?
Janice: Uh, my color? Uh, . . . I'm proud . . . I don't know how to explain it because I don't put things in a category. I can confuse myself when I try to understand it. What does black mean? That is what I want to know. I've had people look at me and go—because I recall this friend of mine. She was real uptight because I was going out with white guys. And I told her: "You have got to stop thinking that way if you want to be my friend." I said color doesn't mean anything. It is spirit. And that is how I am attracted to people. Chemistry. I am not attracted

to a person because of color. Thwang! It's more than color and I am an earthling. I am someone in this universe that wants to be able to follow my intuition, to follow what is real inside of me. Why shouldn't I go with what is real inside of me? I don't want to put labels on anything. I don't want to be labeled as a female, as a black person. I want to be labeled as an earthling. Maybe I want to go to another planet (laughs). I've had it with this planet, I mean it. It's just plain and so immature to me. You get into all these categories and everyone keeps banging their heads against each other and for what!? Why?! So much wasted energy.

But she is African-American. And she has been reminded of this by a white female, one who, ironically, deals in myths and mysticism. Janice's desire is legitimate; but being a trailblazer exacts a high price. Janice has had to pay this in the currency of unwanted pregnancies and abortions.

Janice had two abortions. But she did not understand that she used pregnancy as a means of defining herself, her womanhood, and her relationship with her parents. During each pregnancy she returned home from "out west" and claimed no knowledge of the pregnancy until it was "discovered." Janice disapproves of her father and brother but envies their "freedom from constraint." Paradoxically, they behave like the very "individuals" she wanted black men to be. But they were both "irresponsible" and uncomfortable with "black women." She felt different from them because she could interact with blacks as well as nonblacks. She did not realize that she habitually withdrew from the black community—including her mother and sisters—until she needed them. She did what pleased her (as had the father) and "forced" her mother and others to accept this. Shortly before I left the city in which this family lived, I learned that Janice had returned home pregnant once again. This time she kept the baby; the father was a white musician on his way abroad.

Janice's life at this point seems to replicate Marcia's. Each has tried to modify her racial history and her portrait of black womanhood. Each, despite intelligence, family support, and educational opportunities has had to face single parenthood and dependence on the traditional black family. Each became trapped in the economic and social predicaments of black underclass females from which she had sought to escape.

Marcia's and Janice's accounts suggest a common pitfall—the risk of losing oneself even as one hastens to find or create a new self. It is both necessary and desirable that the limitations racism places on individual freedom and group identity be destroyed. In a better world, it should be possible for a black woman or man to mate without consideration of race. Likewise, it should be possible for individuals to speak of their race as merely an aspect of personal identity. But in a world still dominated by race-conscious power groups, such a move toward an enlarged self-definition does not depend on a simple act of will.

A believable enlargement of identity must include at least two things. One, the individual must recognize that the history of oppression cannot be erased from memory by fiat. The plight of Jews in Nazi Germany has taught us that identifying with the oppressor—becoming German, Christian, or a capitalist—does not protect one from oppression. It is not sensible for a black man to declare that "blackness is not his core" in a country where a black is not safe from harm if he steps out of his home.

Second, the individual must acknowledge that the fulfillment of personal needs may conflict with collective group identity needs. If one cannot integrate these needs, one must squarely face the resulting contradictions. Moreover, private choices have not and cannot change the reality of racism or diminish the collective importance of black racial self-regard.

Could Janice and Marcia, each by herself, have recognized that their choices would increase the personal and collective burdens of racism? Probably not. Only renewed dialogue within the ethnic community can bring the implications of such identity enlargements out into the open. When it does, the path will be clear for a kind of development that benefits the group as a whole. Meanwhile, many minority members will not easily abandon what they see as personal liberation for the sake of a doubtful collective liberation.

Narratives like Marcia's and Janice's and critiques and interpretations such as I have presented constitute a new Middle Passage—a journey between the worlds of black and white in search of new selves and of more fulfilling relationships in a race-conscious society.

NOTES

1. But as a group blacks have been inconsistent in this, some preferring African-American, some white features, and some being indifferent.
2. This is not uniformly true. Many light-skinned blacks avoided mating with darker-skinned blacks in order to remain as white-looking as possible.

REFERENCES

DuBois, W. E. B. 1903. *The Souls of Black Folk*. Chicago, n.p.
Gresson, A. D. 1987. "Transitional Metaphors and the Political Psychology of Identity Maintenance." In *Cognition and Symbolic Structures: The Psychology of Metaphoric Transformation*. Edited by R. E. Haskell. Norwood, N.J.: Ablex.
Lester, Julius. 1982. "The Black Writer." *New England Journal of Black Studies* 2:82–85.
Pinderhughes, Elaine. 1988. "Treatment with Black Middle-class Families: A Systemic Perspective." In *Black Families in Crisis: The Middle Class*. Edited by A. F. Coner and J. Spurlock. New York: Brunner/Mazel.

10 The Family as an
Overwrought Object of Desire

How do couples poised on the edge of parenthood imagine the future? What transformations in their lives do they anticipate? In looking toward the future, how do they remember the family life of their childhoods? This chapter presents accounts given by young couples who have been unable to conceive (Walkover, 1983). Although they are experiencing particular problems, I shall argue that they articulate an ambivalence that virtually all couples feel toward becoming parents. What is most striking about their accounts is a profound and pervasive contradiction—extreme idealizations of child rearing juxtaposed with equally dismaying possibilities. Middle-aged and young adults who appeared otherwise moderate and balanced, and who held in most cases rather unsentimental views of marriage, seemed thrown into an altogether different realm of possibilities when faced with the prospect of having children—a realm animated by longings and dread. As they spoke, their imagery would change abruptly: the idea of providing adequate and reasonable care was suddenly replaced by the staggering responsibility of creating a near-perfect world in which a child's emotional and material needs could virtually always be satisfied. And with that slippage what might have been seen as an appealing challenge became instead an overwrought object of desire, an utterly daunting enterprise but one without which life seemed devoid of meaning.

Why is it so difficult to maintain modest expectations of parenthood? Why do ideas of doing right by one's children lead so inexorably to ambivalence and conflict? One common subtext to emerge from the interviews is an idea of the perfectibility of childhood. When examining meanings of family life as expressed by prospective parents, one encounters not only images of families as they were experienced but also as they were wished for, as well as shared beliefs about what the family is *supposed* to be. It becomes necessary then to address seriously societal and cultural contributions to the imagery of families. Through examining social histories of the family in Western culture and contemporary self-help literature for prospective parents, we can achieve an important perspective on the contradictory themes of gain and loss, growth and stagnation, perfectibility and ruination, that pervade personal accounts. We can then recognize not only what is appropriated from the culture in thinking about children but also what intrudes uninvited to animate particular dilemmas.

This exercise is not only informative but essential to a more integrated psychosocial understanding of parenthood, a conceptualization that is honored in theory more often than in practice. Failing to identify the cultural dimensions of ambivalence about parenthood leaves us unwitting participants in a popular form of "psychologizing," a tacit assumption that individual strength of character can mitigate conflicts that in fact reflect unresolved tensions in society. To anticipate briefly, my reading of social history suggests that our culture promotes a highly idealized vision of family life and that our social structure places the full burden on parents to realize it. The family is expected to be a haven, a sanctuary from the rest of life. It is not, has never been, and cannot be, but the hope of starting fresh with the heartfelt wish to provide for one's child what was lacking for oneself is fertile ground for reproducing the powerful illusion of the ever-elusive perfect family.

The interview data I draw upon here come from a focused inquiry into the fantasies, hopes, and fears of couples who anticipate "starting a family." Looking at meanings before the event preserves a level of abstraction, uncolored by particular experiences with pregnancy, obstetrics, infant care, and so on. I chose as interview subjects couples who were having problems with conception and had sought medical assistance to overcome infertility. They were exceptional then in an important way: parenthood was no longer something they could take for granted.

However, precisely because of their difficulty, they may have been unusually reflective about parenthood. Many had endured intrusive technological interventions; all had been repetitively on the brink of parenthood, in an exaggerated preparatory stance, and this had made them think—longer and harder than their fertile counterparts—about the meaning of having children (Payne, 1978). They are therefore ideal informants in the anthropological sense about the meaning of what remains for them an *imagined transformation*. Their degree of self-scrutiny is undoubtedly atypical. Their repeated failures at conception compelled them to question everything: had they tried too hard or not hard enough? Were unconscious worries in the way? Were they being punished for something?[1] Apart from these concerns, however, their visions of family life should be readily recognizable to everyone, parents or not, who has seriously considered having children.

It is my intention to illustrate and explain the contradictory meanings of parenthood that emerged from these accounts, using both personal-historical and social-historical interpretations.[2] I hope to show how these levels of analysis are complementary. The case studies that follow demonstrate that cultural (idealized) images of family life are internalized along with the experience of being parented and function as inner referents for men and women as they consider creating their own families. Accordingly, this chapter has a phenomenological as well as a conceptual aim—to display the structural conflict of values regarding reproduction not as a structure apart but as a structure within.[3]

Ambivalence and Contradictions—Acknowledged and Denied

My informants were fifteen couples who resided within a thirty-mile radius of a university hospital in the industrial Midwest. They were middle-class, Caucasian, largely Protestant and Catholic. Within the group there was nonetheless tremendous diversity of living conditions, income, occupation, and marital style. Every point on a rural-urban continuum was represented as was the socioeconomic spectrum of the middle class. The men were all employed, some experiencing seasonal layoffs. The women worked as well, at least part-time and several were the primary wage earners. The group comprised retail managers, secretaries, grade school teachers, college professors, factory workers, writers, nurses, accountants, contractors, and systems analysts. The majority were in their late twenties and early thirties, but some a decade or so older. These were mostly first marriages ranging from two to eleven years at the time of the interviews. The couples' relationships reflected a broad spectrum of needs for intimacy, from a high degree of mutual involvement to largely separate pursuits.

Some of these couples, more comfortable with their own mixed feelings about becoming parents, acknowledged their hopes and fears directly. The accounts of others evinced a split in consciousness, an articulation of certain disvalues of having children and a subsequent denial; nothing could be as wonderful as family living, and parenthood was something they had "always wanted."

Yet whether ambivalence was acknowledged or denied, a longing for family, for a sense of regeneration and participation in something larger than but reflective of oneself, coexisted with the fear of losing one's dreams, one's freedom, even oneself through that creation. If the focus was on a deepening commitment to marriage, the fear was of divorce. If the focus was on activity, stimulation, and "staying young" with children, the fear was of constriction, immobility, and existential death. Where children were seen to signify immeasurable enrichment and fulfillment, the same accounts contained imagery of depletion, impoverishment, and deprivation.

Couples' ambivalence about having children revealed itself in their approaches to the decision. As a kind of dialectical antithesis to images of perfectibility, we encountered a dry calculus of affordability, a cost-benefit analysis of childbearing in which the child appeared as a luxury commodity. These oddly dehumanized discussions of costliness contrasted sharply with the nearly sacral tone in which couples spoke about the desirability of children.

The case example that follows illustrates how the anticipation of parenthood can function as a lightning rod for psychological conflicts about the introduction of a third and dependent person into a dyadic relationship.

Russ and Laura Larsen, age thirty-seven and thirty-six, respectively, had been married for nine years at the time of the interviews. They had at first questioned whether they would ever want children. But as they attained "that involuntary sort of lovely, pure love reaction that's very deep and you can't explain it and there aren't any strings attached to it," the wish for a child had blossomed naturally. And yet the Larsens worried about the child's intrusion into their time with each other. They would have to become less "selfish." The child would have to be "number one."

Laura: I'd be sort of frightened. Part of it is because we have seen so many people have kids and have it hurt their relationship. I mean, we've had so many friends get divorced and, um, two of our very dearest friends that we thought had this great relationship had a little girl and a lot of other things happened that year to them, but basically, it was the kid. It just broke 'em apart. Um, they weren't prepared for it.

Laura was also worried about giving up a successful career and becoming a resentful drudge at home—possessive, envious of Russ, drained and drab. As for Russ, his anticipation of having a child was also marked by caution and restraint.

Russ: I would enjoy having a child, our own child as a friend. They're really interesting people, kids are, I think. Ah, and you can learn a lot from them. Maybe that's sort of a selfish attitude, but I just think small people are interesting to be around and, ah, that you sort of grow with them . . . you learn a lot. The goods and bads about being a parent would strengthen our relationship. Not that that's a goal in itself—strengthening a relationship, but it would inherently, and it would be just another facet of our relationship to explore, I think. We're two human beings relating to each other and this would add a new dimension to it, it would be, ah, really interesting and sort of exciting to explore I think.

For this couple, a child signified at once the flowering of their mutual connectedness and a threat to its continuation. Parenting represented an opportunity to grow in sharing responsibilities and at the same time the prospect of being stunted. The child they hoped to have was valued as a catalyst for loving interaction and feared as a wedge that could drive them apart.

Connectedness and Identity: A Culturally Prescribed Struggle

The transition to parenthood, moving from individuated young married adult life to family life, contains a profound contradiction. My informants saw family life as enabling, invigorating, and substantial, with a richness and depth otherwise unattainable. Yet this image existed in constant tension with the obverse possibility; parenting signified oppression, debilitation, and alienation. Informants' portrayals of their own childhood experiences provide abundant illustrations of how the family is both the condition of and greatest threat to the identity and autonomy of its individual members. Before turning to this material, however, it may help to recall certain features of family life that we take for granted.

In the last two decades social historians have described the complex relation between changes in economic and social forces and the structure and function of families. Beginning with the disruption of reciprocal obligations between social groups that had characterized the feudal order, a breakdown in social relations occurred that then accelerated under the impact of industrialization and mass migrations. In this process the family has become ever more exclusively the locus of emotional and spiritual repair. The hope was (and continues to be) that through private satisfactions the family might make up for the collapse of communal traditions and the harsh indignities of a capitalist economy.[4]

The nineteenth-century ideology of the family was that of a refuge wherein the nurturant woman ministered to an exhausted husband, repaired the damage inflicted by the market, and sheltered the children from its corrupting influence. From a structural standpoint, the form of the family was frequently more extended than nuclear. For example, a majority of individuals in this country either boarded with others or took boarders into their homes. Working people shared "family" responsibilities with neighbors and kin, organized mutual aid societies, and focused their social life on street corners, tenement yards, and taverns. And though the middle class increasingly idealized the sanctity of the family in theory, women's friendships and kin networks seem to have remained more central to their emotional lives than did their marriages. It was not until the twentieth century that American families lost their organic connection to intermediary groups and communal functions and developed heightened expectations about the family's role in fostering individual fulfillment. No longer merely a refuge, the family was to provide a whole alternative world of satisfaction and intimacy. Inevitably these new ideals increased the perception of families as failures; the divorce rate skyrocketed, and there has been a recurring sense of "crisis" in the American family ever since. Rage, disappointment, and withdrawal from families often leave the cultural symbol intact—the image of the perfect family as an idealization believed to be realizable.

The appearance of these ideals occurred in relation to other profound changes— the growing role of schools, the mass production of food, clothes, and medicine—resulting in family functions being increasingly organized around the consumption of goods and services. Some have seen the family as losing not only productive functions but authority as well, particularly in the areas of healing and of tutoring children (Lasch, 1980; Donzelot, 1979). Modern family life is often painful, marriage fragile, and parent-child relationships full of hostility and recrimination because relationships stripped of everything save mutual solace and support (in forms continually revised by experts) are frequently problematic. When families are judged by the terms and values of the market and commonly judge themselves in comparative terms of success and failure, their functioning as a refuge from those pressures is vitiated. At the same time, when the indignities suffered in the outside world are not redressed at home, the family is instantly felt to be a failure. As object to both observers and participants, the family is in the position of striving to conform to an externally imposed ideal that is impossible for all but a few to attain. To put it simply, the family, far from being a shelter, has been infiltrated by the outer scourge.

Still, the tensions of modern family life only highlight the decline of community and civic alternatives to family-centeredness. The persistent rise in individualism, which values the capacity to detach oneself from the constraints of community, tends to reject collective sources of aid and solace. Structurally then, there are few alternatives left. The family is the only social institution available as refuge from the pressures of society. Rarely able to fulfill this function, family life will be ambivalently valued. Drained of its power as an independent socializing agent, it also stands as the last bulwark of individuality in an age of mass culture. It is both too weak and too strong, too intense and too fragile. It is at once the realm of nourishment and intimacy, wholeness and sanity, and an overcharged, constricted arena regularly viewed as the cause of much psychopathology.

The strain placed upon prospective parents is therefore considerable. On the threshold of creating a new family, they confront the full weight of these contradictions and experience the full responsibility for realizing our impossible ideal. That pregnancy and parenthood are regarded as choices in a culture dominated by a consumerist mentality seems to add to this complex of conflicting values. Apart from religious and spiritual definitions of childbearing as sacred, parenting has been transformed from a duty to one's family, community, or country into an optional way of living. Desire is therefore the only socially acceptable reason for having chosen parenthood.

Family planning agencies and a vast popular literature on decisions about parenthood offer the well-founded advice that prospective parents should determine whether they *really want* a child. I can think of no better advice, and I regard the right to choice in childbearing as absolutely fundamental. Without questioning that, we can still be mindful of ambiguities in the rhetoric of purposeful parenting. The idea that one expects (and is expected) to be satisfied with one's choice implies that dissatisfaction reflects a miscalculation, an error resulting from inadequate knowledge either of the undertaking or of oneself.[5] Given childlessness as a legitimate choice and given the widely held view that one must not choose what one does not want (or lacks the material or emotional means to bring to fruition), couples take a formidable risk in deciding to reproduce—a risk even graver in a culture that expects families to be perfect.

This has a noticeable effect on subjects' discourse in two important ways. First is the phenomenon of split consciousness, the articulation and subsequent denial of disvalues of children. In the shrewd calculus of a consumer society, one is expected to find what fits. One can change not only cars, homes, wardrobe, and career, but community, friends, and spouse as well to meet ever-evolving needs. But once born, children are supposed to be exempt from this calculus. In conducting the self-assessment appropriate to determining their desires for children, prospective parents are invited to explore ambivalence. Once the choice is made, however, the ambivalence is to be forgotten, and one is invited to repress one's knowledge of the disvalues of children. In this sense, the specific split in consciousness encountered in these interviews could be said to have been socially constituted, if not prescribed.

The second impact of a consumer ideology upon a fundamental life decision is apparent in the ambiguity of subjects' concerns with "selfishness." On one side couples who were clear that they wanted children focused their self-evaluation on the question of "readiness," that is, of personal maturity turning on a repudiation of selfishness: when needs conflicted, could they sacrifice their own for those of the child? On the other side, the subtle expectation of some ultimate satisfaction suggests that the decision to have a child must be selfish (see Russ Larsen's interview above and Rick Kessler's following). Expecting to find certain joys in raising a child and creating a family is quite different from embarking upon parenthood for the *purpose* of deriving *pleasure* from the experience.

The Culture Internalized: Life-Historical
Reconstructions of Family Relations

We can now bring an awareness of cultural contradictions in the meaning of parenthood to our reading of interview data. As we look at particular images of fatherhood and motherhood in the context of personal history, the manner in which childhood experiences color someone's ambivalence toward parenthood will be apparent. The ways in which specific images or complexes of meaning reflect cultural themes is perhaps more subtle. In reading these cases it may be helpful to consider whether these informants, who generally accept their own parents' shortcomings, nonetheless measure their own experience against the ever-elusive perfect family.

The dilemma for some prospective parents was "how to give more than you got." One man, concerned about the financial consequences of his wife's leaving work to devote her time to child care, illustrates how a sense of what childhood should be is shaped by the combination of individual life history and cultural imagery. The life historical background of these worries about being the sole provider, which were both expressed *and* repudiated as unmasculine and immature, provides the context for understanding a split consciousness in terms of both contradictory cultural axioms and personal needs for self acceptance.

Rick Kessler, an amateur karate expert, expressed concerns about losing the income of his wife, Donna. The Kesslers had recently purchased their first house in a small industrial city. They would be unable to make the payments on his salary alone. Donna had been working for ten years and wanted to quit, even though she realized this would not be possible for the time being. Though Rick did not want to deprive his own child in the way he felt he had been deprived, Donna was anxious that these concerns not affect their having a family and tried to dismiss them.

Donna: I know that I won't like it. I'll wish that I could stay home. My mother stayed home when we were all little, and when I was in school and a catastrophe came up, it was always nice to know that my mother was there and she could come and get me. But yet, today is today, and we have what we have and so I have to work. I wouldn't like it, but I could accept that. . . .
Rick: But if you brought a child into the world and tried to maintain it on what we have, you couldn't do it. You know, without taking away from the child. . . . My feeling is I will not deprive my child just for the sake of me having a family. . . . I'm saying if you didn't work. If you *didn't* work. The child—daughter—comes up to you and says, "Mom, I want to go to camp." You'll have to say, "I'm sorry. I don't have the money so you can go to camp." You know. "But I love you, you know. But we're barely making ends meet"—something like that. This, I can't see.

Rick was frustrated by accounts "in the news about people who destroy their baby," stories of abuse and neglect that deeply affected him. He wondered whether he had developed a "reverse attitude [of] not wanting to have children because we might be in the same situation some day."

Donna: I don't think Rick thinks he would be that kind of father; he's just mentioning things on the outside.
Rick: Maybe deep inside—I don't know. I don't even know how to explain it.

In further discussion during Rick's individual interview he clarified that though he felt an "inner conscience" might worry that he could hurt his child, he could not imagine doing such a thing if he were fully conscious. These twin themes of violence and control along with an extreme sense of personal vulnerability were central to this man's sense of himself in the world.

The sixth of eight children, Rick was seven years old when his mother died in an automobile accident. He described his father as a "hard" man. Although he struggled to keep his family together, he often vented his explosive temper on his children.[6] Rick considered himself fortunate to have learned to "just let it roll off." The maintenance of a self-protective stance, a preparedness to fend off any attacker, was vital to his sense of well-being. Most telling were his comments about his intense involvement with martial arts. From his skills in karate, Rick derived a sense of "unlimited power." He said, "It gives you the confidence, you know; a guy could be seven feet tall, you know, it doesn't bother you. If it comes to the point where it's you or him, you always say it's going to be him."

Rick's description of his own disciplined self-control betrays, in its exaggeration, his sense of the absolute precariousness of human survival. His financial concerns were drawn in the starkest terms.

Rick: The first most important thing is money. Yeah, anything that you relate back to always relates back to money. That's like saying, if we didn't have money, we we couldn't be together. We'd die together, but we wouldn't live together. You see? It takes money to live. And it all revolves around money. That's basically, you know, any relationship always revolves around money. You might love each other, you might understand one another, but what it comes right down to is, if you didn't have money, you couldn't live.

He believed any departure from self-sufficiency to be dangerous, almost as though he expected dependency to result in abandonment. He mentioned several times that if he were crippled and unable to do his share, his wife might leave him. Most poignant was an early memory of losing a dog to which he had been attached. Although no one knew for sure, he believed that his father had gotten rid of it.

Rick: Well, my dad he kept hunting dogs, basically, and through that time period we were having a pretty tough time you know and, ah, you know an extra mouth to feed wasn't too cool and considered as being a mutt as it were so, you know, that's probably what happened, but as I look back, you know, now, just one of the things that just had to be.

As a child, he might well have been anxious about his own expendability. Rick had become an avid hunter and felt secure with the means his father had taught him for living off the land. Most satisfying to Rick was the ability to consume something he had procured himself without having to depend on outside sources. As with his skills in martial arts, his "built-in reflex," he liked to think he contained *within himself* the means for survival.

The Kesslers spent little time together, each following independent pursuits with a virtual prohibition from making emotional demands on each other. Both husband and wife in this couple placed extraordinarily stringent demands on themselves to be self-sufficient. Rick imagined that a baby would dramatically disrupt the balance they had achieved. He both expected his world to change and accepted that he would be faced with a new set of demands. He said, "When two grown adults are together with themselves, like my wife and I are, you can meet on equal terms, where with a child there is no meeting on equal terms. You have to go overboard to meet their demands."

He believed that dependency, which he refused to accept in himself or in his wife, would be acceptable in a child who could not be expected to take care of himself. Rick's expectations of himself as a father, despite his sensitivity to the needs of children, required a radical change in his mode of relating to people. He liked to think of himself as a giving and nurturant person. The tension for him lay in first having to have enough for himself. Having suffered sudden and severe deprivations as a child, he had constructed a heroic persona that provided a comforting sense of security and allowed him effectively to regulate his rage. He felt that one could not depend on outside aid for anything so one must have the personal resources to be a loving parent. At the same time, even the most temporary sense of deficiency felt threatening because there would be nowhere to turn for assistance.

While prospective fatherhood commonly raised issues around becoming the primary provider, prospective motherhood raised issues around becoming the primary nurturer. (Given the limitations of space, I have elaborated an example of male dynamics partly because women's issues in this area are somewhat better understood.) The ambivalence of women informants had to do with locating themselves within the realm of the household (as opposed to having to support it from the outside) and the impact this relocation would have on self-image and opportunities for self-care.

It is worth noting that daughters seemed to judge their mothers much more harshly than sons judged their fathers, which again reflects a cultural phenomenon.[7] Perhaps inadequate nurturing is more often regarded as a failure of character than inadequate providing, which is more obviously tied to economic and other forces beyond individual control. Female respondents seemed to fault their mothers for falling short of the ideal—to be there when needed, absent when not, and to maintain a sense of emotional integrity and well-being with clear interpersonal boundaries throughout an eighteen-year developmental process. The validity of a child's needs for such an environment is not in question, but the idea that this could be provided through a single relationship is quite extraordinary.

Many of the women in this study had conflicted relationships with their mothers, struggles with separation and individuation that are not atypical of female development.[8] Those who felt they had not gotten what they needed tended either to deny their own needs, to reject their mother, (and sometimes then to idealize their father's nurturing) or both. Those who replaced dependent needs with autonomous strivings found themselves vulnerable to fears of a child's dependence on them (much as husbands were anxious about their wives' dependence).

Wanda Jordan, a self-described "survivor" of a childhood with a volatile and emotionally abusive mother, focused her negative expectations on pregnancy. An exuberant and expressive "active coper"—a college friend described her as a "walking defense mechanism"—she imagined pregnancy as transforming her into a "beached whale." Although she had had notable success in business, Wanda was concerned about not being entirely settled yet in a career and was anxious that she not "take this out on a child." Not having had a "good" mother herself, she stated frankly that she would be handicapped by feelings of insecurity and inferiority, which she usually concealed from others.

Her coping style was founded on a fiercely defended independence. The value of sharing coexisted in dynamic tension with the disvalue of being "dictated to." She had found that she could diffuse tension and build self-confidence through a larger network of relationships. In fact she felt that her means of surviving her mother's competitive "zapping" came from strong nurturing connections not only with her father but also with her grandparents and other members of her extended family.

Wanda was understandably enamored of nonnuclear images of family life. Her sense of how a family ought to be was articulated in fond recollections of snow-mobiling trips with her husband's sister's family—evenings of intergenerational sharing, adults and children learning from one another, spent miles away from television and telephone and the demands of daily living that otherwise dominate family roles and functions. Here we see the family as a sanctuary and a locus for stimulating growth if only everyone can escape the ordinary conditions of life! It stands as a compelling image—a supremely satisfying self-contained miniature community—but is counterbalanced by the equally impressive emblem of the "beached whale," an image of paralysis, ungainliness, and doom that epitomizes our contemporary horror of inhibited social and physical mobility. The longed-for haven of peaceful communion is invaded by the threat of stasis and helplessness.

Dialectics of Contradiction and Conflict in the Meaning of Becoming a Parent

In becoming a parent one reenters, as an adult this time, the contradictory world of the modern family: the bond to the child is thought to enliven the parent while also being feared as a restriction. Responsibility for offspring, whether emotional or material, animates and mobilizes as well as burdens and enervates the parent. Although adults may well be able to tolerate such contradictions, these become problematic when their social origins are forgotten, as happens so often in our society, and when the cultural ideal of the perfect family—the family that magically escapes these value clashes—is installed as the touchstone of human excellence.

As cultural contradictions are absorbed and reproduced, they impose moral definitions. Life historical studies, like those excerpted here, make clear that parents pass on the logic of their culture as they fulfill the fundamental needs of their children. Rick Kessler's father impressed on him unforgettably that rigorous self-sufficiency is a condition of honorable manhood. Although we do not know in every case what repetitive formative childhood experience gave rise to the significant moral themes of the adult, the general pattern seems clear enough. For instance, Wanda Jordan's lifelong struggle against being a loser, founded in her early years, will in time probably communicate itself to her own children. Values prominent in our culture—foremost among them the various versions of self-enrichment—inform a parental anxiety that perpetuates itself by instilling a pre-emptory code of right and wrong in generation after generation.

Yet culturally potent values are not reducible to individual morality as received in the family. The social history of the family shows that these values are autonomous and exert a pressure not only in the home but also in the contemporaneous cultural discourse. How ordinary people organize their experience of themselves and others, as spouses, parents, or children, is significantly influenced by the terms of this shared discourse. Those who do not raise their children "as children should be raised" are subject not only to pangs of conscience but also to the condemnation of their peers. Even this does not put the matter strongly enough. When peers remain silent, the offender "knows" how he or she is seen! This is what is meant by saying that parents' worries about identity, autonomy, and self-sufficiency have a personal as well as a cultural meaning. They are enforced by the hard lessons of childhood as well as by the might of communal judgment. The study of individual lives in biographical perspective lets us forget that although social-historical contradictions are repeatedly found within the subjective table of values, indexed as the residue of childhood experience, these contradictions are even more potent as a criterion of social adaptation. This duplication creates opportunities for self-misunderstanding.

When Rick Kessler speaks of the all-importance of money, he is not only encoding a neurotic worry about the dangers of dependency but also summoning the specter of poverty, deprivation, neglect, and the hopeless future of the young child we all associate with these afflictions. When he expresses his "frustration" over newspaper accounts of physical abuse, he is not only camouflaging anxiety about his aggressive impulses, perhaps contained by his involvement in karate. Rather, he is also portraying himself as a possible target of public contempt. If Wanda Jordan should waver in her determination to be a success in her ventures, she not only succumbs to a primal internalized devaluing voice; she also disappoints herself and others who look to her as an accomplished woman and a model of feminist aspiration. She might then become vulnerable to an even graver devaluation than her own mother was in the previous generation.

The contemporaneous discourse that frames cultural horrors is less merciful than many a would-be parent's self-doubts. The couples in this study do not impress us as crippled by their childhood experiences. Their private anxieties have not kept them from leading more or less satisfactory lives or from pursuing reproduction despite initial failures. After all, every adult enters parenthood with vulnerabilities too well known to require discussion. Still they are only vulnerabilities and can be moderated, even overcome. But once a parent's uncertainties about his or her capacity for nurturance or tenderness are translated into the stark categories of social evil, they become frightening and unmanageable. Self-doubts that might have been assuaged by experience and accommodation become escalated into grave before-the-fact self-condemnations.

The point is not that one might be able to escape socialization but that the contemporaneous discourse of good and evil presses on sensitivities and squelches potential laid down in earlier years. Nuanced negotiable frailties are magnified and resources dwarfed by the extremity of internalized social judgment—an extremity that reflects the extravagant stakes riding on the modern family.

When private worries are cast into terms of cultural evil, a characteristic irrationality can be seen in the personal accounts. We saw that the Larsens could not escape their own indictment of selfishness: they were selfish either for not wanting a child at all or for using the child to their own benefit. Similar conundrums occurred in other couples' accounts. The inescapability of the charges combined with their moral weight is a sure sign that these people labor under cultural conditions that effectively occlude self-understanding and self-development.

Parents and children become victims of cultural rhetoric if the family is felt to be doomed when parents cannot care for their children perfectly, even while the parents themselves are unprotected against many misfortunes; if the standards of parenting are made criteria of social comparison; if it is believed that a child's every action reflects primarily upon the parent and only the parent; and if the *choice* of parenting implies a pledge to resolve and surmount all contradictions through strength of character and careful planning. Our discourse of reproduction encourages parents to personalize their ambivalence and remain unaware of the cultural contradictions in the meaning of the family. A likely consequence is that moral pressures will be not only preserved in this generation of parents but also passed on to their children while the social origin of these pressures remains unrecognized.

NOTES

1. The interviews were conducted in 1977 and 1978, when medical interventions were limited to hormone therapies, surgeries, and artificial insemination. A concern with "emotional factors" in infertility was an initial impetus for this research. Even now, with in vitro fertilization, reasons for failures of conception remain elusive.
2. The data from which these meanings were drawn were gathered by means of a semistructured interview format over four meetings ninety minutes each in length. The initial and final meetings were with the couple. The second and third meetings were individual interviews of husband and wife. When possible, follow-up interviews were conducted a year later.
3. The final form of this chapter is indebted to George Rosenwald's adept articulation of the translation of idealized imagery into the burdensome form of moral imperative.
4. For more detailed discussion of these complex issues, see Aries (1965), Stone (1979), Degler (1980), Lasch (1977), Levine (1977), Tilly and Scott (1978), and, for an attempt at synthesis, Coontz (1989).
5. The exemplary text in this area is by Whelan (1975).
6. In the process of editing case material in this section I find that I have inadvertently selected informants who were abused by a parent. Abuse was perhaps not as common in the histories

in my sample as we know it to be in the general population. It is, however, an element of experience that rather quickly and compellingly crystallizes contradictions running equally deeply, if less dramatically, through the other accounts of family history.

7. In attempting to address the "crisis of the American family," society has subjected the last several generations of mothers to intense scrutiny and severe criticism. (Excellent discussions of this ongoing phenomenon may be found in Ehrenreich and English, 1979, and Lupenitz, 1988.)

8. In this connection, see an excellent object relations analysis of mother-daughter separation and individuation by Chodorow (1978).

REFERENCES

Aries, Phillippe. 1965. *Centuries of Childhood: A Social History of Family Life.* Translated by R. Baldick. New York: Vintage Press.

Chodorow, Nancy. 1978. *The Reproduction of Mothering: Psychoanalysis and the Sociology of Gender.* Berkeley: University of California Press.

Coontz, Stephanie. 1988. *The Social Origins of Private Life: A History of American Families, 1600–1900.* New York: Verso.

———. 1989. "Families: Myth and Reality." *Seattle Post-Intelligencer,* June 11.

Degler, Carl. 1980. *At Odds: Women and the Family in America from the Revolution to the Present.* New York: Oxford University Press.

Donzelot, Jacques. 1979. *The Policing of Families.* New York: Random House.

Ehrenreich, Barbara, and Diedre English. *For Her Own Good: 150 Years of Experts' Advice to Women.* Garden City, N.Y.: Anchor Press.

Lasch, Christopher. 1977. *Haven in a Heartless World: The Family Besieged.* New York: Basic Books.

———. 1980. "Life in the Therapeutic State." *New York Review of Books* June, 27:24–32.

Levine, David. 1977. *Family Formations in an Age of Nascent Capitalism.* New York: Academic Press.

Lupenitz, Deborah. 1988. *The Family Interpreted.* New York: Basic Books.

Payne, J. 1978. "Talking about Children: An Examination of Accounts about Reproduction and Family Life." *Journal of Biosocial Science* 10(4):367–374.

Stone, Lawrence. 1979. *The Family, Sex, and Marriage in England, 1500–1800.* Abridged edition. New York: Harper and Row.

Tilly, Louise, and Joan Scott. 1978. *Women, Work, and Family.* New York: Holt, Rinehart and Winston.

Walkover, Barbara C. 1983. *Contradiction and Conflict in the Meaning of Becoming a Parent.* Ann Arbor, Mich.: University Microfilms International.

Whelan, Elizabeth M. 1975. *A Baby? . . . Maybe: A Guide to Making the Most Fateful Decision of Your Life.* New York: Bobbs-Merrill.

III

Critical Awakenings and the
Renewal of Narrative Identity

JACQUELYN WIERSMA

11 Karen: The
Transforming Story

If fiction begins in daydream, if it springs from the cramp of the world, if it relieves us from the burden of being ourselves, it ends, if it is good fiction and we are good readers, by returning us to the world and to ourselves.—Robert Penn Warren (1962, 156)

B y the end of his career Freud had essentially abandoned the possibility of recovering an individual past and instead began to formulate that the positive effect of psychotherapy might have more to do with reconstructing one's history. This implies that a story is not static and thus can change, and in that change lies its therapeutic potential. Academic psychology's attention has periodically turned to the construction and reconstruction of one's history in the form of the life story (Murray, 1938; White, 1981), and, more recently, in a movement coming to be known as "narrative psychology" (Sarbin, 1986; Gergen and Gergen, 1986; McAdams, 1985). The stories a person tells about his or her life are recognized to be not only expressive but formative as well. By becoming a part of one's self-image or even one's identity (McAdams, 1985) or personality (Sarbin, 1986), a "central feature of who people know themselves to be" (Ochberg, 1988, 174), these stories interpret our experience for us and shape our lives. They form the text by which we read our lives in much the same way that Sapir and Whorf have demonstrated that language does for its speakers (Mathiot, 1979).

Narrative psychologists and script theorists (Tomkins, 1987; Carlson, 1981) have concentrated so far on the life story as product and on its heuristic value when trying to understand persons. In contrast, I would like to introduce in this chapter the concept of story *as process* by looking at the narrator in stories about one's self as both speaker and listener and describing how this can lead to action, change, and ultimately to an improved story. Earlier sections of this volume have concentrated on the socio-culturally established rules that subtly define and limit the text of a personal story. Given that formal restraints and distortion exist in this process,

The author gratefully acknowledges the contributions of Stanley M. Wiersma, master storyteller, literary critics Gwen and Bill Bronson, and the generous loan of ideas by Rick Ochberg and George C. Rosenwald.

this chapter will address the question of whether the reverse is possible. That is, can a person *by telling her story* rescue her understanding from both accidental and formal mis-construction and heal what was previously a formal self-mis-understanding and inadvertent self-mis-representation? Can life stories be opened up, as well as cramped, in the telling?

This chapter is a story about how one woman interacted with her own story. It highlights the routes for self-transformation made possible by reconstructing one's life history in story form, translating it into a text, and treating it almost as a work of fiction. It focuses on the transformative features inherent in story telling, that is, its ambiguity, defined as its: (1) dynamic tension; (2) virtual experience (the *partial* identification of teller-listener with story); and (3) "as if" mode, the entertaining of multiple possibilities. Most important, this chapter shows how the ambiguity in the story form encourages action and action leads to a transformed story (that is, story leads to action leads back to story, ad infinitum). This chapter will argue that a story can be improved by creating successive dissatisfactions with one's life and thus creating the impetus for transforming a life and the story that describes it.

In doing so this chapter will highlight: (1) How can we "sniff out" a bad story and tell it from a good one? (2) How does the objectivation—the "as if" qualities—of storifying a life enable the transformations of story or even force a new story into being? (3) How can telling a bad story lead to action and action lead back to a new story?

We will see how such a transformation to a better story occurred in one woman's life story—or actually a series of stories—as she attempted to explain her career change along the thematic lines of roles, responsibility, and socialization. We can see how her life changed *as she told it,* in large part *because* she was telling it.

Story 1: The Dutiful Wife

Karen was a thirty-nine-year-old historian, both a graduate student and a junior faculty member at a northeastern state university, at the time we started a series of five interviews over the course of twenty-five months. Her husband was a physicist and worked as an academic; they had two children, seven and ten years old. She was interviewed as part of a study of women who had changed from a domestic career (as wife and mother) to one outside the home. In a series of unstructured interviews Karen and the other women in the study were asked to explain their career move and to describe how they had experienced it and how it affected their sense of identity and life structure.

When we started our interviews, Karen had been a graduate student for eight years, having gone back to school at age thirty-one. In the first interview, she reported that for increasingly convoluted reasons she felt stuck in her graduate student role and unable to complete her dissertation and move ahead toward faculty member status. Exemplifying this limbo was her atypical career pattern: while a graduate student she had written a book in her field and had risen to national prominence through an organization promoting grass-roots historical societies. As Karen's interviews progressed, each successive version of her story was followed by a burst of action, prompted (at least in part) by the preceding story, which helped erode the immobility she reported at the time of our first interview.

Karen's initial explanation for her career move was that it had simply been a better way for her to fulfill the responsibilities of her domestic career. She began our first interview by saying that she originally had gone back to school to become a "responsible" faculty wife. She reflected that she felt her career change had been part of her "socialization" into the supporting role she had to play to her husband's lead. "I was very clear that I should be primarily oriented to my husband. I worried about what people thought of me and whether I was dressed right and whether I was playing the role of faculty wife right. In fact, I think my conception of the role of faculty wife in the department . . . was probably important in my coming back to school, because a number of the wives there were professors. And I said, 'Well, that's what they expect here, so I better go learn how to work.'" Karen had returned to school to study history, with an emphasis on the influence of children on the family, the determinants of family size, and the effects of childlessness. She started school shortly after the birth of her first child.

Karen quite clearly portrayed herself as having played the passive role in the relationship. She described her career as an almost coincidental, certainly inadvertent, "responsible" time commitment—a demonstration of her dedication to the role of dutiful wife: "But I never had it planned. It just happened. I mean you just do what . . . makes your relationship good . . . which could change from time to time." She explained that "In order to be a good wife to my husband, I'd have to become an intellectually adept person."

As Karen described what had happened to her once in graduate school, her insistence on using the passive voice became even more prominent, almost incongruous with the actions she was describing. "I just got *sucked into* making commitments that turned out to be more than I wanted or really needed. . . . Because of the limited number of jobs in this area, [*I was just*] *led on step by step . . . led by the nose.* You know, I was just *socialized* into further academic work [italics added]. She recounted successive, seemingly fortuitous opportunities for advancement in school; she was "thrust up," with the encouragement and support of her husband as well as the academic community. One promotion had led to another, and she accumulated successively more advanced academic degrees—far beyond her original expectations. Repeatedly, she asserted that this had not been her idea. "It *never occurred* to me . . . we [she and husband] *never thought of me as a professional* with a career of my own." (italics mine) And after each such statement I would hear the refrain that she had made each step up the career ladder "because I get support for that at home."

Up to this point in her story, Karen seemed at pains to demonstrate, despite increasing odds against its probability as the plot gained momentum, how she had simply and always been unswervingly dutiful and responsible to her role as wife and mother. Her first story—which began with the return to school and continued up to the day we started interviewing—seemed to read, "I looked around and saw how I should be." Nevertheless, she also described how increasingly split she'd become by the demands of her responsible wife role. She had begun to feel strained and defensive with her peers: "Back in the neighborhood among women, when I first went back to school, I was still acceptable to them because I had children, because I would put up the children; I would emphasize to other people, and also to myself, that I was very mother oriented and home oriented, and give them precedence. . . . But I spoke about it partly because it was a defense, to say to other women, 'See, I'm still OK.' "

After presenting this story about her return to school, Karen began to elaborate on her difficulties with trying to remain the protagonist of this story. She could not keep this version of herself cohesive. Already, almost before the telling was completed, she was ending with a fragmented denouement of conflicting roles instead of a climax. "[At the national level] I'm an authority and a person . . . a recognized leader. . . . And then I come home and there are all kinds of criticisms and flack. . . . So I find it extremely difficult to be an authority one day, a revered authority, some kind of goddess even, and then to come home and to be an everyday drudge."

Theoretical aside

This consideration of Karen's story began with the question, "Can a bad story become good?" However, we have not yet considered just what criteria we might use to make this evaluation. On the most accessible descriptive level, Karen's story did not appear to serve her well. She seemed to be attempting to make part of herself invisible through a voice of exaggerated feminine passivity and to eradicate herself from the plot, which consisted of powerful husband and other academics "sucking" and "thrusting" at Karen's malleable form. She seemed to be holding up a mirror and reflecting only the part of herself that consisted of responsible socialized gender stereotypic roles.

Karen's story appears to be an extreme example of Mary Gergen's (this volume) description of women's stories as being more "relational" than individualistic and Bardwick's statement (1980) that, unlike men, women typically don't have a "dream," that is, a purpose, an action-directing conception of their character that encapsulates past and future. Here is, Karen seemed to be saying, a story of a person without purpose or character, except for what is reactive, externally molded. If one of the intrapsychic criteria we can use to recognize a good story (and routinely do in psychotherapy) is how much agency or effectiveness a person experiences, this story construes Karen as having very little sense of control of her world, not to mention her lack of self-determined purposefulness.

By other intrapsychic criteria as well Karen seems to be suffering at the hands of her story. Karen's demeanor so far was striking: her energetic emotional engagement seemed disgruntlingly incongruous with her dull story. She sounded much like the patient who comes to psychotherapy complaining of acute emotional distress when "nothing is wrong" in her life. To remedy denial or repression, a psychotherapist might ask for the *context* of the feeling, to establish how the past might be reenacted in the present, and to establish a pattern that has become an unconscious part of personal history. But Karen's remains stolidly fixed in a sterile present. And one might also question the congruity of the cognitions themselves; the ironic mute contradiction seems to be that a vigorous assertive intellectual woman who is beginning to achieve national prominence portrays herself as merely fulfilling her husband's imperative to be "responsible."

Quite clearly, then, this story makes neither common nor psychological sense. But even more is missing. This story doesn't "grab" us; as listeners we don't resonate with it.[1] And why we don't can be seen by applying a literary yardstick. Robert Penn Warren notes that the sine qua non of an interesting story is the presentation of a *problem*. "To put it bluntly: No conflict, no story" (1962, 148). Similarly, E. M. Forster describes the backbone of a story as "the constant 'and then . . . and then'" (1963, 41). "We are all like Scheherazade's husband, in that we want to know what happens next" (ibid., 27). Karen's story did not pull us ahead with the dynamic tension of conflict and uncertain outcome because rather than highlighting a problem, which would make it interesting, she was bent on suppressing any potential problem, even to the point of denying her own need or wants. And now a literary criterion helps us explain a psychological fact. Karen, though highly articulate and psychologically sensitive, could not manage her ambivalence. Although she occasionally was forced to mention it, it had no place in her story.

By the intrapsychic criteria noted—a sense of agency, affective and cognitive congruence, recognition of the past's influence on the present, tolerance for ambiguity, and modulation of ambivalence—Karen's story falls short of satisfactory. But a good intrapsychic interpretation would also explain what it is that keeps an apparently sophisticated and capable woman like Karen from using her observing ego to tell a better story. Karen's first story reads like a press release of her official self. Jurgen Habermas's theory of communicative competence offers some beginning clues to this contradiction by suggesting that the source of Karen's repression may have been social or political as well as intrapsychic. Each utterance, he says, situates itself within a recognized normative context, the shared values of a social life-world (Dickens, 1983). McAdams's (1985) version of script theory specifies somewhat the same thing in describing each life story as situated in an ideological context. As a result of this necessity to establish common linguistic territory between speaker and her imagined audience, areas of discourse or story which are seen as beyond the realm of approved social practice may be repressed. And repression, says Habermas, may be best understood linguistically because it might be similar to linguistic excommunication: "the splitting off of individual symbols from public communication would mean at the same time the privatization of their semantic content" (1968, 241–242).

Such systematic repression of what she might say seems to have skewed Karen's story. Uniformly, Karen uses the idea of role to suppress (if not consciously, then at least linguistically) references to her personal history, to her own wishes, to her feelings, and to conflict from her story. She seemed to feel that suggestions of her own autonomy, and a meaningful context in which to place it, were private data that were inadmissible, somehow taboo or uncalled for, in a story about career. In other words, this story also seems to tell us that for Karen her public persona and her private feeling are mutually exclusive and *must* have nothing to do with each other.

Modulation to Story 2: Going from Story to Action

Disidentifying with the first story

How could Karen find her way out of the apparently unambivalent subscription to her wifely "roles" that Story 1 portrayed? The answer seems to lie in her use of the story form itself. We might choose Mead's distinction between the "I" and the "me"—the experiencing, subjective "I" and the objectivated "me," one's view of self from the observing ego, the view one imagines others have of him—as a point of departure. Mead states that the "I" and the "me" are always interacting with each other and mutually formative, that is, one continually sees one's self from others' point of view and this affects how things are experienced (1934). But rarely does one express these private views out loud, that is, tell them to an audience as a story. The story form increases the distance between the "I" and the "me" by forcing the teller to commit himself or herself to a story line and increase his or her capacity as listener. A parallel may be that although we believe we know what we think, we discover the snags, inconsistencies, murkiness, or even downright surprises in our thoughts when we put them into words.

So with Karen. What she heard herself say in the first story took her aback. In the intervening interview material[2] before the next story began, she reflected that after she told—and heard—her first story she immediately began to divorce her identity from the passive protagonist of Story 1. Because we laid out Karen's story *as a story,* she had a previously unavailable means for self-reflection. By objectivating her self, she could step into the listener's role and hear what she was saying from a new perspective. She began to see that she didn't really know herself apart from her "role" stereotypes. As she looked back on her first story, she discovered: "I was not clear about who I was inside or, you know, afraid of confronting that whole thing. You know what I did? I had just gone right straight through from childhood into the different acceptable roles and never had a time when I was by myself. . . . I'm becoming aware that I have been very role oriented. And so, who am I, apart from all those roles? There must be somebody else in there."

This realization led her to pick up on hints she'd dropped outside of the main theme of her first story, questioning whether she had lost her self in her "conflicting segmented roles." "The student role was something that wasn't *really me*," she said. But neither was her family role: "All of the love and the tensions are there because of things that I consider quite apart from my *core personality*" (italics added). She concluded, "I don't know what freedom is. I would just like to be and do. But what that is, I'm not really sure." She wondered, "Would it be better to ignore or demote roles and to be myself—whatever that is?" She'd tried on the first story for size—in perhaps the same way as she might try on a dress—and found that it didn't fit, but didn't yet know what would.

Trying out new actions

But as she gained some distance from the protagonist of her first story, Karen began to see for herself some of the ambivalence that had been almost invisibly buried in the cracks of that story. What also seemed to be happening to Karen between stories 1 and 2 was a psychological development that capitalized on the narrative distance of the "I" from the protagonist (her objectivated "me") of the story. By hearing her story, almost as if it were a work of fiction, Karen was also free to step back, to withdraw her identification with her heroine and let the story proceed as it would—"out there," "as if" to someone else. With the ambiguity of identification that the "as if" mode afforded her, she was able to suspend belief in and tenancy of her habitual "me." Bettelheim points out how children can work through childhood terrors by placing them in another person, time, and place through a fairy tale (1976); similarly, Karen could confront fears and see possibilities that had seemed taboo or at least unthinkable in her first official story. And conversely, she could imagine for her fictional protagonist many alternative possibilities for action, experiencing a kind of expanded en-couraged imagination.[3] She experienced some of the sense of freedom that Robert Penn Warren ascribes to the "mere fact that in imagination we are getting off scot-free with something which we, or society, would never permit in real life" (1962, 153). With what Warren would call her "involvement and noninvolvement at the same time," Karen was able imaginatively to open up for herself a whole new version of possible thoughts, feelings, and actions. In using the story's *as if* mode, she could also start to rehearse different motivation and plot scenarios.

Complementing the possibility that narrative offered for movement were psychological conditions that fueled its progress. Karen, like most people who enter psychotherapy, was suffering from considerable ambivalence and confusion about her roles, felt stuck, unable to move forward in her life, and was in a certain amount of pain. She took to the interview process with a vengeance, despite her first opaque story; in fact, the contrast between the energy of her involvement in the process and the dearth of good initial material provided a kind of spontaneous combustion of the first story. Karen's vigor of engagement in the interview process sounded reminiscent of how Peter Blos (1962) describes the way trauma may be worked out in one's social world: with a feeling of self-evident rightness, determination, meaningfulness, and gratification.[4]

New actions give birth to a new story

Between telling her first and second stories, Karen exploded in a veritable whirlwind of activity, apparently (and by her description) *impelled* into new behavior by the vacuum left by moving her identification out of her first story. Karen realized that not only her story but also her life was unsatisfying. Now her imaginative participation in her "as if" heroine allowed Karen some ideas about how to surmount the feeling of "stuckness" that had characterized the daily life she described in her first story. At this point, action alternated with story. Karen started talking to others, which she never before had thought of doing. "I'm realizing . . . [my feelings] were intense afterward [after the first interview]. . . . I found that I *had* to talk about it. And I would search these people out again to discuss 'What is your self-image?' And I was surprised to hear that . . . they had gone through similar experiences of change in self-image. . . . It stimulated . . . an awareness that this was an OK thing to do, to be going through changes." Karen also initiated a reading campaign of novels and biographies as a way to investigate other women's feelings, especially those who had been able to tolerate difficulties and "tremendous pain," and who felt splits in themselves that were similar to her goddess-drudge dichotomy.

This led her to new courage with her husband. She began to question the priority she'd made of her husband's wishes and confronted him about his family responsibilities. She also discovered, to her surprise, "If I just go out and start marching around doing things [I want] . . . the other people adjust. . . . It turns out they're perfectly OK."

Even more of a contrast was Karen's fantasy life as she began to identify with a more assertive "as if" heroine. She began to entertain the "incredible" idea of taking time for herself, which led her to ponder fantasies of being "totally independent, just on my own," of no family to care for, of having an apartment away from her husband and children that would be "my own turf . . . a safe womb" that she could use as a retreat to get uninterrupted work time. In another of her new-found fantasies she placed herself at center stage, fearlessly leading an interdisciplinary research expedition of women to interpret South American tribal women's experience "from a woman's point of view."

Amid this roiling and fecund turmoil, Karen also began to return to the question of whether she had a purpose and a self beyond her roles. She laid the groundwork for this questioning by sifting through memories of how she'd felt when alone. She recalled positive memories of playing alone happily as a child. But somewhat wistfully, she said, "I was always a very alone person, even as a child." She quickly associated this to the fear she'd sometimes had when leaving her current structure of domestic life on professional trips. She described how she struggled with the "terrors of the night, what it might feel like to be without any supports. . . . I think I was afraid that I would go crazy."

Despite her fear of the dark side of being alone, Karen felt the pull to try it out. It was at this point—after her actions led to the emergence of previously suppressed pieces of her identity—that she launched into a coherent plot that sounded like a new story emerging.

Story 2: Aborted Careers—The Meaning of Children

In our second interview, three months after the first, Karen began to sow the seeds of a second story in the already fertile subject area of fantasies about being alone and independent of family. She did so in response to my question about the first steps she took toward her academic career. And as she did so, a recalcitrant counterstory to the first one emerged.

Karen returned to graduate school when her first child was eighteen months old. Although she described going to school as a "responsible" reaction to feeling tied down, and she could describe her distance from her daughter as a conscious choice to avoid an unhealthy power over her, she soon went on to reveal in a hushed tone and hesitant manner something that didn't fit at all with the dutiful wife and mother role: "I'm just beginning to admit that I had this terrible period with both [of my children]. . . . a terrible difficulty in accepting them . . . even though they were 'intensely' planned." She explained some of her apparently nurturing mothering as overcompensation in the face of an "imprisoning experience": "In the last few years I've really actively rejected them. I thought that to myself and *I've been able to say it to maybe one or two people.* That I just really wish that I didn't have children. And I've fantasized about walking out" [italics added].

Karen herself made the next connection about her ambivalence as a mother, recalling that her mother, she sensed, had a "terrific power struggle" with Karen. "I think she had that hostility and ambivalence about having children as an invasion of her life, just the same as I did."

Karen explained why this was so. At the time of their marriage, both parents had been in training to be professional academics with promising careers ahead of them. "When they were first married, she was *furious and ashamed* when she became accidently pregnant and she blamed my father for it. And now it turns out—I found out last year—that she went to her family doctor and tried to get an abortion, but the oral medicine that he gave didn't do the job." This led to fierce arguments between her parents. Her mother resentfully dropped out of her professional graduate program to care for the new infant (Karen's older brother), and her father stopped short of his doctoral dissertation in order to support the family. Her father eventually gave up hopes of a Ph.D. and of academics altogether and became a businessman. Karen read this move as a generous capitulation to her mother's pressure, out of her long-standing ambivalence, to become a "typical family" in which her mother would play a domestic role. Karen saw what happened to her father as "the same thing that happens to women today . . . 'I must give precedence to other people in my family.'" Because of the initially unwanted presence of children and Karen's mother's conflicted push to play a traditional role, Karen felt that her mother and father gave up their intellectual life and achievement aspirations.

She described herself as losing respect for her mother at that point. "I guess she probably would not challenge herself for fear of failing." Her mother's concerns became garden parties and "what kind of chicken salad to serve at the YWCA luncheon." Karen disgustedly described her mother's powerful intellectual force as focused on trivia, "*not* a responsible use of her time." Now the word *responsibility* used throughout the first story assumed more meaning. Karen had striven to be unlike her mother. "I see myself challenging myself in productive ways that . . . she *should* have done had she really been the person I'd like to have her be."

At this point, Karen's identifications seemed to be clear. She was determined not to be like her mother, who was selfish, domineering, and trivial. Karen had made a strong identification with her father, who she saw as patient, long-suffering, altruistic, and high-minded enough to acquiesce to her mother's demands. Perhaps it is no coincidence that she saw the psychological aspects of her father's role as more traditionally feminine or wifely. She may have maintained this "wifely" identification so strongly in the first story as a way to give him vicarious power over her mother with her idealization of him. Most important, in this story of aborted careers she was able to take more responsibility for her own almost desperate motivation to leave a traditional mother role and to refuse to let her children drain her life. As soon as her daughter was weaned, she "thrust" herself from the home with the force of a speeding bullet but made that move permissible and "responsible" by doing it for her daughter's sake as well. Part of the vacuum that "sucked her up," she could now tell me, was the horror of thwarted careers in her personal history.

Karen's second story is one of polarization of identity and family. She portrayed the pain of conflicting goals and concentrated on telling about separations: be-

tween mother and father, mother and herself, and brother from the family. Yet
even with its somber tone, this story is better than the first one. It gains context,
coherence, and dimension with the addition of personal history data that run
counter to her dutiful wifely role. By telling the first story and opening herself to
her subsequent thoughts and actions, Karen experienced permission to bring in
data that she had previously considered "private" or "personal" and thus inadmissible to a story that I would want to hear. In the act of reflection she successively:
(1) felt dismay at what her heroine sounded like in Story 1; (2) juxtaposed what she
felt to be her present self with the one she portrayed in the story; (3) imaginatively
re-created a fictional character more like the desired self; and then (4) reidentified
with it to produce new behavior. When her action then led into Story 2, the
previous psychological and narrative taboo on the private was lifted, and those
details that had been banned were called into discourse. In what Habermas calls
"de-privatization," a psychological *and linguistic* repression was removed to
allow thought *and talk* of the secrets of a dutiful wife and mother: resentment of
children, a botched abortion, aborted careers. This talk, in turn, led to actions that
allowed her to pull identity fragments from the past to rearrange them and begin to
rebuild a more robust, autonomous, purposive sense of self.

Most important, this "de-privatization" opened up the world of others' personal
experience to her. As she began her talking and reading campaign,[5] she broke out
of a rigid selective attention to permissible roles and considered other alterations
in fantasy and action, which led to a new story. It would be highly improbable that
only one encounter with me could result in such action were it not that Karen's
affect was already in a partially psychologically mobilized state, near enough to
the surface of consciousness to be accessible. Nevertheless, it seems significant
that *telling the story* gave her an opportunity to act and *through the story form* she
began reintroducing lost pieces of her personal history to her current life. Story led
to action, which led to new story, which in turn—as we shall see—led to further
action, ad infinitum, in ever-increasing concentric circles.

In following Karen through this cycle, it became clear that story and action were
not really separate entities, that the action could not be said to be a result of the
story in the sense of a cause. Rather, they seemed mutually interpenetrating.
Action and story created each other and were embedded in each other.

This story now seemed quite complete to Karen. "It's fascinating to think that
this is a relationship thing and more father-oriented. . . . But I really feel comfortable . . . about having buried my mother somehow." Given how much her story
had changed from first to second time, one might question how permanently these
newly defined identifications were fixed and how thoroughly her mother was
buried. Karen attested to the enormity of her emotional upheaval by commenting
that she was literally "shaking" at the end of telling her second story. As we
planned for the next interview, she commented: "In some ways it's unsettling
when we talk but it's probably better to do it and get into depth. I'd get it more

settled, I think, by going back to the same subject over and over. I begin to understand too, at least *I see a different facet of it every time* and God knows what the truth is" (italics added).

Story 3: The Responsible Daughter—Bringing My Family Together

Like Karen's first story, her second also was followed by action, this time of an even more spectacular variety. In Story 2, Karen began to identify her own achievement drive. Story 2 also produced profound regret over the lack of resolution of achievement motives, embodied in her parents' unfinished careers. These two factors appeared to combine and create a kind of spontaneous combustion. When added to her already existing motivation, this combustion seemed to produce a critical mass of the energy she needed to finish her long-procrastinated dissertation.

Karen preceded Story 3 by enthusiastically plunging into what she called her "freedom decision." Shortly after our second interview, in a burst of energy, she retreated to her parents' cabin—a building her father had built by hand, stone upon stone, which she called his "mausoleum"—and finished her long-delayed dissertation in a period of self-imposed isolation. During our third interview, eight months later, she compared (perhaps not coincidentally) the euphoria of her concentration to childbirth. She felt as if she'd gotten rid of her ambivalence, which she said consisted of asking herself whether a goal conflicted "with different things I wanted to do, different parts of my . . . identity. . . . Now I've gotten so much energy out of deciding I really want something! . . . Because I *really wanted* to get that dissertation done! I have never felt such goal attraction in my life!"

In describing the process, she told me how she had not only written in the cabin her father built but also had glued his picture to her typewriter. The result was that she felt her father's comforting presence hovering all around her, "his spirit supporting me." She again confirmed her identification with him in pointing out how her dissertation was on history, that her father was a would-be historian, and that she would graduate from the same university that he would have. As she elaborated, she began to launch into the body of Story 3.

Karen said she felt that the completion of her dissertation was the "rebirth of our family togetherness. It brought together my father, and my mother, and my brother." In explanation, she reflected that she had done something that neither of her parents had been able to do. She quickly moved to wondering whether she was not trying to complete her father's career and thereby resolve his conflict with her mother, correcting some of the injuries to his self-esteem that she felt her mother had inflicted on him and supporting her long-standing alliance with him. "And I have, I mean that is *exactly,* I think *exactly* what I've done for my father [in the dissertation] is say, 'Mother, you are *wrong!*' And in some way maybe I'm going to *prove* that you're wrong even. . . . I think it's the power of my mother that was bothering me. And that I transferred that power to my father."

But the identifications that had seemed so clear in Story 2 were now shifting; her actions were leading her into a new story. Karen realized that she was losing her father as an ideal because she was the one who was now bolstering his strength instead of vice versa.

Karen also felt that she had finally been able to make a critical metaphoric statement to her mother, as if to say, "Mother, you are wrong. You *can* have both career and children." (Parenthetically, Karen noted a further similarity. She was forty when she was finally able to write her dissertation, the age when her mother had finally given up all vestiges of a career outside the home.) Interestingly enough, having made this assertion, Karen now was able to describe her mother as a far more benign figure. Her mother sensitively interpreted how Karen's dissertation had played out a part of her marital conflict. In turn, Karen, through recognizing her own ambivalence, became much more sympathetic to her mother's pull in two different, and nearly mutually exclusive, directions. Her first story, she realized, was a mirror of her mother's plight as well as her own.

This was a highly emotional realization for Karen. And she found that her discovery was not complete. There was an additional way in which her dissertation represented "family togetherness." Karen's dissertation was done on a fairly obscure topic: the meaning of children and population control policy in the political history of a remote South American region. Though esoteric, her topic had great theoretical impact. And now Karen reflected that it also had interpersonal family significance. She was also trying to assuage and repair the harm done to her parents in giving up their careers for children. She hoped to repair whatever damage she had done them by being born—whatever the "cost" of her existence to their ambitions—by allowing them vicariously to experience her achievement. And the point she made to them was that she recognized their pain and that this was a universal pain—other souls suffered as they did. Knowing full well that her ability to do what they had not might also rub salt in their wounds, she first— *without knowing what she was doing*—completed their aborted careers and only then let herself experience her own autonomy and the energy of her goal-directed behavior. Only then, by being dutiful and responsible in her role as daughter, did she feel permission to proceed with her own life. "That's incredible," she said, "but, yes, I needed them so much because they fulfilled a function of making this thing that I was doing for myself acceptable . . . by making it meet other people's needs also."

As she spoke, Karen realized that she had also been trying to incorporate her brother, with his long-standing feelings of rejection, into this "family togetherness." She used his suggestion of topic and invaluable help in finding documents. The region of South America she wrote about was the same place that her brother had fled to at the time of his traumatic separation from the family, the site of his "declaration of independence." Story 2 was a history of separations. This story, in contrast, was a story of reconciliation and unity, achieved by modulating polarized identifications and vicariously reversing losses. Karen could finally acknowledge her ambivalence fully and understand why she'd had to push it from consciousness previously. At this point Karen also could let herself experience her own achievement drive to the fullest extent. And she was quite clear about that being her concealed and repressed motive all along: "There are requirements of the situation that are unexpected, unknown, or—perhaps—*willfully* unknown. I might not have recognized my purpose. But once they're there, they became things I had to do." In gaining her purpose, she felt she'd also recovered the elusive self—tough, independent, and fiercely goal oriented—that had been smothered by the "roles" of Story 1.

Story 3 is an improvement on Story 2 in narrative as well as psychological terms. This pass over the story is not only more comprehensive, with the addition of layers of meaning, but also more satisfying psychologically. Karen had recovered her past and identity fragments, discovered early life historical paradigms for present-day action, resolved the associated ambivalences, and claimed "responsibility" for reestablishing her own sense of control. This story has added dimension to what initially sounded like the clichés of "role" and "responsibility." The narrative distance Karen achieved has paid off with gratifying action. That her story also has dynamic tension goes almost without saying—this story is a rip-snorter!

Putting the story—action—story cycle in perspective, Karen's case can now suggest the following conditions for improving storytelling: (1) there has to be a "bad" story; (2) experience and the constructs that represent it have to be narratively and psychologically opened up through reflection; (3) some psychological readiness or mobilization in the form of discomfort, however subtle, must be present; and (4) the story must be able to lead to action and back again.

An individual psychologist might feel that Karen has arrived at an ultimate explanation. Yet any good psychoanalytic interpretation, as well as any good story, tells us about the human condition as well as about the individual case. It also makes a social or a political interpretation to point beyond itself. And this is what Karen was able to do in her last story.

Story 4: Repressed Autonomy—Roles in Perspective

"I feel like Job," Karen said some months after completing her dissertation. "Is this too visited upon me?" Karen had experienced a feeling of freedom and increased power as she assumed functions of control that she previously had attributed to husband, father, and mother. But now she began to realize that the painful struggle which she experienced in doing so was not only a demonstration of fear or ambivalence about loss of a framework. It was also a reluctance on the part of others to recognize this transformation. Karen's last story shows us that it was not simply an intrapsychic shift occurring through changing story and action but a transformation taking place in every sphere of her interpersonal and social worlds. In contrast to the previous narratives in which action alternated with story, Story 4 unfolds through the interpenetrating step-wise progression of Karen's action and a simultaneous reaction (or nonreaction) from her environment.

Story 4 began in our fourth interview, only one month after the third interview. Karen began her story by talking about how her long-awaited Ph.D. was ignored by her department. "It was one of the crowning blows. Even my supporters did not announce that I had finally gotten this certificate [Ph.D.]. Finally I waited and waited, and I just had to announce it myself. I guess they feel like I'm too much of a hot potato even to discuss." She saw the problem as one of control. She had changed from the student role, which she felt was a passive or even a victim role ("like a little dog you can lead around on a leash"), into one with more autonomy. But she felt this was almost impossible for her department to accept. "They could not understand me and were totally opposed [to my appointment], to such a nontraditional career, a backward career. The problem is they can't control a mature woman, and they're just not going to approve of that kind of career path."

She directed further resentment at her mentor, a man much like her father (in fact, someone she had called a "father figure"), who seemed reluctant to let her go. "My mentor now considers me *invisible*. . . . They think you'll always have the same ideas."

Karen found that the resistance to her development extended into her relationship with her husband. Although he'd expected, even required, her to get a Ph.D., now that she had, he was terribly threatened by her independence. When she wanted to buy her car without his help, he exploded and seemed to feel that her increased sense of competence diminished his own.

By this point, Karen was furious. She said she could imagine nothing more degrading than the kind of invisibility she was experiencing when she now expanded her old role in ways that others refused to recognize. "It's insulting and offensive . . . to avoid [someone] . . . , avoidance is *nothingness*, it's that kind of invisibility."

Karen's dismay at "nothingness" now explains her previously described ambivalence about being alone. Karen used the analogy of "mirroring" her social world by producing the behavior it expected of her. In Stories 2 and 3 she began to address feelings of wanting to look in the mirror to construct a "self-identity." Now as she looks at herself in the mirror of others' acknowledgment, she saw the horror of nothingness. This reminded her that she had perhaps unconsciously known she would have to face this and, fearing it, had invented excuses (including those of the good wife and mother) to remain stuck. "[Before], I don't think I was strong enough [to go ahead with my career]. I don't believe that I could face that identity *without shattering inside*. I don't think I had a strong enough image of who I was to survive, but I know I hated those roles. (Were you hiding something?) A nothingness, I guess. A *fear of nothingness*. It was like the fear of darkness at night, the *fear that there was nothing there*." (italics added)

Karen's last story climaxes vigorously, in the turmoil of stormy emotion. During a follow-up interview, years later, she filled in the denouement. She and her husband had to learn, painfully, to "readjust roles." Their eventually successful struggle had been one of the "costs" Karen had unconsciously anticipated. Her son and daughter lived through this strife apparently none the worse for wear. Her daughter, now launched as an adult, is repeating the intergenerational "declaration of independence"—she is in the Peace Corps in South America. Karen weathered the demise of her department and is now a full professor at a small women's college.

Karen's fourth story leaves one with conflicting emotions: it does not have an unambiguously happy ending. Her stories have progressed from identity confusion to resolution and back; her final story had led us from euphoria to role rigidity and social repression. Yet in a sense the last story is the best story because it tells us more than the others by giving us a perspective that explains all of them. Story 4 looks back to previous stories and tells us not only about what was wrong but also about the *reasons* for the distortions and repressions existing in the first place.

But in the same breath that we congratulate the fourth story on being better, we have to admit that the first story was a necessary clue to it, and that all the stories taken together, coexisting, bring each one of them to life. Rather than supplanting one another, they are interdependent. To understand any one of them, we must hear them all.

Now we can add a final criterion for a good story: the story should point beyond itself. Karen's fourth story explains why linguistic excommunication was necessary in the first place and thereby eradicates it. Karen's final story has achieved this by bringing together the personal and the social. We finally understand not only why Story 1 was a bad story but also why it *had to be* a bad story. Story 4 actually describes the social conditions, what Habermas calls the "recognized normative context," in which Story 1 was told and to which it was addressed. In other words, Story 4 describes both the context and the anticipated audience for Story 1. It tells us that Karen was fearful of the "costs" she would have to pay should she break out of a traditional feminine "role," which society considered her "responsibility." Reading between the lines one can see that Karen actually used Story 1 as a kind of disclaimer or contradiction of her actions and her "willfully unknown" purpose. It became a kind of shibboleth with which to slip under the censorship of social norms. Like the shibboleth password, however, Karen's story rang false enough to alert the sensitive listener to the fact that she was not a true believer in rigid gender roles and was trying to smuggle unnoticed her career change into traditionally male territory.[6] Karen had to hide her true story from herself and others in order for them to let what she was about to do go unnoticed.

Karen's story is now better in that it has taken on explanatory power as well as passion and vigor, context, congruence, and control. Her story is now filled with dynamic tension, encompassing both the good and the bad, the acceptable and unacceptable wishes and roles, motivations and obstacles. It captures the bittersweet ambiguity of her life and of all lives.

But not just Karen's stories are better. As story and action mutually elicited each other, her *life* became better. To apply the truest test of a psychoanalytic interpretation—she *felt* better: happier; freer to exercise independence, autonomy, and agency; more knowledgeable, mature, and self-confident; and more able to cope with her life. Karen had now discovered a purpose and in that purpose, recovered her sense of self.

From the vantage point of the fourth story, Karen could see that repression had been lifted in her life as well as in her story. Reflecting on the interview process through which her stories had evolved, she realized how meager had been the support in her life for examining her experience. She said, "I had never really talked to people about myself." And her reflections on the process confirmed the speculative link made earlier in this chapter about how placing the "me" in a story form can "open up" a life and lead to action and change. "I recognized that every day my mind was changing about various things, not that they were contradictory but that it was a developing process."

A final interview, which took place a year after the fourth interview, formed a coda to Story 4. In that interview, Karen testified to the effect of telling her story on the way she now felt and lived her life. "I felt that the interviews really were formative for me," she said, because she felt that the interviews were "responsible for creating the idea that I have a self-image of my own." "So," she concluded, "it was critical," to her changing self-concept probably because "it's like a freedom; *by articulating*, I get a lot of power."

Karen felt that by the end of the interviews she'd learned much about the rules that had suppressed the language available for her story. She volunteered advice to other people who might also begin to feel that something wasn't right in the way they had to live or had to speak, thereby offering a nice synopsis of what this chapter starting out asking: how do we sniff out a "bad story" and what to do about it. "It [the thing wrong] doesn't even have to be so blatant. . . . It's just [that] I think it would be useful [to] always have your antennae out into the atmosphere, find out what's going on. Pick up clues that are dissonant with what you think should be going on. Go read a book, talk to other people, go to church groups or any groups that are useful, think about it, set aside a time to think about it during a shower or walk or anything. And it may be unresolved for a year or ten years. But anyway, it's something that doesn't fit, and sometime you're going to need to know about that and try to make it fit."

That Karen could transform her story has implications reaching far beyond a single life. This phenomenon concerns us as researchers, as social scientists, and as citizens of the world. In careful listening to how the stories evolved—why it could not be known or told initially and how it was gradually transformed—we can see, in microcosm, a telling indictment of how communication, sometimes subtly or unconsciously, is constricted by the ideological setting. And in seeing the reversal of this process, we see how such systematic privatization may be undone. Karen's story restored the multiple meanings of her words to her speech, her purpose to her self, and a realization of political realities to her life. In good story telling, to reiterate Robert Penn Warren, we are returned to ourselves and to the world.

NOTES

1. We have no sense of moving inevitably, excitingly forward in this story because it has the same static quality that Kris describes in the "personal myth," a nearly unassailably rigid idealized distortion of the past, usually created to deny or suppress awareness of trauma and consequent ambivalence to persons or events in one's history (1956).
2. Karen and I began each interview by thinking about the preceding one. She would refine my paraphrase of what she'd said and offer her own analysis of her story up to that point. Karen and I picked out the first story's theme from the surrounding material in much the same way that Elliot Mishler describes doing in analyzing interview narrative (1986). Note that each story roughly—not exactly—corresponds with each successive interview, i.e., the bulk of Story 1 occurred in interview 1, and so on.
3. Rosenwald has termed this *aesthetic differentiation* (unpublished ms.).
4. The reader will note that this is the second time trauma has been suggested, even if in an aside. This is more than coincidental and suggests that Karen is suffering from repressed pain of traumatic proportions and that one of the functions of her first story has been to deny this pain. The reasons for it, however, remain unclear so far. For further discussion of this point, see Wiersma (1988).
5. The other eighteen subjects in this study who were interviewed in depth also reported that one of the effects of telling their first stories was that they began communication campaigns to ask other people about what they had previously considered taboo subjects.
6. For further explanation of this phenomenon and its occurrence in the other subjects in this study see Wiersma (1988) and Rosenwald and Wiersma (1983).

REFERENCES

Bardwick, J. M. 1980. "The Seasons of a Woman's Life." In *Women's Lives: New Theory, Research, and Policy.* Edited by Dorothy G. McGuigan. Ann Arbor: University of Michigan, Center for Continuing Education of Women.

Bettelheim, B. 1976. *The Uses of Enchantment.* New York: Alfred A. Knopf.

Blos, P. 1962. *On Adolescence: A Psycho-Analytic Interpretation.* New York: Free Press of Glencoe.

Carlson, R. 1981. "Studies in Script Theory: I. Adult Analogs of a Childhood Nuclear Scene." *Journal of Personality and Social Psychology* 40:501–510.

Dickens, D. R. 1983. "The Critical Project of Jürgen Habermas." In *Changing Social*

Science. Edited by D. R. Sabia and J. Wallalis. Albany: State University of New York Press.

Forster, E. M. [1927] 1963. *Aspects of the Novel.* London: E. Arnold. pp. 25–42.

Gergen, K. J., and M. M. Gergen. 1986. "Narrative Form and the Construction of Psychological Science." In *Narrative Psychology: The Storied Nature of Human Conduct.* Edited by T. R. Sarbin. New York: Praeger.

Gergen, M. (this volume).

Habermas, J. [1968] 1971. "Self-reflection as Science: Freud's Psychoanalytic Critique of Meaning." In *Knowledge and Human Interests.* Translated by Jeremy J. Shapiro. Boston: Beacon Press.

Kris, E. 1956. "The Personal Myth: A Problem in Psychoanalytic Technique." *Journal of the American Psychoanalytic Association* 4: 653–681.

Langer, S. K. 1953. *Feeling and Form: A Theory of Art.* New York: Charles Scribner's Sons.

Mathiot, M., ed. 1979. *Ethnolinguistics: Boas, Sapir, and Whorf Revisited.* New York: Mouton.

McAdams, D. P. 1985. *Power, Intimacy, and the Life Story: Personological Inquiries into Identity.* Chicago: Dorsey Press. (Reprinted by Guilford Press.)

Mead, G. H. 1934. *Mind, Self and Society.* Chicago: University of Chicago Press.

Mishler, E. 1986. "The Analysis of Interview Narratives." In *Narrative Psychology: The Storied Nature of Human Conduct.* Edited by T. R. Sarbin. New York: Praeger.

Murray, H. A., et al. 1938. *Explorations in Personality.* New York: Oxford University Press.

Ochberg, R. L. 1988. "Life Stories and the Psychosocial Construction of Careers." In *Psychobiography and Life Narratives.* Edited by D. P. McAdams and R. L. Ochberg. Durham, N.C.: Duke University Press.

Rosenwald, G. C., and J. K. Wiersma. 1983. "Women, Career Changes and the New Self: An Analysis of Rhetoric." *Psychiatry* 46:312–229.

Sarbin, T. R. 1986. "The Narrative as a Root Metaphor for Psychology." In *Narrative Psychology: The Storied Nature of Human Conduct.* Edited by T. R. Sarbin. New York: Praeger.

Sherwood, M. 1969. *The Logic of Explanation in Psychoanalysis.* New York: Academic Press.

Tomkins, S. S. 1987. "Script theory." In *The Emergence of Personality.* Edited by J. Aronoff, A. I. Rabin, and R. A. Zucker. New York: Springer Verlag.

Warren, R. P. 1962. "Why Do We Read Fiction?" *Saturday Evening Post,* Oct. 20, 148–158.

White, R. W. 1981. "Exploring Personality the Long Way: The Study of Lives." In *Further Explorations in Personality.* Edited by A. I. Rabin, J. Aronoff, A. M. Barclay, and R. A. Zucker. New York: John Wiley.

Wiersma, J. K. 1988. "The Press Release: Symbolic Communication in Life History Interviewing." In *Psychobiography and Life Narratives.* Edited by D. P. McAdams and R. L. Ochberg. Durham, N.C.: Duke University Press.

RICHARD L. OCHBERG

12 Social Insight and Psychological Liberation

One of the central ideas that guides the interpretation of life stories, at least for those of us gathered in this volume, is that self-understanding is always shaped by culture. The tales we tell each other (and ourselves) about who we are and might yet become are individual variations on the narrative templates our culture deems intelligible. This has implications for both private lives and the social order itself. For the cultural circumscription of self-understanding controls—more intimately than overt power—our sense of our character and our allegiance.

All communities, of course, set rules of conduct, which members violate at their peril. But there is a more deeply binding loyalty. Every society also presents a vision of the world: an image of what is permissible and admirable—and what is illicit and inferior. Members in good standing align their own desires with those their culture prizes. By contrast, whatever thoughts, emotions, behavior, and even physical self-images cannot be cropped to the cultural template may become a source of embarrassment and guilt. In turn, those who trim their desires to the cultural standard and ascribe their occasional dissatisfaction and rebellion to personal maladjustment are unlikely to rock the social order that constrains them.

This skeptical view of socially constricted self-understanding holds out an optimistic corollary. For the narrowing of psychological and political horizons depends, in part, on the invisibility of the rules that shape discourse. (It also depends on material reality, which is why telling better life stories is no substitute for political change.) If individuals grow skeptical of social authority, however, they may reassess not only what we ordinarily mean by "politics" but also their own characters. Desires that once seemed illicit may now seem reasonable; strategies of circumventing social rules that once seemed proof of dishonesty may now appear as civil disobedience. In turn, such a revised self-estimate may embolden some people to resist—or even change—the constricting social order itself. There may be, in short, a reciprocal tie between psychological and political liberation.

This chapter explores the potential for self-reclamation that exists when people grow skeptical of social authority. It focuses on what I will call "social strategy"— that is, the way individuals may wrest power and authority from the various social groups to which they belong.

Briefly (and here I must modify the picture of total social control described a moment ago), membership is not an all-or-nothing affair. Further, there is no simple correspondence between the perfection of one's membership and one's self-regard. Dissidents may see themselves as fearful of punishment or cheerfully defiant, bitterly cynical or members of the loyal opposition, apathetic or creatively iconoclastic, and so on.

What one makes of one's dissent no doubt depends on subjective estimates of *power* and *authority*. Individuals who feel (for whatever combination of accurate social perception and psychodynamic sensitivity) that their rebelliousness places them in danger are likely to feel anxious. Even where the threat of punishment is minimal, those who take for granted the moral authority of the group may feel that the imperfection of their membership is proof of their personal deficiency.

In this way social discreditation may appear to ratify the most fundamental doubts people entertain about their weak morals, poor ability, or even, in the primitive logic of psychodynamic symbolism, defective bodies. But if, on the other hand, one concludes that dissent is a vigorous and legitimate counterattack on an illegitimately constrictive social order, all the other signs may be reversed as well. A style of social opposition that once confirmed one's deepest self-doubts may now become the means by which those doubts are allayed and a new selfhood reclaimed.

The case history I present here illustrates this possibility. It is drawn from an interview study of students who dropped out of college and took up temporary residence in exotically alien communities (Ochberg, 1986). Many of these students, on their return, described what might be called a lesson in "sociological insight." They became aware of how societies are organized—perhaps more exactly, aware *that* societies are organized. This lesson, discovered by some in Third World villages and by others in the grittier sections of urban America, clarified something about their own position in a web of social organization. Thus Greg described his dawning perception:

> I started a schedule of observing. I got a bike and went riding around Boston, especially around the docks and railyards and factory districts. And I visited some other cities: New York, Chicago, and Minneapolis. I started seeing some kind of big pattern. The configuration of the factories and railways, the turnpike and stuff around the inlets of water, was very similar. I knew how to find that in every city, so I'd just go down and check it out, and take more pictures. I got an idea of how that configuration in every city tied in to the experiences I'd had growing up a long way from any urban center. The way anyone survives in a rural setting is that they are in a network that basically consists of a telephone line, a highway, an electric line, and maybe a gas main. For the first time I realized what it was that went on in cities that made it possible for me to live very comfortably in a rural setting. Working with film at the time made it a lot

more coherent. It was like I was taking notes on it. It involved tracing things back and trying to find intersections.

Of course, there is something overly elemental about Greg's discovery. Social structure is not only gas mains and electric lines. It is also—even more fundamentally if less palpably—the institutions and codes that preserve social power. These pieces of the social machinery are considerably less visible than literal infrastructure.

Further, social insight does not inevitably make one critical. Greg's articulation of the social skeleton did not make him a revolutionary. What he read in the large bones of gas mains and electric lines was a lesson in social support. But someone with a different agenda might have discerned a different moral. For the discovery of social arrangement—the insight that social life *is* an arrangement—carries with it the understanding that life might be arranged otherwise. The vast welter of details, the million unaligned particulars, take form. And it becomes clear that if the gas mains—or the habits of banks—were altered, the lives of those caught up in these ever so man-made webs would alter as well. The elucidation of social power is simultaneously the demystification of authority. This is what Catherine, who spent two years with the Peace Corps in Africa, understood.

This may be the moment to forestall a possible confusion. Although Catherine told me her story, sitting many evenings over a tape recorder, this is not an analysis of narrative. My concern will not be with the rhetorical strategy Catherine brought to her telling of the tale but with her self-understanding. Still, this case bears upon issues that frame the narrative interpretation of life stories. I assume that the narrative strategies available to individuals are shaped by public discourse and may be enlarged when the hidden cultural assumptions that limit discourse are made visible. Catherine illustrates the relation between enlarged understanding of society and the self and in this sense speaks to the larger interests that motivate the cultural critique of narrative.

Catherine

The developmental history I will sketch focuses on Catherine's "social strategy" —her way of being a member of various social groups and gradually taking control of the quality of those memberships. The quality of her membership, in turn, influenced her sense of self: her sexuality, her competence, and her moral character.

It may be most useful to begin this history in the middle, with Catherine's high school years and her first years of college. For it was the doubts of this age (incorporating, to be sure, the residue of earlier self-doubts and partial resolutions) that her years in Africa redressed.

In high school, then, Catherine found herself facing a common problem of bright, ambitious women. It seemed to her that it would be extremely difficult to combine a family and a career. The problem was not simply that each demanded time and energy (real as that struggle promised to be, it was a separate issue) but that men seemed unable to think of women as simultaneously feminine and competent—and that women seemed to agree. This conclusion had been forced upon her by the evidence of her parents' lives and her own experience.

As Catherine saw it, her mother had achieved only a self-abnegating, second-class citizenship in a family that revolved around the father's work. (He was a professor of religion.) "Both my mother and I were peripheral. Her failure to get out from under my father's shadow meant that the only way out for me would be by marriage, and then again being under someone's shadow. If my bad self-image has a role model it is her. She was always putting herself down relative to him. . . . One reason I respected her opinion so little is that she respected herself so little."

Although in this passage Catherine concentrates on her mother's subordination, she suggests that she too felt "peripheral." Elsewhere she elaborated on the idea, saying, "All my friends were faculty brats." The phrase was striking enough for me to question; she explained "that is what people called us. It is fairly descriptive of being a peripheral part of something, and not a particularly valuable one; connected to the core through a relationship."

Catherine's sense of being dismissed was heightened by her father's preoccupation with his work and possibly his emotional distance. She recalls him as an affectionate father when she was very young, writing little stories about his daughters—they were mostly about her older sister, Cindy—that he would read to them. As they got older and Cindy became more of a troublemaker, "He withdrew more and more from being a father," leaving his family increasingly on the margins of his attention.

There was no sharing this part of his life. As a teenager Catherine tried. She recalls asking her father about his work and that he would always turn her aside with a joke or an anecdote. "His students could get answers, but I always felt unworthy." Speaking of her loss of religious faith in eighth grade she said, "I just couldn't get an answer. I prayed my heart out, 'Show me you're there,' but I got no answer. I have never been much good at these one-sided conversations." In part she was talking about God (in part, her frustration with my saying little in our interviews), but I imagine I hear the echoes of her frustration with her unreachable father.

Catherine's father dominated the family by virtue of his professional stature. This is not in itself a matter of sexual politics, though Catherine surely observed that the three women in her family were minor planets around a masculine sun. The incompatibility between serious intellectual competence (the apparent domain of men or, at best, asexual women) and feminine frivolousness took shape only as she grew older. By high school, however, it seemed clear that femininity and intellectual competence were an unlikely mix.

She was smarter in unfeminine math (and everything else) than the boys in her class. They honored her by never asking her out. In response to this dilemma Catherine perfected a strategy of presenting different images of herself to different groups of admirers. At school and at home she was the perfect scholar. At the same time she began dating a boy from across town and then several of his friends, who went to different schools. There was a secret club room stocked with liquor, and she had her first experiments with sex. To make it all work she carefully kept apart her different circles of friends. School and parents knew nothing of her teenage rebelliousness; her boyfriends knew nothing of her academic success.

By dividing her world in this way Catherine seemed to have everything: she could be smart and ambitious at school, sexy across town. But her success was spoiled by her self-recrimination.

There were two parts to me, the goody-goody and the more daring, less bound by parents' and others' wishes. That was the real me, flirting with evil. But I had also begun to reject my parents' notion of evil; it was just too all-encompassing. The only way I could cope with that was to compartmentalize; lie to my parents about the club room. . . . I took pleasure from concocting good lies, from manipulating the system, from being unique, which I couldn't be at home. It was a complex balancing act, manipulating impressions, yet it seemed to confirm that I was evil at the core, the way my parents would have thought. The only reason they were pleased with me was false; it was an image I created, SATS and so on.

To understand why Catherine might have felt "evil at the core" we need to consider her history of childhood doubts, whose incomplete resolution cast a shadow on this otherwise promising solution. These doubts, as I have suggested, concern the relation between her sense of her self and her sense of being a member in good standing.

Catherine's doubts about herself go back to earliest childhood and perhaps to what she feared inheriting. Her sister Cindy, three years older, was adopted after her mother had a series of miscarriages. Until the birth of her own children set her fears at rest, Catherine worried that she too might have difficulty bearing children. Aside from her feared maternal inheritance Catherine had her own history of physical self-doubt. As a young child she had scoliosis, had to have several operations, and wore a brace. "It was painful. I felt that there was something basically wrong with me, that all this money, and pain, and time might possibly cure."

I find Catherine's turn of phrase suggestive. "Money, pain, and time" hint at expiation. Did she think, as a child well might, that her physical disability was in some way a moral defect as well? The connection between bodies in their literal sense and as moral symbols is one that will recur.

Catherine's history became more explicitly moral—and social—in the next few years. As we have heard, Catherine felt that both she and her mother were peripheral in the family. But it was her sister Cindy who provided the most striking example of how moral discreditation could lead to social extrusion.

What Cindy thought of her family status we will never know. From her behavior it seems possible that she tried to test the adopted child's predictable fear of being "sent back." Whatever her reasons, by fourteen Cindy was sexually promiscuous, using drugs, drinking, staying out all night and sleeping all day. In response her parents sent her to a special school for the emotionally disturbed and then, briefly, to a psychiatric hospital.

Cindy sinned brazenly and was punished; Catherine observed and learned to be discreet. As a child, she recalled feeling forever on the edge of doing something unforgivable and straining not to slip. Cindy kept a box of fishing tackle and extra socks under her bed in case she had to escape; several times she did run away. Catherine "figured to be real careful, and not make anyone upset with me."

I feel the pain now; I've talked about this in therapy. I don't know what I felt then. The result, in terms of fearfulness, was needing to curry favor. Feeling that anything I was likely to do might be wrong. Some things I knew were right, like going to Sunday school, or not eating with my mouth open. I thought, if I could just do the things I know how to do, then maybe things would be okay.

She pictures herself back then "a scared, mealy-mouthed little girl, tied to my mother's apron strings, who panicked when anything got out of control." One story: she and a young playmate set some waxed paper aflame. Catherine panicked; the friend calmly put out the fire. Later Catherine kicked herself: she should have been as cool.

These memories of early childhood sketch a first relationship between social membership and selfhood. Catherine feared she might be banished like her sister and imagined she might turn into "another bad daughter." (Her sense of potential "badness" drew force from her earlier conclusion that something—physical? moral?—was "basically wrong.") There is a certain ambiguity here. Is she speaking of how others might see her or of how she saw herself? The essential point is that these are intertwined. If Catherine's worst fantasies came true and she incurred her family's condemnation, her self-estimate would also turn. In her own eyes as well, the "basically wrong" part of her would take over the field.

Her first, fearful sense of membership reflects a child's powerlessness. As she grew older and more self-reliant her sense of both membership and self changed. A memory from a few years later shows a different portrait. She got lost and wandered the streets for hours until, by herself, she found her way home. "It never occurred to me that I could just sit down and cry; I was looking for something. I could have thrown myself on the mercy of the first passing adult and gotten out of the situation. But I never saw myself, even as a little kid, as having so little responsibility." She recalls putting herself to a hundred little tests (Peace Corps itself was one) to bring the panic under control. It was, she said, like "holding myself up to something like a buffing wheel. Being honed."

With her growing self-assurance came rebellion, but more discreet than Cindy's. For a time Cindy saw a therapist, who reported back to her parents everything said in confidence. Catherine profited from the example: she would make sure that secrets told in one part of her world would not find their way back.

She gleefully recounted an elaborate hoax to get an extension on a class project. The library of the college where her father taught was taken over by students protesting the Vietnam war. Every newspaper covered the story. Of course, she said, it was not at all newsworthy that the protesters left the next morning. Catherine claimed that her notes had been locked in the library during a three-day siege and won her extension.

The previous year her high school class spent six months studying in France. Bored in a math class that she found too easy, Catherine found herself the leader of a cheating ring. She said, "Their rules seemed ridiculous. They didn't apply to me; I was from somewhere else."

In her early years of high school, then, Catherine began to develop a social strategy of divide and conquer. French rules had no power over her because she was "from somewhere else"; she could circumvent the rules in her own school because they did not understand what went on at her father's college. By this point in her life Catherine had largely overcome her fear of the *power* of social institutions. She no longer feared outright punishment. But her fear of banishment had been replaced by something else: her uncertainty about moral *authority*.

Sometime in junior high school Catherine began to have doubts about religion. She recalled writing a paper in eighth grade about Catholicism. "I was fascinated by their idea of the difference between mortal and venial sin, because in my family it did not seem that there was anything less than a mortal sin, and that was, you know, not brushing your teeth well enough. And that if I got caught in something minor their whole view of me would shift, and I would become like Cindy, another bad daughter."

Her exaggeration (not brushing your teeth was a mortal sin) makes it clear that this was no longer her own view of delinquency. Yet if Catherine no longer accepted her parents' brand of religious orthodoxy she very much admired their moral commitment. The problem was that moral commitment needed to be built on some solid ground. For her parents that ground was established by religious faith. Having rejected their faith, Catherine wondered where she could find a replacement of equal moral solidity. Her discomfort is suggested by her description, a few years later, of her radical college friends. She said she admired their commitment but felt "their beliefs were ad hoc, baseless; I couldn't build them up from anything solid."

To return, finally, to Catherine's high school strategy of living in divided worlds and the moral anxiety it evoked: she had come a long way from the mealymouthed kid she now remembers with disdain. Unlike Cindy or her mother, she could be sexy *and* competent—living effectively (if dangerously) in a world in which these are usually mutually exclusive options for women. Yet her "divide and conquer" social strategy ran afoul of her need for grounded commitment; it seemed to cast her as an opportunist. Like her radical college friends, she seemed to herself all too willing to make the most of what any situation offered: "It seemed to confirm that I was evil at the core."

The history I have sketched so far focuses on two themes. One is the doubt Catherine had about herself as a woman: doubt about her body, about whether men would find her attractive, about whether marriage would restrict her career. The other was her moral uncertainty: having turned away from her parents' religious faith, could she discover an alternative basis for conviction, or was she adrift on a sea of opportunism?

I must emphasize that each of these concerns was partly a matter of how Catherine saw herself and partly how she experienced her relationships with others. For example, by her first years of college Catherine had half-concluded that she did not want children. This decision (which she reached with considerable reluctance) drew its force partly from her doubt about herself: could she be, did she want to be, sexual? But the image we hold of ourselves is not strictly distinct from our sense of our relationships with others. Catherine's experience of her own sexuality (and morality) might change through a shift in her sense of being connected to others. As I'll try to make clear, Africa altered Catherine's sense of herself in both these individual and relational ways.

Now we should not assume too quickly that we know what an improvement in relatedness means. Catherine, of course, had felt on the margins of various groups all her life. The problems she anticipated, both in combining family and career and in working out her own view of moral commitment, were each related to her sense of wanting to do something socially unorthodox. We might imagine, therefore, that what Catherine most needed was to find a community of like-minded souls: one where men find smart, ambitious women sexy, and where careers and families are simultaneous possibilities. And of course this might have helped. But saying this oversimplifies things, psychologically and socially. Speaking psychologically, Catherine had reversed her earlier fear of banishment; her marginality was now purposeful—a source of pride and competence. Discovering a more perfectly fitting community might not have reassured her—it might have robbed her of her élan. From a social point of view, Catherine would eventually have to live in a world where careers and families forever tear at women's commitment. If she was going to maneuver successfully in these social conditions she would need all her skill at manipulating divided worlds. In short, though Catherine did indeed need to feel related to the world in something better than a marginal, opportunistic fashion, more perfect membership, in the conventional sense, would not be her answer.

Africa

Starting the summer after her graduation from college Catherine spent two years in a village in Uganda, where she taught school and organized a rural health center. Occasionally she visited other Peace Corps volunteers (the closest a day's bus ride away) and went back home one Christmas, but for the most part she spent her time in a world dramatically removed from the United States. In that time her conception of the world—and herself—shifted.

In part, rural African culture offered Catherine an image of life—women's lives in particular—that she could imaginatively try on for size. Back home, femininity and competence had seemed irreconcilable. Tribal culture, however, expected hard labor of women no less than of men. Vigorously physical women were seen as both competent and sexual. Catherine said: "It made having children and being feminine seem more legitimate, because both could be good? In more ways than just attracting men; it expanded what being feminine is all about. Fear of success was just about not having dates on Saturday—nothing about other aspects of femininity."

Of course, African images of womanhood could not solve the problem Catherine would encounter the moment she returned home. She would again face a world in which social roles segregate men's work and women's domesticity, men's aggressive ambitiousness and women's tender self-effacement. But if Catherine could not bring home with her Africa's social organization she could at least borrow local images to reinterpret for herself her own desires and capacity. She could envision motherhood as a form of female competence and in this way reclaim her own desire for a family.

If Africa offered an alternative to previously segregated images of femininity and competence, tribal culture was less directly helpful on the score of moral commitment. When Catherine set off for Africa she had every intention of immersing herself in whatever worldview local culture might offer. Still indignant at the coerciveness of American orthodoxies (her parents', her schoolmates') she said, "Americans don't even have a word like *Weltanschauung*. They can't imagine there could be more than one." As for Africa, "I did not want to study that culture; I wanted to look with its eyes at the world."

As it turned out, tribal culture did offer an alternative to Western cosmology but one so alien to Catherine's beliefs that it proved indigestible. She was shocked to discover, for example, that several of her closest (and best educated) friends in the village believed in magic. How could she not have known this? The only explanation, she ruefully admitted, was that she never really did enter into their worldview.

If tribal culture did not offer Catherine an acceptable alternative to Western systems of belief, it did, in a less direct way, allow her to rethink her position on social authority. In the end, the conclusions she reached about cultural relativism altered not only her conception of political orders but her own character. First, rural Africa laid to rest whatever lingering doubt she still entertained about religion. It became obvious that Western beliefs were not only incongruous in tribal Africa but downright oppressive. She said:

There was a real caricature there of Western religion. The missionaries wouldn't dance, or wear stockings, or talk about birth control. The Salvation Army was so much a force for evil. They built schools for boys but not for girls; they downgraded African culture. Western religion just looked so bizarre there. Western hymns with African words and a big drum, and chickens for the offering. The caricature made things stand out in sharper relief.

Elsewhere she said, "I was in a culture where the physical was closer to the surface, and trying to see with their eyes, and not reject immediately. Seeing that perhaps there was some reason for female circumcision, and that the missionaries who were trying to change that were wrong. I have had enough labeling as evil from missionary types."

The clear evidence that Western orthodoxy had its limits was important in itself, but alone it would not have been enough. By the time she went to college Catherine had already become skeptical—and not only of religion. The African caricature of Western religion supported her skepticism but did little to provide an alternative faith. Catherine was becoming uneasy with her own opportunism— African beliefs in magic could not provide an alternative faith—so where then could she turn?

My sense is that Catherine began to discern an answer in the idea that tribal culture was built up "from the ground." "Ground" was, for her, a symbol with multiple reverberations. It referred to literal ground: soil instead of city streets, and all that soil implied of an earthy, physical fertility. "Ground" also suggested bedrock, the sort of moral certainty that religion provided her parents and that Catherine had found wanting in her own urbane sophistication.

She talked about feeling in touch for the first time with a simple, very physical world—a world not of processed foods and ethereal academic games but of people carrying water on their heads and growing things. When I asked if her father was an ethereal academic, she retorted that he was a farmer. (He gardens in the summer: arguably a minor facet of his identity, but then we all reinvent those who matter to us as we reinvent ourselves. If Catherine could reclaim the physical side of herself she might also reclaim this part of her identification with him.) She recalled trying to grow corn, having tomatoes grow up among the stalks, and joking that it must have been genetic because her father also grew tomatoes.

In some ways I was getting more back to those parts of my own family. My father as a social activist is certainly more of this world than most academics; that is a tension I come by honestly. Maybe Africa made me more of this world, more rooted, more able to live without anything you don't understand. I don't understand how electricity works, but it's real clear how water gets up the hill: on people's heads. I was much more in touch with my body and the day-to-day aspects of living. All that may have given me more foundation. I mean, part of being unsure of yourself and superintellectual and not wanting to have kids is a bit of rootlessness. I don't have roots in Africa, but people, human beings, have roots in the land, and simple things. . . . This is sounding too 1960s hippyish, but I was a long way from that. I wasn't into sports or cooking or growing things. I used to say, "I'm from the city; I can tell the difference between the grass and the trees." There is a real sense of being of this world, or connected to it, to the not-so-ethereal parts. I felt real uncomfortable with the elegant, slippery ideas in college. . . . I am not sure how all this fits together, but I think it fits with the physical parts of being a woman, with some of the notions of competence, that I am not dependent on this elaborate superstructure of so-ciety, that it is possible to live more simply, without all the fancy footwork and worrying about slipping, but by standing on something that is firm, that is the ground, and smelling sweat.

In this long, emotional passage Catherine drew together a series of images that have been important throughout her life. Partly, she referred back to an earlier idea: a physical tribal culture helped her reclaim her own physicality. Her body, which she half-suspected was inadequate and had largely disowned for offering an unpromising future, seemed more worthy of being taken seriously. But in this passage Catherine also said something we have not heard before. She linked her previous disinterest in children to a sense of rootlessness and suggested that she discovered roots—not exactly in Africa, but "in the land." How are we to under-stand this?

The clue seems to lie in her earlier comment "Africa made me more of this world." For until she lived in Africa she was not of this world. Her estrangement was double-sided: she was at home neither in the various communities to which she was always peripheral nor in her own body. In the past, these two experiences of alienation seemed to confirm each other. Her detachment from the ordinary social world echoed and thus amplified her sense of being a stranger to her own physical self. Now Africa provided a way of overcoming this double estrange-ment, by allowing her to feel reconnected to the world. In this way she could also overcome her alienation from her own body.

The sort of connection Catherine claimed is of a special sort. She carefully observed that she does not have roots in Africa. Although she did not say so, Catherine was not likely to claim roots in America either. Her roots, she said, are in the land—an image that seems prior, more elemental, than any community. In the same vein, to speak of "human beings" is to call attention to something more basic than any social group. To put the matter in a phrase, she reclaimed her *social* connectedness while defending her *societal* autonomy. In this way she rescued herself from the alienation—physical and social—she once felt while preserving what was vital in her communal marginality.

Catherine's conclusion about all of this seems to leave her somewhat short of her own aspirations. True, Africa settled whatever remaining doubt she had about escaping her parents' religion. She also was convinced that tribal beliefs were "grounded" in something fundamental. One might reject Western religion or the other certitudes of her childhood without necessarily abandoning all anchor. But if part of what she wanted was an alternative to her parents' faith, African cosmology was not an answer. She was left short of discovering an alternative worldview, with only the promise that she would eventually create one of her own. "Africa provided a consistent way of looking at things. Not one I could adopt, but at least it was possible there was more than one. My friends' radical politics seemed too ad hoc, baseless; I couldn't build it up from the bottom. Africa proved that it was possible, and that one could forge yet another. I was choosing what I would study in a framework that would be mine."

We can read Catherine—as she understood herself—as feeling hopeful but not yet arrived. But I think this does her insufficient justice. For when Catherine notes that African worldviews are "consistent," unlike her friends' "ad hoc politics," she hints at a much more profound shift in her conception of relativism and commitment. In brief, she became comfortable with pluralism.

Pluralism is not simply another belief, at least not in the sense that religion and magic are. It is, rather, a point of view of another order: the conviction that more than one way of looking at the world may be appropriate. At the same time, Catherine's new view of pluralism was not the same as the anxious (or amoral) relativism she had previously espoused.

She now seemed to feel that though truth may indeed be various, each variety is "grounded" in local conditions and traditions. Along these lines she could preserve what was valuable in her skeptical detachment and at the same time feel that she was not morally adrift. In turn, pluralism led her to a new way of thinking about communities and her own style of social engagement.

Vocation

On returning to the United States Catherine started graduate school in economics at a program known for its Marxist orientation. She imagined herself heading toward a career as an economic consultant to neighborhood-development projects but soon discovered that even in this leftist department the discipline was designed to produce university professors. Frustrated, she enrolled in a master's program in public health while continuing to work toward her Ph.D. Five years later she was teaching at an urban university and organizing women's neighborhood health centers.

In both graduate school and her subsequent career the old themes are evident. Constrained by the limits of one academic community, she sought redress in another. (And perhaps, given her born-again enthusiasm for materiality, it is not strictly coincidental that what annoyed her about economics was its coolly intellectual indifference to practical application.) Her solution, again characteristic, was not to switch fields but to establish herself in both.

Still, if Catherine's approach is familiar, there is something distinctly new and better about it. When Catherine described her family or her high school or the school in France, she emphasized their parochialism and her own escape. But when she spoke of economics and public health, she emphasized the merits of each. And now, rather than picturing herself merely as an escapee, she saw herself as straddling disciplines.

She suggested that sometimes creativity is not so much a matter of coming up with a truly novel idea as of bringing an idea established in one context to another. Standing between disciplines, she might become a "linking pin."

> What is important is not the one group you are marginal to but the groups you span. The consultant is *not* a member of the community but *between* the university and the community. It is a multiple membership, though of necessity not a full member anywhere. There are advantages: you have a lot of freedom. When there are pressures on two sides you can choose how to balance them.

This partial continuation and partial transformation of old themes appears not only in Catherine's description of her mixed career but also in her approach to community consultation itself.

> I had wondered what to do with my life, what to study and so on. There was that need for righteousness and commitment. In community organizing your values are real important; they are right up front. You don't get involved in what is ethereal; you focus on action that will be useful to people immediately. It is OK not to stay with the common wisdom. You can take a new perspective: doing and thinking in the same breath, proactive instead of reactive. I didn't have all the ideas but I could see there were bold new ways of thinking of things, and that environments were real important. That in this country you don't die of scoliosis, except that you might, if you are poor.

In this passage Catherine refers back to the old themes of her life: her preoccupation with values, her disdain for the "ethereal" (read: disembodied), her distaste for orthodoxy, her admiration for agency. She even illustrates the power of social environments—a power she herself has felt keenly—with her own scoliosis.

If the themes are familiar, however, her sense of empowerment is new. She suggests that as a community consultant she could liberate other people who find themselves oppressed as she had been. This, of course, is a familiar turn in psychological growth. As the analysts say, she imagines turning passive into active: doing better, *for* others, what was once done badly *to* her.

But to put this in terms of a familiar psychodynamic transformation risks missing the connection between Catherine's social insight and her psychological growth. She had come to a new vision of the world—and this is what altered her conception of herself. Here we must retrace, one last time, Catherine's moral history of social engagement.

As a young child, Catherine could only imagine that her parents were right and that her own occasional naughtiness would make her "another bad daughter."

As an iconoclastic teenager, she thought no one was right and so became a clever manipulator: an amoral agent in an amoral world. But she was uneasy about this conception of the world and herself.

After Africa, she could imagine a different possibility. The clear evidence that cultures differ in their cosmology was no longer proof of moral chaos. Instead, she concluded that local worldviews could each be grounded in their own bedrock of tradition and material necessity. If this were true, the values of local communities might be taken seriously, not merely evaded. Finally, she could now view her own style of living between divided worlds not as opportunism or estrangement but as her own way of being effectively and morally committed.

From this new understanding of the world and her place in it she arrived at a particular view of community consultation. She was scornful of traditional consultants, who see themselves as resources of technical expertise. Instead, she explained, a good consultant should help local communities clarify their own desires and grievances and their own approach to a solution. She saw herself not as a provider of information but as a skilled elucidator of local points of view.

And yet, if Catherine now saw the virtue of local truth, I must emphasize that she herself was not about to become a member of any community. As always, she remains apart, and her detachment is essential. Psychologically, it preserves her vigor, her autonomy, her clarity of vision. Vocationally, it preserves the way she can be of use to others. For her power as a consultant depends on the ability to bring a fresh point of view—or to see the patterns where insiders get caught up in the details.

Would it work? Catherine herself was all too clear about the risks of divided careers and marginal memberships. Speaking of the tension involved in pursuing a joint degree she said,

> You take it in strain. There are pressures from each side to be one of them, and not the other, if you are at all liked. Or to exclude you. It is walking a tightrope; you have to scrounge. One article I read worried me; it was about predicting schizophrenia. It said those people tended to be loners, or to have friends who did not know each other. I have stopped trying to separate people, but I have not

stopped trying to span things. Maybe that is what wanting a family is about. I want a husband, a family, a place of my own.

She underscores the strain of pursuing a vocation divided into camps that have little use for each other. (I don't think she was literally worried about schizophrenia but about the emotional strain such a divided vocation would inevitably entail.) Her description shows us what has changed and what remains the same. True, she is no longer separating people—no longer escaping their clutches by keeping distinct circles of admirers ignorant of one another's existence. But this does not at all mean that she has become a conventional member of any single community. She is still standing in the middle, trying to pull together disciplines that have little regard for each other.

(In passing, she also described, as if taking it for granted, how much her view of family life has changed. Not too long ago, a husband and family seemed an obstacle to her career. Now they are the emotional base that would support such a strenuous vocation.)

As it turned out, the problem of a divided career became evident all too quickly. Her dissertation, written to satisfy both her degrees, set the members of her interdisciplinary committee at odds with one another. Upset, she turned to a trusted friend on the faculty, who said, "You knew this would happen when you chose the committee." To me she concluded, "I suspect I would be bored not doing it this way."

Conclusion

Catherine's history is, of course, likely to be exceptional. Her need for autonomy, her resources of energy and intelligence, her transformative experience abroad, and her ultimate creation of an iconoclastic career are all well beyond our expectations for average lives. If she is to teach us anything beyond her own highly idiosyncratic history, she must serve as something other than an example in the usual, normative sense. Perhaps she can direct our attention to ways of thinking—of paying attention to lives—that we ordinarily overlook. Here, then, is what I take to be the lessons of her experience.

The account I have sketched of Catherine's life is a developmental, psychosocial history, but it is development plotted against a different coordinate than the one we usually consider. What we ordinarily mean by psychosocial development is the passage from one stage to another. These stages are partly established by social norms—those of family, school, neighborhood, and the larger culture in which they are embedded—and partly the unfolding of physical and psychological capacities. In the developmental scheme that Erikson has made famous, the schedules of emerging psychosexual themes and social opportunities are fitted to each other. To describe development within this framework is to plot an individual's passage from one bio-psycho-social constellation to another.

It is possible to tell a portion of Catherine's story within this outline. Following Erikson, we can point to the conjoining of physical, psychological, and social forces that shaped her experience of herself. We can examine how the residue of earlier developmental passages infiltrated later crises. Along these lines we would reencounter Erikson's familiar sequence: Catherine's childhood scoliosis provoked a sense of shameful inadequacy (and perhaps a fear that her body was basically untrustworthy); her early teenage rebelliousness left her feeling guilty; her high school strategy of compartmentalization led to a fragmented identity and finally to her anticipation of an unhappy choice between marital subservience or isolation.

But by itself, this way of recording her history seems to leave something out. For Catherine not only "developed" in the inevitable sense that her concerns at twenty were different from those at ten. She also "developed" in the sense that she made progress, improved, got better. To register this improvement we need to consider another dimension of psychosocial development, one that describes the relation between a sense of membership and sense of self.

Catherine has always considered herself something other than a member in good standing of any group; this imperfect membership is the constant in her life. But the quality of her outsidership changed: from her earliest fear of banishment, to covert disobedience, to the constructive marginality of multiple membership. As she revised her view of social power and authority her style of social engagement and her view of her own character changed as well.

The theoretical point I mean to underscore is that Catherine's progress is visible only if we examine not just the effect her various social memberships had upon her self-understanding but also the way this social influence was modified by her own growing ability to resist the coercion of these memberships. Here the relationship between insight and action flows in both directions. Because even as a young child Catherine developed self-reliance—she could find her way home alone—she became more willing to question her parents' beliefs. What she could do altered what she could imagine. Much later, in Africa, her new conception of local truth changed not only what she thought about herself but her style of social action as well. Instead of merely escaping the authority of various communities she could become a social activist. This time, a change in social insight altered her real power in the world.

This margin of freedom—between self-regard and the judgment of the groups to which one belongs—bears not only on psychological theories of development but on political theories of social control. From a political point of view, psychosocial theory emphasizes the power of culture over self-understanding. Because specific cultures make available only certain opportunities, certain styles of interaction, certain forms of discourse, only a limited range of self-understanding is possible. What counts as worthwhile, plausible, even intelligible is culturally delimited. This influence is not restricted to the subjective interpretation of obviously social life: careers, families, and so on. The most seemingly private of "self" experiences—our emotions, our bodies, our autobiographies—stand revealed as the work of cultural mediation (Berger, 1963; Gergen and Gergen, 1988).

The problem with this theoretical optic, powerful as it is, is that it seems to rule out the sort of critical reflection and self-reclamation that are the heart of Catherine's history. It is surely true that the "I" I know myself to be is shaped by my sense of how I appear to others. But it does not follow from this that I am forced to accept their evaluation uncritically as my own. I am also, to some admittedly limited extent, capable of reflecting critically on the cultural milieu that proposes to tell me who I ought to be. To the extent that any of us grow skeptical of cultural authority—recognizing the power but disputing the legitimacy of particular social arrangements—we may reclaim the legitimacy of our alienated desires and strategies of social engagement. This is the type of progress Catherine illustrates.

None of this, of course, promises to be easy. As Catherine herself illustrates, liberative social insight must always struggle against the alliance of social and psychodynamic self-reproach. Though she was ready by high school to break the rules of ordinary membership in order to expand her opportunities, she suspected herself of having a defective character. Further, even if individuals become convinced that their own dissident desires are legitimate, they must still contend with social resistance. If Catherine reclaimed her desire for family and career, she still faced the long odds of social arrangements—little day care, flextime, medical insurance for maternity leave, part-time work for men and women—stacked against her. The psychological liberation of individuals, and even the larger liberation of public discourse, are only first steps toward institutional change. This is a historical chapter waiting to be written.

REFERENCES

Berger, P. L. 1963. *Invitation to Sociology: A Humanistic Perspective*. Garden City, N.Y.: Anchor Books.
Gergen, K. J., and M. M. Gergen. 1988. "Narrative and the Self as Relationship." In *Advances in Experimental Social Psychology,* vol. 21. Edited by L. Berkowitz. San Diego: Academic Press.
Ochberg, R. L. 1986. "College Leaves of Absence: The Developmental Logic of Psychosocial Moratoria." *Journal of Youth and Adolescence* 15:287–302.

13 Making Sense
of Marital Violence:
One Woman's Narrative

All sorrows can be borne if you can put them in a story . . . tell a story about them.—Isak Dinesen

How does a woman tell about a life of marital violence, rape, and her decision to divorce? How does she make sense of her experience in a marriage in which, instead of being honored and protected, she was devalued and demeaned? What does her way of telling teach us about the emotions and actions of women who are sexually abused and how they make the transition from victim to survivor?

Marital rape is not legally considered a crime in more than half the states in the United States (Margolick, 1984). The cultural and legal ideology of marriage is that sex is consensual. Further, marriage is viewed as the normal and preferred state for adults, so one cannot walk away from it lightly—especially a woman with young children. As for other decisions that go against the social grain and often bring new hardships in their stead, a divorcing woman must make her motives and emotions believable to others through forms of symbolic expression. Her situation also derives its meaning from the framework of interpretation by which listeners judge it (Burke, 1935). In other words, legitimating divorce—especially on the grounds of marital rape—must be accomplished in social interaction, through talking and listening.

Through narration the teller can persuade a listener who was not there that a marriage was seriously troubled and that she was justified in leaving it. As Sacks (1970–1972) notes, stories are ways of packaging experiences, and in them the teller can figure as hero. Tellers draw us into the world of the story through

This research was jointly conducted with Naomi Gerstel and supported by a fellowship from the National Institutes of Mental Health (5F32MH09206). I thank Susan Bell, Uta Gerhardt, Ann Hartman, Joan Laird, Elliot Mishler, Richard Ochberg, George Rosenwald, and Dennie Wolf for helpful comments. An earlier version of this chapter appeared in *Smith College Studies in Social Work* 3(1989):232–251.

particular narrative structures. They build tension by describing the setting, characters, dialogue, and unfolding plot. Imposing a narrative line on the disparate images of our lives is not limited to biographers or novelists; as Joan Didion says in *The White Album,* "we tell ourselves stories in order to live." Narrative allow us to create who we are and to construct definitions of our situations in everyday interactions.

But narratives are not simply Machiavellian devices to persuade listeners (Riessman, 1990b). Creating a narrative about one's life is an imaginative enterprise, too, in which an individual links disruptive events in a biography to heal discontinuities—what should have been with what was. Stories are a kind of cultural envelope into which we pour our experience and signify its importance to others, and the world of the story requires protagonists, inciting conditions, and culminating events. A near universal form for ordering our worlds, narrative allows us to make connections and thus meaning by linking past and present, self and society. Psychoanalytically oriented investigators (Cohler, 1982; Schafer 1981; Spence, 1982) and scholars in family therapy (Laird, 1989) articulate how narrative retelling heals in the psychotherapeutic process. By storifying a life we bring order to random happenings, make sense by reconstructing and reinterpreting. (For more on narrative theory see Mitchell, 1981; Polkinghorne, 1988; Sarbin, 1986.)

In this chapter I analyze the narrative of a divorcing woman to show how, in the context of an interview with a supportive listener, she reconstructs and reinterprets her husband's sexual abuse of her. Narrative retelling enables her to transform her consciousness: to name the abuse, to interpret it as oppression, to reexperience her anger, and to make the transition from victim to survivor. The narrative also persuades, for it draws the listener into the teller's point of view. She renders the events in her life meaningful by constructing a storied account; she finds a language for her husband's domination and rejects the definition of the situation that he, as well as others in her social world, offers to rationalize the abuse. I argue that the narrative is both an individual and a social product; she goes into memory to reexperience the violence and to try, once again, to make sense of it. At the same time her consciousness is shaped in important ways by a cultural discourse and the interactional context of the interview itself. She interprets her experience in the specific terms that American culture provides in the 1980s, which are taken for granted between teller and listener. Yet there is a contradiction in this background knowledge that is evident in her talk: contemporary feminism has opened up new possibilities for action by women, but there are continuing limitations on the emotions they may legitimately display. Women are not supposed to express rage, even when raped.

There is much that is generalizable in the woman's narrative. It displays many of the features common to battering situations in general. The family is the most frequent single locus for violence of all types in American society, and most of such violence is directed against women. Nonetheless, practitioners who work with women often overlook the battering (Walker, 1984; Gelles and Straus, 1988; Stark, Flitcraft, and Frazier, 1979). To see how one woman challenges prevailing social definitions, I examine her long reply to a question in a research interview about divorce. The narrative preserves her way of organizing the account, displaying her talk as a text to be interpreted. Narrative analysis is particularly well suited to understanding the process of making sense of difficult experiences because it lays bare the interpretive work narrators do in collaboration with listeners (Mishler, 1986). I attend to the linguistic coding of the text and argue that there is a relation between the *way* the story about abuse is told and personal and cultural meanings.

The detailed method of transcription used here may not be familiar to all readers. This representation of speech facilitates an analysis of the relationship between narrative form, meaning, and social context. To see how a narrator actually constructs her account—the linguistic choices she makes, the structural function of specific clauses, the role of the listener—"cleaned up" speech is not sufficient. The transcripts must be as complete as possible and thus include both lexical and nonlexical utterances (the actual words and other sounds, like "uh-huh") and pauses in the interview interaction (long pauses of more than three seconds are noted as P and shorter ones as p). The lines are numbered for easy reference. The narrator's utterances are indicated by N, and the interviewer's by I. There are alternative forms of transcription (Mishler, 1986). This one type preserves features relevant to theory.

A Case Analysis

Tessa is a twenty-three-year-old white woman who has been living apart from her husband for two and a half years. She looks much older than she is. It was her decision to separate; he "was completely against it," she says. Though she lives in a dilapidated housing project, her apartment is clean and colorful. Her son from her marriage, a preschooler, lives with her, and an older child from a previous relationship is in foster care. Tessa has held a variety of unskilled jobs, mostly in the fast-food industry, is on welfare, and has just begun to attend a community college part-time. She has always loved music, and her ambition is to be a music teacher some day.

Here is the full text of the first of three episodes of Tessa's narrative account of why she divorced.

Transcript 1

01   I: Would you state in your own words what were the main causes of your
           separation, as you see it?

02   N: (P) um the biggest the biggest thing in my mind was the fact that I had
           been raped three times by him (I: mm-hmm)
03   but at that time it didn't, it wasn't *legal* in a probate court (I: mm-
           hmm)
04   you you couldn't get a divorce on those grounds
05   but that was my biggest (p) (I: uh-huh) complaint (I: uh-huh)
06   total disrespect for me (I: uh-huh) (P) (I: mm-hmm)
07   I: Can you tell me a little bit more about that? I know it's hard to talk about
08   N: (laugh/shudder) Well, um (p) when it was time to go to bed it was really
           rough cause (p)
09   it was like we had to go together (p) (I: uh-huh)
10   and (p) if I wanted to go to bed while he was watching TV
11   he'd say "No, stay up with me" (I: uh-huh), you know
12   and um sometimes I just wanted to stay up
13   but he would insist that I go in with him (I: mm-hmm)
14   so it was like we had to do it together (p) (I: uh-huh)
15   um when I, you know, when I finally *was* in bed I'd just roll over and I
           just wanted to go to sleep
16   I mean scrubbing the floor every day is kinda rough, you know,
           you're pretty tired (laugh) (I: uh-huh)
17   I guess I'm a little sarcastic about it (I: uh-huh)
18   I: Uh-huh, I know what you mean
19   N: He'd just grab my shoulder and roll me over
20   and I knew what he was I knew what it was what it was doing
21   I said, "I just don't want it tonight," you know,
22   "don't you understand, I just don't want anything tonight"
23   "No, you're my wife and in the Bible it says you've got to do this" (I:
           uh-huh)
24   and ah, I'd say, "I just I just don't want it," you know. (I: uh-huh)
25   And after debating for fifteen or twenty minutes
26   I'm not getting any less tired
27   I'd grab a pillow
28   I'd I'd say, "I'm going to sleep on the couch, you're not going to leave
           me alone"
29   I'd get the pillow and a blanket (I: uh-huh)
30   and I went and laid on the couch.
31   Two minutes later he was up out of bed
32   (p) and one particular time he had bought me a dozen roses that day (I:
           mm-hmm)
33   and they were sitting on top of the television which was at the foot of
           the couch (p)

34   and he, he picked up the vase of roses
35   threw the roses at me
36   poured the water on me (I: mm-hmm)
37   and dragged me by the arm from the couch (I: mm-hmm)
38   to the bedroom
39   and then proceeded to (p)
40   to make love to m.e. (I: uh-huh) (p)
41   And uh (P) I didi.'t know what to do (I: mm-hmm)
42   I tried to push him off me
43   and I tried to roll away (I: uh-huh)
44   ah I tried to cross (laugh) my legs (laugh)
45   and it didn't (p) work. (I: uh-huh)
46   He's six foot seven (p) and I'm five eight. (p)
47   And uh (P) I just had I just closed off my head (I: mm-hmm)
48   all I could do was shut off my brain (p)
49   and uh (p) I got very hostile, I— (p)
50   there was no outlet for those feelings. (p)
51   You know that even my neighbors as far as they were concerned
52   you know, they *they* figured that, you know, when people are married
53   that they love each other
54   I think, was the assumption.
55   That wasn't so.

The reason she gives for divorcing is rape; as she puts it, her husband by his actions showed "total disrespect" for her. Yet the point she wishes to make is that she escaped her husband's domination and brutality.

Tessa's account makes explicit the difficulties of leaving a marriage because of sexual abuse ("you couldn't get a divorce on those grounds"). Her recourse to protection from the courts was limited by the law's casual treatment of rape (Estrich, 1988). Until quite recently, in the state in which she resides a husband could not be prosecuted for forcing sexual intercourse upon his wife as long as they lived together. Far from a rare event, sexual abuse of women in marriage remains a closet crime in large part because women are considered the sexual property of their husbands (Russell, 1982; Gordon and Riger, 1989). Yet because of legal reform Tessa is able to name the form of her oppression as rape; sexual abuse is a legally defined reason for divorce in the state in which she filed. Thus an evolving legal discourse shapes her personal discourse and legitimates her experience of sexual abuse.

How does Tessa construct her compelling account and draw the listener into her point of view? If we look at the structure of the narrative, we see that it is saturated with pattern and reveals a woman who is now in control. In the first six lines Tessa gives a plot summary, or abstract, for the three episodes she will subsequently relate (on the structural parts of a story, see Labov, 1982). Here, she also sets forth the key contrast that organizes the narrative—the tension between two realities. At this point, the specific contrast is between her current reality (she was raped) and the reality of prevailing legal doctrine (marital rape isn't a crime). Using verbal emphasis ("it wasn't *legal* in a probate court"), she draws attention to these contrasting points of view. From Tessa's perspective, which the listener is invited to share, she was a victim of both her husband's sexual violence and the legal system. Her opening also introduces the main characters of the drama about to unfold: Tessa, her husband, and, importantly, the social others (in this instance, the legal system) whose definitions of reality Tessa will ultimately overturn. The way she introduces the narrative conveys its overall message—she triumphed over others' definitions of her situation. The narrative she wants to tell is how she made the transition from victim to survivor, how she is now in charge of her life.

Although Tessa controls the flow of talk in her opening statement, the woman listener-interviewer is by no means passive. The narrative is frequently punctuated by her nonlexical utterances ("mm-hmm" "uh-huh") which signal interest and invite the narrator to say more. Also notice how the listener responds to Tessa's long pause at the end of the abstract. Rather than using this as an opportunity to back off from the highly charged subject of marital rape, she waits and, after a pause, conveys through a question that she expects to hear more. ("Can you tell me a little bit more about that? I know it's hard to talk about.") Without this affiliative comment, Tessa might have stopped after her summary statement. Instead, she goes on to tell a long narrative in which she constructs meaningful totalities out of scattered events (Ricoeur, 1981).

Tessa's account is consistent with the five-stage process of victimization that Trudy Mills describes (1985), though not in sequential order. She analyzes victimization as a gradual process with five stages: (1) women usually enter the relationship at a time when they are feeling particularly vulnerable and are searching for intimacy; (2) women attempt to manage the violence by attaching meanings to it and developing strategies to cope with it (such as placating violent husbands and/or constructing justifications for maintaining the relationship); (3) women experience a loss of self as they withdraw from social interaction in shame—their various social identities are diminished and they lose the observing self; (4) at some point women who leave reevaluate the violent relationship (often a specific event triggers this, jarring the previous definition of the situation); and (5) in time, women restructure the self. An important manifestation of the final step is taking on the identity of a survivor rather than seeing oneself as a victim.

Tessa invites the listener into the narrative world on lines 8–14 by orienting her to time, place, and situation. Substantively, she tells about the general case of the bedtime ritual: her husband's rule was that they go together and he would not allow her to go earlier or to stay up alone. Tessa attempts to manage the sexual violence by placating her husband, acquiescing to his demands—the second stage Mills (1985) describes. Structurally, Tessa communicates the routine and repeated interaction through the habitual narrative genre, indicated here by the conditional past tense ("if I wanted," and "he would insist"). In the habitual narrative genre, events are not unique to a particular moment in time but instead stand for classes of events that happen over and over again. They tell of the general course of events over time rather than what happened at a specific moment in the past (Riessman, 1990a). Tessa continues in the habitual mode by describing in lines 15–31 the usual sequence of events once they were in bed.

Tessa moves in and out of the voices of the characters in the narrative she is building:

```
20        and I knew what he was I knew what it was what it was doing
21        I said, "I just don't want it tonight," you know,
22        "don't you understand, I just don't want anything tonight"
23        "No, you're my wife and in the Bible it says you've got to do this" (I:
          uh-huh)
24        and ah, I'd say, "I just don't want it," you know. (I: uh-huh)
```

Strategically, by embedding a dramatization within a narrative, Tessa draws the listener in and by reenacting the typical argument over sex, mobilizes support for her point of view. She communicates in a vivid way the verbal struggle that preceded the physical struggle—her attempts to resist her husband's unwanted sexual advances with repeated strong statements about her wishes. In line 20 "he" becomes "it"—she merges the man with the act.

In lines 15–31 Tessa also reintroduces the organizing theme—the contrast between two realities. Her juxtaposition of his and her voices achieves this in a powerful way. But the conflict between two realities goes beyond their private conversation, which she suggests here by invoking the Bible. The patriarchal church, as well as the state, colludes with her husband to deny her rights.

Several important interactions take place between the two women, teller and listener, in this section. Tessa makes repeated use of the phrase "you know"— affiliative appeals suggesting that the listener should understand the implications (and thus the truth) of Tessa's reality. Perhaps Tessa is also appealing to the listener's experience with men and marriage, thereby creating an intersubjective world of meaning between them. There is some evidence that she is successful, judging by the interviewer's nonlexical expressions. Even more, the narrator steps out of the role of storyteller in the midst of a highly dramatic episode (which one might think of as uninterruptable) and, as a woman, makes an active alliance with the woman interviewer. The interviewer responds in kind:

```
15        um when I, you know, when I finally was in bed
          I'd just roll over and I just wanted to go to sleep
```

16   I mean scrubbing the floor every day is kinda rough, you know,
            you're pretty tired (laugh) (I: uh-huh)
17   I guess I'm a little sarcastic about it (I: uh-huh)
18   I: Uh-huh, I know what you mean

Tessa's statements strike a responsive cord in the interviewer; "I know what you
mean" suggests a solidarity between the women is developing. They share the
understanding that women are vulnerable, do housework that is often grueling,
repetitive, and boring, and have to deal with sexually demanding men. (For more
on women interviewing women see Riessman, 1987.)

Out of this growing affiliation, perhaps, Tessa goes deeper into memory:

32   (p) and one particular time he had bought me a dozen roses
            that day (I: mm-hmm)
33   and they were sitting on top of the television which was
            at the foot of the couch (p)

Tessa moves from recapitulating the general situation of coercive sex in her
marriage to a particular and dramatic instance of it—rape. As the content shifts, so
must the form of the narrative. Tessa changes genres from a habitual narrative to a
story, the first of several she will ultimately tell. (In contrast to habitual narratives,
which encode a general state of affairs, "a story can best and most simply be
thought of as a specific past-time narrative that makes a point," often a moral one
[Polanyi, 1985, 189]). She uses the story form in this episode to create a unique
past-time world and by reenacting sequential events, tells of a significant change
in that world.

She makes the transition to the story in line 32; it emerges in an almost seamless
way from the habitual narrative that preceded it. A short pause signals the shift.
(Tessa's speech is fluent, and pauses carry meaning. They had been largely absent
from the previous twenty lines of text.) She begins the story by providing the
listener with the necessary information needed to follow it. Because the roses will
figure prominently in the rape, Tessa introduces these props and their exact placement in the living room, just as a skilled novelist might make the reader aware of a
particular physical object that will be used in a later scene.

But the roses are more than a prop. They have symbolic meaning, as do the
television set and the couch—Tessa's refuge from her husband's sexual demands.
The mention of flowers also introduces an ambiguity into the text. Tessa does not
explain why her husband "bought her a dozen roses that day," but such gifts are
often a way in American society for men to demonstrate romantic love or ask for
forgiveness. Because Tessa's husband has a working-class job, the purchase of a
dozen roses may have caused financial strain. In other words, there is a gap in
Tessa's story, though the value of the gift is suggested by her displaying the roses
on the living room television—the centerpiece of the modern American home.

Whatever may have "really" happened, Tessa's juxtaposition of the roses and the rape in the narrative makes *her* interpretation evident. The linguistic choice emphasizes the clash between two realities—romantic love in marriage and Tessa's actual experience, as she has come to define it.

The narrator brings the roses and the rape together in the climax of this first story, told in a series of short, terse clauses in the simple past tense:

34   and he, he picked up the vase of roses
35   threw the roses at me
36   poured the water on me (I: mm hmm)
37   and dragged me by the arm from the couch (I: mm hmm)
38   to the bedroom
39   and then proceeded to (p)
40   to make love to me. (I: uh huh) (p)

The story is poignant and effective not only because of its content but also because of its expression, and by its contrast to the earlier (habitual) form of the narrative. There is every evidence that the interviewer gets caught up in the story, judging by the frequency and placement of her nonlexical utterances.

But this episode is more than the factual reporting of events. Tessa distinguishes key events in the story in several ways. When describing the rape (lines 39–40), she uses a loaded phrase ("make love") rich in tenderness, positive connotation, and cultural meaning to describe what she earlier referred to as "rape." As with the roses, there is an ambiguity and a paradox here. Tessa pauses to punctuate and thus mark the significance of these lines. She pauses even longer at two other critical points in the story:

41   and uh (P) I didn't know what to do (I: mm-hum)
47   And uh (P) I just had I just closed off my head (I: mm-hum)

Because long pauses are not characteristic of her speech, they draw attention. Structurally, they re-create in the listener the state of feeling of the storyworld and, in this case perhaps, the futility the narrator experienced in trying to protect herself from her husband's sexual advances. Consistent with the victimization process Mills describes (1985), there is a loss of self. Tessa "closed off" her head and "shut off" her brain—the observing ego in the language of psychoanalysis.

Battered women rarely experience their anger directly. As Elaine Hilberman (1984, 225) observes, there is "a constant struggle with the self to contain it and control aggressive impulses." Yet Tessa says in line 49 that she "got very hostile," a statement that, like earlier ones, is ambiguous and invites multiple readings. It may refer to her resistance to the sexual abuse—that she fought back; yet the previous lines suggest otherwise. The line can also be read as a more generalized statement about her emotions—both at the time and as she has reinterpreted them.

The abstract, clinical language ("hostile") is noteworthy and suggests control, not rage.

Structurally, the clause also signals a shift in genres; Tessa is gradually moving out of this particular story and into a "way of the world" moral telling. She justifies her lack of effectiveness in resisting the rape in line 46 through reference to men's physical size and associated strength and women's consequent vulnerability to abuse. Feminists have argued that a woman is likely to be sexually victimized not only because she is physically weaker than her opponent but also because she is socially less powerful (Bart and O'Brien, 1985; Gordon and Riger, 1989). Tessa develops her account in the context of these contemporary understandings. She also draws on another aspect of contemporary American culture when she explains both her passivity and her "hostility" by drawing on an explanatory scheme widely available in our psychologically oriented society—strong feelings require expression. ("There was no outlet for those feelings.")

By communicating her moral attitude, Tessa solves the teller's problem (Riessman, 1990a). She convinces the listener (as well as herself, perhaps) that she is a good person, that she behaved correctly, and that she did the best that could be expected under the circumstances.

Tessa concludes the first episode by returning to the theme of two realities. This time she invokes her neighbors' views:

51   You know that even my neighbors as far as they were concerned
52   you know, they *they* figured that, you know, when people are married
53   that they love each other
54   I think, was the assumption.
55   That wasn't so.

The neighbors, like the legal and religious systems earlier, stand for definitions of the situation that differ from Tessa's own. Through these contrasts between public ideology and private experience, she further defends her reality over that of her husband and others. She also says explicitly that she didn't love her husband, a theme to which she later returns.

Structurally, lines 51–55 function to bridge the first episode—about her husband's physical domination—and a second and closely related episode—about her economic inequality. The episodes are linked by the common theme of powerlessness. Tessa continues:

Transcript 2

56   N: I, you know, I married my husband because I wanted to escape
57   but I didn't know that then, I couldn't—
58   I: Escape from what?
59   N: Poverty

60   I had, you know, my first apartment when he proposed to me
61   was two rooms, flea-ridden (p) (I: uh-huh)
62   and (p) it had a leaky roof (p) (I: mm-hmm)
63   it was just *awful*
64   and I I sort of expected higher, you know, better things. (I: mm-hmm)
65   It improved a little bit but (p) there was still very little money and uh (p)
66   he was gone for a couple of weeks at one point
67   with nothing, and there was no food in the house
68   and he couldn't get any money to me cause he was out on a camping thing with the army (p)
69   and uh (p) his friends (p) went and got some food for us
70   from the kitchens of the (p) the mess halls, I guess
71   and they brought my son and I a whole great big box of food.
72   You know, it wasn't the best, there wasn't any fresh (I: mm-hmm) vegetables or fruit
73   but it was meat and cake and stuff like that
74   so we ate. (p)
75   But I was totally uh dependent (I: uh-huh) and powerless at the same time (I: uh-huh)
76   I was just like I was when I was raped. (I: uh-huh) (p)
77   And those things, you know, those things happen.
78   As far as I'm concerned, I was raped I was raped from the first day (p) (I: mm-hmm)
79   but I didn't feel so hostile about it at that point. (p) (I: mm-hmm)
80   I just felt like it was something that you had to go through because you were married.

The second episode, which comes immediately after the first, is tightly structured and, also like the first, begins with a plot summary: Tessa says she married to escape (lines 56–57). Because of the interviewer's interruption ("Escape from what?"), Tessa elaborates. As in the first episode, she orients the listener to time, place, and social circumstances—the flea-ridden apartment with a leaky roof that was all she could afford before she married. Going back in time and shifting scenes, Tessa seeks to explain her divorce to her listener by explaining why she married in the first place. In this flashback she again sets up a contrast: her reason for marriage as she understands it now, compared with what she thought then. She says she married her husband to escape her poverty, not because she loved him. (Listeners may begin to feel some empathy for Tessa's husband at this point and reinterpret her earlier story about the roses. Was he trying to woo her, to persuade her to love him?)

The content of the second episode is consistent with Mills's (1985) analysis of the first stage of victimization. Tessa entered into the relationship at a time when she was feeling particularly vulnerable. Like other women before and since, Tessa's susceptibility to poverty was, in large part, a consequence of her gender. She had the sole responsibility for care of a child, an inadequate welfare allowance, and limited job possibilities. As a member of American culture, however, she "expected better, you know, higher things." Her solution, consistent with the American dream for white women, was to find a man; she thought the traditional conjugal family would improve her circumstances. Although marriage hardly proved to be a protective haven for her or her child, it did help their economic situation. Yet, she says, "there was still very little money."

In this episode too Tessa moves into the story form, on line 66, providing an illustration to persuade the listener how difficult things were. She tells of a sequence of events: her husband could not provide for her financially and his friends did, getting food from army mess halls. Although the story lacks the linguistic elaboration of the first story about the rape, and hence the associated tension and drama, it nevertheless makes its point. If we have any doubt about the causal link that ties the two episodes together, Tessa states it explicitly:

75   But I was totally uh dependent (I: uh-huh) and powerless
        at the same time (I: uh-huh)
76   I was just like I was when I was raped. (I: uh-huh) (p)
77   And those things, you know, those things happen.
78   As far as I'm concerned, I was raped I was raped from the first day (p)
        (I: mm-hmm)
79   but I didn't feel so hostile about it at that point. (p) (I: mm-hmm)
80   I just felt like it was something that you had to go through because
        you were married.

In these lines, Tessa tells the listener directly how to interpret the two stories and, more generally, her episodic narrative. She creates her own private image to give meaning to her past: the metaphor of rape epitomizes her total domination—financial, psychological, and physical. She moves away from the specific events with interpretive meanings, contrasts how she felt about them then and how she feels about them now. Through metaphor, Tessa makes a moral point: marriage based on women's subordination is not the way marriage ought to be. In creating a narrative to explain her particular separation, she has produced a discourse about inequality in marriage in general.

But there may be another meaning here. In addition to linking powerlessness and rape metaphorically (to refer to women's structural subordination in the institution of marriage), Tessa may be referring more specifically to her experience of sex: "It was something you had to go through because you were married." Again, the ambiguous meaning may lead some listeners to their own interpretations of the roses, and even the rape. Tessa also reintroduces the topic of her anger here, again choosing clinical language that distances ("I didn't feel so hostile about it at that point").

Tessa has not yet mentioned precisely when she left her husband. The listener, sensing a missing piece, pauses and asks about it. ("And then what made the difference so that you wanted to get out of that relationship?") Tessa responds by developing a third narrative episode:

Transcript 3

81 I: (p) And then what made the difference so that you wanted to get out of that relationship?

82 N: (p) Oh, when I found myself, when I realized that I was throwing myself at him be—

83 out of hostility (p) rather than out of self-defense (I: uh-huh)

84 it was a little bit of both.

85 But I was so angry at one point when he was moving his things out (p)

86 he had promised, he had told me

87 as an example, he *told* me he'd give me the TV, okay.

88 At the last minute he decided he wanted it. (p) (I: mm-hmm)

89 And I was so *mad* (p)

90 I threw myself at him

91 I went to punch him (I: mm-hmm)

92 and I passed out (I: mm-hmm)

93 I was so mad. (I: mm-hmm)

94 (laugh/shudder) It's, my God, there's nothing like it

95 I don't *ever* want to feel that again, never (p) (I: mm-hmm)

96 I'd sooner scream at somebody and (p) and pound

97 I've punched my fists into walls

98 I punched in the front door in that apartment on Main Street (I: uh-huh)

99 and unlocked it.

100 He put my son out on the front porch at one point and I was

101 it made me so violently angry

102 that I I literally punched in the front door

103 and it was just about as thick as the front door here. (I: uh-huh)

104 (p) And uh (p) I, you know, after that incident

105 I lived in Rocky Falls with my mother (I: uh-huh) and my father, my stepfather, for three weeks (p)

106 and I tried to get a restraining order

107	and the and the person at the courthouse said it's not worth it. (p)
108	But he did tell me that what I *could* do is go back to him, to my husband
109	and say "if you're not out of here I'll have the police after you." (I: mm-hmm) (p)
110	So I did that
111	and he left reluctantly (I: uh-huh) (p)
112	but he did leave. (I: uh-huh)

The third episode returns to the topic of violence, but this time it is hers, not his. She has hinted at the theme several times earlier. She says that she went beyond "self defense" and began "throwing" herself at him "out of hostility."

In this episode, Tessa moves into the story form to recount a specific instance (lines 85–95) but, unlike her controlled way of telling in the previous episodes, here her control slips. The emotions of the last days of her marriage break through as she reenacts the events in the story. She intimates that the trigger event—the fourth stage in Mills's model—was her own rage, and she no longer uses clinical language to refer to it ("I was so angry at one point"). Although the precipitant for her anger is seemingly minor (certainly when compared to the sexual abuse in the earlier story), her husband's change of mind about the television provokes a violent response, which she describes in a series of staccato clauses that contrast with the measured way she told earlier of the rape:

89	And I was so *mad* (p)
90	I threw myself at him
91	I went to punch him (I: mm-hmm)
92	and I passed out (I: mm-hmm)
93	I was so mad. (I: mm-hmm)

Her rage (which perhaps includes her pent-up rage about the rapes) disturbs her, even in the retelling. She makes her current disturbance clear in the series of affect-laden evaluative clauses that follow. Unlike her discourse earlier, here there is a cluster of rhetorical devices, including verbal emphasis, an explicative, and expressive speech (a shudder).

| 94 | (laugh/shudder) It's, my God, there's nothing like it |
| 95 | I don't *ever* want to feel that way again, never (p) (I: mm-hmm) |

This moment is the peak of the action in the narrative. We learn later in a series of story fragments that this dynamic—his actions provoking rage and physical violence in her—had occurred through the marriage (lines 97–103). But there is a difference: previously she had punched walls and doors. This time she went to punch her husband.

Hilberman's (1984, 225) observations of sixty clinical cases of abused wives are relevant here: "The violent encounter with another person's loss of control of aggression precipitates great anxiety about one's own controls. . . . In the life experiences of battered women, there is little perceived or real difference between affect, fantasy, and action. Thus is it not surprising that fear of loss of control was a universal concern [in her sample]. These fears were often expressed in vague, abstract terms but were unmistakably linked to aggression." Social conventions do not allow women to express their rage easily. Tessa does vent hers, and this is the turning point in the narrative. She leaves her husband and goes to her parents for protection (and the court, again unsuccessfully). Tessa can no longer contain her *own* aggression, so she moves out. She has begun to take on the identity of survivor rather than victim—the change that is the final stage in Mills's analysis.

Conclusion

Through her narrative, with its three distinct but related episodes, Tessa has provided a coherent interpretation of the connections between rape and violence, her feelings of powerlessness and ultimately uncontrolled rage, and her decision to separate from her husband. Her point is that she surmounted powerlessness and victimization. Ironically, she took control by losing control and broke out of a violent relationship when she could no longer contain her own violence. She became a survivor and filed for divorce, even though her husband "was completely against it."

Tessa realizes these themes through language and story. She organizes the narrative she tells around her definition of the situation, set against the contrary definitions of others—her husband, the state, the church, her neighbors. She gives shape to her experience and makes it meaningful by talking about power and subordination. She tells a series of linked stories (Bell, 1988) in three episodes that focus on highly memorable intolerable moments set against a backdrop of how intolerable her marriage was in general. The rape story is quintessential, a dramatic incident that illustrates her overall theme of powerlessness. Through narration Tessa not only reconstructs the temporal sequence of the events that led to separation but invests these events with meaning and morality. She constructs a reality and a surviving self that are sealed inside the narrative—a reality that is accomplished as much by the way she structures the account as by what she says.

Why are the episodes of the narrative told in such different ways? Although both the rape episode and the punching episode about the television set use story structure and build to a climax and resolution, there are subtle contrasts between them. The rape story is tightly assembled, told by a controlled narrator who is describing events that, most likely, she has narrated often. From a present vantage point of mastery and freedom from abuse, she tells of a time when she was physically overpowered. The punching episode about the television set, in contrast, presents another dimension of the same protagonist—a woman who is not in charge nearly to the same extent, either of the narrative or the emotions it relates. Just as her rage toward her husband erupted through the constraints of marriage, so does her recounting the rage disrupt the form of narrative. Terror at the idea of losing control of murderous impulses momentarily breaks the story apart. We sense that though Tessa may have reinterpreted and resolved some of the events, the associated emotions have not been put to rest nearly to the same degree.

But cultural meanings influence the extent to which each can be "privately" resolved. The first episode is about rape—a trauma that has undergone a marked social redefinition because of the contemporary women's movement. The culture is increasingly providing women with a language for talking about and reinterpreting sexual abuse. The punching episode about the television set, by contrast, lacks a normative context. Being "mad" and physically attacking a husband challenge social definitions of women's proper role in marriage. Society provides for women's depressed emotions but not for their rage. Thus, as an individual, Tessa must make sense of emotions and actions that are deviant for her gender. Her difficulty with this cultural problem is revealed in the way she tells the third narrative episode.

Tessa's text is also a cultural product in other ways, situated historically, with assumptions and formulations that could not have been made in another age or by women in many parts of the world today. At numerous points a specifically American cultural discourse shapes her reconstruction of self. For example, she can be sarcastic about who does housework, she can leave an abusive marriage, and most obviously she can articulate the form of abuse as marital rape. Going beyond a formalist analysis of the text, I suggest that a narrative cannot be fully interpreted without investigating the condition of the person in the society that produces the text (Lennox, 1989). The narrative is contextual in this additional sense because it speaks to the aspects of a survivor's identity with which gender is intimately intertwined, namely race and class. Tessa's narrative does not reflect some essentialist view of women in general (Spelman, 1988) but speaks of the unique experiences of a white, working-class woman who came to define her marital experience as rape. The narrative also was told to a white, middle-class feminist interviewer who "heard" the account in a particular way and shaped the narrative by her questions and nonlexical responses, just as it was told in a cultural context where feminism and personal psychology provided legitimating vocabularies of motive (Mills, 1940). The narrative implies how extensively some psychological concepts and assumptions about women's rights have fed back into popular thought in the United States (Linde, 1986). Tessa's "private" story is embedded in a social discourse in which it is taken for granted that strong feeling requires expression and marital rape should be a crime.

In my analysis of Tessa's narrative, I stayed close to the text as she constructed it and suggested some aspects of the assumptive world that was contained in it and the structural ways she accomplished her communicative aims. To emphasize the performance aspect of language is not to undermine the "truth" of what Tessa said. Although all texts may be interactionally produced, coauthored by listener and teller (Bell, 1985; Paget, 1983), the marital experiences Tessa's text relates certainly are not. Whatever "actually" transpired in the marriage, we must assume that Tessa's selection represents a reality. An interpretive approach need not entail what Paul Ricoeur (1981) calls a hermeneutics of suspicion—a skepticism toward the given, a "distrust of the symbol as a dissimulation of the real" (Thompson in Ricoeur, 1981, 6). Yet, at certain points, I noted ambiguities and paradoxes in the text, intimating that there may be a more complex reality than the narrative itself could encompass. Of course, narratives are always edited versions of reality, not impartial descriptions of it, presentations of the world, not copies of it (Schafer, 1981). Edward Said's (1979, 272–273) views about issues of representation have bearing for all narrative accounts:

> The real issue is whether indeed there can be a true representation of anything, or whether any and all representations, because they are representations, are embedded first in the language and then in the culture, institutions, and political ambience of the representor. If the later alternative is the correct one (and I believe it is), then we must be prepared to accept the fact that a representation is *eo ipso* implicated, intertwined, embedded, interwoven with a great many other things besides the "truth," which is itself a representation.

In a word, we don't know all that happened in Tessa's marriage; all we have is her embedded representation of it in the narrative, just as in therapy the client and clinician only have access to narrative truth, not historical truth (Spence, 1982).

Through talking and listening, a woman has rendered the sorrows in a life heroic and meaningful. Her decision to divorce signifies a transformation in this life. This teller has attempted to heal wounds that only narrative can bind.

REFERENCES

Bart, P. B., and P. H. O'Brien. 1985. *Stopping Rape*. Elmsford, Mass.: Pergamon Press.
Bell, S. E. 1988. "Becoming a Political Woman: The Reconstruction and Interpretation of Experience Through Stories." In *Gender and Discourse: The Power of Talk*. Edited by A. D. Todd and S. Fisher. Norwood, N.J.: Ablex.
———. 1985. "Narratives of Health and Illness: DES Daughters Tell Stories." Paper presented at annual meeting of Sociologists for Women in Society, Washington, D.C.
Burke, K. 1935. "Motives." In *Permanence and Change*. Edited by J. B. Gusfield. New York: New Republic.
Cohler, B. 1982. "Personal Narrative and the Life Course." In *Life-Span Development and Behavior*, vol. 4. Edited by P. B. Baltes and O. G. Brim. New York: Academic Press.
Dinesen, I., quoted in Arendt, H., 1958. *The Human Condition*. Chicago: University of Chicago Press, 175.
Estrich, S. 1988. *Real Rape*. Cambridge, Mass.: Harvard University Press.

Gelles, R. J., and M. A. Straus. 1988. *Intimate Violence*. New York: Simon and Schuster.

Gordon, M. T., and S. Riger. 1989. *The Female Fear*. New York: Free Press.

Hilberman, E. 1984. "Overview: The 'Wife-Beater's Wife' Reconsidered." In *The Gender Gap in Psychotherapy: Social Realities and Psychological Processes*. Edited by P. P. Rieker and E. H. Carmen. New York: Plenum.

Labov, W. 1982. "Speech Actions and Reactions in Personal Narrative." In *Analyzing Discourse: Text and Talk*. Edited by D. Tannen. Washington D.C.: Georgetown University Press.

Laird, J. 1989. "Women and Stories: Restorying Women's Self-Constructions." In *Women in Families*. Edited by M. McGoldrick, F. Walsh, and C. Anderson. New York: W. W. Norton.

Lennox, S. 1989. "Feminist Scholarship and Germanistik." *German Quarterly* 62:158–170.

Linde, C. 1986. "Private Stories in Public Discourse: Narrative Analysis in the Social Sciences." *Poetics* 15:183–202.

Margolick, D. 1984. "Top Court in New York Rules Men Can Be Charged with Rapes of Wives." *New York Times*, Dec. 21, 1984, p. 1.

Mills, C. W. 1940. "Situated Actions and Vocabularies of Motive." *American Sociological Review* 5:904–913.

Mills, Trudy. 1985. "The Assault on the Self: Stages of Coping with Battering Husbands." *Qualitative Sociology* 8:103–123.

Mishler, E. G. 1986. *Research Interviewing: Context and Narrative*. Cambridge, Mass.: Harvard University Press.

Mitchell, W. J. T., ed. 1981. *On Narrative*. Chicago: University of Chicago Press.

Paget, M. A. 1983. "Experience and Knowledge." *Human Studies* 6:67–90.

Polanyi, L. 1985. "Conversational Storytelling." In *Handbook of Discourse Analysis: Discourse and Dialogue*, vol. 3. Edited by T. A. Van Dijk. London: Academic Press.

Polkinghorne, D. E. 1988. *Narrative Knowing and the Human Sciences*. Albany: State University of New York Press.

Ricoeur, P. 1981. *Hermeneutics and the Human Sciences*. Edited and translated by J. B. Thompson. New York: Cambridge University Press.

Riessman, C. K. 1987. "When Gender Is Not Enough: Women Interviewing Women." *Gender and Society* 1:172–207.

———. 1990a. *Divorce Talk: Women and Men Make Sense of Personal Relationships*. New Brunswick, N.J.: Rutgers University Press.

———. 1990b. "Strategic Uses of Narrative in the Presentation of Self and Illness: A Research Note." *Social Science and Medicine* 30:1195–1200.

Russell, D. 1986. *The Secret Trauma*. New York: Basic Books.

Russell, D. E. H. 1982. *Rape in Marriage*. New York: Macmillan.

Sacks, H. 1970–1972. Unpublished lectures. As quoted in D. Bogen and M. Lynch. 1989. "Taking Account of the Hostile Native: Plausible Deniability and the Production of Conventional History in the Iran-Contra Hearings." *Social Problems* 36:201.

Said, E. W. 1979. *Orientalism*. New York: Vintage.

Sarbin, T. R., ed. 1986. *Narrative Psychology: The Storied Nature of Human Conduct*. New York: Praeger.

Schafer, R. 1981. "Narration in the Psychoanalytic Dialogue." In *On Narrative*. Edited by W. J. T. Mitchell. Chicago: University of Chicago Press.

Spellman, E. V. 1988. *Inessential Woman: Problems of Exclusion in Feminist Thought*. Boston: Beacon Press.

Spence, D. P. 1982. *Narrative Truth and Historical Truth: Meaning and Interpretation in Psychoanalysis*. New York: W. W. Norton.

Stark, E., A. Flitcraft, and W. Frazier. 1979. "Medicine and Patriarchal Violence: The Social Construction of a Private Event." *International Journal of Health Services* 9:461–493.

Walker, L. E. 1984. *The Battered Woman Syndrome*. New York: Springer Verlag.

WILLIAM R. EARNEST

14 Ideology Criticism
and Life-History Research

One focus of the preceding chapters is on how social forces shape subjects' reflections on their lives. A life history is more than a simple autobiographical register, a statistical summation, of this influence; it is the landscape for a subject's orientation to his or her needs, potentials, and frustrations and the social order in which they develop. We have seen how reflective dialogue, involving a dialectic of intrapersonal and interpersonal communication (Arlow, 1987; Habermas, 1970), is the medium of this reflective activity. Social forces not only impose certain contents upon individuals—for example, "proper" work behavior or gender identities—but also shape and constrain reflective dialogue concerning those prescriptions.

The concept of ideology is frequently used to frame this process of shaping and constraint. As Geuss has noted, confusion associated with the concept has obscured the reflective dimension we are interested in here (Geuss, 1981). Attempts to define ideology criticism typically mire themselves in the question of whether the critic of ideology can posit the "true" beliefs and values deemed appropriate to a subject living in a particular social context (McLellan, 1986). Two related lines of argument have been made against a critical standpoint defined in these terms. First, for a subject's rendering of their own interests to be "untrue," their "true" interests must be specified within a philosophy of history positing objective values, for example, socialism as a "higher" stage of social development. Along with the epistemological issue of whether one can derive objective values in this way, the plausibility of such a system can be further questioned because historical experience with such philosophies has involved so much coercion that the transparency implied by their purported "objectivity" is obviously lacking. Thus, Thompson and Gintis point to the experience of socialist movements and argue that instead of mandating ever-broadening and open-ended discussions of social alternatives, the concept of ideology criticism has been associated with limiting discussion in favor of supposedly indisputable interests, generally defined in strategic terms (Gintis, 1980; Thompson, 1978). Thus ideology criticism can extinguish critical reflection instead of enhancing it.

It is possible however, to establish a more modest standard of reflection which, although lacking the imperative mandate provided by an objectivist philosophy of history, does justify ideology-critical dialogue (Geuss, 1981, 88–95). To do this, we must return to the motives for critique, grounded in routines of suffering, that inspire the questionable leap to an objectivist philosophy of history.

We start with Bowles and Gintis's observation regarding complex social systems: the different institutions people participate in contradict one another in the sense that the rights, privileges, and norms of respect and reciprocity that are regarded as legitimate and appropriate in one institution are institutionally regarded as illegitimate and inappropriate in others (Bowles and Gintis, 1986). Capitalist democracies provide a vivid example of this form of institutional, or structural, contradiction. In capitalist democracies, "socialization" to work involves not only learning the hierarchically framed role expectations and obligations associated with capitalist production. Socialization to work also involves learning that the role expectations and obligations associated with institutions and practices that are of a more democratic and/or egalitarian nature—for example, in voluntary organizations, formal aspects of electoral politics, personal relationships—are either prohibited from the sphere of work or subordinated to hierarchical command structures.

The telos of ideology is the maintenance and reproduction of the ensemble of such contradictory relational models, and it interworks two processes—the "onsite" affirmation of the relationship prescribed for the institution and the exclusion of alternatives. These processes do not resolve the contradiction, and suffering and conflicts remain endemic to it. The history of worker resistance to capitalism indicates that a principal grievance has been the hierarchical, authoritarian form of capitalist production relations (Blumberg, 1968; Gutman, 1977; Montgomery, 1977; Thompson, 1963). Demands for increased worker control are routinely generated within the dialectic of: (1) working conditions—the hierarchically imposed physical experience of work mediated by sociocultural interpretations; and (2) the real violation of codes of personal rights lived out in other institutions. Variously expressed as a protest against the progressive intensification and degradation of work or the general "despotism" of the factory, worker resistance to hierarchical relations of production reflects workers' experience of those relations as enforcing physical suffering and routinely violating rights and privileges they have "lived out" in other spheres. Dahl and Lindblom put it this way: "Workers cannot accede to control of management without damaging their own sense of self-respect. In a culture like that of the United States, where the goal of reciprocal control is highly valued, there is bound to be a deep-seated conflict between the control of a 'private' management and the ordinary citizen's conception of legitimate control" (1953, 480).

In keeping with a popular theory of mobilization (Tilly, 1978), we might regard reflection and action based upon it as determined by the availability of a variety of resources such as information about alternatives, power, "repertoires of contention," and so forth. These are essential, of course. But the theory shallowly

assumes that in the intrapersonal and interpersonal aspects of the process participants are rational, albeit tradition-bound, actors. Thus the theory is most articulate
regarding how worker-citizens seek to act on perceived interests and contentiously
limit the institutionalized power of employers. But it merely notes that critical
reflection is enhanced in the relatively unconstrained interpersonal and organizational space developed as part of the mobilization. Critical reflection is thus
understood to be directly enhanced by the power accumulated by those mobilizing
and simply to involve the elaboration and rationalization of interests. Beyond this
truth the theory does not go.

Of course, a motivating context and some freedom from external coercion are
prerequisites of critical reflection. But is this all? Consider the following example,
taken from my experience as a labor organizer.

Angry about wages and supervisor harassment, an assembly worker talks with
an organizer. The organizer sketches a context for his problem, the un-
necessarily hierarchical command relations of work. The worker is interested
in the organizer's analysis, including his ideas about increased worker participation. But later he reflects on his situation. Recognizing the possibility that
criticism of management invites sanctions, including the loss of his job, he
shrugs his shoulders and decides to continue as before.

The discontented worker finds support for his discontent and for consideration of
plausible alternatives. He forgoes action, however, in the face of real and anticipated constraints.

At this level of characterization, the worker's consideration of an alternative to
the relations of production apparently corresponds to the rational actor model of
decision-making psychology (Sloan, 1986, ch. 3). Having weighed the costs and
benefits, he has made his decision. Why should we presume to complicate this
account of his critical reflection, an account that might well correspond with his
own, by considering whether it is constrained? Further, in what way could this
constraint be said to be ideological?

Again, the contradiction between democratic and authoritarian relational forms
is not merely formal but generates experiences of suffering. The worker's decision
to continue on at the job is an important but by no means conclusive step in an
ongoing process of handling his difficult existence. How he represents the relationship between himself—his needs and aspirations—and the coercive forces
arrayed against him and potential allies as he lives in this matrix of experience
becomes the terrain of ideology. On this terrain ideology criticism proceeds as a
reflective inquiry into the play of coercion, *both as actually experienced and as
anticipated,* within the worker's handling of experience.

Ideology criticism moves upstream from the cost-benefit stage of representing
experiences to reconstruct the ebb and flow of cognitions and emotions that swirl
within contradictions. In this process, reflection is drawn to examine how experi-

ences that potentially upset the worker's accommodation to the relations of production and associated working conditions are handled. Ideology criticism is directed not simply at beliefs but also at the process within which experience is prevented from informing belief.

Ideology criticism asks the individual to pause to consider just how freely they arrived at their ongoing stance toward a contradiction, whether coercion deflected them, and whether a representation of coercion holds their stance together. Ideology criticism thus questions not only beliefs about contradictory relationships but also the nature of the dialogic relationship within which those beliefs were formed. Relatively open and unconstrained critical dialogue inevitably reveals and establishes a counterpoint to an ideological rendering of communicative relationships—for example, restrictive definitions of "free speech"—that obscures the conditions within which dialogue about suffering actually occurs.[1]

Depending in part upon the prevailing level of social coercion, the individual's standard of adequate consideration will varyingly approximate what might be argued constitutes full consideration.[2] In the above example, the worker may remain aware of having given up, however "sensibly"; when asked why he gave up, he might bitterly explain, "They'd have fired me." This asserts a costly truth because he maintains an awareness of his anticipated experience of coercion, along with concomitant tension with management. However, there are plenty of culturally available "reasons" for his decision that can either immediately or subsequently blot out the coercion that lay behind his giving up, thereby reducing tension: he has made a "necessary" sacrifice to further other goals, regards the organizer as only a "troublemaker," simply forgets about it because it hurt his pride, and so on. Each standpoint varies regarding the extent to which coercion shapes the worker's conception of himself and others, of his interests and theirs, and of his awareness of coercion itself in his ongoing construction of his grievance and how he handled it.

Psychoanalytic Theory and Ideology Criticism

How might we develop a more precise understanding of the impact of experienced and anticipated coercion on the assembly worker? And if he is willing and interested, how might this understanding be employed in dialogue with him?

Psychoanalytic theory and its therapeutic application incorporate a critical sensitivity to, and exploration of, the impact of forms of coercion on subjects' experience and their awareness of it. This is part of a project in which reified conceptions of desire and the objects of desire, along with associated anxiety and depressive affect, are explicated, allowing subjects to make more deliberate decisions about their fears and strivings (Barratt, 1984, ch. 4; Brenner, 1982, chs. 3–4).

I would distinguish my use of psychoanalytic theory from a well-known alternative. As I will elaborate, my emphasis will be on the microanalysis of defensive maneuvers that develop as the subject tries to express grievances. One alternative approach informing attempts to bring psychoanalytic theory to bear on social problems involves identifying character types suited to institutional requirements, for example, the "authoritarian personality" of Adorno et al. (1949) or Fromm's democratic character type (1947). I would question such a characterological orientation because: (1) it assumes that a high degree of character-institution "fit" either prevails or is necessary to either institutional functioning or individual adaptation to institutional life; and (2) it assumes that enhancing the subject's capacity for reflection on their adjustment will be difficult because the psychological obstacle to reflection, the institutionally determined characterological mode of adaptation, is such a dominant element in the subject's ego functioning.

Instead of assuming congruence between individual psychology and institutional structure, it is more judicious to assume only that in handling their experience a subject will bring to bear a variety of mental operations, some of which may be both crucially effective and unconscious. Accordingly, it is more pertinent to note that the conflicts and coercion associated with core structural contradictions tend to heighten defensive psychological functioning in subjects, infusing a more automatic reflection-resistant, hence reified, quality into their handling of their experiences.[3] The prescribed thoroughness of the "fit" is determined within a socio-individual dialectic, with one extreme defined by characterological congruence and the other by the formal contingency of the wage labor contract (Edwards, 1984).

I will present sections of hour-long interviews with a twenty-year-old Chrysler assembly worker, "Pat," done in the summer of 1978. I interviewed him once a week for eight weeks, and these sections are from the first and fourth interviews.[4] They adequately illustrate only the opening phase of an ideology critical process, the sort of grievance recovery that would be preliminary to a focus on the defensive maneuvers typically directed against them. Given my role, talking with Pat in a critical-interpretive vein would have been irresponsible, possibly leaving him feeling worse about his job and without the opportunity for significant changes.

My approach was as follows: in talking with him generally about his life at the plant and his grievances, I would try to use his own terminology when eliciting more information. After he presented his stance, to get his reaction I would at times ask him a question reflecting another perspective available to him, as in the case of my question about time and motion studies in the first interview. In the fourth interview I directly raised the question of workplace democracy and encouraged him to talk further. We shall see that as he talked he went through a series of shifts regarding the grievances, shifts that can be appropriately interpreted as being defensive. Our rapport was good, and though usually tired from having just gotten off work, he was fairly spontaneous.

I will begin about five minutes into the first interview, in which he talked about the pace of his work:

Pat: They have a rate set up . . . [denotes pause] you know, for normal production and how many parts a person can run an hour, and if I run over that . . . like the rate on my machine is 3189. If I hit 3189 two hours early I don't have to work any more, and if they make me work they have to pay me time and a half for the hours worked . . . so I just quit when I hit production.

RE: So you can work a varying number of hours per day?

Pat: Yeah, there's a lot of people who work like five hours a day, every day.

RE: You mean you can go in there and work hard for five hours . . .

Pat: Yeah, and then you go sit in an air-conditioned cafeteria, or out in the sun.

I conveyed surprise that people had to remain at the plant after they met their quota. Pat replied:

Pat: Yeah . . . it strikes me as funny, but, I don't know, I suppose it's to keep down cheating and things like that 'cause a lot of people would like to leave early. . . .

RE: Let me follow this up some. How would you cheat if they know you've done 3189?

Pat: They really can't tell because the parts I make don't go directly to somebody. They sit in a bin and someone else puts parts on top of those so they couldn't tell if it was mine or theirs or somebody else's. My counter, I push the counter by hand, so . . . there's lots of jobs like that.

RE: Do you mind staying at the plant after you've done your quota?

Pat: Not really. You know there's people always saying, "Boy, I wish we could leave after we got done," but they really can't bitch because they get paid for doing nothing . . . you know . . . I mean the work isn't really that hard. I mean, most places, if you hit the . . . like Ford's, if you hit the production you're on call even if you are done.

Deciding to see how he would assess a justification for leaving the plant upon reaching the quota, I referred to the time and motion studies by which expected output is nominally determined:

Pat: Yeah, well it's supposed to be no more than a normal pace, is how it reads, the contract. . . . Yeah, it does sound reasonable, but . . . uh, yeah . . . I don't see why they don't work it that way. . . . It's just the way it's been since I've been there.

RE: I see.

Pat: Sounds, yeah, they're just confining people.

RE: Hmm . . .

Pat: That's what they're doing. . . . I don't think they like the system they have there, really.

I asked if people planned to finish early.

Pat: People do that with the remainder of their time . . . there's always a card game you can get into. . . . I used to get done every day, but they raised my rate and I won't . . . I won't run it. I mean, you know it's inhumanly possible [his phrasing] so I start slowing down.

Moving into the discussion of production rates, Pat focuses on the possibility of getting off as much as two hours early—he can "just quit when he hits production" and then "go and sit in an air-conditioned cafeteria, or out in the sun." When I ask why people are kept at the plant after they've finished their quota, Pat momentarily questions the policy and then guesses that "it's to keep down cheating" that would occur if people were allowed to leave early.

This interview section raises the following question: is Pat simply guessing at management's rationale, or does his hypothesis stand in a more complex relationship to what is coming out as he talked with me? As I talk with him, is Pat randomly throwing a spotlight on aspects of life at work, or does the sequence of illuminations follow an underlying rationale in which defensive processes play a significant and yet unacknowledged role?

After he has talked about cheating, culminating with a broken-off reference to his own situation, I ask him if he minds hanging around the plant after he has done his quota. His response, "Not really, I'm getting paid for it," is not conclusive—is he getting paid for work done, or for time spent at the plant? Again we can ask: does this statement reflect a simple lapse in Pat's putting together a sound justification? Should we simply infer from this that Pat "really" regards himself as getting paid for time spent, contradicting the earlier emphasis on work done? Or is an underlying rationale suggested?

Pat shifts to people who "bitch" when they have to stay, a denigrating term suggesting the standpoint does not merit serious attention. He follows by saying work is not "all that hard," an absolute argument he then relativizes through a reference to conditions at Ford. To see how he might respond to a justification of his coworkers' complaints, I referred to the time and motion studies commonly used to determine, or at least "objectively" justify, a day's labor. Pat refers to the contract's insistence on a "normal pace" of work, a concept that, however fluid, supports a "pay for work done" argument. As he thinks of this he begins to move unsteadily into a more critical stance—"it does sound reasonable [to be able to leave the plant after the quota is met], but . . . I don't see why they don't work it that way"—and then momentarily suspends its development by referring to the policy as a fact, also possibly implying a different situation in the past.

After he stops, I neutrally let him know I am still listening, which seems to encourage him to develop the critical stance further to "they're just confining people." He stops once more, I again make a neutral utterance, and he reaffirms the criticism but then immediately relieves management of responsibility by doubting that "they [really] like the system they have there." I inquire blandly to find out if groups of workers plan to hurry through their work to pass the time together later. Pat addresses that question generally but then drops it to begin voicing his own grievance, which strikingly contradicts the previous image of easy work: he can't actually run the rate, and because it is so high, he refuses to run it and slows down.

This surprising statement, closely following Pat's claim that management doesn't like their own system, sheds light on earlier portions of the section. Before the "denouement," Pat's articulation of his grievance is *suppressed*—not *repressed,* in that he seems to remain preconsciously aware of his grievance even as he affirms notions that occlude it—through the invocation of the standpoint of management as it contends with Pat's coworkers. An earlier section illustrates this well:

Pat: Yeah . . . (1) it strikes me as funny
            (2) but, I don't know
            (3) I suppose it's to keep down cheating and things like that be-
               cause a lot of people would like to leave early.

My asking why people are kept at the plant after they finish their quota appears to have resonated with objections voiced equivocally in (1). In (2) Pat cuts off further articulation of his grievance with the objecting "but" followed by "I don't know," which might reflect uncertainty regarding management's rationale—"I don't know [for sure]. I suppose. . . ." In light of what follows, it is more plausible to regard it as a self-effacing statement, roughly equivalent to "Who am I to say?" It reflects Pat's "reorientation" to his experience, a blotting out of his grievance, which then reappears in criticized form in (3), conflated with the behavior it might set off in other employees—"cheating."

Pat maintains this orientation, which in light of the shift occurring across segments 1, 2, and 3 and his conclusion, can be regarded as *suppressive.* As part of this he adopts the "pay for time spent" rationale over the "pay for work done" rationale, talking of other workers "bitching" about "work that really isn't all that hard" and is at least better than at Ford. When I rearticulate a critical standpoint, not explicitly justifying it but offering it as another perspective, Pat's grievance wells up again. He does articulate it, however, only after management has disappeared as a responsible agent—"I don't think they like the system they have there really." Thus Pat's final statement of his suffering is abstracted from the social relations of the workplace. It hangs in midair, as much one of the unavoidable discontents of coordinated production as it is of the capitalist workplace.

Psychoanalytic theory informs my "second reading" of this interview section. I emphasize, however, that those concepts serve to deepen our understanding of a dialogue that is already mundanely problematic. Just as Freud (1901) would begin an investigation by asking why a name could not be remembered, we start from the simple question of why Pat's route to the articulation of his grievance is so circuitous, beginning with a rosy perspective, then self-effacement, criticism of other workers, sympathy for management rationales, and the final absolution of management. To pose this question is not to ask more clumsy and brutal ones— such as "Why is Pat so muddled?" or "Why is his consciousness false?"—that Thompson and Gintis see inescapably tied to ideology criticism. Instead, we inquire into the nature of his intrapersonal and interpersonal processes of representation and how those processes are distorted by intertwining subjective and objective constraints.

In this connection we can usefully draw upon the psychoanalytic theory of the therapeutic process for a parallel. When listening to a patient the therapist seeks to identify the conflicted locus, or loci, of their presentation and to make an interpretation that helps make them aware of the defensive occlusion of conflict. The subject's passage through this "hierarchy of resistance and defense" (Greenson, 1967, 78), culminating in the expression of a wish, is roughly congruent to Pat's route to the expression of his grievance. I offer Pat no interpretation, but the real diminution of constraint in the interview situation—although I was a stranger, I probably seemed at least sympathetic, certainly more so than his supervisor— coupled with my focusing on a problematic aspect of work allows Pat to "get past" resistances and defenses that he normally uses to adjust to the work situation. This is not to say that Pat never feels angry about the work rate. Rather, he regularly manages his anger through the various defenses evident in the interview: *denial* of the problem, *projection* onto other workers of his critical stance, *displacement* of his anger, and perhaps most relevant to our concern with ideology criticism, a likely *identification with the aggressor,* in which the series of defensive maneuvers can culminate in Pat adopting management's standpoint to blot out his own. His adjustment to his work incorporates "defensive maneuvers" (Wallerstein, 1983) that, by occluding essential aspects of his experience at the plant, support oppressively one-sided conceptualizations of the social relations of production.

In the fourth interview I raised the topic of democratic-egalitarian social relations by first talking about some political questions and then asking what he thought most important about a democracy:

Pat: I think the freedom to do anything you want. That's about it, or the most important.
RE: Could you expand on that?
Pat: It's just that, you know, in nondemocratic countries people are oppressed and aren't able to say what they feel, whereas in this country you can. We can also go just about anywhere we want at any time, or just about anywhere, more places than any nondemocratic country. That's about all.

We continued to talk generally about democracies, Pat expressing frustration with anonymous "politicians who line their pockets instead of serving the people." I then shifted into a discussion of workplace democracy by asking him how he would characterize the way the plant was run. He said it wasn't a democracy.

Pat: Far from it, I think. . . . At Chrysler, you mean? No, I mean you can voice your opinion to the union, but the company can only hear so much. I mean, if all the employees were for something and the company were against it the company would win unless everyone went out on strike for it. It seems close to the way democracy is running right now, you know, where people have to go to extremes to get their way, but I don't think it's run as a democracy, the company has the final say, really the major say. Employees can only gripe to a certain extent. Suppressed . . . [his phrasing, and I had not used the term]

RE: How do you feel about that?

Pat: Seems like that's the only way they could run the company and still make any money. I mean, if they let the employees decide everything they wanted to do they could probably decide not to work or work two days a week or something, so they have to. . . . Company prides itself, well, it doesn't pride itself but their way of getting things done is to be strict on the rules. That's the only way the company could run smoothly, because if a democracy was used in the company the employees would be voting on everything . . . bringing up their proposals on the way they want the company run.

I asked him why he thought the employees would work only two days a week.

Pat: Because it seems like everyone there gets everything they want and still doesn't have enough . . . bad example. . . . People are never satisfied with what they have, they always want more.

Pat went on to speculate about the causes of the "crazy" behavior of other employees, wondering about their challenges to rules and how they would "take things to the limit." I asked when he had first met people like that.

Pat: I suppose when I started working for Chrysler, you know, that's the first place I really noticed it workwise, you know, union companies in general. Chrysler was the first place I ever worked where they kind of pushed things to the limit.

RE: And that struck you as crazy. . . . Uh, were there any other feelings that you had toward them at that time?

Pat: Yeah, well I first noticed it when they were voting on a new contract and everyone seemed dissatisfied with what they had, you know, to me it sounded like a really good, a great contract. And I thought they were all crazy, that they were pretty greedy at that point.

Pat initially formulates democratic rights as "the freedom to do anything you want," and then restricts this to the freedom to "say what you feel" and to "go about anywhere you want," a restriction carried out with a relativizing reference to "nondemocratic countries." This passage is significant in light of both Pat's characterization of other employees later in this section and how he previously projected his wishes onto others and then condemned them. Instead of considering the "freedom to do anything you want" a mere slogan, it is more appropriately seen as expressing a fantasy of impulsive freedom that contemporary capitalism both cultivates and condemns. This is not to portray Pat's personality as simply determined by the social order in cookie-cutter fashion. Rather, the social order stimulates, highlights, and interrelates psychological trends in a way that encourages an understanding of them as antagonistic.

Concomitantly, institutional positions are imbued with this naturalized antagonism. This is clearly reflected in Pat's discussion of worker/union–company relations and the possibilities of workplace democratization. When Pat begins, the tone is realistic (although the idea that "the company can only hear so much" suggests both Pat's cool appraisal of the constraints upon then-floundering Chrysler and a willingness to absolve them of responsibility once more). Thus Pat draws a nice parallel between the nature of political and economic conflict under state capitalism and indicates that militancy—"going to extremes"—is necessary. But after I ask him how he feels about the situation, he briefly points to the profit rationale guiding the company's behavior and then imagines the resulting chaos if workers ran the plant. Pat interpretively posits generalized traits of craziness and greed—"People are never satisfied with what they have, they always want more"—to be the problem. A proud management thereby becomes the sole available source of rules and discipline. Thus, although the company and the workers may be motivated by the same greed, the company's enforcement of rules is the only guarantee that anything will get done and that the company will survive.

The sociopolitical underpinnings of Pat's perspective are so glaringly obvious that they can obscure how Pat's personality trends are implicated. Under state and corporate coercion, unions have largely foresworn any interest in controlling the production process and, what is more, discourage workers from formulating demands to that end (Davis, 1986; Montgomery, 1977). This encourages workers to defer to management control.

All of this facilitates the ideological project of excluding democratic-egalitarian relational forms, forms within which the grievances of the first interview segments would either not develop or could be remedied. Real coercion and its threat encourage a dovetailing of Pat's psychodynamics with representations of this level of social relations. Pat draws from the store of culturally available rationales ideologically relevant ideas concerning "human nature," emphasizing those that are personally resonant. Key defensive maneuvers include *repressively* denying his frustrations and wishes, *projecting* them onto other workers, and then *identifying* with management as he condemns the proposal. Easily misconstrued as obsequiousness, this pattern was replicated throughout the interviews.

Within the coercive relationship between wage labor and capital, Pat constructs a rationale for "the way things are" that mediates between his more personalized view of life and the distribution of rights and obligations formalized in the "accord" between management and labor. Intensified by the demands of adjustment,

Pat's defensive processing concludes in a personalized standpoint that is congruent with ideology, or *ideology syntonic,* while ideology seems to incorporate lived, experienced truth because it is *defense syntonic.* Put differently, this process entails a *reciprocal reification:* the reification at the social level of institutional relationships is supplemented by their interpretation through defensively distorted relational frames and, in turn, defensively grounded reifications are institutionally rationalized. The one-sided, problematic aspects of Pat's defensive processing are obscured, their results simply regarded as "his view of things," while to him relations at the plant appear to be determined by natural forces.

But the ideological circumscription of Pat's reflection is just that—a circumscription. In the course of our dialogue his representation of suffering within the contradiction is not completely occluded; instead, it is encapsulated and denied elaboration and relevance to action. The first interview segments, in which Pat momentarily adopted an occlusive stance only to drop it in favor of an explicit acknowledgment of one grievance against the company, indicate how even within the interview's inexplicit and fragile relaxation of constraints his mode of adjustment to work hierarchy could be suspended, giving rise to an unexpected avowal of his refusal to run the rate.

If even this relaxation of constraints is effective, it is reasonable to anticipate that a deliberate relaxation would be more so. What form might that take?

1. As indicated above, I might have directly addressed defensive trends by highlighting them via the shifts in his presentation. In addition to familiarizing him with his way of handling his grievances, the risks Pat associated with more sustained articulation of his grievances—risks that he momentarily pushed aside—could be more explicitly identified. This form of defense analysis might lead into:

2. A search for the relational ground of defenses in his life history (Kernberg, 1987). For example, he talked of his divorced father's infrequent visits in this way:

Pat: I didn't really think about it because I was usually pretty busy playing baseball. I didn't think about it until I got older.
RE: What did you think about it then?
Pat: I thought he was kind of a heel for not coming around too often. That's about it.
RE: . . . Why do you think he didn't come around too often?
Pat: Busy . . .
RE: Uh, doing what?
Pat: I'm not really sure. If he's anything like me, he didn't do it until it crossed his mind to . . . I mean, I wouldn't go and visit relatives regularly. I can see if I was single, I would be busy. . . . He also had a lot of hobbies. Like he built airplanes, bought 'em and rebuilt 'em and flew 'em. And he was usually busy with other hobbies.

It is likely that his pattern of accommodation to that relationship transferred and informed his accommodation to plant relations. With his father, as with management, his recounting is strongly shaped by identifications with the aggressor. Here they: (a) contain Pat's anger by tarring him with the same brush of paternal neglect; and (b) probably allow him both to participate vicariously with and be like the father as he engages in his exciting hobbies. Interpretive exploration of this likely transference might contribute to a more realistic revision of his sense of management's power and his relation to it. In particular, this would allow us to address the contribution of wishful fantasies to his defensive maneuvers, wishes having little real applicability to plant relations.

3. Such an interpretive exploration could greatly extend the scope and duration of the critical dialogue. Although the literature on short-term psychodynamic therapy indicates that in some cases a narrow, consistent interpretive focus is highly effective (Malan, 1976), unpacking defensive operations into their relational antecedents is often the stuff of lengthy analyses. This probably would be unnecessary. Drawing upon existing, contradictory relational frameworks for its critical power, ideology critical dialogue facilitates the transition from a demobilized state to one in which group solidarity, affirming relational alternatives, limits the impact of defensive processing and supports articulating grievances. In another area of his life Pat had already begun this transition: remarkably enough, he told me of his activity in a local environmental group protesting nuclear power and of his willingness to face arrest. Such contentious participation, not personality change as such, is a more appropriate outcome of ideology critical dialogue.

NOTES

1. Habermas's work (1979, ch. 1) on a "universal speech pragmatics" may be regarded as a formal inquiry into the presuppositions of an ideology critical dialogue. Unfortunately, his turn to universal pragmatics has lost the edge of his earlier work (Habermas, 1970) by obscuring how ideology criticism derives both its motivation and validation from concrete human suffering and the experience and anticipation of intrapersonal and interpersonal relationships remedying it. Lorenzer's criticisms (1974, 71–75) of a parallel dialogic formalism in Habermas's reading of psychoanalysis inform and support my reservations.

2. Social psychologists have given extensive attention to factors limiting individual rationality. Two of the more significant areas are individual conformity to group pressure (Santee and Maslach, 1982) and cognitive processing (Nisbett and Borgida, 1975). The psychoanalytically oriented approach I will take converges with these literatures, perhaps most interestingly with work on biases in individual self-reports of mental processes (Nisbett and Wilson, 1977; Wright and Rip, 1981). However, social and cognitive psychologists need to reconsider their theoretical and methodological rejection of at least the more defense-oriented elements of psychoanalytic theory, marginalized in academic psychology since at least the early 1960s. Mischel (1973) and Wachtel (1973) have outlined the grounds for marginalization; Rosenwald (1985) provides a strong argument for reconsideration.

3. Kahn et al. (1964, ch. 13) are among the few authors to consider fluctuations in defensive functioning relative to ongoing variations in occupational "role conflict." Less immediately related to the present work, Kohn and his associates (Kohn, 1969, 1973; Kohn and Schooler, 1973) have studied the impact of job characteristics on more general personality traits and attitudes ("authoritarian conservatism") and intellectual flexibility.
4. Pat volunteered in response to a card I placed on the union bulletin board. He was paid five dollars an hour, about two-thirds of his hourly wage.

REFERENCES

Adorno, Theodore, et al. 1949. *The Authoritarian Personality.* New York: W. W. Norton.
Arlow, Jacob. 1987. "The Dynamics of Interpretation." *Psychoanalytic Quarterly* 56:68–87.
Barratt, Barnaby. 1984. *Psychic Reality and Psychoanalytic Knowing.* Hillsdale, N.J.: Lawrence Erlbaum.
Blumberg, Paul. 1968. *Industrial Democracy.* Schocken: New York.
Bowles, Samuel, and Herbert Gintis. 1986. *Democracy and Capitalism.* New York: Basic Books.
Brenner, Charles. 1982. *The Mind in Conflict.* New York: International Universities Press.
Dahl, Robert, and Charles Lindblom. 1953. *Politics, Economics, and Welfare.* New York: Harper and Row.
Davis, Mike. 1986. *Prisoners of the American Dream.* London: Verso.
Edwards, Richard. 1984. "Work Incentives and Worker Responses in Bureaucratic Enterprises: An Empirical Study." In *Research in Social Stratification and Mobility,* vol. 3. Greenwich, Conn.: JAI Press.
Freud, Sigmund. 1901. "The Psychopathology of Everyday Life." In *The Standard Edition of the Collected Works of Sigmund Freud,* vol. 6. Edited by James Stratchey. 1957. London: Hogarth Press.
Fromm, Erich. 1947. *Man for Himself.* New York: Rinehart.
Geuss, Raymond. 1981. *The Idea of a Critical Theory.* New York: Cambridge University Press.
Gintis, Herbert. 1980. "Communication and Politics: Marxism and the Problem of Liberal Democracy." *Socialist Review* 50–51:189–232.
Greenson, Ralph. 1967. *The Technique and Practice of Psychoanalysis.* New York: International Universities Press.
Gutman, Herbert. 1977. "Work, Culture and Society." In *Industrializing America.* New York: Random House.
Habermas, Jürgen. 1970. "On Systematically Distorted Communication." *Inquiry* 13:205–218.
———. 1971. *Knowledge and Human Interests.* Boston: Beacon Press.
———. 1979. *Communication and the Evolution of Society.* Boston: Beacon Press.
Kahn, Robert, et al. 1964. *Organizational Stress: Studies in Role Conflict and Ambiguity.* New York: John Wiley.
Kernberg, Otto. 1987. "The Ego Psychology–Object Relations Theory Approach to the Transference." In *Psychoanalytic Quarterly* 56:197–221.

Kohn, Melvin. 1969. *Class and Conformity.* Homewood, Ill.: Dorsey.

———. 1973. "Occupational Experience and Psychological Functioning: An Assessment of Reciprocal Effects." *American Sociological Review* 38:97–118.

Kohn, Melvin, and Carmi Schooler. 1978. "The Reciprocal Effects of the Substantive Complexity of Work and Intellectual Flexibility: A Longitudinal Assessment." *American Journal of Sociology* 84:24–52.

Lorenzer, Alfred. 1970. *Sprachzerstorung und Rekonstruktion.* Frankfurt: Suhrkamp.

———. 1974. *Die Wahrheit der Psychoanalytischen Erkenntnis.* Frankfurt: Suhrkamp.

———. 1976. "Symbols and Stereotypes." In *Critical Sociology.* Edited by Paul Connerton. New York: Penguin.

Malan, David. 1976. *A Study of Brief Psychotherapy.* New York: Plenum.

McLellan, David. 1986. *Ideology.* Minneapolis: University of Minnesota Press.

Mischel, Walter. 1973. "On the Empirical Dilemmas of Psychodynamic Approaches: Issues and Alternatives." *Journal of Abnormal Psychology* 78:335–344.

Montgomery, David. 1977. *Worker's Control in America.* New York: Cambridge University Press.

Nisbett, Richard, and Eugene Borgida. 1975. "Attribution and the Psychology of Prediction." *Journal of Personality and Social Psychology* 32:932–943.

Nisbett, Richard, and Thomas Wilson. 1977. "Telling More Than We Know: Verbal Reports on Mental Processes." *Psychological Review* 84:231–259.

Rosenwald, George. 1985. "Hypocrisy, Self-Deception, and Perplexity: The Subject's Enhancement as Methodological Criterion." *Journal of Personality and Social Psychology* 49:682–703.

Sandler, Joseph, et al. 1973. *The Patient and the Analyst.* New York: International Universities Press.

Santee, Richard, and Christina Maslach. 1982. "To Agree or Not to Agree: Personal Dissent and Social Pressure to Conform." *Journal of Personality and Social Psychology* 42:690–700.

Sloan, Tod. 1986. *Deciding: Self-Deception in Life Choices.* New York: Methuen.

Thompson, Edward. 1978. *The Poverty of Theory and Other Essays.* New York: Monthly Review Press.

Tilly, Charles. 1978. *From Mobilization to Revolution.* Reading, Mass.: Addison-Wesley.

Wachtel, Paul. 1973. "Psychodynamics, Behavior Therapy, and the Implacable Experimenter: An Inquiry into the Consistency of Personality." *Journal of Abnormal Psychology* 78:324–334.

Wallerstein, Robert. 1983. "Defenses, Defense Mechanisms, and the Structure of the Mind." *Journal of the American Psychoanalytic Association* 31 (suppl.):201–226.

Wright, Peter, and Peter Rip. 1981. "Retrospective Reports on the Causes of Decisions." *Journal of Personality and Social Psychology* 40:601–614.

GEORGE C. ROSENWALD

Conclusion: Reflections on Narrative Self-Understanding

T he introduction to this book sets out a theory: that life stories play a significant role in the formation of identity, that these stories may be constrained by oppressive cultural conditions, and that these stories—and the lives to which they relate—may be liberated by critical insight and engagement. It has been noted that this theory is at odds with a current theoretical orientation in narratology according to which no story is "worse" than any other. This orientation makes critical theory radically impossible. By contrast, the chapters in this volume can be read as commending a critical theory of narrative. I therefore return to the philosophical issues that such a theory involves.

The process by which narratives evolve so as to broaden understanding and action may be conceived as follows. When people tell life stories, they do so in accordance with models of intelligibility specific to the culture. Without such models narration is impossible. These models are consonant with the forces that stabilize the given organization of society. Stories that comply with such cultural models are generally recognized as sensible. Their formal compliance with these models goes unnoticed: they simply make sense. By contrast, stories that fail to conform to the models are more or less alarming.

Personal accounts may communicate a speaker's beliefs and commitments to others. They may also reflect these back to the speaker and thereby add to his or her conviction. In this way, accounts bind individuals to the arrangements of the society enforcing the models, whether the accounts feature circumscribed reactions to situations or an entire life course. The political and other arrangements typical of a society are implicated in the conventions of discourse. These arrangements come to be seen as natural and inevitable to the extent that the conventions allow us to communicate (Berger and Luckmann, 1966). Furthermore, these arrangements are renewed and strengthened each time they become manifest in a narrative. Not only acceptable behavior but also acceptable accounts of behavior are thus socialized. Through such narratives people are brought to the point of wanting what they must want in their society as well as to regard these wants as reasonable.

These relatively stable and stabilizing patterns are opposed by the force of subjectivity, by the restlessness of desire. Socialization, which seeks to commit desire to the offerings of the culture, forces compromises on the subject that the subject seeks to repudiate endlessly. Accordingly, subjectivity has a potential range extending beyond any temporary settlement it may have entered. Its dissatisfaction jeopardizes the aims of socialization not only in the domain of behavioral, but of narratory compliance. For the stories people tell about their lives are themselves compromises undergone on demand, arbitrary stopping places in a ceaseless groping toward fulfillment and completion—like still photographs that seem to freeze a continuous motion.

The desirous person is therefore bound to be more or less dissatisfied with any such self-objectivation. By undoing compromises the subject again and again takes the risk of violating models of intelligibility. In doing so, narrators draw attention to their own deviance and to the cultural model as one that discomfits. This double awareness permits desire to push the action and narration toward ever new compromises. It should be noted that in this social-psychological model of development progress is not assured. Models of intelligibility, supported by the odium of deviance, constrain the subject's spontaneity. The narrative compromises by which this balance between restless desire and stabilizing conventions is achieved may take the form of routinized thought supporting the existing organization of society. At several points in this chapter I shall allude to factors that help speakers to progress beyond confining models as well as factors that inhibit such progress.

To make the contribution of narratives to enlightenment plausible, I will address some issues in current theories of narrative and autobiography. In linking the stories people tell about themselves to the social conditions of human development, one is hard put nowadays to find a suitable theoretical approach. Traditionally it was assumed that it is possible to recount one's past more or less accurately and to relate it significantly to the experience of the present. It was also assumed that a speaker can give us a picture of the world around him or her and relate this to his or her thoughts or feelings. But these assumptions are no longer tenable in this simple form.

Today theorists commonly discuss narrative as productive of effects rather than as portraying an objective or even a private psychic state of affairs. These postrealist assumptions give rise to conceptual difficulties, some of which I take up in this chapter. In the first section I address difficulties posed by the recent social-constructionist agenda, in particular regarding the relation of the narrating subject to his or her stories and to the situation in which these are produced. This will be followed by comments on a recent skepticism expressed within psychoanalysis concerning the possibility of retrieving the past in order to relieve present suffering. Here one can note an ahistorical, adaptationist trend, which complicates the conceptualization of lives and of their development over time. In the third section, I comment on the concept of narrative situation. It is sometimes assumed that narratives are crafted chiefly to influence the relationship between narrator and audience. But when subjects seek clarification of their lives in society, the inter-locutory dyad may exert a facilitative or retardant effect because of its dependence on social factors beyond its own boundaries. Last, because postrealists reject faithful representation as a criterion for the evaluation of personal accounts, they often classify life histories as a kind of fiction. Accordingly, I ask how this might be reconciled with the notion of a narrator's stories getting "better," freer of misunderstandings.

I shall often refer to psychoanalytic thought and practice. No other discipline has articulated the social formation and malformation of the individual more finely or more deeply, and none has taken the life-historical view of this formation so seriously. That is why the elaboration of the psychoanalytic life story can serve as a model for a broader concern with social-developmental aspects of personal narratives. Throughout I shall refer to the essays in this volume selectively in order to illustrate various arguments, but I do not wish to imply that the authors share the views I offer or approve my comments on their work.

The Relativity of Teller, Tale, and Situation: Critical Possibilities

In democratic societies progress is often thought to depend on an interaction of individual and collective-institutional advances. Individuals reflecting on their social experience can exert their influence so as to direct or redirect social history through concerted action. Of course, the actual political practices of various societies may fall short of this vision. My comments bear on only one impediment to the realization of this ideal social development: when individuals' reflections on their social existence are blocked or impoverished, corrective action will be para-lyzed or disoriented. We may look to the narrative accounts people give of their life experience to obtain insights into typical sources and forms of such perplexity (Rosenwald, 1988a).

Framing the issue in this way raises a prior question. Our interest is in the development of lives, but our access to lives is through stories about them. If we do not believe that such stories are reports of objective reality, how are they nevertheless informative? As social constructionists see it, the stories people tell about themselves—for instance, about their experiences, memories, intentions, or understandings—are erroneously taken as reports of psychic realities. Instead, they are said to reflect social conventions in every detail. There are socially specific models for telling the story of one's growing up or of one's making an important decision. At the same time, social constructionists point out the per-sonal advantages to be reaped if one abides by these rules and the price to be paid if one does not.

Certainly no reader of these essays will feel disposed to make light of cultural forces. But the issue of human development is obscured if these forces are de-clared to be sovereign, as is commonly done by constructionists. In the ideal case, as conceived by these theorists, society is a collection of perfect speakers exercising their mastery of the regnant conventions so as to maximize their personal advantages. The narratives so produced reflect as well as ratify the conventions by which they are constituted—regardless of whether these rules favor or hinder human development.

It is as though the conventions pressed the narrator into their service and, through his or her composition of narratives, reproduced themselves. The narrator takes dictation from the conventions; there are no terms within this approach for conceiving any tension to arise between the narrator's own agenda and the conventions. This represents an oversocialized conception of personality (Wrong, 1961). For example, Slugoski and Ginsburg propose to oust the concept of personal identity from the theoretical vocabulary of psychology altogether. Their argument begins with the social-constructionist premise that what people say bears an indeterminate relation to any supposed personal reality. From there the authors proceed to the proposition that people are commonly judged to have launched a successful identity if they manage to present the events of their lives in a coherent and compelling narrative. By contrast, people who lack the requisite rhetorical skills are said to fall short of this stage of development (Slugoski and Ginsburg, 1989). The argument continues with the observation that certain disadvantaged groups in our society do not dispose of these rhetorical resources and are therefore falsely held to be developmentally arrested. In other words, we cannot say more than that the groups are deficient in how they tell their lives.

It should be noted that although this argument apparently aims at protecting disadvantaged groups against disadvantageous judgments, it ends by limiting their damage to the situation in which they account for their lives; only as they speak are they handicapped.[1] This notion is not likely to find favor with anyone who has closely witnessed the pain and toil undergone by members of oppressed groups who are struggling, often in vain, for a sense of personal direction and continuity and for a relationship of mutual assent between themselves and the larger communities (Erikson, 1974). Furthermore, the argument raises a concern about the strategy of scholarship: why orient—and thereby subordinate—our conceptions of human development to the historical actualities of discrimination? The identity concept gives expression to an ancient dream of humanity—the dream of a congruence between social and personal fulfillment. In the world as we know it, some groups and individuals no doubt have a lesser chance than others of attaining this ideal. Should we therefore scuttle the ideal? It seems that the discriminatory conditions, not the concept, should bear the burden of reproof.

Just as social constructionists treat a tale as a facet of a social situation, they also regard the teller as a construction projected on the basis of a conventionally acceptable tale. For instance, Rom Harré proposes that "people are what they believe they are."[2] He seeks to substantiate this assertion by, among other things, showing that many if not most propositions about the self are manifestations of grammatical necessity rather than empirical statements. This formulation is more than "potentially misleading" (Harré, 1989, 22). Either it expresses a creed devoid of all hope, since it appears to annul the distinction between the actual and the possible on which all progress depends, or else it assumes that the impetus to human betterment will come from somewhere other than human desire. It certifies stasis as normal.

If people are identical with their beliefs and narratives, then only beliefs and narratives can ever be bruised. Since these are under the control of social conventions, a socially deviant narrative might well have to be ascribed to the narrator's linguistic ineptitude rather than to the conditions that have antiquated the old rules of composition. On this account, values yield pride of place to conventions.[3] If people were nothing more than what they believe they are, their lives could be improved with exercises in rhetoric. Further, one must ask what happens to a major insight of social science, namely, that we can be systematically deceived about the world and ourselves in it—without knowing that we are so deceived. If the teller is reducible to social demands and conventions, repression becomes a *façon de parler.*

For constructionism to become useful as a theoretical framework within which to analyze social, political, and economic impediments to human self-comprehension and development, it would have to allow for a socially intelligible and consequential critique of social conventions—including the conventions of critique. But such a critique is inconceivable so long as narrator, narrative, and narrative situation are telescoped into one another. If a life is no more than a story and a story is governed only by the situation in which it is told, then one cannot declare a situation unlivable or a life damaged. Social development ceases to be a significant category. If the narrator is one with the narrative and with the conventions that shaped it, then social harmony and psychosocial identity are assured by definition or by grammar rather than achieved by historical action.

Several chapters in this book suggest that teller and tale can both be damaged or enhanced by a situation. It does not follow, however, that they are one and the same. What chiefly emerges from these essays is that narratives exhibit the mediation between the person and the situation and reflect critically on both because they are not reducible to either. Every narrator recognizes a difference between the self and the story, though for some that difference feels too small. For example, Jan, one of the choreographers presented by Evans, declines personal revelations for fear of jeopardizing her artistic resources—resources that are otherwise protected by the nondiscursive medium of her creativity. She wants to keep her distance from the narrative. Yet it is this untold narrative, not the silence, that defines her. Karen, the scholar followed by Wiersma, reminds us that the teller leads a life separate from but not independent of her tale, and that the two promote each other's development. By the time of the last interview Karen not only had a richer, more inclusive tale but also had become a more competent narrator and a more self-possessed subject of her life.

Social constructionists have dealt a powerful blow to the common-sense view that life stories are created by the mere exercise of competent introspection and forthright communication. Instead, they have highlighted the role played by social convention (Gergen, 1990). But there are reasons not to enthrone these conventions. Although they are powerful, their power is not absolute. Unless we believe this, we must conclude that speakers are doomed to remain locked within the circle of existing norms. If social, political, and economic realities mandate and sustain narrative conventions and these determine not only narratives but, through these, what the members of society are capable of thinking and communicating, then subjects can never free themselves from these realities—even in thought—so as to move beyond them.

The contributors to this volume show that a narrator can become aware of narrative conventions as problematic.[4] In our culture racist and sexist language are commonly experienced this way. These collected essays suggest that the grip of these norms is firm but not tight. If anything, the conventions are hospitable and therefore underdetermine the stories people tell about themselves. This has two sides: first, in an individualistic culture that places a premium on privacy the rules of decent communication make it possible to represent oneself adequately to an audience, for instance, stating one's reasons, intentions, and so forth, without giving a very searching accounting to oneself. What is socially acceptable may well fail to provide the narrator with a self-understanding beyond clichés and bromides. The conventions of communication predispose us all to evaluate what we hear ourselves say in accordance with how it is received by others. This suggests that demanding narrators must rise above degraded conventions and that complacent narrators will be led astray by them.

The second sense in which we can say that narrative conventions underdetermine stories is that one can deceive oneself or prevaricate quite effectively while still observing the conventions. The birthparents discussed in Modell's chapter illustrate this point. One cannot read their accounts without fretting that they may have fashioned politically effective reminiscences of coercive adoption by censoring incompatible narrative elements, for instance, those relating to the obvious advantages offered by adoption. What makes for a plausible, pragmatically effective story may end by fostering the narrator's self-deception. It does not follow, of course, that a more inclusive, balanced account would necessarily violate narrative conventions. But it is conceivable. The full complexity of human experience often tests the limits of what passes as everyday talk.

Whereas the birthparents may have surrendered self-understanding in order to press their claims against social institutions, the couples interviewed by Walkover seem to have paid an even higher price. These couples render such lavish tribute to topics on the current political agenda—child neglect and abuse—that their own tender potential for growing into parenthood is jeopardized.

Social development is promoted not by the conformity of narratives to convention but by the tension between them. What presses to be said beyond the merely acceptable can become a stimulus to critique and innovation. A conceptual framework within which narratives' role in development can be discussed must not conflate teller and tale. But, as I argue in the next section, neither must they be torn apart.

Historicity and the Development of Lives

One need not assume that narrators represent their lives accurately or that this is even possible. It is enough to note that they believe they are doing so. This belief is at the base of their struggles to tell their stories correctly—struggles that are abundantly illustrated in this book. No narrator is indifferent to his or her account; narratives play a role in the life they recount—if only by the dissatisfaction they cause the speaker and the stimulus they provide for the redirection of life and life story. In this sense, *they are both about the life and part of it.* This double relevance gives them their motivational and cognitive power to transform lives— their formative potential. Since the organization of these chapters is governed by an interest in human development, I propose to look at any given life story as provisional, poised to antiquate itself. It is a potential impulse to future development. A narrator's orientation to the past serves commonly to reorient his or her present to a desired future. In psychoanalysis this view is an indispensable working assumption.

But it has provoked the following objection. Human development does not pursue a prefigured end point but unfolds its unforeseen possibilities sequentially. Further, accounts of the past cannot be certified as corresponding to an elapsed reality. Therefore, one ought to think of them as fictions, perhaps retroactively installed so as to justify the narrator's next tactical move. This view has several variations (Geha, 1989; Spence, 1982; Wyatt, 1986) that boil down to a retreat from realist claims in favor of pragmatic criteria of narrative excellence. For example, Spence, the most visible of these critics, argues that the adequacy of a psychoanalytic narrative is attested by its consequences in living (1982).

He holds that memory is unreliable and that the so-called reconstructive operations of psychoanalysis are encumbered by various cognitive, inferential, and interactive disturbances stemming from the process itself.[5] Because of these interferences, historical truth—the accurate retrieval of the life course—is said to be unattainable. What remains is a construction rather than a reconstruction, and this, it is argued, exerts a favorable emotional impact and entails salutary consequences by virtue of its "aesthetic" characteristics—its "narrative truth." Presumably, such consequences occur in the short run, from one psychoanalytic session to the next, as well as in the long run, as a cure is effected.

The technical and probative difficulties cited by Spence undoubtedly deserve close attention. But the solution he offered involves grave difficulties of its own. To begin with, the aesthetic requirements of an effective construction are elusive. Also, the theory Freud formulated linking the genesis of neurosis with the process of therapy has been voided without replacement. We are left to wonder whether there is any methodical correspondence between the details of an aesthetically impressive construction of a psychoanalytic life history and the lifelong suffering it helps abate. Is knowledge of the past helpful in understanding the present?

What is at stake in this last question is not "historical truth" in the sense of radical retrieval but historicism as a central attitude behind all biographical inquiry— psychoanalytic or otherwise. What determinism is to the study of nature, historicism is to the study of lives.[6] It commits us a priori to the expectation that the meaning of any moment in a life's development—any event, any experience, any action—can be better understood if we recognize earlier moments surviving and resonating within it. The past is alive in the present. Historicism also means that we understand the meaning of any past moment retrospectively by tracing its subsequent fate.[7] To illustrate, the shocking significance of Freud's teachings about infantile sexuality is not merely that human sexual life begins earlier than suspected but that the adult is never fully freed from these earliest experiences.

In other words, historical truth was never a claim limited to the reconstruction of the past; it was and remains the possibility of understanding accounts of the present as transformations of past accounts. Spence's concept of narrative truth apparently has jettisoned more than was intended: the past is shown to be not only empirically irretrievable but also theoretically irrelevant. The new thinking about narrative truth not only repudiates the reliability of memory but also cuts the ground out from under the life-historical approach to meaning. This new ahistorical trend in the social sciences must be powerful indeed if it could take hold in psychoanalysis, the discipline that, since its inception, has stood as the model of all historicist understanding in the study of lives in society.

The dialectic of telling and living life

But we can mitigate these theoretical difficulties if we distinguish between narration and consequence somewhat differently: first, the adequacy of a narrative is revealed by the new cycle of stories and consequences it generates. That is to say, stories do not relate to consequences in living as a promissory note relates to hard cash. Rather, the consequences inform ever new updated stories that, in the ideal case, stir up further advances in living.[8] Psychoanalysis has no monopoly on the living-telling alternation. Self-conscious life, as we value it in our culture, always depends for its growth on such punctuating narrations. We stop to take stock of our past development before we move on.

Seen in this light, "consequences" do not only follow stories but precede them as well. For this reason, I refer to them as *new living action*. In psychoanalysis this is the work inside and outside the treatment situation from which new life accounts eventually grow. Accordingly, consequences cannot be evaluated in themselves any more than can narratives. A living action or condition of living can be judged restrictive if, at a minimum, it arrests reflection rather than generating accounts that make innovative action possible. The alternation of telling and living is extended in time and, as I shall suggest, constitutes a causal chain of sorts. But this kind of alternation does not occur in a closed system. Innovations in living depend on factors other than the narrator alone, for instance, on power relations and the costs of exploratory action. Similarly, the new narrative growing out of such innovation depends on reflective and interlocutory conditions at the individual and collective levels.

Second, the relation between narrative and living action must be clarified. So-called favorable consequences in living are never self-evidently favorable. This can be illustrated in respect to the ultimate consequence of psychoanalysis—the cure. Let us say, the analysand now works more productively than before, his nightmares have ceased, his body no longer hurts, he has become potent. At first glance, these outcomes appear as a "real" proof of a speculative story. But on closer examination it becomes evident that the distinction between telling and living is not categorical. Outcomes are evaluated by *how* they are told. A cure that is not narratively continuous with the preceding sequence of narrations may well be judged specious—a resistance to continuing analysis, a flight into health. Credible cure-accounts must evolve out of the illness-accounts they transform.

In the social sphere too we judge innovative action by referring to the prior instigating account of a problematic world. The adequacy of a social action intended to alleviate suffering can only be evaluated if the reasons given for the action correspond to the explanation given for the suffering. In short, living action too is known to us through narrative accounts.

In a different connection, Wittgenstein offered an image that helps clarify the progressive alternation of telling and living: "My propositions are elucidatory in this way: he who understands me finally recognizes them as senseless, when he has climbed out through them, on them, over them. (He must so to speak throw away the ladder, after he has climbed up on it.) He must surmount these propositions; then he sees the world rightly" (Wittgenstein, 1922, 189).

To "see the world rightly" and yet no longer need the ladder evidently means to have become transformed. The achieved new vision has become independent of the steps by which it was reached. Yet this analogy is incomplete; the prototype of a "good" conversation offers a refinement: Many dialogues are judged worthwhile because the speakers wish to continue them and not because a truth has been attained, a problem solved, or a bargain closed. Nor do we necessarily mean that there has been a convergence of minds on a single belief. Often the speakers feel rewarded because the dialogue has turned into an as yet unplumbed opportunity for understanding themselves more fully. We say, it is a promising conversation. In the typical case the earlier conversational exchanges are rendered uninteresting by the more recent ones they helped instigate. Yet, although they lose immediacy, it is their obsoleteness that provides the significance of the later ones. Further, unlike a ladder, a conversation need not stop—ever. But the dialectic alternation between new living action and new narration is not inevitable, as several chapters in this book make clear.

What counts as a development in living and, accordingly, as a better story? The answer depends on how one theorizes about the causes of stasis. To illustrate, in psychoanalysis most types of maldevelopment are attributed to the patient's characteristic ways of avoiding psychic pain. The analysand's initial account of his or her life is as a rule unsatisfactory, showing omissions, distortions, and confusions. But these flaws are gradually corrected as they are shown to have been historically necessary and systematic. Later accounts are more satisfactory because self-damaging ways of avoiding pain have been obviated. Such accounts allow continued development in the sphere of narration as well as in that of living action.

The evolution of more satisfactory accounts is generally correlated with the enhancement of the narrator-analysand. He or she is apt to develop a wider range and a greater tolerance of affective experience and expression, a subtler and more differentiated mode of self-observation, and less automatized, stereotyped representations of self and others. Schafer argues that the analysand's life narrative emerging from a psychoanalytic treatment reflects the history of the treatment itself: "The analysand's stories of early childhood, adolescence, and other critical periods of life get to be retold in a way that both summarizes and justifies what the analyst requires *in order to do the kind of psychoanalytic work that is being done*" (Schafer, 1981, 49, italics mine).

This formulation does not assign pragmatic effects to the life story; rather, the work of analysis follows its own requirements, and the life story is generated by the work, which is in turn complicated by the evolving accounts of the past. We can speak of evolution in the sense that new accounts do not only complete and reorganize prior accounts; they also provide an understanding of the reasons, which are no longer compelling, for the previous accounts' curtailments. That is, each account of the life refers to the preceding accounts implicitly or explicitly. They are not discontinuous fictions tailored to unrelated successive situations, as a pragmatistic approach might suggest.

New living action follows a new story partly as a way of catching the life up to the account of the life and partly to express what is missing from the story. Each story falls short of expressing the full potential of the subject, and each action is somewhat false to the story it bodies forth.

Life experience is larger and more ambiguous than any of its accounts. This is suggested by Mishler's chapter in this volume. Commitments made at successive points in one's life may generate alternative versions of one and the same past event. What is "on-line" in one telling may be "off-line" in a subsequent revision. Each revision of the story reflects a sense of self and generates new actions coordinated with this. This is not a sign of interlocutory opportunism; life experience revises the values we hold.

Actions undertaken when new versions of the self are formulated inevitably complicate these versions in unforeseen ways and prepare the ground for yet newer versions. When Fred Wharton, in Mishler's chapter, follows the call of his talents and sensitivities, he cannot anticipate the deterrent consequences for his livelihood. These, in turn, will press him to articulate what he most wishes to rescue and carry forward from an abandoned commitment to a new one in the making. But unpredicted effects can be triggered by the narrator's own reaction to the story. Karen's alliance with her father helped her to write her dissertation and "to prove her mother wrong." Unforeseeably, this victory placed the mother in a new, gentler light. Not only does the past live in the present, but it also appears different at every new turn we take.

The expression of the political in personal narrative

In Schafer's formulation regarding psychoanalytic narratives the therapeutic praxis supports an account's elaboration and becomes its point of reference. But what sort of praxis is required for the overcoming of misunderstandings resulting primarily from socially typical perplexities rather than neurotic conflict? Putting the question in this way creates a false disjunction. Socialization mediates commonly held social values along with more singular ones. Once part of the person's firmly held outlook on life, values exert their regulatory force without reference to their genealogy. Indeed, they become mutually implicated.

Such an intricate entanglement of private and public sentiments and conflicts is documented in Earnest's discussion of Pat. The common unconscious defenses with which this worker holds the rebellious impulses of childhood in check become mobilized by the authority structure at the workplace. By taking on certain, though certainly not all, aspects of the parental role, organizations mobilize contradictory tendencies of loyalty and rebellion in the employees. As a consequence, irrational beliefs and attitudes, sustained by ego-defenses, serve the arbitrary arrangements endorsed by labor and management. One would not expect Earnest to have much success in restoring flexibility to Pat's adult beliefs because the infantile anxieties persist and receive continual support as Pat wards off the real risks of betraying the unspoken labor-management pact. Infantile and adult conflicts perpetuate each other and serve as cement for the relations of production.

Despite the interweaving of the socially shared and the personally specific, one can draw a lesson from psychoanalytic therapy to the "curing" of socially perplexed subjects. In the case of psychoanalysis the necessity of the earlier defective accounts is clarified through the steady analysis of defenses and resistances, the reintegration of the history of various danger situations into the account of the past, the elucidation of the analysand's complex and multiple identifications, and so forth. But in other settings other sorts of pressure account for the defective narratives. As several of these chapters suggest, in order to achieve a satisfactory understanding of themselves, individuals must at the very least evolve a conception of those features of culture that narrow their vision.

In analogy to the therapeutic situation, an individual's or group's emergence from culturally typical perplexities depends on an understanding of the mystifying structures they have surmounted. The later accounts of their social existence should not only remedy the inadequacies of the earlier ones but also help them (and us) to understand why those defects were necessary. Although subjects who reach a more satisfactory understanding of themselves do not as a rule become social critics, several of the narrators presented in this volume seem closer to appreciating how their personal predispositions linked up with the "social facts" they appropriated. For instance, Catherine, in Ochberg's chapter, appears to have experienced a simultaneously psychological and social liberation. As she grew more skeptical of cultural orthodoxy she became more self-accepting: Her marginal life-style no longer seemed proof of inner corruption. In turn, self-acceptance allowed her to envision a more rewarding career as a community organizer.

Janice, a woman interviewed by Gresson, does not seem to sense such a connection. She reminisces about her special relationship with her mother: "I gave my mother a hard time . . . I took advantage of her . . . I am so much different than my sisters . . . I am not a conventional person at all . . . I deliberately go against the grain . . . It was like a challenge to me." The early sense of being an exception, one who can get away with breaking the rules, reverberates in Janice's evident disdain for her ethnic history. Gresson, commenting on the privatized, self-limiting ideas voiced by Marcia and Janice, calls for the articulation of political sources of self-misunderstanding, arguing that this alone can coordinate and synchronize personal and collective development.

Wiersma's narrator, Karen, seems closer to an awareness of how her personal experience predisposed her to a politically significant developmental paralysis. Her personal progress from the earliest to the last account appears correlated with her awakening to the facts of academic sexism. The parallel between doing "what was expected of faculty wives" and her submission to the felt dictates of her parents seems—first to us and then to her—nearly inescapable. By the last interview she had gained a much wider perspective not only on her own life but also on the political situation of women in universities.

In this section I have taken up problems raised by the new pragmatistic thinking about life stories. I have argued that (1) stories are neither less significant nor less "true" than the living action that supposedly vindicates them; (2) life stories and actions provoke each other in turns; and (3) *both* are narratives and, as turning points in development, must be evaluated in relation to what comes before and after.

The historicity of lives is not reducible to dubious claims about what happened in the past. It is a methodological commitment that enables us to understand the developmental dialectic between lives and life stories. Each subject confronts the record of life as a narrative *challenge*. For to ask the meaning of a life is always to ask for a way of extending it. How this relates to the problem of truth and fiction is a question I shall address at the end of this chapter.

The "Situation" and the Foreclosed Dialectic

So far my discussion of narrative development has focused on the dialectic of the narrator's self-objectivation. Each of the evolved accounts initiates its obsolescence. Yet as several of these essays show, the creation and transcendence of personal accounts depends on more than an internal dynamic. It occurs—or fails to occur—in social situations. Of these, the interlocutory dyad is the most obvious and immediate. But this must be seen in relation to the narrator's other group memberships in family, subculture, and larger society. In this section I point out a few of the social-interactive factors that influence the occurrence of formative effects, citing illustrations from the essays. In particular, I focus on bonds of allegiance.

Immobilization

The twofold dialogue—narrator and interviewer, telling and living—is fragile. Not every dialogue results in advances. Earnest's questioning of Pat's rationalizations came up against seemingly unyielding patterns of representation and defense. Pat dug himself into ever-deeper irrationalities, and these protect his loyalty to his employers as well as to his father. Not that he had much choice; challenges to workplace practices were by convention out of the question. Compromises between labor and management had put them beyond the bounds of acceptable discourse. We have speculated that this subordination complicates Pat's engagement in the issues of workplace democracy.

Several chapters suggest potential resources from which greater self-understanding might be refined. To begin with, it may help to rearticulate the concept of dialogue along some relevant dimensions. Both Fred Wharton (in

Mishler's chapter) and the Reverend Cantrell (in Harding's chapter) related portions of their lives to interviewers. Wharton took pains to justify his career choices in the questioner's eyes but sought no commitment from him. The benefit of his account would fall mostly to himself. He articulated the values guiding his past choices and thereby gave expression to aspects of his ethical self-conception. From the interviewer he seemed to expect relevant questions and acceptance of the reasons he gave for various past decisions. The Reverend Cantrell offered a more impressive account, which strikes one as the polished performance of a set piece. The evident purpose of this recital was not to cleanse his conscience of the accidental killing of his son but to save his listener's soul. The minister sought no new self-understanding; the interviewer was his target. What he wanted was not a reasoned dialogue but an unquestioning conversion. It may well be that Wharton entertains more self-doubts than the minister and that he therefore feels a greater need for self-understanding and self-affirmation. We deduce this largely from the role into which each of them cast his audience.

To achieve greater self-transparence Wharton took advantage of two opportunities every interlocutory situation offers the speaker—opportunities which, if they are taken, support a renewal of self-understanding. Dialogue *may* enforce steadier standards of rationality than are faced by a solitary actor and *may* confront the narrator with the listener's skepticism. To meet these twin challenges simultaneously means having to build a bridge to a divergent set of assumptions and to make sure the bridge holds up.[9] Either the reverend cannot afford such bridge building or he does not need it; he would risk his authority and hence his religious mission if he used the interview to seek self-understanding. Wharton, by contrast, who seems ready to question and reformulate himself at every turn, cannot hope to convert anyone to a cause. Narrative effects, it appears, are not regulated by linguistic considerations alone; they depend on the extranarrative context, including relations of power (Rommetveit, 1974). This, too, must influence the kind of self-understanding to be attained through narrative.

Other intersubjective dimensions codetermine formative effects. Wiersma has speculated that several of her respondents spoke especially frankly because they felt a kinship with the interviewer, who was entering on a new career just as they were themselves. Riessman too draws attention to the lubricating effect of a woman interviewer's sympathetic response to tales of marital oppression. Shared interests make self-examination safer by creating a context in which an interviewer can be skeptical without appearing incredulous.

A different sort of common ground may retard self-understanding. The Russo family described by Rosenberg et al. protected its formal integrity by observing a selective silence. The brunt of this loyalty was fatefully borne by their daughter, Nancy. To free her from her burdens, all the members of the family would have to loosen their bonds of allegiance and deal with one another on new terms. However, the authors make clear that these bonds are in turn the product of historical changes taking place in the culture at large. The very opposite interpretation appears in Gresson's analysis. Here it is the betrayal, rather than the observance, of a common history that portends the individual's ruin. These reflections on social sources of narrative immobilization bring us to the threshold of a social-psychological taxonomy: Some families, groups, and associations leave their members more room than others for the revision of their personal histories.

If it is true that formative effects are favored by the literary genre of confession, they may equally depend on the extranarrative setting, that is, on a setting in which the presumption of innocence is entertained. Esperanza, in Behar's chapter, chose a stranger as her confidante, one who would confess up the line to God and bring back from "beyond the river" the salvation Esperanza cannot extract from her own community. But a stranger may not be able to free us from burdens we acquired in dealing with our peers. Though Esperanza remains in search of an audience that can grant her absolution, Jan, the taciturn choreographer, seems to distrust certain kinds of self-revelation regardless of the audience. And approaching the possibility of dialogue from the audience's viewpoint as well as from the narrator's, it seems inconceivable that the Holocaust survivors studied by Greenspan would ever get the redemptive hearing one wishes for them. It is the nonnarrative inter-subjective dimensions of narration that are decisive in these failures.

These questions confront us with a besetting paradox: To climb the ladder to a better account of one's life one needs a perspective on the constraining circumstances, for instance, on the supporting and inhibiting roles played by the various loyalties in one's life and by the available genres and audiences. That perspective remains obstructed, however, until one has reached the top of the ladder. If Marcia and Janice could fully appreciate how loyalty to their ethnic history might extricate them from their respective troubles, if the Russos knew what relief they could get from moderating the false accounts each gives of every other, they would already have escaped their troubles and enhanced their lives.

Not that such an ascent is limited only by the subject's imagination! It would be arbitrary and romantic to draw the limits of narrative self-enhancement no wider than the interlocutory context. No doubt the greatest encumbrance to self-formation must be sought in the limits that feasible action sets to the dialectic of telling and living. Most conspicuously, the members of disadvantaged groups work with shorter opportunity ladders than Karen did. Material conditions place a low ceiling on the development of living action, and this must inevitably curtail the revelatory experiences the members of these groups can find to process in their narratives.

As for the narrative constraints, they too are not limited to the interlocutory situation. The categories of social experience current within a culture specify the scope of possible understandings in ways which may, in retrospect, appear as impediments. For example, not so long ago women who today attribute their social handicaps to gender discrimination might have interpreted these as personal defects. Marcia and Janice are apt to run afoul of their own best interests by longing to "feel the future in the instant." They appropriate integrationist rhetoric as though it had already been translated into practice.

These examples illustrate how the fate of personal understanding is hedged in by subjects' social commitments of various sorts. They make clear as well why an analysis of life histories patterned on therapeutic models lacks the power to untangle the web. Private life-historical and contemporaneous social bonds and representations potentiate each other. Social perplexities are especially intractable when the dangers of social dissent are felt more acutely because of correlated archaic fears surviving from childhood. To the extent that this is so, they cannot be righted merely by providing "correct" information. Rather, they remain entrenched as long as they provide the subject with a sense of elemental protection. In order for social understanding to evolve, the conditions of social as well as psychic safety must be addressed.

Escape

In our approach to increased understanding we gain confidence from other cases. One might have supposed that Catherine, the woman studied by Ochberg, was doomed. She seemed pinioned by a merciless morality borne in upon her by her family experience. How could she escape? But Catherine seemed to elude the stranglehold of her socialization. She overleapt her culture and drew from her psychosocial moratorium not only temporary respite but also a permanent new vision of all culture and of herself and finally returned to the very context she had found intolerable at the start—putting her old sensitivities to new rewarding uses.

She is not the only subject in this volume who reasserts her small voice against the din of nearly overwhelming social prohibitions. Tessa, Karen, Esperanza, Nancy Russo—they might all have been subdued by the various oppressive forces in their lives. But they endured, and this is due to something more than personal fortitude.

Renewals of public discourse create opportunities for self-possession. Constantly energized by the various collective struggles, new categories for understanding social life endow stammered, vague complaints with a recognized topicality. Tessa finds expression for her husband's barbarism: marital rape. Thirty years ago she might have been unable to escape from her marriage. That she can do so today is only secondarily a statement about changes in the divorce rate. Chiefly it attests to changes in the self-interpretive possibilities—the semantic practices— open to mistreated women (Rorty, 1990). It is the hope—and the likely effect—of studies like Gergen's and Greenspan's to sharpen our sensibilities and to offer various muffled stories a first hearing.

Schafer spoke of a psychoanalytic life story as summarizing and justifying the "work that is being done." Overcoming obstacles to social understanding also requires work. In this section, I have sketched the linked psychological and sociological factors that must be addressed. In comparison with the psychological treatment of one individual at a time, this social-psychological work must be carried out on many levels. It touches on institutional life, economic and social relations, public discourse and the mass media, education and governance. In parallel fashion, the social-psychological accounts that summarize and justify the work will point to new turns that work must take. Reports of participatory research have documented this in suggestive ways (Brown, 1983; Hall, 1981; Kassam and Mustafa, 1985).

Misunderstanding, Ideology, and Formative Process

In the first section I argued for separate concepts of narrator, narrative, and narrative situation and for a theoretical linkage of these concepts. In the second section I showed how the narrator uses his narrative capacity to objectivate himself in successive narrations and how dissatisfaction with each given account can generate a new cycle of living action and narration. In the third section I filled in what is meant by the narrative situation and indicated that development does not occur in abstraction from social processes. Finally I wish to examine whether one can properly speak of the growth of understanding when narratives give way to one another. To do so, I begin with a brief discussion of ideology.

Content and process

Since Plato the concept of ideology has functioned in social philosophy as linking the individual's beliefs to the functioning of social arrangements. Authors in the Durkheimian and Weberian tradition discuss ideology as the collection of knowledge and beliefs necessary for the cohesion of social life, while theorists who regard society as moving through a history of conflict and crisis identify ideology with false or alienated concepts imposed by the dominant classes on others to the detriment of the latter's class-consciousness. Others who do not posit a systemic-functional falseness nonetheless grant that no individual or group can have other than an incomplete and fragmented vision of the social world (Mannheim, 1955).

   Political theorists who recognize false beliefs as a major obstacle to political progress commonly call for the reeducation of the deluded. But given a conception of the human subject as spontaneous and restless, such a sociotherapeutic regimen is apt to become oppressive. It subordinates human development to the rigors of a party line and is therefore unlikely to facilitate individuals' search for fulfillment (cf. Althusser, 1970). Instead, I will argue that socialized perplexities must be overcome by remobilizing formative processes. This requires restoring the individual's reflective capacity, or, as one might say imprecisely, the capacity to learn from experience.

   The phrase is imprecise because the term *learning* has been defined narrowly to mean increasing one's efficiency in securing desired rewards. This definition

presupposes an essentially acquiescent attitude—the attitude of an apprentice—
toward the given arrangements and the rewards actually available. By contrast,
when learning processes are supported by a restored capacity for self-reflection,
they lead to unpredictable outcomes, including the reordering of known and novel
needs and incentives.

Two recent theoretical contributions are relevant to my discussion of learning
processes. The first of these shifts the traditional focus from ideological beliefs to
cognitive-psychological capacities. Seventy years ago relatively compact ideological belief structures could still be called upon to defend the status quo. Those
structures are no longer needed or available to perpetuate the social situation. The
defense has been taken over by what Leithäuser has called "everyday consciousness," a mentality equally shaped by the conditions of late-capitalist relations of
production and by the "consciousness industry." Centered in the mass media but
winning support from family, school, and workplace, this industry creates
cognitive-affective systems in the members of contemporary society that are
neither capable of nor in need of coherent worldviews. Rather, everyday consciousness operates with mere remnants and fragments of erstwhile ideological
formulations.

Its characteristic is not to be found in its contents but in the form of its processes.
What these accomplish, in a word, is to preserve the human subject by restricting
its scope and purview: "Everyday consciousness flattens contradictions until they
appear as mere conflicts [to be] mitigated and harmonized or simply forgotten.
Contradictory and mutually exclusive conceptions are seen as mere differences in
concept or opinion. Conditions . . . that have been forged or produced are converted into and represented as conditions of nature." The mind narrows the world
and becomes equally narrow itself. "Everyday consciousness defends itself in
principle against critical reflection and comes to easy terms with the world precisely because it ignores the latter's edges and corners. The contours of experience
have been polished away. The procedure of everyday consciousness is not that of
reflection as detached deliberation, critical or precise definition, but rather *reduction* toward diffuse and vague notions which are presumed as familiar and thence
in no need of examination" (Leithäuser, 1976, 11–12, my translation). Pat's
impressionistic and faulty thinking and his smoothing over of the conflict between
labor and management may serve as an illustration of "everyday consciousness."
Leithäuser's analysis of social misunderstandings, including misunderstanding
oneself, draws our attention away from false beliefs to formative processes.

The second contribution relevant to the view I shall offer is contained in a
discussion of democracy in the workplace. Earnest (1982, and in this volume)
shows that ideological thinking is maintained by the accord—anchored in a
metadiscourse—that labor has entered with management to limit its reasonable
demands. Workers like Pat pay obeisance to this accord by giving unreasonable

accounts of their lives and of the organizational conditions shaping them. To reach self-understanding and self-realization the workers would have to address this limiting metadiscourse itself, namely, the mandate to limit reflection, conceptualization, and communication (Earnest, 1982; Habermas, 1970; Rosenwald, 1988b).

Leithäuser and Earnest agree that misunderstandings of self and others do not hinge on false beliefs but on a comprehensive stultification. Individuals lose their ability to revise existing categories for the interpretation of social experience, coordinate new appreciations of self with new conceptualizations of the other, substantiate their beliefs, resolve interpretive contradictions, act on their insights, or comprehend their own actions. In short, there are many ways to run aground, and all of them are formally defined rather than with reference to a privileged doctrine. This does not imply a value-neutral approach so much as one that is centered on process. These two conceptions are consistent with the present view that reflective processes evolve historically—on the individual and collective levels—through an exchange of views and through the alternation of and reflection upon living and telling life. What these processes require above all is an open, speculative attitude. Karen concluded her second story: "I see a different facet of it every time and God knows what the truth is." What protects the subject's learning processes against excessive tolerance is the desire driving it and creating dissatisfaction with the compromises culture seeks to impose on it.

This dissatisfaction is discussed by Barratt in a valuable essay on psychoanalysis as an epistemological and ontological model for the critique of ideology. The human subject, that is, the "I" of reflective consciousness, is always unhappily split within itself because representation and desire proceed within a relation of nonidentity. The objects given to consciousness are not merely ambiguous (because interpretively elusive) but "contradictorily polysemous": That is, they signify not only what they manifestly feature but also the desire they help to repress. This desire strives forever toward the undoing of the contradiction, that is, toward the reclamation of what it has been forced to renounce. Accordingly, it "continually indicts the representational world . . . as insufficient and hence impels the movement of constructional and significational activity and the shifting locus of its subjectivity" (Barratt, 1985, 461). In short, desire is never reconciled with its objects of the moment, and this inextinguishable fact maintains the movement of subjectivity toward new positions.

This sort of self-emancipatory movement is, however, commonly arrested by the "general semiotic system" that the culture enforces in order to maintain and propagate itself. When the nonidentity of desire and representation is frozen in a given subject's life, the subject is said to be alienated. It wants what desire will never embrace. The psychoanalytic method is typified by its uncompromising interrogation of self-consciousness. This interrogation militates against "the alienation of self-consciousness in ideological forms by restarting the dialectical movement" that seeks to undo this "estrangement of representation and desire" (Barratt, 1985, 467). Without the pressure of suffering—that is, the pressure of unfulfilled desire—neither psychoanalysis nor the enhancement of social existence can proceed.

"Better" stories and the idea of fiction

In consonance with these authors, I argue that ideology is not a matter of erroneous or rigid beliefs but the mark of psychological processes that stunt critical capacities and hence lives. Given social processes and institutions that suppress these capacities, one should not expect coherent knowledge to be typical in the population. Rather, fragmentary and discontinuous accounts are the most authentic witnesses to such a social order. Seen in this light, Pat's fumbling during his interview with Earnest mirrors perfectly the irrationality of his working conditions. We have reason to believe that he deals more effectively with other domains of his life.

Having outlined the abatement of misunderstanding as occurring through the restoration of a dialectical movement rather than through the authoritative installation of correct beliefs, we are now prepared to examine what would be a "better" story. For Pat, it would be one in which he could reflect on the irrationality of workplace arrangements, rather than to display the scars they left on his mental life. Further, satisfactory stories—stories that can advance living action—excel through comprehensiveness. They contain more detail of every kind. Narrative generalizations are supported with instances. Instances are set in historical context, showing how the past reverberates in the present and how the present retrospectively illuminates the past's potential. History is seen as interactive—made as well as suffered. One's relation to the world and relationships with others and oneself are recognized as being ambivalent and contradictory. The future is seen as an unfulfilled and unpredictable possibility but not without limit. Most of all, (later and) better accounts help comprehend the (earlier) defective ones. Better stories tend to be structurally more complex, more varied and contrastive in the events and accompanying feelings portrayed, more interesting and three-dimensional. Even though better stories are richer in detail, they are also more open to further detail—the opposite of a "press release" (Rosenwald and Wiersma, 1986).[10] They are a retelling of the course by which they were attained. They are stories about stories. To consider them in this way places the concept of fiction in a new perspective.

Recent developments in epistemology (Collingwood, 1946; Rorty, 1982; White, 1978) have supported the notion that history does not mirror the past but is a kind of fiction that helps the historian cope with the problems of his time. On this view, stories do not get better in an absolute sense; at best they are adequate to the situation that must be coped with. But does a story become better because its elements have been conveniently reshuffled to fit the occasion? If this were all, it would be rightly called fiction. But can a fiction reduce suffering?

As fiction is often defined, it does not correspond to the work by which it is created. For instance, Geha defines fiction as the activity—or the product of the activity—of "constructing, forming, giving shape, elaborating, presenting, artistically fashioning: conceiving, thinking, imagining, assuming, planning, devising, inventing." The emphasis in this definition is on freedom from restraint: "All psychic reality is fictional, a *free* creation of the human mind" (Geha, 1989, 273, italics mine).

In evaluating this notion, several points must be noted. First, when narrators improve their life accounts in the course of several tellings, whether in psychoanalysis or in the kind of exploration with which I am concerned, they do not merely reorder a given set of elements into ever greater coherence. They also change the elements, add new ones, and delete or deemphasize old ones. Accordingly, improving the coherence of a life history is not a process akin to finding the best fitting curve for a set of points on a graph.

Second, life stories consist of elements on different levels—generalizations (for instance, patterns of events, attributions of traits to oneself and others), episodes (specific instances substantiating a generalization), acts (components of episodes), emotions (affects, moods), mementos (present residuals of earlier events), and so forth. A good story must not only be horizontally coherent—episodes hanging together to warrant generalizations—but also vertically—episodes warranted by acts, feelings, and so on. In short, better stories must be coherent in several planes; they must become *compact*.

Let us say, an adult is told that his deafness stems from a childhood accident caused by his father's negligence. The deafness is a memento, the accident an episode, and the negligence a constructed trait. Although each of these narrative elements rests on an interpretation rather than on a theory-neutral observation, each is subject to different sorts of doubt and corroboration. For instance, the deafness might be hysterical or feigned; the accident might have been witnessed by others; and the alleged negligence is a synthesis of many strands of evidence. Taken together, they support each other in one direction more than in the other: if the deafness proves imaginary, the alleged accident and the negligence become doubtful. And yet a pyramid of evidence is rarely toppled by the presence of a few crumbly bricks. This is so because in more fine-grained accounts, the demand for compactness is usually more stringent. The "better" story must be *more coherent despite being more comprehensive*. We may still insist that no single version is the ultimate truth, but the note of free-wheeling arbitrariness, frequently sounded by constructionists, has been dampened.

Third, there is an even more important sense in which the creation of such fictions is constrained. In psychoanalysis this work commonly involves the confrontation of numbing fears and draining sorrow. Insights are wrested from the flesh. To overcome culturally common perplexities, one must confront personal anxieties as well as other obstacles, as shown in various of these essays. To discuss the successive accounts as "free creations" belittles this work. They are not free in any ordinary sense. By this I do not mean simply that they require effort; a novel, too, is not written easily. What I mean is that they are neither freely given by the interpreter nor freely accepted by the subject of the narration. This is as true of the narrators referred to in this book as it is of analysands. The accounts are paid for with work and are no more fictional than this.

What keeps the narratives from being free fictions is not that they represent anything in particular but that they "summarize and justify" the work from which they arose and our comprehension of the obstacles that had to be surmounted in the construction of these narratives. Further, in psychoanalysis it is usually the most concrete elements of narration—childhood memories of wishful fantasies, anxious imaginings, affective tensions of all sorts—that require the hardest work. This is why the vertical coherence of the "better" story is never cheaply bought. A narrative will lead to new actions and new narratives to the extent that it was hard won. The truth of a narrative is therefore not representational and not pragmatic but dialectical: the narrative is true in that it enshrines the toil of undoing repression and social perplexity—both forms of routinized suffering; it is true as the laborious negation of the prior self-consciousness.

This conception reflects on our notion of subjectivity. The narrator of a life history appears as the pole in a dialogic relation. He or she responds to the particular terms of the interaction by producing successive versions of himself or herself in the given sequence, with the given unfolding of detail, the given increase of complication and simplification, the given versions of past, present, and future, the given conceptions of self and other. Subjectivity is activated only in such a context; there is no other, more direct way of broaching it. It displays its momentum by oscillating between telling and living. But it is never reducible to particular manifestations; it is always ready to repudiate what it has asserted as it alters the outer and inner conditions of the assertion itself.

What makes for identity does not quell the restlessness of desire. For identity, as it is usually discussed, is itself a compromise with conventions. It can now be seen that it is the difference between subjectivity and its obsolescent narrative manifestations that moves life forward in a search for new more satisfying identities: the life story is always false; it contains both more and less than the subject's potential. This falseness is neither accidental nor a liability, as some critics imply; it is essential. The endeavor to extinguish the falseness—the subject's longing to become identical with its story—is the impetus to development. Although subjectivity defeats our efforts to predict the course of its tellings and livings, we may glimpse the scope of its secrets whenever we attend closely to its untiring pursuit of a ceaseless, arduous self-creation.

NOTES

1. Social constructionists do not believe that social ills are unreal in the sense of imaginary. But the impact of such ills on human beings is ascribed to social convention. A constructionist might point out that under different social conditions the same state of affairs could be interpreted as a benefit. For instance, unemployment might be regarded as massed leisure.
2. Not all constructionists go to this extreme. Some stop short of equating "the account with its putative object" (Gergen and Gergen, 1988, 18). But to the extent that constructionists subscribe to an "ontology of discourse," narrating subjects are abstracted from narratives. Tellers are constructions in a sense in which the tales and situations are not. Narrators no longer figure as authors; they have been displaced by the conventions.
3. For instance, "the possibility for adjudication within a single, isolated relationship is minimal. Isolated relationships, within themselves, have no necessary trajectory, no essential goals to which they must aspire. Adjudication arises primarily . . . where comparisons among coordinated sequences are possible. . . . On this account, the master-slave relationship is not intrinsically undesirable for the slave; it becomes so primarily as advantageous alternatives become salient" (Gergen, 1990, 586–587).
4. A much milder version of this quandary is sometimes felt by a bilingual speaker who finds it onerous to express in one language what is so easily conveyed in another—a critical consciousness of linguistic conventions. In extreme cases, the conventions are politically supported to such an extent that they become taken for granted and as imperceptible as the air we breathe.
5. A recent paper by Kerz-Rühling argues that Freud never subscribed to the naïve realism attributed to him in connection with the "archaeological model" (1989).
6. Rapaport's discussion of "psychological continuity" is relevant to this notion of historicism (1967).
7. Freud's history of the Wolfman illustrates the interpretive application of this methodological commitment (Freud, 1918).
8. This criterion may be recognized as the one that governs the clinician's distinction between therapeutically integrative action and neurotic acting-out. (For a review of these issues, see Abrams, 1990).
9. Excessive tact and "empathy" are not an interviewer's most useful tools if they relieve the respondent of making his views plain.
10. This normative statement is not intended as universal. It is based on the typical disfigurement of discourse resulting from repression in contemporary Western culture.

REFERENCES

Abrams, S. 1990. "The Psychoanalytic Process: The Developmental and the Integrative." *Psychoanalytic Quarterly* 59:650–677.

Althusser, Louis, and Etienne Balibar. 1970. *Reading "Capital."* London: New Left Books.

Barratt, Barnaby B. 1985. "Psychoanalysis as Critique of Ideology." *Psychoanalytic Inquiry* 5:437–470.

Berger, Peter L., and Thomas Luckmann. 1966. *The Social Construction of Reality: A Treatise in the Sociology of Knowledge.* Garden City, N.Y.: Doubleday.

Brown, L. D. 1983. "Organizing Participatory Research: Interfaces for Joint Inquiry and Organizational Change." *Journal of Occupational Behavior* 4:9–19.

Collingwood, R. G. 1946. *The Idea of History.* Oxford: Oxford University Press.

Earnest, William R. 1982. "Work and Its Discontents: The Ideological Containment of Social Contradictions." Ph.D. diss., University of Michigan.

Erikson, Erik H. 1974. *Dimensions of a New Identity.* New York: W. W. Norton.

Freud, Sigmund. 1918. "From the History of an Infantile Neurosis." In *The Standard Edition of the Complete Psychological Works of Sigmund Freud,* vol. 17. Edited by James Strachey. London: Hogarth Press.

Geha, Richard E. 1989. "On Psychoanalytic History and the 'Real' Story of Fictitious Lives." *International Forum of Psychoanalysis* 1:221–291.

Gergen, Kenneth J. 1990. "Social Understanding and the Inscription of Self." In *Cultural Psychology: Essays on Comparative Human Development.* Edited by J. W. Stigler, R. A. Shweder, and G. Herdt. Cambridge: Cambridge University Press.

Gergen, Kenneth J., and Mary M. Gergen. 1988. "Narrative and the Self as Relationship." In *Advances in Experimental Social Psychology.* Edited by L. Berkowitz. San Diego: Academic Press.

Habermas, Jürgen. 1970. "On Systematically Distorted Communication." *Inquiry* 13:205–218.

Hall, B. L. 1981. "Participatory Research, Popular Research and Power." *Convergence* 14(3):6–17.

Harré, Rom. 1989. "Language Games and the Texts of Identity." In *Texts of Identity.* Edited by J. Shotter and K. Gergen. London: Sage.

Kassam, Y., and K. Mustafa. 1985. *Participatory Research: An Emerging Alternative Methodology in Social Science Research.* New Delhi: Society for Participatory Research in Asia.

Kerz-Rühling, Ingrid. 1989. "Die psychoanalytische Erzählung." *Psyche* 43:307–330.

Leithäuser, Thomas. 1976. *Formen des Alltagsbewusstseins.* Frankfurt: Campus.

Mannheim, Karl. 1955. *Ideology and Utopia: An Introduction to the Sociology of Knowledge.* New York: Harcourt Brace.

Rapaport, David. 1967. "The Scientific Methodology of Psychoanalysis." In *The Collected Papers of David Rapaport.* Edited by M. M. Gill. New York: Basic Books.

Rommetveit, R. 1974. *On Message Structure.* New York: John Wiley.

Rorty, Richard. 1982. *Consequences of Pragmatism.* Minneapolis: University of Minnesota Press.

———. 1990. "Feminism and Pragmatism." The Tanner Lecture presented at the University of Michigan, December 7.

Rosenwald, George C. 1988a. "Toward a Formative Psychology." *Journal for the Theory of Social Behavior* 18:1–32.

———. 1988b. "A Theory of Multiple-Case Research." *Journal of Personality* 56:239–264.

Rosenwald, George C., and Jacquelyn Wiersma. 1986. "Women, Career Changes, and the New Self." *Psychiatry* 46:213–229.

Schafer, Roy. 1981. "Narration in the Psychoanalytic Dialogue." In *On Narrative.* Edited by W. J. Y. Mitchell. Chicago: University of Chicago Press.

Slugoski, B. R., and G. P. Ginsburg. 1989. "Ego Identity and Explanatory Speech." In *Texts of Identity.* Edited by J. Shotter and K. Gergen. London: Sage.

Spence, Donald P. 1982. *Narrative Truth and Historical Truth: Meaning and Interpretation in Psychoanalysis.* New York: W. W. Norton.

White, Hayden. 1978. *Tropics of Discourse.* Baltimore, Md.: Johns Hopkins University Press.

Wittgenstein, Ludwig. 1922. *Tractatus Logico-Philosophicus.* New York: Harcourt Brace.

Wrong, Dennis. 1961. "The Oversocialized Conception of Man in Modern Sociology." *American Sociological Review* 26:183–193.

Wyatt, Frederick. 1986. "The Narrative in Psychoanalysis." In *Narrative Psychology.* Edited by T. R. Sarbin. New York: Praeger.

Index

Abraham (biblical figure), 67–73

Absence: presence of, in Russo family, 49; of Cain's descendants (from Bible), 157–58. *See also* Silences

Achievement: male models for, 130–32, 136; women's, 136, 139–40, 206–8

Adoption: and birthparents' stories, 10–11, 76–92; reform movement for, 77–80; as exploitative system, 78–79, 87–89; Cindy's, 218–19

Adorno, Theodore, 254

African-American unity, 165, 167, 169, 176

African-American men, 169–70, 173–74

African-American women, 13, 165–77

Agoraphobia, 45

Allegory: Victor's prosecution of God as, 160

All Is Well (Lester), 165–66

Allport, Gordon, 5

Allusions: biblical, in born-again discourse, 63–64, 66–72, 73

ALMA (Adoptees' Liberty Movement Association), 77

Alter, Robert, 70

Ambiguity: as transformative feature of storytelling, 196

Ambivalence: about parenthood, 10–11, 178–91; choreographers', toward narrative clarity, 95–107; in Victor's relationship with God, 160; racial, 166–67. *See also* Ambiguity; Contradictions; Duality; Roles: conflicting

American Adoption Congress, 77

Analogies: in Holocaust survivors' stories, 150, 154–56, 158–60. *See also* Enactment

Androcentric order: in narrative line, 127–42

Anger: Pat's management of, 258. *See also* Rage

Architect, 27, 28

Artist: and craftsperson, distinction between, 26–27. *See also* Choreographers

Audience: and teller of life stories, relationship between, 1, 3, 5, 9, 247, 266–67, 277–80; in minister's tale, 10, 11, 60–61; in birthparents' tales, 11; for Esperanza's stories, 11–12, 113, 115, 118–19; lack of, for Holocaust survivor tales, 13, 150–53, 162–63; in craftsperson's tale, 26, 35–36; through dance, 95–107; lack of Mexican, for Esperanza's tale, 113, 115, 119; importance of, in women's life stories, 136, 152; teller of story *as*, 200–201; in legitimating divorce, 231–32; in rape tale, 233–34, 236–38, 241, 243. *See also* Listener; Narrator; Researcher

Auerbach, Erich, 70

Augustine, 12

Autobiographies. *See* Life stories

Bakker, Jim, 73

Bardwick, J. M., 198

Barratt, Barnaby B., 283

Barrows, Sydney Biddle, 135, 136, 138, 139–40

"Beached whale" metaphor, 187–88

Behar, Ruth, 11–12, 108–23, 279

Benstock, Shari, 133

Berger, B., 41, 42, 43, 46, 58

Bettelheim, Bruno, 201

Bible: relation between Old and New Testaments in, for born-again Christians, 66, 69–71; as Victor's evidence in his prosecution of God, 157; violent husband's invocation of, 237. See also *Names of biblical figures*

Contributors

RUTH BEHAR is associate professor of anthropology at the University of Michigan.

WILLIAM R. EARNEST is a clinical psychologist in Tallahassee, Florida.

JEFFREY E. EVANS is coordinator of clinical training in the Division of Rehabilitation Psychology and Neuropsychology, University of Michigan.

MICHAEL P. FARRELL is professor of sociology at the State University of New York, Buffalo.

MARY GERGEN is associate professor of psychology at Pennsylvania State University, Delaware County Campus.

HENRY GREENSPAN is a lecturer at the University of Michigan and a psychotherapist in private practice.

AARON DAVID GRESSON is associate professor of education and director of the Center for the Study of Equity in Education, College of Education, Pennsylvania State University.

SUSAN HARDING is professor of anthropology and chair of the Board of Anthropology at the University of California, Santa Cruz.

ELLIOT G. MISHLER is professor of social psychology at Harvard Medical School and chief psychologist at the Massachusetts Mental Health Center.

JUDITH MODELL is associate professor of history and anthropology at Carnegie Mellon University.

RICHARD L. OCHBERG is assistant professor of psychology at the University of Massachusetts, Boston.

CATHERINE KOHLER RIESSMAN is professor of sociology and social work at Boston University.

HARRIET J. ROSENBERG is an instructor in clinical psychology at Dartmouth Medical School.

STANLEY D. ROSENBERG is professor of psychiatry at Dartmouth Medical School.

GEORGE C. ROSENWALD is professor of psychology at the University of Michigan and a psychotherapist in private practice.

BARBARA COX WALKOVER is a clinical psychologist in Seattle, Washington.

JACQUELYN WIERSMA is a clinical psychologist in private practice, associate core faculty member at the Minnesota School of Professional Psychology, and assistant clinical professor in the Department of Psychology, University of Minnesota.